The Teahouse

*Small Business, Everyday Culture, and
Public Politics in Chengdu, 1900–1950*

DI WANG

Stanford University Press
Stanford, California

Stanford University Press
Stanford, California

© 2008 by the Board of Trustees of the Leland Stanford Junior University. All rights reserved.

This book has been published with the assistance of Texas A&M University's College of Liberal Arts.

No part of this book may be reproduced or transmitted in any form or by any means, electronic or mechanical, including photocopying and recording, or in any information storage or retrieval system without the prior written permission of Stanford University Press.

Printed on acid-free, archival-quality paper

Library of Congress Cataloging-in-Publication Data

Wang, Di.
 The teahouse : small business, everyday culture, and public politics in Chengdu, 1900-1950 / Di Wang.
   p. cm.
 Includes bibliographical references and index.
 ISBN 978-0-8047-5843-7 (cloth : alk. paper)
 ISBN 978-0-8047-9103-8 (pbk. : alk. paper)
  1. Chengdu (China)--Social life and customs--20th century.
 2. Tearooms--China--Chengdu--History--20th century. 3. Chengdu (China)--Politics and government--20th century. I. Title.
 DS797.77.C48W35 2008
 951'.38--dc22
                                            2008002788

Typeset by Bruce Lundquist in 10.5/12 Bembo

Printed and bound in Great Britain by
Marston Book Services Ltd, Oxfordshire

In Memory of Steve Averill

Contents

List of Tables, Maps, and Figures   ix
Acknowledgments   xi
A Note on Currencies   xv
Abbreviations   xvii

Introduction: The City, Teahouses, and Everyday Culture   1

Part One. The Teahouse

1. A Small Business   27
2. The Teahouse Guild   57
3. Labor and Workplace Culture   84

Part Two. Teahouse Life

4. Public Life   113
5. Entertainment   135
6. All Walks of Life   167

Part Three. Teahouse Politics

7. Conflicts in Public   203
8. A Political Site   224

Conclusion: The Triumph of Small Business and Everyday Culture   249

Appendix: Comparison of Tea and Rice Prices, 1909–1948   265

Character List   267

Notes   285

Works Cited   323

Index   341

Tables, Maps, and Figures

Tables

1.1. Teahouses in Chengdu, 1909–1951   *30*
1.2. Population of Chengdu, 1910–1949   *31*
1.3. Streets, teahouses, and population in Chengdu, late 1920s   *33*

Maps

1. Chengdu, its wall, and its gates, 1900–1950   *5*
2. Some frequently mentioned streets and places, 1900–1950   *32*
3. Chengdu and its districts, 1910s–1940s   *33*
4. Some frequently mentioned teahouses, 1900–1950   *45*

Figures

I.1. Sand-filled vats   *19*
1.1. A food peddler   *36*
1.2. A typical rural market on the Chengdu Plain   *41*
1.3. Cry of the Crane Teahouse   *44*
1.4. Warm Spring Road   *46*
1.5. The Commercial Center   *46*
1.6. A teahouse in the Smaller City Park   *48*
1.7. A teahouse next to Xue Tao Well   *48*
1.8. The Flower Fair   *49*
1.9. A teahouse with a beautiful view   *49*

3.1. A skillful waiter   85
3.2. A teahouse stove   90
3.3. Regulations of the Union of Chengdu Teahouse Workers   94
4.1. Sketches of teahouse life   116
4.2. A bird fight in the late Qing era   124
4.3. An earwax picker serving a customer   125
4.4. "Sitting operas"   129
5.1. A local opera performance in the Elegant Garden   137
5.2. "Beating the Daoist drum"   139
5.3. A storyteller   140
5.4. The Joy Tea Garden today   152
5.5. The Joy Tea Garden and its stage   153
5.6. "Electric-light operas"   156
5.7. The grand stage of Warm Spring   158
6.1. A fortune-teller   173
6.2. The Peace and Happiness Temple Teahouse   179
6.3. "Tea bowl formations"   181
6.4. A street-corner teahouse   187
6.5. "Local opera craze: Watching the show or watching women?"   192
6.6. "Shameful! Women watching male performers"   193
7.1. "Doing violence"   216
8.1. Policemen and residents on a commercial street   229
8.2. A crowd in the Imperial City   230

Acknowledgments

THIS BOOK BEGAN as a research paper I presented at the Institute of Global Studies in Power, Culture, & History at Johns Hopkins University in March 1998. I owe special thanks to Bill Rowe, who has inspired and encouraged my study of this topic and given me many helpful suggestions and much support during the long gestation of this book. I would like to especially thank Joe Esherick, a reader for the Stanford University Press, who read the entire manuscript twice and offered the most comprehensive, detailed, and constructive comments, which helped me shape and sharpen some important arguments and greatly improved the book. I also want to thank the two other, anonymous, readers for their comments and suggestions. I am very grateful to Akinobu Kuroda for inviting me to and arranging a seven-month research and writing sabbatical at the Institute of Oriental Culture of the University of Tokyo in 2005, where I made crucial progress on the manuscript. Many scholars have supported this study in various ways at different stages, and I would like to thank Timothy Cheek, Kishimoto Mio, Perry Link, Tobie Meyer-Fong, Murata Yujiro, Susan Naquin, Jonathan Ocko, Sakamoto Hiroko, Kristine Stapleton, Richard Smith, Sun Jiang, Suzuki Tōmō, Shuo Wang, Jeffrey McClain, Wen-hsin Yeh, Seiichiro Yoshizawa, and Madeleine Zelin. I am grateful to the history writing group of the 2006–7 fellows at the National Humanities Center, including Robert Beachy, Francesca Bordogna, Christopher Browning, Jan Goldstein, Sally Hughes, Benedict Kiernan, Sheryl Kroen, Jann Pasler, William Sewell, Sarah Shields, James Sweet, and Rachel Weil, for their comments and suggestions on my manuscript. I thank Terry Anderson, Troy Bickham, Olga Dror, Chester Dunning, April Hatfield, Carol Higham, Andrew Kirkendall, Adam Nelson, David Vaught, and Lora Wildenthal—my colleagues at Texas A&M University—for reading portions of my earlier drafts or otherwise generously providing help. I thank Walter Buenger, head of my department at Texas A&M and Ben Crouch, executive associate dean of the College of

Library Arts, for their consistent support in providing research funds, releasing me from my normal teaching duties, and allowing me leave to work on this book.

During the years when the manuscript was taking shape, I was invited to give talks on the teahouses of Chengdu at several institutions: Academia Sinica (Taipei), Nankai University (Tianjin), the Hopkins-Nanjing Center (Nanjing), Hitotsubashi University (Tokyo), University of Tokyo, University of California-Irvine, Sichuan University (Chengdu), Ecole des Hautes Etudes en Sciences Sociales (Paris), and University of Texas (Austin). I thank the scholars and students who attended my presentations for their stimulating comments. I also owe thanks to Jiang Mengbi and Xiong Zhuoyun, long-time residents and teahouse-goers in Chengdu, for telling me of their own experiences in the teahouses. I thank John E. Knight for permitting me to use the photos of Chengdu taken by Luther Knight, a missionary who taught in Chengdu in 1911 and 1912, and photographer Wang Yulong for helping me get permission to use Knight's photos. I also want to thank Jean Elliott Johnson for providing and giving me permission to use the photos taken by her father, Harrison S. Elliott, in 1906 and 1907. I owe additional thanks to photographer Chen Jin, who generously permitted me to include his excellent photos in this book. My thanks also go to Sun Bin, Zhang Youlin, Li Wanchun, Liu Shifu, Xiong Xiaoxiong, Pan Peide, and Xie Kexin for granting me permission to adopt some details from their great scroll painting, *Old Chengdu* (Lao Chengdu). I thank Ann Kellett for her expert copyediting. I would also like to express my gratitude to senior editor Muriel Bell at Stanford University Press for her encouragement and expert direction through the entire publication process, to editorial assistants Joa Suorez and Kirsten Oster for their valuable help, to senior production editor Judith Hibbard for guiding me through the production process, and to Richard Gunde for his meticulous copyediting and insightful comments on the final manuscript.

This project received financial support from the American Council of Learned Societies/National Endowment for the Humanities; the Japan Society for the Promotion of Science; the Institute for International Research at the Hopkins-Nanjing Center; and the American Historical Association, which provided a Bernadotte E. Schmitt Grant for Research in European, African and Asian History. I was also supported by fellowships for this project from Texas A&M University, including an International Research Travel Assistance Grant, Department of History/Center for Humanities Research Fellowships, and funding from the Program to Enhance Scholarly and Creative Activities. I want to thank the National Humanities Center, which provided an excellent environment for revising this manuscript as I also worked on the second part of my teahouse project ("Public Life under Socialism: Teahouses in Revolutionary and Reformist Chengdu, 1950–2000") there during the 2006–7 academic year. I thank the staff of the Chengdu Municipal Archives for allowing me access to their massive archival collections, which are the foundation of this project, and for providing good service when I did research there. My thanks also go to the Sterling C. Evans Library at Texas A&M University, Sichuan Provincial Archives, Sichuan Provincial Library, and Sichuan University Library. Earlier versions of Chapter 3 and Chapter 7 have been published in the journals *Twentieth-Century China* and *European Journal of East Asian Studies*, respectively. Figures 5.1, 6.5, 6.6, and 7.1 were used in my article published in the *Journal of Urban History*. I thank the editors and publishers for permission to reuse the materials here.

I dedicate this book to my friend and teacher Steve Averill (1945–2004). I first met him when he was conducting research at Sichuan University in 1989, and he later worked with Ernest Young to invite me to the University of Michigan and Michigan State University as a visiting scholar, supported by a Young Chinese Scholar Fellowship of the Committee on Scholarly Communication with the People's Republic of China (sponsored by the American Council of Learned Societies), in 1991. Steve was the one who led me into Western historiography and helped me as I transitioned from being a China-trained historian to an America-trained historian during my early years in the United States. After I left Michigan, he continued to give me his generous support in all possible ways, carefully reading every paper I sent him and offering inspiring and constructive comments. He gave me many invaluable suggestions and generously shared with me the benefits of his experience and teaching materials pertaining to East Asian history. Even after he became very sick, he devoted a great deal of time to editing my paper "Masters of Tea" (which became Chapter 3 of this book) and published it in the final issue of the journal *Twentieth-Century China*, for which he was editor. I saw him for the last time at the 2004 annual meeting of the Association for Asian Studies in San Diego. Although very weak, he attended my panel and gave comments on my paper about the teahouse guild (an earlier draft of what became Chapter 2) and advertised my forthcoming article in the journal *Twentieth-Century China*. He expressed high expectations and put forth a great deal of energy on this study and his spirit has always inspired me to work very hard toward its completion.

Finally, this book would not have been possible without the support of my family. My deepest gratitude goes to my wife, Wei Li, and my son, Ye Wang, who made life much more fun and meaningful during the years when I was deeply focused on this project. My heartfelt thanks also go to my parents and my older brother, who have always been among my most enthusiastic supporters.

D. W.

A Note on Currencies

CHINA'S MONETARY SYSTEM underwent several changes between 1900 and 1950. In the Qing, currency consisted of silver yuan (*yinyuan*) and copper yuan (*tongyuan*), and wen (cash), the most basic unit of currency. Wen roughly corresponds to "cents," though they are not identical. In the late Qing, the official exchange rates were one silver yuan to one hundred coppers, and one copper to ten wen. However, coppers were constantly devalued from the late Qing to the Republican period. In the 1910s, the rates were one silver yuan to about fifteen hundred to two thousand wen, and in the 1920s, about two thousand to three thousand wen. In November 1935 the government introduced *fabi* (literally, "legal tender") and prohibited the circulation of silver yuan coins. In August 1948, in response to hyperinflation, the government replaced the fabi with golden yuan (*jinyuanjuan*), at the rate of one golden yuan to three million fabi yuan.

Abbreviations

FOR COMPLETE author names, titles, and publication data for the works cited here in short form, see Works Cited. These abbreviations appear in the captions and the Notes. All citations of documents in the Chengdu Municipal Archives follow the Archives' cataloging conventions: numbers following the abbreviation (e.g., CSZGD) refer to category (*quanzhong*), catalog (*mulu*), and volume (*juan*) (e.g., CSZGD, 38-11-982). If there are only two groups of numbers after the abbreviation, it means this archive has only category and volume and no catalog (e.g., CSSD, 104-1388).

CDKB: *Chengdu kuaibao*
CDTL: Fu Chongju, *Chengdu tonglan*
CDWB: *Chengdu wanbao*
CGTGD: *Chengdu shi gehang geye tongye gonghui dang'an*
CSGJD: *Chengdu shi gongshang ju dang'an*
CSGXD: *Chengdu shi gongshang xingzheng dengji dang'an*
CSJJD: *Chengdu shenghui jingcha ju dang'an*
CSSD: *Chengdu shi shanghui dang'an*
CSWHJ: *Chengdu shi wenhua ju dang'an*
CSZGD: *Chengdu shi zhengfu gongshang dang'an*
GMGB: *Guomin gongbao*
HXRB: *Huaxi ribao*
HXWB: *Huaxi wanbao*
JSWS: Li Zhuxi, Zeng Dejiu, and Huang Weihu, *Jindai Sichuan wujia shiliao*
SZSC: *Sichuan sheng zhengfu shehuichu dang'an*
TSRB: *Tongsu ribao*
XMBWK: *Xinminbao wankan*
XXXW: *Xinxin xinwen*

The Teahouse

Introduction:
The City, Teahouses, and Everyday Culture

A teahouse is a little Chengdu and Chengdu is a big teahouse
(*Chaguan shige xiao Chengdu, Chengdu shige da chaguan*).
—A local saying

THIS SAYING CONVEYS an image of Chengdu as unique, as a place where teahouses were found on every block, where residents depended on the teahouses, and where teahouse life was a genuine expression of the city and its people. Chengdu is the capital of Sichuan Province—a land in the upper Yangzi region surrounded by mountains, relatively isolated, famed as a "Kingdom of Tea and Teahouses." Few other institutions in Chengdu in the first half of the twentieth century were more important in everyday life than teahouses, and no other city in China had as many of them as Chengdu. The teahouse was a microcosm of the larger society. The images brought together in this work paint a comprehensive picture of everyday culture in the most basic unit of public life and unearth narratives of events that took place in the teahouse. An examination of the teahouse and public life from the perspective of microhistory can take one into the depths of a city and create an opportunity to put urban society under a microscope. A study of teahouses also provides a new way of looking at the Chinese city and at everyday culture.[1]

This is the first book-length history of Chinese teahouses, in either English or Chinese. It examines economic, social, political, and cultural changes as funneled through the teahouses of Chengdu during the first half of the twentieth century. Its major theme is that during the first half of the twentieth century long-standing local culture and customs constantly resisted the relentless waves of Westernization, which tended to impose a uniformity of modernist transformation, parallel with the state's growing role in public life. In other words, two major developments coexisted in the course of urban reform and modernization in this period: the growing role of the state and the decline of the uniqueness of local culture and customs. In these processes, everyday culture, in which the teahouse played a major role, showed both tenacity and flexibility. Modernization constantly chipped away at diversity in local life and culture and transformed the city as it followed a unified model, such as widening roads to improve the flow of traffic, reconstructing urban space to create "modern" landscapes, setting up standards of hygiene to prevent disease, taking the poor off the streets to enhance an image of "progressiveness," enacting many kinds of regulations to maintain public order, manipulating popular performances to "civilize" citizens, promoting patriotism to shape a new national identity, enforcing national policies to strengthen state control, and so forth. Although various studies have focused on one or another aspect of urban reform in different cities, all these measures could be found in a single city during the late Qing and Republican China, reflecting the trend toward national unification.[2]

The development of most premodern Chinese cities was governed by geography and networks of transportation and marketing. Physical space and culture emerged organically, without a "master plan" or national template. The result was diverse appearances, lifestyles, customs, folk traditions, economic functions, and local governance, which underscored a rich and colorful local culture. However, under the impact of modernization and the growing role of the state, this uniqueness and variety faded, either dramatically or gradually. From a political perspective, the city of Chengdu was the site of a struggle between localism and nationalism in which, in the late Qing, reformers and the government regarded local customs as "uncivilized" and "backward" and tried to change them according to Western or Japanese models; during the post-1911 era, local military leaders and warlords resisted unification with the central government; and by 1936 and 1937 the Nationalist Party (the Guomindang; hereafter GMD) and the Nationalist government finally expanded their power into Sichuan. The battle of local culture in resisting modernist uniformity reached a new zenith in the War of Resistance (1937–45) and the Civil War (1945–49).

This theme will help us understand how and to what extent daily life changed in this inland city while the nation underwent economic, social, and cultural innovations in the face of the dramatic political turmoil of the late Qing and Republican periods. A thorough examination of teahouse life in Chengdu reveals the complex relationship between public space and everyday culture. As a microcosm, the teahouse was a good example of the small businesses that dominated the city's economy and an ideal lens through which to scrutinize the issues of management, competition, and employment; the teahouse was a complex establishment that provided a venue for leisure activities—public talks, recreation, and entertainment—but it was also a much larger multifaceted worksite and arena for local politics where ordinary people could adopt public personas, live out the drama of social interaction, and create a rich culture. The teahouse was a center of communication and social activities, and the headquarters of numerous social organizations; it was also an indicator of economic, political, and cultural conditions and transformations. Because of its complex role, the teahouse was always a target of both social reform movements and government control, becoming the one venue that people at every level of power sought to influence and occupy.

Based on this theme as its foundation, the book is built of three parts: the teahouse as a small business, its contributions to everyday life, and its role in public politics.[3] First, I identify how small businesses were the most important segment of commerce in late Qing and Republican-era Chengdu. No other shops were so thoroughly woven into the fabric of people's everyday lives as the teahouse. The teahouse not only represented a unique method of business operation and management, but it also shaped a vibrant and enduring consumer culture. I reveal the external and internal issues the teahouse faced and examine the connection between teahouses and their patrons, and between teahouses and the local government. An analysis of the roles of the Teahouse Guild and the Union of Teahouse Workers explores how the guild and union became the agencies between local authorities and this business sector, and between the government and workers. Second, I investigate the roles the teahouse played as a center of communication and community or neighborhood life. Various social groups used the teahouse for a wide range of economic, social, and cultural purposes: a market where people could earn a living, a gathering place for social and business transactions, and a theater for entertainment. I also examine how this space was used differently based on customers' social group, profession, and gender. Finally, by focusing on conflicts and the struggle for power, I explore how politics was pursued in the teahouse. Political changes were immediately obvious in the teahouse, which became a political arena and a measure of the transformation of the local and national political process. The government, concerned about public order, tried to impose many regulations on the teahouse, from the hours of operation to the number of teahouses permitted in the city. During the War of Resistance and then the Civil War, the government and other social forces used the teahouse in unprecedented ways for political ends, bringing a new element of politics to everyday life in Chengdu. The deterioration of the economic, social, and political situation and the government's increasing control had a dampening effect on the teahouse as a forum for the free discussion of politics and other sensitive topics, thus reflecting changes in society at large.

The City and the Teahouse

The Chengdu Plain was "one of the richest, most fertile, and thickly populated areas in the whole of China." Unlike North China, where farmers lived in villages, the country people of this area were scattered and their farmhouses were surrounded by bamboo groves. Yet, the provincial capital was a sophisticated place. Westerners left many accounts praising Chengdu as "among the finest cities," "a second Peking," with a "classical atmosphere like that of Kyoto." By the late nineteenth century, when coastal cities experienced dramatic change, Chengdu remained a traditional Chinese city with little Western influence. Until just before the turn of the twentieth century, Europeans were surprised to find that Chengdu owed "absolutely nothing to European influence."[4]

Chengdu had one of the largest populations of the country's inland cities in the late nineteenth and early twentieth centuries. In the 1900s–1920s, its population was 340,000–350,000, and in the 1930s–early 1940s, 440,000–450,000. In 1945, its population reached its highest point, 740,000, before falling to 650,000 in 1949.[5] Chengdu was surrounded by a wall. During the Qing dynasty, it had only four gates for communication with the outside world, but three others were opened during the 1910s and 1930s. Within the city wall, Chengdu had two smaller walled subdivisions—the Smaller City (Shaosheng, also called "Manchu City") and the Imperial City (Huangcheng). The Smaller City, home to the Manchus, was in the west section of Chengdu; the wall that separated it from the larger city was dismantled after the 1911 Revolution. The Imperial City, a historical site of the Han dynasty (206 BC–AD 220) rebuilt during the Ming (1368–1644), was located in the central area east of the big city and surrounded by the Imperial River (Yuhe). The Imperial City featured the Examination Hall (*Gongyuan*), where provincial civil service examinations were given; the Imperial City was destroyed during the Cultural Revolution in the 1960s (see Map 1).

Drinking tea has been part of Chinese daily life for millennia. An old Chinese axiom states that "there are seven things you need as soon as you get up in the early morning: oil, salt, firewood, rice, soy sauce, vinegar, and tea." Tea drinking in fact originated in Sichuan and can be traced back to the Western Zhou (c. eleventh to eighth centuries BC). The practice spread to other regions after the unification of the Qin dynasty (221–207 BC).[6] Scholars liked to drink tea in a quiet environment and to write essays and poems describing the feelings that tea inspired. Zheng Banqiao, one of the greatest Chinese painters of the Qing dynasty, always included both tea and bamboo in his works. His idea of bliss was "to live in a thatched-roof cottage," where he could paint and sip a cup of "pre-rain tea" (*yuqiancha*)

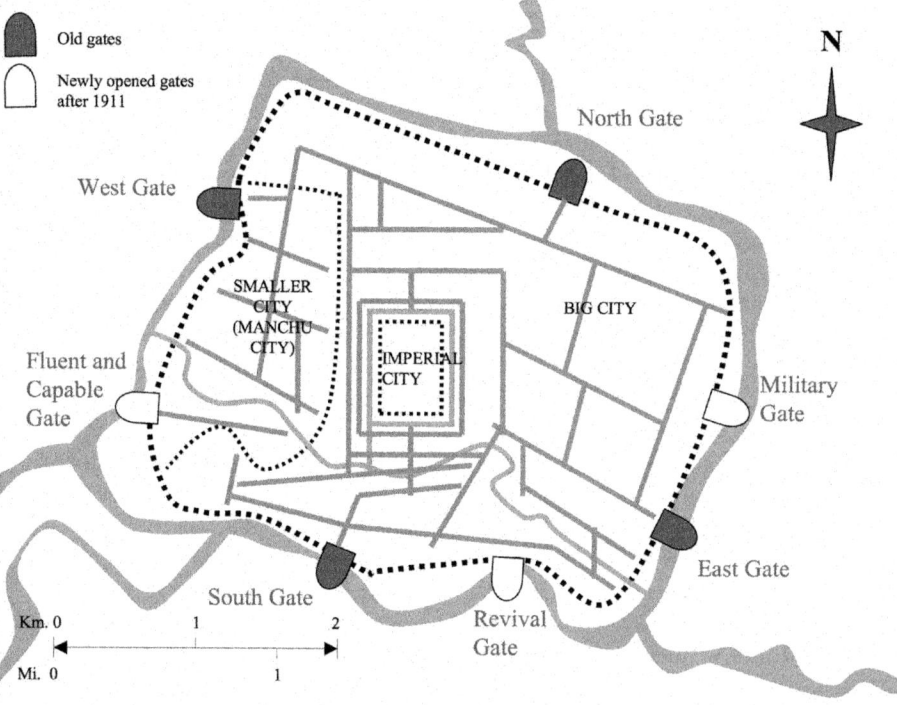

MAP 1: Chengdu, its wall, and its gates, 1900–1950. Adapted from Di Wang, 2003: 26.

while looking through the window at green clouds of bamboo.[7] Zheng Banqiao's apparent desire to escape human society and live closer to nature was often expressed in the inscriptions on his paintings. Yet, he would not have found such tranquility in the teahouses of Chengdu. Although teahouses had both tea and bamboo (bamboo chairs or actual bamboo), they were usually noisy and crowded as patrons participated in public life as well as drank tea.

Various historical records provide us with rich accounts of tea, tea drinking, and tea culture, but little is known about the teahouses themselves. It is clear that they have a long history, but we do not know precisely when and how they originated. Documents mention many kinds of tea-drinking places, including *chashi* (tea chambers), *chatan* (tea stalls), *chapeng* (tea sheds or tea booths), *chafang* (tea rooms), *chashe* (tea societies), *chayuan* (tea gardens), *chating* (tea halls; tea pavilions), *chalou* (tea balconies), *chapu* (tea shops), and so on. In different places and times such places went by different names. Because of a lack of detailed information, we do not know how similar these places were to our contemporary *chaguan* (teahouses). We do know that the earliest form of public tea drinking—in "tea chambers" (*chashi*)—appeared in the Tang dynasty (618–907).[8] Later, Bianjing, capital of the Northern Song (960–1127), and Hangzhou, capital of the Southern Song (1127–1279), had many "tea rooms" (*chafang*). These drinking places also hosted business meetings as well as gatherings of performers and prostitutes. The literature of the Ming dynasty (1368–1644) also contains references to tea shops, especially in such cities as Nanjing, Hangzhou, and Yangzhou.[9]

In Chengdu, the earliest record of tea-drinking places dates from the Yuan dynasty (1271–1368).[10] *A Record of Festivals* (Suihua jilipu) of the Yuan mentions "tea and wine shops" (*chafang jiusi*) in Chengdu, where people drank tea while entertainers sang "tea poems" (*chaci*).[11] However, little detailed information about teahouses is found in pre-twentieth-century sources; a few brief references are found in poetry. Li Diaoyuan, a well-known scholar of the Qianlong period (1736–95), wrote a poem titled "Rest at the Four-Horse Bridge" (Simaqiao xiaoqi), which describes how he stopped his horse cart and bought a bowl of tea at the end of the bridge.[12] The poet did not state whether he bought the tea from a formal teahouse or a crude tea stall, but at least we know that tea was commonly available at tea establishments during that time. A bamboo-branch poem printed in 1805 offers more information: "A new teahouse has been opened on Confucian Temple Street, / with flowers sending forth a delicate fragrance during all four seasons. / At night, it attracts even more visitors, and bustles / with noise and excitement under bright goat-horn lanterns."[13] This poem not only describes the location and atmosphere of the teahouse, but also provides the first known use of the term *chaguan* (teahouse). Though comparable to modern teahouses, *chaguan* did not become popular until the late nineteenth or early twentieth centuries. Zhou Xun, a late-Qing official, wrote that "Every street had a teahouse, but no official and member of the gentry would go to one that placed tables with four stools each on the sidewalks and did not have private rooms and armchairs." Until the early twentieth century, teahouses still used high square tables, stools, and benches, but after the 1911 Revolution, the teahouses in the Smaller City Park began to use low tables and bamboo chairs, a trend later adopted by all others.[14]

Chaguan is now the most common term for China's teahouses, but in Sichuan, especially before the People's Republic, the most frequent term was the generic and informal *chapu*. "Let's go to a *chapu*" was often heard in Chengdu to refer to all sorts of teahouses. Whereas *chapu* referred to a certain kind of public space, *chashe* or *chashe ye* often referred to the teahouse profession itself. Early in the twentieth century, more elegant teahouses known as *chayuan* (tea gardens) and *chalou* (tea balconies) began to be seen;

the former often staged performances of local operas and the latter were usually located on the second floor of a building.

In the Republican period, many visitors to Chengdu, whether Chinese or foreign, were impressed by the city's teahouse life and culture, and included descriptions of teahouses in their travel notes.[15] Some described old Chengdu as a city of "Three Plenties": plenty of idle people, plenty of teahouses, and plenty of lavatories.[16] The city was best known for having the most teahouses, the most patrons, and those who spent the most hours each day at a teahouse. Visitors often compared the teahouses in Chengdu to those in other regions. For example, a Westerner found that in Chengdu, "there are also restaurants and tea-drinking saloons open to the street. The latter take the place of the public-houses in England, and are a great deal less harmful. Friends meet there for social chat." He also noted that "a large proportion of the business is also done there." The most detailed descriptions of teahouses came from Chinese travelers. When Shu Xincheng, a famous educator in the Republican period, visited Chengdu in the 1920s, the most remarkable characteristic he found was the feeling of "special leisure in people's lives." The outbreak of war did little to change this. Xiao Jun, a well-known leftist writer who came to Chengdu in 1938, was surprised by the large number of teahouses and exaggeratedly proclaimed that "there is a willow tree every ten steps in Jiangnan, but there is a teahouse every ten steps in Chengdu." Wu Zhihui, an important figure of the Nationalist Party who once studied in Paris, said in 1939, "Teahouses in Chengdu are as popular as coffeehouses in Paris."[17]

He Manzi, one of China's most prolific contemporary writers and literary critics recalled: "When I was a child, I thought that Jiangnan had the most prosperous teahouses. After I grew up and visited Yangzhou, I found that it had many more teahouses than Jiangnan. But upon my arrival in Chengdu during the war, I found that the teahouses there were the best to be found anywhere on earth or in heaven!"[18] He likes to discuss teahouses in Chengdu although he was born and reared in Jiangnan and has spent almost all of his life there except for a few years during the War of Resistance. Teahouse life, however, is one of his favorite topics, and he has written extensively about his most memorable experiences in the teahouses of Chengdu.[19] In fact, He Manzi was just one of many visitors to Chengdu who were surprised to discover the richness of its teahouse culture and found that the teahouse was a complex social institution that served various economic, social, and cultural functions.

In 1943 an author wrote a very interesting article, "On Teahouses" (*Guanyu chaguan*), which describes his experiences in the teahouses of different cities. The author, not a Sichuan native, arrived there during the war. As a child, he wrote, his parents did not allow him to go to the teahouse because it was a place for "lower society"—opium users and gamblers. His parents would beat him for merely standing at the door and watching the show inside. Therefore, although he was curious about teahouses, he never entered one until he was eighteen years old and moved to Wuhan. Teahouse-goers in Wuhan were "indecent" people too, and from them he learned to gamble, feed birds, and speak the language of hooligans. He became known as an "young ruffian" (*eshao*). Later, he traveled to many cities and towns but seldom visited teahouses, except in Shanghai and Nanjing, where the women singers who performed on the stage to an audience of well-dressed men made a deep impression on him. Then, during the war, he went to Sichuan and lived in Chongqing for five years, spending "more than one hundred nights in the coffeehouses," which were nicknamed "foreign teahouses" (*waiguo chaguan*). Eventually, he arrived in Chengdu and was surprised to find that teahouses provided a comfortable setting for customers of all social classes. He wrote that "the teahouses in Chengdu are the greatest among all cities" and that a teahouse there was probably the "only place today where one could spend more than half a day at a cost of five yuan."[20]

These writers had different backgrounds and their observations came from a variety of angles, but their impressions of teahouse life were remarkably similar. They all believed the teahouse was an especially important part of daily life in Chengdu, and that teahouse culture in Chengdu was prominent and unique because teahouses there were more accessible, were open for longer hours than anywhere else in China, and served all classes of customers.

Debate over Patronizing Teahouses

Throughout the first half of the twentieth century, debate raged over the popularity of teahouses, which could be divided by the War of Resistance in 1937 into two periods. The first ranged from the late Qing and the early Republic, when criticism was primarily internal, a part of local elites' urban reform of popular culture and so-called local backwardness, while some outsiders showed greater appreciation of teahouse life. After the war broke out, however, major criticism of teahouses and everyday culture came from immigrants from East China, while local people strongly reacted to this criticism, revealing cultural conflict between the inland and costal regions. This debate shows how reformist elites and government officials evaluated and manipulated the teahouse and teahouse life. Elites' debates on the teahouse reflected their different attitudes toward popular culture, which determined their policies.

Elites criticized the teahouse through official documents, newspaper reports, and other writings they produced. This large-scale criticism originated in the social reform of the late Qing era and became more obvious and stronger in the Republican period. Criticism generally concentrated on three aspects of teahouse life: gambling, watching folk performances and local operas, and loitering. Elites paid special attention to women's appearances in public. Their opposition to women patronizing teahouses may contradict our assumption that China's new, Westernized elites were open-mind about women's public activities. Reformers, on the one hand, orchestrated many economic, educational, and social changes based on agendas adopted from the West or Japan; on the other hand, they regarded women's public activities as "uncivilized."[21]

There were more intense attacks on popular culture after the collapse of the Qing empire. In 1912, for instance, the new governor of Sichuan Province ordered the police to close the Joy Tea Garden. The *Citizens' Daily* (Guomin gongbao) published an essay supporting this measure, stating in response to the argument that operas served an educational purpose that they in fact promoted "nothing but passing leisure time." The Joy, criticized for not segregating men and women, argued that men and women in the West studied together at school. But the article retorted that the teahouse "damaged China's rituals" just as did the custom of Japanese men and women bathing together in public bathhouses. This article denied the accepted late Qing notion that opera served an educational function, which had led to the reform of local operas. This anti-teahouse and anti-theater sentiment became so widespread that it gave rise to a popular saying: "Don't enter teahouses and don't watch local operas; just cultivate the land and plant rice. Plant one seed but harvest ten thousand grains."[22]

Throughout the late 1910s and 1920s mainstream elites continued to criticize teahouse life, although some defended it by emphasizing its social functions. The custom of frequenting teahouses had a long history and met a real social need. Shu Xincheng, a prominent educator, who visited Chengdu during the 1920s, understood why Chengdu people loved the teahouse:

When I consider the leisurely lifestyle, I think of the men and women who spend their lives rushing around in industrialized and commercialized society and of my own rushing about to make a living, but without having a real life. Several decades or even a century ago, before the West touched our country, China was not pressured to enter the twentieth century under the reach of science and we were free. Yet now that has changed and everything is controlled by global trends, and even the leisurely life found in Chengdu could be lost to the railroads of Sichuan and Hubei and highways of Chengdu and Chongqing. We should feel lucky to see the agrarian life described by Zhang Shizhao and exhort our friends in Sichuan to cherish this life.[23]

Shu admired the slow-paced, traditional life found generations earlier and the cheap entertainment that the teahouse provided. According to his estimate, people in Chengdu could enjoy tea, lunch, and operas all for less than people in Shanghai spent on cigarettes. He also pointed out that it is hypocritical to condemn ordinary citizens for wasting time when no one criticizes government officials and others for doing the same. Unlike most Westernized scholars, Shu yearned for the traditional lifestyle that had all but disappeared along the coast. Of course, Shu came from a coastal area where prices and labor costs were much higher, and while he did not consider the cost of drinking tea, eating noodles, and watching operas in first-class seats expensive, these were a significant—although not insurmountable—expense for most people in Chengdu.

During the War of Resistance reformist elites and the government all framed their constant attacks on teahouse culture in the larger context of the war. Their basic point was that when the very fate of the nation was at stake, people should devote their money and energy to saving the country rather than squandering them in the teahouse. They often compared the plight of soldiers fighting on the bloody battlefields with people whiling away the hours at teahouses, turning leisure pursuits into shameful activities. According to the author of the essay "The Social Situation in Wartime Chengdu" (Zhanshi Chengdu shehui dongtai) published in 1938, the second year of the Japanese invasion, Chengdu's residents seemed to care little about the war. The essay stated that there were two kinds of "special people": those who played mahjong and those who lingered in the teahouse. Sitting in the teahouse was "surely the pastime of Chengdu's people." Although some might go to the teahouse to conduct business, 50 to 60 percent of teahouse-goers, the essay claimed, went "purely to drink tea" (weichicha er chicha), ensuring that teahouses always did a good business. This essay urged those who were selfish and insensitive to wake up and care more about the fate of the nation.[24]

Some elites, however, treasured and defended teahouse life in Chengdu. They pointed out that tea was the cheapest of all drinks and that teahouses were not the exclusive domain of gossip and rumors. They acknowledged that teahouses had many problems and that it was necessary to limit the number of teahouses, enforce registration and hygienic standards, and forbid gambling and "lecherous" shows, but they disagreed with the radical measure of permanently closing teahouses. A writer gave some concrete examples of teahouse culture's good qualities, one of which was that a man who quarreled with his wife was likely to forget his troubles after a few hours spent chatting with friends or reading a few newspapers at a teahouse. Another author explained that the many young people who were unemployed found the teahouse to be the cheapest place to kill time, relieve frustration, and even find a job if they were lucky.[25]

The most passionate defense of teahouse culture came from a writer who used the pen name Lao Xiang (Old Folk) in a long series, "A Discussion of

Tea Drinking by Chengdu People" (Tan Chengduren chicha) published in the *West China Evening News* (Huaxi wanbao) in 1942. The author pointed out that drinking tea had always been a part of daily life in Chengdu, where it was "neither cherished nor despised," and that it had not become a "serious issue until some people began to talk about it." In response to the criticism that people wasted too much time in the teahouse, the author wrote mockingly, "It seems these people treasure every minute but sometimes they let the cat out of the bag because they also like to play cards, chat, and watch local operas, spending more time in these activities than people in Chengdu do drinking tea." Those who had different hobbies and preferences joined the critical chorus of teahouse-goers. Lao Xiang, responding to the description of the teahouse as the "devil's den" (*moku*) where students ignored their studies, argued that "we cannot claim that all bad things originate in the teahouse." He suggested that educators find out why students liked to go to the teahouse and pointed out that "everything has both advantages and disadvantages," and that "we do not destroy an entire society just to get rid of a few bad people." Lao Xiang further stated that many teahouse-goers were poor and liked to relieve their fatigue by meeting friends at the teahouse and conversing about things "as big as space to as small as a fly; from Aristotle to the shape of a woman's body; and from skyscrapers in New York to the Peace and Joy Temple (Anle si)." While some people discussed topics at random and some conducted business, others just sat alone, reading books. He even gave a foreign example to support his point: "The great French writer Balzac drank foreign tea and coffee while writing his book, *The Human Comedy*." Even commoners might be inspired to do great things while drinking tea: "They do not gamble, drink much alcohol, watch local operas, or frequent prostitutes, so who are we to say they have enjoyed themselves too much?"

Lao Xiang also addressed the claim that "mere talk hurts the country" (*qingtan wuguo*) by writing that critics considered the national interest a top priority, but while they despised "mere talking," they never volunteered to go to the frontlines to fight the Japanese, but only engaged in empty talk themselves. The author placed opposing ideas in extreme juxtaposition. If the claim that "mere talk hurts the country" were correct, then "teahouse-goers would be traitors and should be put in jail" and "given the death penalty." The article claimed that critics either did not know the cause of the country's calamities or "they know but pretend not to see." The author added sarcastically, "They should follow Hitler and burn all books on tea." Lao Xiang further asked, "Is drinking tea [in the teahouse] really a crime?" There were reasons that Chengdu had so many teahouses, tea gardens, tea balconies, and tea halls. A teahouse functioned as a market, where people traded goods and settled disputes. Teahouses on both sides of the road provided a resting place for travelers and traders from outside the city. Therefore, teahouses provided a convenience for travelers and others who regularly went there to drink "early tea" (*zaocha*), "noon tea" (*wucha*), and "evening tea" (*wancha*). "They are addicted," Lao Xiang argued, "so spending 20 cents on tea is not a luxury." The article asks why drinking coffee in a coffee shop was "fashionable," but drinking tea was considered "backward." Both activities were similar; those who praised coffee but ridiculed tea were "too snobbish" (*guoyu shili*) and had "the face of a Western dog" (*xizai xiang*). The author even noted that he wrote the article from a teahouse balcony and that

> if more public spaces are built for appointments and gatherings of friends in the future, people will spend less time in the teahouse. We do not cry out, "Long Live Teahouses!" but we also disagree that teahouses should be forbidden. When a better alternative emerges, teahouses may fade away. In the meantime, however, we have to go to teahouses to drink, rest, chat, do business, meet friends, and so on. We still repeat the old saying, "Let's drink tea on the street corner."[26]

Lao Xiang's article is the most comprehensive defense of teahouses and teahouse life that I have found. Although it was a lone voice in a tidal wave of criticism, it at least reflected the opinion of most Chengdu residents, who resisted the attempt to change their lifestyle. His article also suggested that a gap existed between Chengdu natives and outsiders. Although some outsiders, like Shu Xincheng, held a positive view of the teahouse, Lao Xiang's article implied that most critics were outsiders. Lao Xiang believed that these critics were do-nothings who came to Chengdu after the war and, because they could not criticize the rich and powerful, found a convenient target in Chengdu's teahouse culture, which they attacked as "senseless" (*wuliao*) and "harmful to the country" (*wuguo*). In mocking critics as having "the face of a Western dog," he suggested that only those who embraced Western attitudes attacked Chinese tradition, a view that reflected his own hostility to the "other," underscoring ethnic and geographical conflict. Therefore, during the war, the debate over the teahouse was actually a debate over issues far beyond the scope of teahouse life, a cultural conflict that reached a new level with the influx of downriver people (*xiajiang ren*) to Chengdu. When the elites from downriver picked the teahouse as their target of criticism, the debate to some extent became a fight between Sichuanese and coastal people over the evaluation of culture and lifestyle. Lao Xiang's article, however, indicates that Chengdu people lacked the confidence to defend their teahouse life and culture. Even though Lao Xiang enthusiastically championed teahouses, he believed that a new type of public facility would eventually replace them. Although he repeatedly emphasized teahouses' useful functions, he seemed to agree that they were an artifact of "old society" that would be abandoned as society became more "progressive." He likely never anticipated that more than fifty years later, when society had indeed become much more "progressive," teahouses would flourish to an unprecedented degree.[27]

The Teahouse in Urban History

Scholars have emphasized the significance of the teahouse in urban history; however, scholarship to date has not accounted for the broader importance of the teahouse in Chinese society and culture. The scholarship on Chinese teahouses has followed three approaches. The first, taken by Japanese scholars beginning in the early 1980s, offers a comprehensive view. Suzuki Tōmō published an article on the teahouses in late Qing Jiangsu and Zhejiang, describing how people used the teahouse for social activities such as leisurely passing time, dispute resolution, and gambling. But, as he recognized, because of a lack of sources, "the analysis is not adequately developed," and could not answer questions about how teahouses were managed, for example.[28] The few subsequent studies of teahouses basically followed the same path, including an article on teahouses in Chengdu by Nichizawa Haruhiko, which opened a window to the social life of China's vast interior.[29] A profound study by Wang Hung-tai traces the origin of the teahouse and examines the rise, fall, and subsequent renaissance of the teahouse from the Song (960–1279) to the Qing (1644–1911) dynasties. Wang's study largely focuses on coastal cities such as Nanjing and Hangzhou. The major argument of all these scholars is that the development of teahouses reflected the expansion of urban public space and that teahouses played a complex role in urban society.[30]

The second approach considers the teahouse a basic unit of social structure and one of many factors shaping Chinese urban history. According to this approach, teahouses were often used as the "turf" where disputes were settled by various associations of clans, professions, and societies, which included nearly every member of the influential local elites. Teahouses, in the words of William Rowe, were "the forums of 'private talk' among preselected and like-minded members of the urban elite."[31] William Skinner, in his classic study of marketing and social structure in China, found that teahouses in market towns on the Chengdu Plain served the same social functions as wine shops, restaurants, and other shops, with facilities that were very basic. He noted that teahouses became a gathering place for the Sworn Brotherhood Society (*Gelaohui*), of which most adult males were members.[32] Skinner paid more attention to the social network of the teahouse, while William Rowe emphasizes its role as a social club. Rowe finds that in Hankou, teahouses were a place for men. Teahouses were the site of "freewheeling and non-class-restrictive discussions of current news and events, the city's poetry societies, like the exclusive men's clubs that began to appear in early modern London and Paris." It is significant to note these similarities between Chinese teahouses and comparable Western venues, and although Rowe did not analyze the differences, he emphasizes the importance of the opportunity for social interaction in such places as teahouses.[33]

The third approach, taken by more recent studies, considers the teahouse as an arena of social, cultural, and political conflict between elites and ordinary people and between the state and society. This approach emphasizes that during the modernist movement of the early twentieth century, local elites employed new media such as newspapers and "mercilessly attacked the teahouse and its culture as outmoded and harmful to the Republican order." This movement became part of modern nation-building. Superficially, the teahouse and teahouse culture seemed weak and vulnerable—subject to ceaseless regulation, attack, and subsequent reformation—but in reality they proved vibrant and enduring.[34] In her article "Tempest over Teapots," Qin Shao examines how the new elites and modern media in Nantong "tried to police the public arena." Shao explores the relationship between teahouses and urban development, social changes as seen through teahouses, and the new elites' criticism of teahouses.[35] Joshua Goldstein's "From Teahouse to Playhouse" describes how Peking opera shaped the teahouse and the theater in early Republican Beijing and Shanghai, how teahouse theaters served as centers of amusement, and how teahouses shaped the relationship between theaters and their audiences. Goldstein argues that the transformation of Chinese teahouse theaters into Westernized playhouses reflected "changes in fundamental principles of daily social and political practice" in the early twentieth century.[36] In my article "The Idle and the Busy," I analyze the teahouse as a class-conscious and gendered place and a political arena where various groups promoted their agendas and where the government enforced its policies. Although modernization in the early twentieth century had a profoundly negative impact on the folk traditions and popular culture of the previous centuries, the teahouse survived by adapting to the new social and political environment.[37]

These studies that examine one or a few aspects of this extraordinarily complex public space have built a foundation for us to understand Chinese teahouses, showing that teahouses played a multifunctional role in urban life, became a basic unit of social structure, and were attacked and changed by the state and social reformers alike during the modernist transformation. All these studies agree on the importance of the teahouse in Chinese society. Although they have addressed many aspects of the teahouse, they have focused heavily on coastal areas and concentrated on the Qing and early Republic. We basically know little about the effect of the GMD and Nationalist government, especially during the War of Resistance and Civil War. Many questions remain: How did local culture resist the uniformity of modernity along with the growing role of the state in teahouse life? Why could teahouses survive such high density and what was the secret for running a successful business? What liaison role did the professional organizations of teahouses play between the government and teahouses? What were the working conditions and what was the workplace culture in the teahouse? Why and how did so many people, social groups, and organizations rely so much on the teahouse? How did the teahouse become a place for negotiating social conflict? Why and how did reformers and the government want to control the teahouse and how did concrete policies influence teahouse life? To what extent did the teahouse connect with politics and play a political role? In sum, the most basic questions are three: What role did the teahouse play in the city's economic life? How did people use this public space in daily life? And how and to what extent did the teahouse become an arena for various political and social struggles? To answer these questions requires us going inside the teahouse for a close examination.

The Teahouse in Comparative Perspective

A local matter is, to a certain extent, often generalizable to a national pattern. Teahouse culture is an example: the teahouses of Chengdu reflect a common phenomenon in Chinese culture and public life. In fact, teahouses in Chengdu and in Shanghai, Hangzhou, Yangzhou, Nantong, and elsewhere shared many features: people used these largely male sanctuaries as a space for leisure activities, as a market, business office, entertainment venue, and as a place to settle disputes. From this perspective, it can be said that teahouses throughout China were "Chinese teahouses."[38] Yet, we can still find some unique characteristics in the teahouses of each region or city. In the teahouses of Shanghai, for example, there was much less gender separation, and women gained entry to teahouses much earlier, than in Chengdu. In the 1870s, women in Shanghai increasingly ventured into teahouses, theaters, opium dens, and other public places. Of course, some were prostitutes, but many were not; young women liked to have dates in teahouses, for example. Middle- and lower-class women frequented teahouses and theaters during the 1880s, when it was common for women to mingle with men there and in opium dens, although upper-class women still did not feel comfortable in such places.[39] In Beijing, theaters emerged during the seventeenth and eighteenth centuries, much earlier than in Chengdu, and teahouses grew out of Peking opera theaters, the opposite of what happened in Chengdu, where teahouses became the early stages for performances. Under the verandas or in the shadow of trees of Beijing's parks, for instance, were round or square tables covered with white cloths upon which sat platters of fried seeds, peanuts, and other snacks. These places sold soda, beer, and all kinds of snacks in addition to tea. Tea in fact was not their primary business. Northerners usually drank plain boiled water or cold well water; only old men or gentry drank tea. One seldom saw teahouses in Hebei, Henan, Anhui, Shaanxi, or Northeast China. In many places, such as Tianjin, rather than drinking tea in a public teahouse people went to facilities called "tiger stoves" (*laohu zao*) where they bought hot or boiling water, which they took back home to make tea.[40]

Teahouses in south China were much more sophisticated. Guangdong had a kind of tea balcony that superficially looked like those in Sichuan, but they obviously catered to a "bourgeois" clientele, unlike the "popularized" (*pingmin hua*) tea balconies of Sichuan. These establishments had four or five floors, and the tea served on the higher floors commanded higher prices because everything there was better: the tables, chairs, cups, saucers, and even the sunshine. These floors were reserved for wealthier patrons, usually rich merchants and gentry, who liked "putting on airs." They usually bought snacks as well as tea, and used these places to meet people or to discuss business, just as people in Sichuan did. In Yangzhou, the teahouse and public bathhouse were combined, usually serving tea in the morning and opening for bathing in the afternoon. Nanjing had far fewer teahouses than Chengdu, and people visited them only in the morning. Moreover, the majority of teahouse-goers in Nanjing belonged to the middle and lower classes. Nantong had three kinds of teahouses: *dianxin* (which served snacks with tea), *qing chaguan* (which served only tea), and *tangshui luzi* (or *laohu zao*, "water stoves," which sold hot and boiled water). All the teahouses in Nantong were for lower-class people; elites were not among their clientele.[41]

People wrote that teahouses in Chengdu were well known for being "commoner oriented." Although in Chengdu "there's not a single street that has no teahouse," none of Chengdu's teahouses was as splendid as those in Shanghai and Guangdong. He Manzi recalled that he did not have the courage to enter teahouses in other cities, but this was not a problem during his sojourn in wartime Chengdu, where people from both high and low society could sit in the same teahouse with little concern about class.[42] Another famous modern writer, Huang Shang, compared teahouses in Sichuan with those in other regions, stating that

> I could envision laborers in short jackets sitting under the shadow of the big trees in Zhongshan Park in Beijing. In Suzhou, teahouse-goers were almost exclusively people who carried birdcages and wore the small "melon-skin caps" typical of old China that often appeared in the cartoons of Feng Zikai, the best known cartoonist during the Republican period. Almost all of Feng Zikai's cartoons depicted the "idle class" (*youxian jieji*) who killed time in the teahouse.

But teahouses in Sichuan were different. "All sorts of people could be found there. A policeman could share a table with a common laborer, and next to him might be a man in a Western-style suit and leather shoes. College students come here to study and merchants to conduct business."[43]

Although tea is China's national drink, found everywhere throughout the country, and teahouses were found in most cities, towns, and even country markets, in no other place were people's lives as intertwined with the teahouse as in Chengdu. Anthropologists have found that "tea drinking in north China is less sophisticated than in the south," and that teahouses and teahouse life were more important to southerners than northerners.[44] The descriptions in the literature of ancient cities such as Hangzhou and Nanjing in *A Record of the Dream* (Menglian lu) and *Unofficial History of Academic Circles* (Rulin waishi) also focused on the south. The travel notes and memories of Shu Xincheng, Huang Yanpei, Zhang Henshui, He Manzi, Huang Shang, and others again focused on the south. Yet, when comparing teahouses in different southern cities, these writers expressed surprised over the size and number of those in Chengdu, as well as the number of their customers and the fact that their clientele included all social classes.

Environment and Lifestyle

The physical environment often dictates lifestyle; it certainly contributed to the development of teahouse culture in Chengdu and elsewhere throughout Sichuan. Unlike the people in most other regions in China, the rural inhabitants of Sichuan, especially those on the Chengdu Plain, lived in relative isolation on their farmsteads, which inhibited the cultivation of village or community life. Because of this, they relied on rural markets more than did people elsewhere. They bought and sold goods at the nearest market on trading days and usually stopped by a teahouse to socialize with friends, take a break, or entertain themselves. Some even found buyers or sellers there.[45] Other environmental factors also contributed to the prosperity of teahouses. The Chengdu Plain had an ancient but well-developed irrigation system that made agriculture highly productive. Farmers did not need to work in the fields the entire year and had ample free time for trade and leisure activities. During the idle seasons, usually summer and winter, they spent a great deal of time in the lower-class teahouses in the market towns and cities. Regarding the pace of life in Chengdu in the 1930s, Xue Chaoming wrote, "a meal can be eaten relatively quickly, but drinking tea in a teahouse takes at least three to four hours." Furthermore, some people theorize that Sichuan's famously spicy food, which stimulates thirst, is popular because the climate of Sichuan is humid. Xue Chaoming, in his travel notes, repeated this theory: "It is a routine process of life for every person in Chengdu that after a meal in a restaurant he goes to a teahouse."[46]

The geography and modes of transportation on the Chengdu Plain also played a role in the prosperity of teahouses. Wang Qingyuan observed that in North China horse- or ox-cart drivers usually stopped at teahouses only long enough to drink a bowl of water, and would not stop at all during short trips. However, the narrow footpaths on the Chengdu Plain made drayage or the use of pack animals rare. Men using shoulder yokes, wheelbarrows, and sedan chairs were much more prevalent. In this area, coolies depended on teahouses as places to take a break, quench their thirst, and, following folklore, drink tea with ingredients that eased sore muscles. Along the roads of the Chengdu Plain, handcarts belonging to coolies were lined up in the front of teahouses all day long. Wang noted that teahouse managers obviously catered to their clientele of carriers and cart pullers and pushers.[47] The soil of the Chengdu Plain was conducive to tea cultivation, but Sichuan's location made exporting tea leaves very difficult, and transportation costs made export to the east coast unfeasible. Therefore, Sichuan tea was sold almost exclusively within Sichuan, and at prices that were affordable for ordinary people.[48]

Its poor water and dearth of fuel made Chengdu particularly dependent on teahouses. Well-water in the city was highly alkaline and bitter. For drinking water, residents depended on water-carriers who brought river water from outside town. Every day, hundreds or even thousands of water-carriers transported water to residences and teahouses on shoulder yokes from which a wooden bucket hung on each end. It was said that "the city would come to a standstill if the water-carriers did not work for even one day." River water was more expensive than the foul well water; in the late Qing era, two buckets of river water cost about the same as four pancakes (*guokui*). In the late 1930s, people began to use wheeled carts and huge wooden vats to transport water into the city. Because obtaining river water was so difficult, many ordinary families bought boiled drinking water directly from teahouses. Nearly all teahouses advertised this service by hanging a sign on which four Chinese characters—*he shui xiang cha* (fragrant tea made with river water)—were written. Many teahouses also sold hot well water for washing, and teahouses usually had two huge vats, one for river water and the other for well water (see Figure I.1).[49]

Firewood, the major fuel in Chengdu, was expensive; many ordinary families lit fires only to cook. When Xue Chaoming visited Chengdu in the 1930s, he found that many families patronized restaurants and teahouses in order to conserve firewood, and bought their hot water for washing from neighborhood teahouses. As mentioned, many Chinese cities, such as Shanghai, had "tiger stoves," which sold only boiled and hot water, but Chengdu had no such facilities. Instead of using precious firewood, residents went to teahouses for such services as boiling medicinal herbs and stewing meat. Access to hot water was so important that proximity to a teahouse was a major consideration when choosing a place to live. Usually, a lack of hot

FIGURE I.1: Sand-filled vats. River water had to be filtered through sand-filled vats. Photo by Chen Jin, 1980s. Photo courtesy of Chen Jin.

water was a problem easily solved: "There will be a teahouse not far from your front door. Buying ten coppers of hot water will be enough for the whole family to wash their faces and feet, and buying a pot of tea will be enough to satisfy the thirsty."[50]

The lifestyle of Chengdu's residents also contributed to the popularity of teahouses. The city had many absentee landlords and property owners who every day had plenty of leisure time to while away in teahouses.[51] Even those who had only a moderate income spent time at the teahouse; it appears that they were not strongly motivated to earn more money. Lower-class people who lived hand-to-mouth also frequented teahouses as long as they could afford to buy a bowl of tea. Teahouses thus became the ideal place for the idle of Chengdu to kill time. The growth in the number of teahouses was also an inevitable outcome of urban development; as more immigrants moved to the city, they needed more places to look for a job, conduct their social lives, or take a break. They did not have permanent homes in the city, so teahouses became something of a home away from home.

Sources

The difficulty of finding sources is one of the major reasons for the dearth of scholarly studies of the teahouse. Although Chinese and foreign visitors often wrote about their impressions of Chengdu's teahouses in their travel notes, reports, and memoirs, these records provide only superficial and general descriptions, and are often devoid of real insights or concrete details.[52] However, this study relies on a massive amount of archival materials about teahouses in the Chengdu Municipal Archives. Valuable records about teahouses are scattered throughout the archives of the police force, the chamber of commerce, and government bureaus that regulated commerce.[53] None of these materials has ever before been explored by either Chinese or Western scholars. This treasure provides a plethora of information about teahouses, including how teahouses were managed, where their capital came from and how much each had, and how they competed for customers. We can also find records detailing taxation and pricing, the number of teahouses in Chengdu, how many tables each had, and tallies of their daily sales, which makes it possible to estimate the average number of patrons each day. There is a complete account of the Teahouse Guild, from which we can reconstruct the role of this organization and its connections with government. The police were involved in many incidents in teahouses—disputes, thefts, robberies, gambling, smuggling, fights, riots, and even murders—and left documentation about their activities. Throughout the Republican period, local government and the police enacted many regulations to deal with issues ranging from security, public decency, political propaganda, and hygiene, to service. All these archival sources offer reliable evidence with which to analyze teahouses and issues related to them.

Although these archives are an invaluable source of material, they are also limited. First, sources are unbalanced. Some periods have extensive archival records and others have much less. There are no archival records before the twentieth century, and very little from the late Qing and early Republic. In 1932, during a local war in Sichuan, most official documents and archives were destroyed. This has made the study of early Republican Chengdu very difficult and constructing a complete historical narrative of Chengdu's teahouses impossible. There are significantly more materials from the 1930s and 1940s, and hence this book is able to provide a relatively detailed account of teahouses during this period. Second, it is difficult to gain a complete picture of teahouse customers. For example, how many customers did a typical teahouse serve per day? At best, we can only estimate this based on information found in other sources, as I try to do in Chapter 1. Also, who were typical customers and what were their social backgrounds? What were the percentages of men and women customers, and what were their age distributions? All these questions are unclear due to a paucity of evidence. Third, many records are incomplete. The final outcomes of many of the disputes cited in this book are unknown. In some cases, only one side of a dispute is recorded, which prevents us from knowing the whole truth. Therefore, I am very cautious when I use these archival sources and try to distinguish facts from the claims made by the people involved.

Of course, when possible I have used other sources, such as newspapers, travel notes, and personal accounts, to overcome these limitations. The reports on teahouse life found in local newspapers, though brief and incomplete, in some ways help fill this unfortunate gap, and are as valuable as archival records. This situation has required me to check sources as thoroughly as possible and to the extent possible find potential links in other fragments. Local newspapers routinely published articles on teahouses, some of which were in serial form.[54] These articles were based on the authors' own observations and investigations and provide important sources that can be regarded as oral histories that help us expand our view of teahouse life in the past. Of course, the authors had their own subjective and highly selective viewpoints. Many of the vivid descriptions of life in everyday Chengdu, and especially teahouse life, were written by travelers or visitors. As soon as a traveler entered Chengdu, he or she would be attracted to the city's unique landscape and culture, and would often be motivated to write down impressions and feelings. Thus, visitors left us our most precious records from which to recover Chengdu's past.

Because of the centrality of the teahouse in everyday life, some historical novels set in Chengdu feature plots that revolve around the teahouse. For example, Li Jieren's novel *Great Wave* (Dabo), first published in 1937, gives a detailed picture of the 1911 Sichuan Railroad Protection Movement and includes many stories from teahouses, reflecting the vibrancy of teahouse life in late Qing Chengdu. Although *Great Wave* is fiction, it is based on the author's personal experiences. His descriptions of Chengdu's landscape, place names, social customs, major events, and historical figures are taken from reality. His novel, according to some critics, lacks imagination, but for scholars of social and cultural history, it is a useful source of information about a society and culture that are long gone. Sha Ting, another great novelist, wrote extensively on daily life and power struggles in the market towns near Chengdu. In 1940 he wrote his well-known short novel *In the Fragrant Chamber Teahouse* (Zai Qixiangju chaguan li), and in 1941 and 1944 he published two more novels based his experiences, *Digging Gold* (Taojin ji) and *Caged Beast* (Kunshou ji).[55] The teahouse became his favorite setting for depicting social conflict, and many of his plots unfold there. While some historical novels can be used as a kind of oral history, we should distinguish between historical facts and a writer's creations when we use fiction as a source for historical research. Novels may provide rich depictions of teahouse culture and life, but they are seen solely through the writers' eyes and are not intended to be objective. Therefore, it is necessary to use them with caution.

This book is organized topically rather than chronologically, which has two benefits: First, it provides structure to otherwise disorderly and unsystematic materials, and second, it gives a more complete picture of the various aspects of the teahouse. Nonetheless, careful attention is paid to chronology within each topical chapter. Sichuan, like the rest of China, suffered great turmoil during the Republican period as its capital city of Chengdu experienced a radical political, economic, and social transformation, which can be observed through the teahouse. Because cultural change can occur very gradually and can appear continuous even if it occurs during times of radical political upheaval, I hold the approach that chronology is more important when addressing emerging social issues, but less so when discussing cultural phenomena that remain relatively unchanged. This thread—the resistance of local culture to the bland uniformity of modernity and the growing role of the state in teahouse life—will be woven through each of the chapters, although from difference angles.

The three chapters in Part One focus on the teahouse itself. Chapter 1 analyzes the teahouse as a business: the size of business; its method of operation, management strategies, and employment practices; its ownership, profitability, and capitalization; and its physical location and setting. Chapter 2 examines the Teahouse Guild's important role as liaison between the government and the trade, and how the guild functioned and handled matters such as its relationship with the government and its control over the trade. Pricing and taxes were the most important issues the guild dealt with, and were a constant source of conflict between the government and the organization. Chapter 3 sheds light on labor issues, particularly the interactions between business, labor, working conditions, and workplace culture. Teahouse workers dealt with social relations, and their experiences embodied various social conflicts played out in a public arena. They and their workplace culture thus became a window through which to observe the workforce and working environment in a Chinese small business, and to understand gender, popular culture, and public life.

Part Two shifts the focus from the teahouse to teahouse-goers. Customers were the major occupants in this public place and were like actors performing on a public stage that became part of everyday culture. Chapter 4 examines the various people in the teahouse and their public lives. Teahouses became the place where many people lingered to socialize while others went to teahouses to conduct business or other purposeful activities. Although Chapter 5 deals with the notion of leisure, its focus is teahouses as an early form of theater and the local operas that were performed there. From these teahouse performances we can look into the lessons this form of popular entertainment taught those who lacked formal education; this became one of reasons elites and the government tried to reform and regulate popular entertainment. Chapter 6 covers the social functions of the teahouse and the issues of class and gender. The teahouse was an arena for all sorts of people and social organizations. People settled their disputes and conflicts in the teahouse, a place where justice could be meted out under public scrutiny. And the Sworn Brotherhood Society adopted teahouses as their headquarters. Traditionally, female customers were prohibited from patronizing teahouses, but early in the twentieth century women challenged this custom, and since then the teahouse has been a constant battleground in the struggle for gender equality.

Part Three examines how social conflict and national and local politics influenced teahouses, teahouse life, and teahouse culture and how teahouses, as a public space, were controlled by the government and elite reformers. Chapter 7 discusses conflicts in the teahouse, which increased dramatically along with social disorder during the Republican period. In the teahouse, lower-class people struggled to make a living, local toughs bullied patrons, soldiers destroyed property, thieves and robbers stole the belongings of patrons and teahouse items alike, and so on. I also examine how the government sought to control public places under the guise of "keeping public order." Chapter 8 explores politics in the teahouse. Reform became a goal of both the government and the elite, although the specific content of reform varied over time. Throughout the late Qing and Republican eras, the teahouse was always a political arena for both local and national politics. During wartime, when teahouse politics reached its zenith, teahouses became a place for mobilization and propaganda, and to an unprecedented extent everyday life became intertwined with national politics.

Finally, the Conclusion presents an overview of how growing state power influenced public space and public life and the extent to which local culture responded to and resisted modernist uniformity. I examine the teahouse as a microcosm or reflection of society at large and how local knowledge could be indicative of a national pattern. I compare the teahouse with the Western tavern, café, coffeehouse, and especially saloon and analyze the differences and similarities of public space and public life between China and the West. I also evaluate the vitality of the teahouse and the degree to which the teahouse, teahouse culture, and teahouse life changed, yet remained the same, during the first half of the twentieth century.

PART ONE

The Teahouse

CHAPTER 1

A Small Business

Teahouses in Sichuan were unique. Teahouses as a topic of conversation seem trivial; they can be found everywhere in Shanghai, Suzhou, and Beijing. . . . But none of them can match those of Sichuan. . . . I entered Sichuan from the north and saw teahouses beginning in Guangyuan, a northern city. The deeper inside Sichuan I traveled, the more teahouses I saw. When I arrived in Chengdu, I found more teahouses than I had ever seen before. There were many streets in Chengdu, and nearly every one had two or three teahouses, always full of customers. In the large teahouses, such as those on Warm Spring Road (Chunxi lu) and by Jade Belt Bridge (Yudai qiao), which could serve a few hundred people, waiters carrying kettles—there were a few dozen kettles of boiled water in each teahouse—quickly ran from one table to another. The teahouse bustled with activity; the atmosphere in no other place was comparable.
—Huang Shang, "Chaguan" (Teahouses)

HUANG SHANG'S DESCRIPTION from 1943 hints at the importance of the teahouses of Sichuan in general, and of Chengdu in particular, in daily life and in commerce. The teahouse in every respect was a small business because it operated with little capital, occupied a small space, had few employees, and generated meager profits. Most teahouse proprietors were small traders who were precariously balanced on the line between the poor and middle class. The term "small business" (*xiao shangye*) was applied universally to the teahouse; that term appeared in official documents, local newspapers, and daily conversations. Moreover, teahouse owners identified themselves as "small business" proprietors. Petitions to the local government for help often emphasized teahouses as "small businesses with little capital" (*xiaoben shangye*). Large teahouses, which had more capital, occupied huge spaces, served hundreds of patrons, and earned more in profits, constituted only a small percentage of the teahouses in Chengdu. The teahouse as an institution succeeded because teahouses found ways to survive and even thrive in the face of severe competition from other teahouses.

Studying the teahouse offers an opportunity to scrutinize small businesses as a whole. Economic historians of China have undertaken significant studies of the operation of modern factories and big companies, but few have analyzed small shops. The few studies of traditional firms focus on large, successful establishments. Teahouses were an important part of the small business trade in Chengdu and developed unique approaches to management issues such as accumulating capital and attracting customers.[1] Therefore, a study of the teahouse trade can shed light on the role of small businesses in general in urban commerce and economic life. This chapter examines the business aspects of teahouses, from their number to the size of their operations. This chapter identifies the forms of capital and ownership of the teahouse and shows that establishing a teahouse did not require a large financial investment; ordinary people could enter the business, and most proprietors were simple people who struggled to make a living. It also analyzes how teahouses were taxed and how teahouse owners sought to ease their tax burden, questions that were closely aligned with the profitability and survival of teahouses. Through a close examination of some representative teahouses, we can see that to survive a teahouse had to be very competitive and that while teahouses shared some common business experiences, each also implemented unique practices.

This chapter reveals how traditional small shops fought to retain their trade in the face of new industries and new government regulations. Through the first half of the twentieth century, Chengdu was basically a world of small shops, of which the teahouse was emblematic, and did not have many modern factories or large companies until the establishment of the People's Republic in 1949. Small shops accounted for the vast majority of the city's economic activity and could be found on almost every street, from commercial centers to remote alleyways. Handicrafts and items for daily use—shoes, hardware, textiles, bowls, wooden wares, clothing, and so forth—were made and sold on the spot. On the main streets, row upon row of small shops sold domestic and imported goods, ranging from food and utensils to medicines. People lived very close to these shops. These small businesses provided a livelihood for many lower-class people and made the city seem prosperous and vital.

Beginning at the turn of the century, foreign products, new industries, and growing state power increasingly influenced Chengdu's economy, resulting in a confrontation between traditional shops on the one hand and modern factories and companies on the other. Although the wave of modernization and Westernization failed to dislodge Chengdu's traditional economic structure, the state power that pushed the trend was sufficient to interfere with many aspects of small business operations. This intervention can be seen in three stages. The first wave of the new economy that washed over the city occurred during the New Policies promoted by the Qing government early in the twentieth century. This involved the introduction of new industries into Chengdu as products, especially foreign goods, gradually entered the Upper Yangzi region, but ultimately it had little overall impact on small businesses in Chengdu.[2] The second stage stretched from the collapse of the Qing in 1911 to 1937, during which Sichuan was relatively independent from the central government, but also fell prey to profound internal chaos. From about the 1910s to the 1930s, warlords, in order to expand their economic power, tried to develop local production. Nonetheless, most of industries established during this period, including those in the fields of energy, machinery, textiles, chemicals, and printing, and the production of daily items, were actually small workshops with only twenty to fifty or so workers. This new development was undertaken with the support of the local government before 1937 but after that was conducted under the national standards of the central government. Chengdu in 1934 had 17,497 shops; in 1936 five trades alone—teahouses, butchers, public baths, barbers, and restaurants—operated 3,290 shops. The third period was from 1937 to 1950. After war broke out, many factories, along with a large number of refugees, government offices, and educational institutions, moved into Chengdu. There were 105 modern factories in 1942 and 330 in 1945, but this did not substantially shift the city's economic structure. After the war, many firms either moved away or closed, ending Chengdu's brief period of prosperity through "industrialization." In 1949, the city's 28,480 small shops and trades continued to dominate the city's economy.[3] From these numbers, we know that throughout the first half of the twentieth century every fourth or fifth household managed a shop, which was engaged in either trade or handcraft production. This basic pattern was not disrupted by wars, political movements, and other external developments, reflecting the enduring strength of small businesses.

An Overview of the Numerical Data

There are no systematic statistics of teahouses in Chengdu, but based on a variety of sources, including archival materials, newspapers, journals, and other records, we can get a rough picture of the overall state of the teahouse business from the late Qing to the fall of the Nationalist government. The number of teahouses in Chengdu remained relatively constant at between five hundred and about eight hundred, except in the year of 1921 (see Table 1.1). Shanghai, the largest and most prosperous city in China, had only 164 teahouses in 1919, while Chengdu had more than six hundred.[4] The number of teahouses in Chengdu did not decrease until 1921, but this was the

TABLE 1.1: Teahouses in Chengdu, 1909–1951

Year	Number of teahouses
1909–10	518[a]
1914	681
1921	1,000+[b]
1929	641
1931	620
1932	600+[c]
1934	748[d]
1935	599
1936	640
1940	610[e]
1941	649[f]
1942	614
1946	623
1949	659[g]
1951	541

SOURCES: 1909–10: *Sichuan guanbao* 2, 1910; 1914: CSJJD, 93-6-2635; 1921: Lai Yeyi, 1932; 1929: CSJJD, 93-5-1046; 1931: GMGB, Jan. 15, 1931; 1932: Lai Yeyi, 1932; 1934: *Chengdu shi difang zhi*, 2000: 42; 1935: XXXW, Jan. 11, 1935; 1936: *Jingwu xunkan* 3 (Aug. 1936); 1940: CSZGD, 38-11-1539; 1941: CSSD, 104-1388; 1942: CSSD, 104-1406; 1946: CSZGD, 38-11-1465; 1949: CSZGD, 38-11-97; 1951: CGTGD, 52-128-2.

a This figure is from a police investigation in 1909, but *An Investigation of Chengdu* (Chengdu tonglan) shows only 454 (CDTL, II: 253).
b The source indicates "more than one thousand."
c The source indicates "more than six hundred."
d Another source says 747 (*Sichuan jingji yuekan* 3, 1934)
e Qiu Chi's report of 1942 stated that Chengdu had 611 teahouses in 1940 (Qiu Chi, 1942).
f There were 39 Level A firms, 399 Level B, and 211 Level C. The number Chen Maozhao cites from the Municipal Government was 614 (1983: 178).
g Other sources note that in 1949, Chengdu had 598 teahouses (Gao Shunian and Wang Yongzhong, 1985: 110; Yang Zhongyi, 1994: 116).

result of the control exerted by the Teahouse Guild and the local government rather than a response to a decline in demand.[5] According to a 1932 article in *Latest News* (Xinxin xinwen), after the 1911 Revolution, the number of teahouses in Chengdu grew to more than one thousand by 1921 but fell dramatically after that. However, this figure is questionable.[6] Based on various other available statistics, Chengdu never had more than about eight hundred teahouses, even as the city's population nearly doubled, from more than 340,000 to more than 650,000, between 1910 and 1949 (see Table 1.2). Even during the War of Resistance, when the refugees who flocked to the city pushed Chengdu's population to its highest level ever up to that time—more than 747,000 in 1947—there were only 614 teahouses. Chengdu had 659 teahouses in 1949, but that number dropped to 541 soon after the establishment of the People's Republic.[7]

Relatively complete records exist for some years, including 1914, 1924, 1929, and 1951, which give the distributions and total number of teahouses, how many tables each had, and the amount of taxes collected. From the 1914 record, we see that Chengdu was divided into six districts with a total of 681 teahouses. Of the 516 streets in Chengdu at the time, only 311 had teahouses.[8] In 1929, the number of districts was reduced from six to five, and the number of streets with teahouses increased from 311 to 336, but the number of teahouses decreased slightly, from 681 to 641. Of the 336 streets that had teahouses, 180 had one teahouse and 91 had two, while others had more.[9] For example, Shaanxi Street (Shaanxi jie) and Laundry Street (Jiangxi jie) each had seven teahouses; Little India (Xiao Tianzhu) had six; and East

TABLE 1.2: Population of Chengdu, 1910–1949

Year	Number of households	Population
1910	67,764	345,867
1926	68,453	302,895
1934	82,177	438,995
1936	78,664	488,563
1937	81,081	463,145
1938	82,656	466,295
1939	67,607	303,104
1940	77,855	355,326
1941	88,088	377,938
1942	97,479	456,536
1943	100,891	441,023
1944	109,970	538,668
1945	239,631	742,188
1946	234,145	726,026
1947	241,404	747,793
1948	125,603 [a]	647,877
1949	126,247 [a]	656,920

SOURCES: Shi Jufu, 1936; XXXW, Apr. 5, 1934, Nov. 25, 1935; CDKB, Nov. 29, 1938; CSJJD, 93-1-900; He Yimin, 2002: 574, 578, 581–82; Zhang Xuejun and Zhang Lihong, 1993: 229–30; Qiao Zengxi, Li Canhua, and Bai Zhaoyu, 1983: 12.

a The numbers of households in 1948 and 1949 are incomplete (Qiao Zengxi, Li Canhua, and Bai Zhaoyu, 1983: 12).

Great Street (Dong dajie), thirteen (see Map 2).[10] The central business district and some areas on the outskirts of the city had a high concentration of teahouses; for instance, the Green Goat Market (Qingyang chang), a marketplace with three streets and only about two hundred households, had nineteen teahouses.[11]

Teahouses were relatively evenly distributed throughout Chengdu (see Table 1.3). In 1929, when Chengdu had more than three hundred thousand residents, there were 641 teahouses distributed across 336 streets in five districts, for an average of 2.12 teahouses per one thousand residents (see Map 3).[12] Districts 2 and 4 had the largest populations (75,739 and 74,177, respectively) and number of teahouses (133 and 136, respectively). However, a district outside the East Gate (Outer East) had the highest density of teahouses, with three teahouses per one thousand people. As for the districts within the city walls, the West had the highest density, with more than 107 teahouses for 46,195 residents on 44 streets, or 2.31 teahouses per one thousand residents. The West District became a major recreational

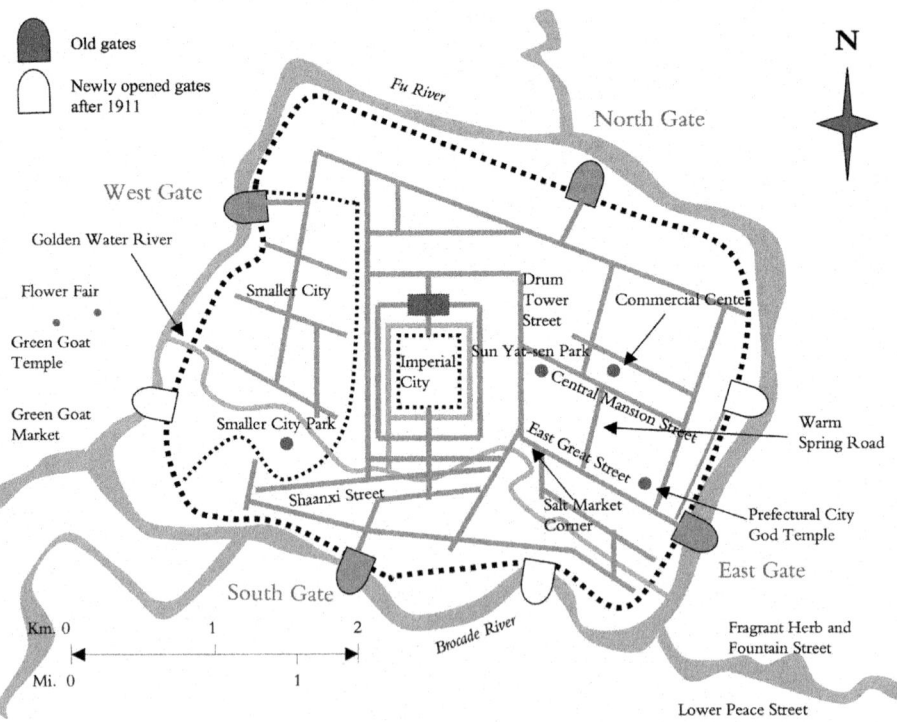

MAP 2: Some frequently mentioned streets and places, 1900–1950

TABLE 1.3: Streets, teahouses, and population in Chengdu, late 1920s

District	Streets with teahouses	Number of teahouses	Population	Teahouses per 1,000 residents
1 (East)	78	128	65,525	1.95
2 (South)	73	133	75,739	1.76
3 (West)	44	107	46,195	2.31
4 (North)	83	136	74,177	1.83
5 (Outer East)	58	137	41,259	3.32
Total	336	641	302,895	2.12

NOTE: The definition of districts in Chengdu changed a few times during the Republican period. Sometimes districts were identified by numbers (such as District 1), sometimes by location (such as East), and sometimes by police branch (such as the First Branch). In 1929, when a survey of teahouses (from which this table draws) was conducted, districts were formed according to police branch, but in 1926–27, when a census was undertaken, they were defined according to their location (such as East District). However, both systems were roughly parallel; for example, District 1 was largely the East District and District 5, the Outer East District.
SOURCES: Streets and teahouses (1929): CSJJD, 93-5-1046; Population (1926–27): CSSD, 1927: 711.

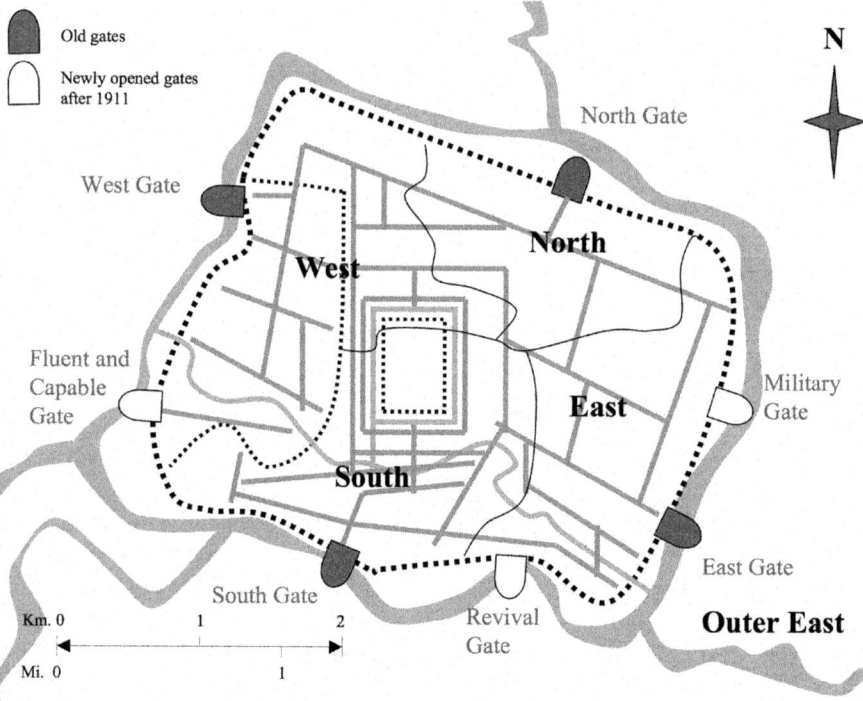

MAP 3: Chengdu and its districts, 1910s–1940s

area beginning in the late Qing, and attractions such as the Flower Fair and Smaller City Park brought many visitors even though this district was relatively poor.

Some accounts include the size of teahouses based on the number of tables and the number of customers they could seat, giving us a clue to the total number of patrons they served each day. In 1914, teahouses had a total of 9,958 tables, for an average of 14.6 tables each, indicating that most teahouses were very small.[13] However, this is only the number of tables that were taxed, so the actual figure likely is much larger. It was common to add tables and chairs according to customer demand, but not to report this in order to avoid tax. In addition to the amount of taxes paid, the number of teahouses and tables gives us insight into how many patrons were served each day. Since we know there were ten thousand tables in 1914, with each table serving an average of ten people, we can determine that one hundred thousand customers, or more than one-fourth of the population of Chengdu, went to teahouses each day.[14]

In early 1942, a local scholar counted four hundred teahouses, each having a maximum of twenty customers per hour, or a total of eight thousand customers. Assuming that teahouses were open an average of ten hours a day, they would have a total of eighty thousand customers per day. The scholar wrote, "It is shocking to see that eighty thousand people waste their precious lives, all at the same time, in teahouses."[15] Using the number six hundred (Chengdu had 614 teahouses; see Table 1.1), and counting by the same method, the total number would reach 120,000. A record of teahouses' daily sales in 1949 provides the most reliable count of daily customers. In that year, Chengdu had 598 teahouses. Of them, sixty were large, selling more than three thousand bowls of tea daily. The seventeen largest teahouses sold a total of 42,700 bowls of tea daily. There were 370 medium-sized teahouses, which sold an average of two hundred bowls per day, for a total of 74,000. There were 168 small teahouses, which had average daily sales of eighty bowls, for a total of 13,400 per day. Using these estimates, we can state that more than 130,000 people visited teahouses daily.[16] If every male head of household went to a teahouse, the number would be near 130,000 (there were over 126,000 households in 1949).[17] Therefore, it seems to me it is a conservative estimate that at least one hundred thousand to one hundred thirty thousand people (that is, one-fifth to one-fourth of the population) visited a teahouse every day. There are many different ways to count or estimate the number of customers, but these numbers give us a rough estimate. Chengdu had a large "floating population" that came and left the city often for business or other activities and depended on the teahouse as much as permanent residents, but the number is difficult to count.

How many people depended on teahouses to make a living? In 1909–10, for example, there were more than sixty-seven thousand households in Chengdu (see Table 1.2); among them were 518 households that ran teahouses, 931 tobacconists, 9 opera troupes, 111 performers, and 589 water carriers, making a total of 2,158 households that depended on teahouses. Because the average family at that time had five members, 2,158 households represent about eleven thousand people. Adding the people such as petty peddlers and barbers who used teahouses as their market or worksite, this number becomes much larger.[18] These people also include teahouse keepers and their family members who worked as helpers, but not necessarily for pay. The Teahouse Guild confirmed in 1932 that there were more than six hundred teahouses in Chengdu, with more than sixty thousand family members and a few thousand workers who depended on them for their livelihoods.[19] In 1941 teahouses ranked fifth in the number of employees among all industries and commercial enterprises.[20]

Teahouses became one of the most important businesses in Chengdu, especially in terms of providing lower-class people a place to earn a living. But what percentage of the total number of small shops in Chengdu were teahouses? Of the known total of 6,615 shops in 1935, restaurants were the most numerous (2,398), food stores were second (910), and teahouses were third (599), or 9 percent of the total number of shops.[21] When Shu Xincheng visited Chengdu during 1924–25, he estimated that teahouses accounted for one in ten shops.[22] His estimate in the 1920s was close to that of the study done in 1935, which may suggest that the percentage of teahouses out of the total number of businesses in Chengdu remained stable.

Capital, Ownership, and Income

Opening a teahouse did not require a large amount of capital and the return on investment was comparatively good. The most basic requirements were tables, chairs, utensils, and of course, a space, which could be rented.[23] Some people believed "if one had a good plan, one could open a teahouse even without any capital," although this might be a slight overstatement. A common practice was to profit from others who benefited from the teahouse, such as farmers, who used the excrement from the toilets as fertilizer, and barbers, who rented a corner of a teahouse to ply their trade. Those who provided services such as hot towels and tobacco usually paid the proprietor as well. These "pre-deposits" were often enough to cover the costs of the initial rent and start-up supplies. Some proprietors even asked those who polished shoes or sold newspapers or other petty goods to invest in the business in exchange for exclusive rights to peddle their wares there (see Figure 1.1).[24]

36   The Teahouse

FIGURE 1.1: A food peddler waiting outside a teahouse. If a patron wants something to eat, he can conveniently buy food from the peddler. Photo by Chen Jin, 1980s. Photo courtesy of Chen Jin.

While there is a lack of detailed records about the capital investments in teahouses in Chengdu before the 1930s, we do have an incomplete figure for 1937—457 teahouses had a total capital of 58,400 yuan, or only 120 yuan per teahouse.[25] However, archival material gives a very reliable and detailed account of the capital invested in teahouses in 1940. The source shows that the lowest investment of capital was 300 yuan, and the highest, 2,500 yuan. In fact, of 610 teahouses, 450 were financed at the minimum level; in other words, 74 percent of teahouses only had 300 yuan as start-up capital. If we add the teahouses that had 300, 400, and 500 yuan of capital, the total is 581, or 95 percent of all the teahouses in Chengdu. Only twelve, or 2 percent of the total, had 1,000 yuan or more of capital. The total capital invested in the 610 teahouses amounted to only 227,200 yuan, or an average of only 373 yuan.[26] This material suggests that 300 yuan was a standard minimum amount required to open a teahouse in 1940, but what was the buying power of 300 yuan? The price of rice was always a major indicator of markets and inflation, and therefore, it is reasonable to put 300 yuan into the context of the price of rice. In August 1940, one dan of rice cost 141 yuan.²⁷ Therefore, 300 yuan could buy 2.1 dan of rice (about 294 kilograms or 650 pounds).²⁸

Some teahouses were limited partnerships that had a much larger capital investment. For example, the Brocade River Pavilion (Jinjiang ge) in Salt Market Corner (Yanshi kou) had 30,000 yuan (*fabi*) in 1942. This was divided into ten shares, each at 3,000 yuan, held by six people; one had four shares (12,000 yuan), one, two shares (6,000 yuan), and four, one share.²⁹ The "partnership agreement" indicates how the teahouse was run and how it distributed financial bonuses. The teahouse had one manager, one bookkeeper, and one salesman, and three supervisors, selected from among the stockholders. The manager was in charge of all business-related matters and was not paid a salary (although his business expenses could be reimbursed), while the bookkeeper and salesman received salaries. The manager had the authority to hire and fire workers. The teahouse reported its business matters, including costs and profits or losses, to shareholders twice a year. Profits or losses were equally divided by each share. At the end of each year, 20 percent of the pure profit could be taken out as a bonus. Decisions on any change, such as an increase or decrease in the amount of capital, were made by consensus of the shareholders. This method of operation was different than that of most other teahouses, which were run more like a family business. This teahouse, as a limited partnership, dispersed risk and expanded capital, which increased its competitive advantage.³⁰

Although opening a teahouse did not require a large amount of capital, capital was turned over quickly. In 1910, investors in the Joy Tea Garden (Yuelai chayuan) received 1.67 taels for every 10 taels invested, and 0.8 percent interest monthly. Adding the interest the investors received in 1909, they gained nearly two to three taels for every 10 taels of investment, which was a very nice profit indeed.³¹ Of course, profit largely depended on the larger economic situation as well as the quality of management decisions. When the economy stagnated or declined, teahouses earned much less in profits or even suffered losses.³² In the early 1930s, the outlook for teahouses turned increasingly negative. Higher costs caused some teahouses to lose money. The Teahouse Guild reported that fuel costs took 50 percent of a teahouse's total income, tea 20 percent, labor 20 percent, and miscellaneous costs 10 percent, and that first-tier teahouses lost 30 to 40 *qianqian* (one qianqian was a thousand wen or a thousand cash) each day; second-tier, 20 to 30, third-tier, more than 10, and the lowest tier, 6 to 7 qianqian. More than forty teahouses went out of business in that single season.³³

In 1931, the more than 620 teahouses in Chengdu were classified into four levels based on their sales and number of wage workers. The first included more than twenty teahouses, each of which employed twenty or more workers and water-carriers and had daily sales of more than 200 qianqian. The second had about ninety teahouses, each of which hired a dozen or more workers and had sales of more than 100 qianqian. The third level had around three hundred teahouses, each with only five or six wage earners and daily sales of 40 to 50 qianqian. At the fourth level there were about two hundred teahouses, which usually had a single room, three to four workers, and daily sales of 20 qianqian.[34] In 1949, the Teahouse Guild grouped its 659 members into three classes: Class A, which had 39 teahouses; Class B, 399; and Class C, 221. The guild's criteria for these classifications are not clear, but they probably were based on size, because the biggest and most well-known teahouses are listed in Class A.[35] The amount of capital might also have been an important criterion. According to a record from 1940, two Class A teahouses, the Sleeping Stream and Three Sages, had 2,000 yuan in capital each, and another, the Cry of the Crane Teahouse, had 2,500, when most teahouses had only 300 to 500.[36]

During the war, most teahouses claimed they faced a financial crisis. A source outlines the financial situation of four teahouses based on the forms they submitted to the government to request permission to raise their prices. From those forms, we can see that all four teahouses claimed a loss. It is possible that some of the teahouses deliberately underreported their income to the municipal government. Those forms also show that tea leaves, fuel, and wages were major expenditures. These teahouses were located in different areas; the first two on Warm Spring Road, called the "special area," and the last two in the "regular area." There are a few notes on these reports. According to one, the "True Entertainment Garden (Zhengyu huayuan) opens late and closes early, and customers are sparse when it is cloudy or raining." Regarding the Two Fountains Tea Hall (Erquan chating), a note said, "its labor costs are high, and it issued ten thousand free coupons on its grand-opening day, so it therefore gives away 400 yuan worth of tea every day."[37]

A source itemized overall income and costs for Class A teahouses in 1945. If a Class A teahouse sold five hundred bowls of tea at 15 yuan per bowl, its income would be 7,500 yuan. Teahouses usually had other sources of income, such as serving hot towels to customers and hot water to nearby residents. This created an additional 150 and 1,000 yuan, respectively, of income, which at 13 percent was only a very small portion of the total income of 8,650 yuan. We can see, however, that the average costs of 13,210 yuan exceed the average income, which meant that a Class A teahouse lost 4,560 yuan for every five hundred bowls of tea sold. We also can see that fuel (coal and charcoal) was the biggest single expenditure, at 7,250 yuan, or 55 percent of total costs, and that the cost of fuel was much higher than the cost of tea leaves, which, at 2,400 yuan (18 percent), was the second-highest expenditure. The cost of wages was relatively low, at 1,150 yuan (9 percent), but teahouses generally provided meals in addition to wages, and the cost of meals should be included in the total cost of labor. Wages and meals added together cost 2,150 yuan, or 16 percent of total expenditures. Other costs include rent (2 percent), taxes (2 percent), equipment maintenance (2 percent), interest on loans (2 percent), and donations (less than 1 percent), which add up to less than 10 percent of the total costs of running a teahouse. Because the Teahouse Guild used this document to support its application for a price increase, it is possible that it overstated the difficulty facing the teahouses.[38] While teahouses faced a slump in sales, the situation might not have been as dire as was claimed, and the guild and teahouses might have overstated their losses to get a bigger tax cut.

The membership lists of the Teahouse Guild offer some information regarding teahouse proprietors' backgrounds, including their age, place of birth, sex, level of education, membership in the GMD, and so on. The list in 1940 shows that 349 teahouse keepers had an education from traditional private schools (57 percent) and 239 from elementary schools (39 percent), but only 22 had gone to middle school (4 percent), and none had gone past middle school.[39] From this, we know that while small shop owners were ordinary people, most (and in the case of teahouse owners, all) received at least a basic education. Most shopkeepers had a basic level of literacy, and as some scholars of Chinese popular culture have noted, "by late Imperial times there were many people who could read, and even write, who were not members of any elite."[40] This background probably helped teahouse owners make informed decisions on everything from the decor and the name of their teahouse to accounting and management practices. The list in 1951 reflected that Sichuanese dominated the teahouse trade in Chengdu; there is no indication that a single teahouse was operated by a non-Sichuan native. For example, none of the proprietors of the 541 registered teahouses were from outside Sichuan.[41] Although it is not clear why outsiders stayed away from the teahouse business, as we have seen, the teahouse in Chengdu was a strong symbol of local culture and tradition, so it would have been difficult for a proprietor who did not speak with a Sichuan accent to attract many customers. This is why teahouse keepers were considered purveyors of local culture who not only provided services to residents but also were a prominent symbol of folk customs. When the twin waves of coastal culture and Westernization washed inland, teahouse keepers were the ones at the frontline of resistance.

Management

The teahouse trade was less affected by economic downturns than other businesses. Also, teahouses conducted their best business at night, when most other shops were closed. As one observer wrote, "Business is slack for markets at night, and customers ignore shops and stalls. Only the teahouses enjoy prosperity, when all guests are engrossed in storytelling." Teahouses had this additional advantage in competing with other small businesses, but competition among teahouses was fierce. Local elites criticized the opening of new teahouses within areas that already had a high concentration of teahouses, and the high concentration of teahouses in commercial areas such as the Commercial Center (before 1910 it was called "Center for Promoting Industry and Commerce"). In response, the Teahouse Guild tried to limit the number of teahouses. It gained support for this from the government, which enacted many regulations (discussed in Chapter 2). On the other hand, competition resulted in better service, a better product, and more efficient management, which helped the teahouse trade thrive.[42]

Insofar as possible, most proprietors kept business practices, such as the amount they paid their workers, how much profit they made, and their business strategies, secret. They tried every way to sell more bowls of tea and hot water. Teahouses usually were open from 5 AM to 10 PM, but some opened earlier and closed later. For example, the Peaceful and Prosperous (Taiheheng) Teahouse on Cotton Street (Mianhua jie), located in a vegetable market, opened at 3 AM to accommodate the vegetable dealers who stopped for their early morning tea before or after taking their goods to market. These were known as "ghost teahouses" (*gui chapu*) because they were open during the time of night when ghosts were thought to wander. A teahouse in Hubei and Hunan Guild Hall Street (Huguang guan) was open until midnight to serve restaurant workers from Warm Spring Road (Chunxi lu) and East Great Street (Dongda jie), who came in very late after a long day of work.[43] Some teahouses operated on different business cycles based on location. Nineteen were concentrated in the Green Goat Market (see Figure 1.2), a small marketplace with about two hundred households on three streets. Their patrons were exclusively the farmers and peddlers who sold their goods there. The markets were open only on the second, fifth, and eighth days of each ten-day trade cycle, which meant that business for the teahouse was good only nine days each month.[44] Although these teahouses still opened for business every day, their profits were made during the market days. Teahouses also had their own daily rhythms. Morning and night were peak points, when customers crowded in, which was known in Chengdu as "rushing into the hall" (*yongtang*). Business in the early afternoon was relatively slow; this time was called "hanging around the hall" (*diaotang*). Of course, this rhythm also depended on the location and nature of the teahouse in question. Those in the vegetable markets might have their peak hours before dawn, while those in commercial areas had their busiest times later in the morning, when nearby shops opened. A teahouse had to adjust its business strategy based on its location and the needs of its customers in order to be profitable.

FIGURE 1.2: A typical rural market on the Chengdu Plain. On trading days, when farmers went to the market to sell and buy goods, teahouses did their best business. Photo by Luther Knight, 1911. Knight, an American, taught at Sichuan College (Sichuan gaodeng xuetang). Photo courtesy of John E. Knight.

Another strategy was the cultivation of regular patrons. Teahouses paid more attention to early-morning patrons and gave them more tea leaves because they tended to be repeat customers. Teahouses sought to provide a pleasant atmosphere; the more elegant ones in particular polished their brass kettles to a mirror-like sheen and kept the tables and chairs clean and neat. While service was important in attracting customers, the quality of tea was even more important. The same kind of tea could be made a more pleasing color, fragrance, shape, and taste using different techniques of drying and compounding.[45] A high-quality, unique compound could become the magic weapon that guaranteed prosperity.

Teahouses typically bought their leaves from tea shops. Next to retail customers, teahouses were the largest single buyer of tea leaves from these shops. Shopkeepers knew that teahouses had different requirements and often served the same teahouses for years or even decades. Most small teahouses, however, had little purchasing power. They often had to buy tea or coal on credit. Some small teahouses that were able to pay cash bought only the smallest quantities needed for daily use, two to three jin (1 jin = 1.1 pounds) of tea, or even one or one-half jin.[46] In the early 1930s the tea trade in Chengdu was controlled by the Official Tea Leaf Store of Chengdu (Chenghua chaan guancha dian) and the Yuanheng Tea Firm (Yuanheng chahao); the local government granted both the power to buy tea leaves from producers and resell them at much higher prices, a continuation of the quota system from the Qing, in which both the local government and privileged merchants enjoyed high profits. Merchants resented the rapidly rising cost of doing business. To protect their interests, the Teahouse Guild swore to "fight the evil tea merchants and ask the government to treat teahouses fairly." The quota system was abandoned in 1942. Some larger teahouses that had a great deal of capital, such as the Prosperity Tea Hall (Huahua chating), bought an entire year's supply at bargain prices directly from the producers when the leaves were ready to be harvested. They usually bought more than they needed and sold the surplus to other teahouses.[47]

Cooperation between teahouses and the peddlers who served their customers was also important. These small venders—butchers, restaurant owners, barbers, and food stand operators—might be shareholders or have other economic ties to a particular teahouse. Food peddlers and butchers usually set up stalls in front of teahouses so that customers could take a piece of meat home after enjoying a bowl of tea and camaraderie with other teahouse-goers. Similarly, people often went to a teahouse after dinner in a restaurant to prolong their fellowship. Teahouses, butchers, and restaurants did not see themselves as competitors, but as a kind of business partner. As for customers who wanted a haircut, "almost 100 percent," it was said, drank tea not only while they waited for their haircut but also when their hair was actually being cut. Barbers took advantage of the availability of hot water in the teahouse and rented space there.[48]

The introduction of electric lighting and other new services also brought customers to teahouses. In the past, teahouses used vegetable oil lamps, which provided dim lighting at best. The Center for Promoting Industry and Commerce attracted many visitors when it began using electricity in 1909, and many new teahouses opened in the area as a result. Business was so good that a local newspaper commented, "Development of teahouses in Chengdu is moving at a tremendous pace."[49] To attract patrons, some teahouses emphasized their modern facilities and some offered novelties never before available in Chengdu. For example, when the Happy and Carefree Pavilion (Taoran ting) was opened in 1912, it claimed five attractions: delicious tea and food; elegant decor; large and even private rooms; "civilized games" from the West for "healthy leisure," such as bowling and table tennis; and access to telephones and newspapers. The Thick Shadow (Nongyin) in the Smaller City Park attracted customers through its exotic

Southeast Asian–style sunshades. In the same park, the Green Sky Teahouse (Lütian chashe) provided patrons with newspapers, magazines, and books from Shanghai and Beijing, as well as a record player that played "elegant and beautiful" music and songs to entertain people and "refresh their spirit." Some teahouses provided private "family rooms."[50] Although this kind of private space was not popular in Chengdu, it indicates the growing trend of meeting the needs of patrons, especially elites, who always sought to distinguish themselves from commoners. Providing performances was another major strategy for generating business, especially among teahouses that were not in popular locations. Folk entertainers often performed in the tea room; the most popular genres were storytelling and singing, while the fancier teahouses presented Sichuan operas.[51]

New services and features were more in evidence during the 1930s and 1940s, with the opening of a few combination teahouses and coffeehouses, such as the Violet (Ziluolan) on Main Mansion Street (Zongfu jie) and White Roses (Baimeigui) in the Commercial Center. These were small but clean establishments, with round tables covered with white tablecloths and vases filled with flowers. The wooden chairs were small and exquisite, and lidded cups were used instead of the usual tea bowls. They served many kinds of tea as well as milk, coffee, and Western-style snacks, and had record players that provided popular soft music and songs. Most customers were young students who liked the "modern" atmosphere. These teahouses were part of a new trend, especially strong among the younger generation, that increasingly embraced Western culture. Some teahouses also offered lodging, and some offered space for social organizations, which appealed especially to those that could not afford an office and did not have a permanent address. This arrangement not only brought more income in the form of rent, but also more customers who drank tea while attending the meetings of these organizations. According to one observer, many teahouses had signs advertising the "So and So Union" or "So and So Guild" hanging above their doors. Teahouses provided their patrons with as many conveniences as possible. For example, they invited many employees of government and social organizations to become investors or shareholders with the privilege of setting up accounts that could be paid at a later date.[52]

In China, one's social network also contributed to business success. Without support from people who shared his social status, from local power brokers, or from residents in the neighborhood, a teahouse manager might not have enough customers or might become vulnerable to local thugs. For example, the Cry of the Crane Teahouse (Heming chashe) was on the verge of closing down when a certain Xiong Zhuoyun took it over. To attract customers, he cultivated friendships with people in all social groups, including the secret societies, government officials, and military officers (see Figure 1.3).[53]

FIGURE 1.3: Cry of the Crane Teahouse. This old teahouse still enjoys good business. Photo by the author, summer 2003.

Location, Setting, and Sanitation

Every aspect of a teahouse, from its name to the items found inside it, reflected local tradition and social customs and became an important part of a local culture—what I call "teahouse culture"—which was an inseparable part of everyday culture in Chengdu. The name of each teahouse was carefully chosen based on elements of natural beauty and literature and to convince people that it was the best place to enjoy tea and spend their leisure time; these names included the Joy Tea Garden (Yuelai chayuan), Hibiscus Tea Balcony (Furong chalou), Bamboo Garden (Zhuyuan), and Fragrant Taste Tea Garden (Pinxiang chayuan).[54] Location was always important, with different criteria for different teahouses. Large teahouses could be found in commercial centers or prosperous districts, where the rent was much higher but where there were many more patrons seeking a place to conduct business or socialize. Warm Spring Road and East Great Street had the highest concentration of teahouses in town; the former had seventeen and the latter, thirteen, mainly large ones. The Commercial Center also had several teahouses that could hold one hundred to two hundred patrons each (see Map 4 and Figures 1.4 and 1.5).[55]

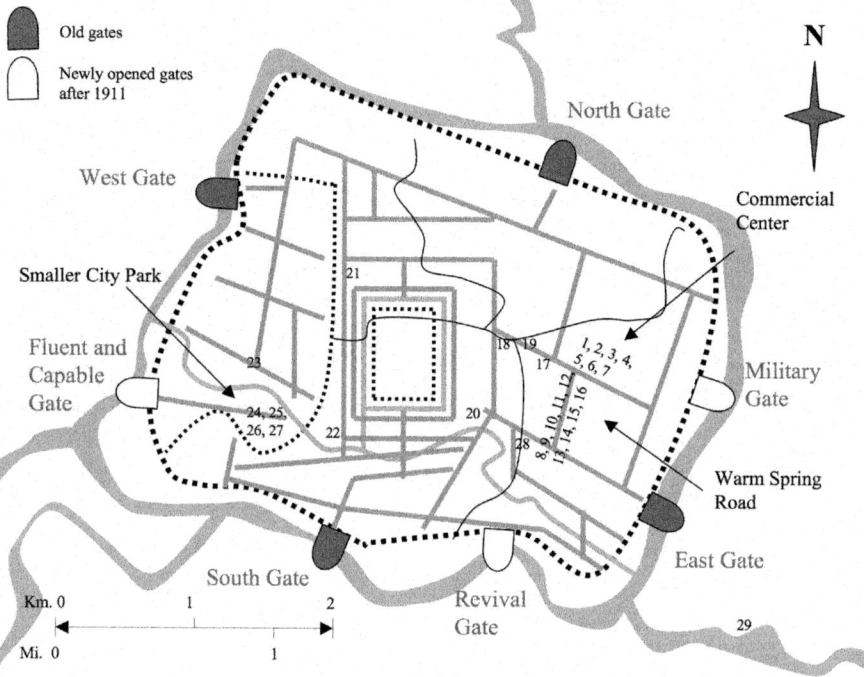

MAP 4: Some frequently mentioned teahouses, 1900–1950

1. Joy Tea Garden (Yuelai chayuan), in the Commercial Center
2. Spring Tea Balcony (Tongchun chalou), in the Commercial Center
3. Happy and Carefree Pavilion (Taoran ting), in the Commercial Center
4. Memorial Garden (Huaiyuan), in the Commercial Center
5. Pleasant Spring Balcony (Yichunlou), in the Commercial Center
6. Two Fountains Tea Balcony (Erquan chalou), in the Commercial Center
7. Elegant Tea Garden (Keyuan), on South Festival Street
8. First Tea Balcony (Diyilou), on Warm Spring Road
9. Fragrant Taste Tea Garden (Pinxiang chayuan), on Warm Spring Road
10. Three Sages (Sanyigong), on Warm Spring Road
11. Rinsing Fountain (Shuquan), on Warm Spring Road
12. Drinking Waves (Yintao), on Warm Spring Road
13. Pleasant Garden (Yiyuan), on Warm Spring Road
14. Great Wisdom Tea Balcony (Yizhi chalou), on Warm Spring Road
15. True Entertainment Garden (Zhengyu huayuan), on Warm Spring Road
16. Oriental Tea Balcony (Dongfang chalou), on Warm Spring Road
17. Hidden Garden (Yangyuan), on Brocade and Prosperous Hall Street
18. Pleasant Wind Teahouse (Huifeng chashe), in Sun Yat-sen Park
19. Hibiscus Pavilion Teahouse (Furongting chashe), on Drum Tower Street
20. Peace and Happiness Temple Teahouse (Anlesi chashe), in the Peace and Happiness Temple
21. Brocade Spring Tea Balcony (Jinchun chalou), on East City Corner Street
22. Water Containing Teahouse (Anlan chaguan), on West Imperial Street
23. Eternal Spring Tea Garden (Wanchun chayuan), on Ancestral Hall Street
24. Green Shadow Pavilion (Lüyin ge), in Smaller City Park
25. Thick Shadow Tea Balcony (Nongyin chalou), in Smaller City Park
26. Sleeping Stream Teahouse (Zhenliu chashe), in Smaller City Park
27. Cry of the Crane Teahouse (Heming chashe), in Smaller City Park
28. Prosperity Tea Hall (Huahua chating), on East Great Street
29. Wind and Cloud Pavilion Teahouse (Fengyunting chashe), on Fragrant Herb and Fountain Street

FIGURE 1.4: Warm Spring Road in 1997 before its large-scale reconstruction. Photo by the author.

FIGURE 1.5: The Commercial Center, formerly known as the Center for Promoting Industry and Commerce, built late in the Qing era, was home to several well-known teahouses, among them First Balcony, Two Fountains, Memorial Garden, Happy and Carefree Pavilion, and Pleasant Spring Balcony. None has survived to the present day. Photo by the author, summer 2003.

Traffic hubs were also ideal locations for teahouses. Lower Peace Street (Taiping xia jie), for example, stretched along a river and became a landing for commercial boats from all directions. Nearby teahouses provided good places for coolies to rest and refresh themselves with tea and a meal. This street had only about two hundred households, but seven were turned into teahouses. At the central hub of the street, there were four teahouses, owned by the He, Jiang, Yu, and Huang families, respectively. These teahouses, called "hanging balconies" (*diaojiaolou*) were built half on the river bank and half over the water, supported by pillars.[56] Small teahouses were usually simple and crude, and served mainly the lower classes that lived nearby; therefore, most were located in residential areas and on small alleys off of the main streets. In the eastern part of the city, where markets were relatively prosperous and the population density was high, each street had several teahouses. In the western part, by contrast, one teahouse might serve several streets.

Teahouses often were located where the view was good or where people liked to gather. Parks also had a relatively large number of teahouses; for example, the Smaller City Park had six (see Map 4). Teahouses in parks took advantage of the pleasant environment and scenery and served visitors from all social classes. Shu Xincheng found that teahouses became the centers of almost all parks and that the "teahouses were crowded but the playgrounds were empty." He was surprised to see that "a teahouse in Central City (Zhongcheng) Park occupied most of the northern area," Zhiji Temple Park was "entirely a big teahouse," and the teahouses in the Smaller City Park were "the largest among many other facilities." The teahouses in the Smaller City Park, with its beautiful surroundings, were full of customers from early morning to night. The Green Sky Teahouse was built under a thick canopy of trees, which provided a beautiful natural environment; it served tea from the top of the Mount Meng (Mengshan) with the high-quality water from Xue Tao Well. One man said, "Every time I come to the Smaller City Park, I see one hundred to two hundred people filling each teahouse, which could serve at least three hundred patrons on average every day."[57] (See Figures 1.6 and 1.7.)

Some suburban teahouses with beautiful scenery became destinations for people who sought fresh air and natural beauty. In a 1938 diary entry, Wu Yu, a famous writer during the New Cultural Movement, describes a Sunday when a teahouse by the river outside the West Gate was crowded with customers and likely sold seven or eight hundred bowls of tea. Wu noted that "there are many leisure teahouse-goers in Chengdu." Temple fairs also brought good business. The Flower Fair every spring, for example, was the largest seasonal gathering in the city. The fair was traditionally held near Green Goat Temple (Qingyang gong) outside the West Gate, where many temporary teahouses were set up. Some of these establishments also offered performances by local opera troupes and other forms of folk entertainment (see Figures 1.8 and 1.9).[58]

FIGURE 1.6: A teahouse in the Smaller City Park. Detail from the scroll painting *Old Chengdu* (Lao Chengdu) by Sun Bin, Zhang Youlin, Li Wanchun, Liu Shifu, Xiong Xiaoxiong, Pan Peide, and Xie Kexin (2000). Courtesy of the artists.

FIGURE 1.7: A teahouse next to Xue Tao Well. Detail from the scroll painting *Old Chengdu* (Lao Chengdu) by Sun Bin, Zhang Youlin, Li Wanchun, Liu Shifu, Xiong Xiaoxiong, Pan Peide, and Xie Kexin (2000). Courtesy of the artists.

FIGURE 1.8: The Flower Fair. The Flower Fair, which was held near the Green Goat Temple outside the West Gate, was the largest public gathering place in Chengdu. In the late Qing era, it was renamed the Promoting Industry and Commerce Festival, and many temporary teahouses were built there. Photo by Luther Knight, 1911. Photo courtesy of John E. Knight.

FIGURE 1.9: A teahouse with a beautiful view. Detail from the scroll painting *Old Chengdu* (Lao Chengdu) by Sun Bin, Zhang Youlin, Li Wanchun, Liu Shifu, Xiong Xiaoxiong, Pan Peide, and Xie Kexin (2000). Courtesy of the artists.

Many teahouses within the city did not have the advantage of natural beauty, but offered man-made ornamentation and elaborate landscaping. Liang Garden (Liangyuan), for example, had a pavilion and a pond. In the Pleasant Garden (Yiyuan), seats were placed on tiers of rocks, giving customers a sense of sitting in a garden. The Brocade Spring Tea Balcony (Jinchun chalou) was in an old-style building that featured miniature trees and rock gardens with fragrant flowers throughout. Evergreen trees flanked both sides of the entrance. The main hall, more than sixty-five feet long and thirty feet wide, led to a courtyard filled with chrysanthemums. The counter for placing orders, to the right of the gate, had thirteen hanging wooden boards with the names of well-known teas, and thirteen kinds of highly finished tea bowls. Matched couplets by well-known scholars decorated the walls and there was a stage at the rear center of the hall where folksingers performed.[59] Teahouses like this were usually expensive, in sharp contrast to the crude street-corner teahouses that mainly served the lower classes.

Most lower-class and street corner teahouses did not have a pleasant environment; this was not their major concern. Sanitation in teahouses, especially lower-class ones, was a serious problem before the police issued regulations concerning hygiene in the late Qing era. Contaminated water, dirty tables and chairs, spitting on the floor, haircuts and pedicures given at the tables, and filthy toilets were common. More sophisticated teahouses spent the money to address these problems because their clientele could afford to pay more for pleasant surroundings. Lower-class teahouses that served ordinary people, however, had to cut costs as much as possible just to stay in business, and sanitation was a low priority. Teahouses were common at the sites of temple fairs and other events. At the Flower Fair, for instance, customers crowded into the temporary teahouses that were built specifically for the fair in the sheds that lined both sides of the roads in the area. An observer called them "dens of bedbugs" because of their vermin, debris, and bad smells. Various traders, performers, and ordinary folk thronged around these teahouses. These crude and simple teahouses had serious hygiene problems and became a major target of the sanitation regulations.

From the early twentieth century, elite reformers and the government regarded sanitation as an issue involving the city's image and "civilization." Locally and nationally, hygiene became an important part of urban reform and the state's involvement in urban affairs.[60] In Chengdu, improving hygienic conditions drew attention immediately after the police force was established in 1902 and continued after the 1911 Revolution.[61] A 1926 regulation specifically targeted teahouse hygiene, requiring that all employees had to be free of venereal disease and other infectious diseases; tables, chairs, and utensils had to be kept clean; spittoons had to be provided and spitting on the ground was prohibited; toilets had be kept clean and odor free; pedicures were prohibited, and barbers had to be licensed. In 1931, the police ordered the teahouse guild to provide a list of all the teahouse workers in the city so that it could give them training in hygiene. The next year, the municipal government enacted regulations requiring that river water be filtered three times in sand-filled vats; water be boiled to over one hundred degrees Celsius; no teahouse be located near a toilet; and leftover tea be poured into a special bucket instead of on the floor. Any teahouse that violated any of these rules would be punished. The previous regulation prohibiting pedicurists and barbers from plying their trades in teahouses had apparently been ignored, so in 1934 the police reissued the ban in response to an anonymous letter signed by "a citizen of the city," which complained that in crowded teahouses where pedicurists and barbers worked, the odor of feet was overwhelming, hair clippings flew everywhere, including into tea bowls, and dirty water flowed on the floor.[62]

The issue of hygiene became even more prominent during the New Life Movement.[63] In August 1938, the Committee to Investigate Hygiene in Chengdu (Chengdu weisheng jiancha weiyuanhui) worked with the hygiene office of the police and the Committee of the New Life Movement to examine the state of hygiene in parks and other public places of leisure. Their investigation revealed that many teahouses had very poor sanitary conditions, and that "teahouses are full of beggars, petty peddlers, and pedicurists," who affected hygiene. The committee asked the police to enforce hygiene standards through frequent inspections. Additional regulations enacted required that waiters at teahouses, restaurants, and inns wear white jackets or aprons, and badges on the left side of their chests that listed their job titles and identification numbers in red. People who had pulmonary diseases or other contagious diseases such as syphilis and leprosy were not allowed to be waiters; furthermore, waiters had to keep their hands clean at all times.[64] Under these rules, each teahouse had to obtain a certificate of hygiene.

This standard was further enforced during the early 1940s. In 1942, the Institute of Hygienic Affairs of the Chengdu Municipal Government (Chengdu shizhengfu weisheng shiwusuo) issued an order regarding hygiene in teahouses, and the municipal government enacted several hygiene regulations for service providers such as restaurants, teahouses, barber shops, and public bathhouses. Based on the regulations, the institute required that all teahouses be inspected and issued certificates of hygiene and that they register information such as their business name, the date of the application, and address. The institute issued a "Plan for Inspecting the Sanitation of Restaurants and Teahouses in Chengdu" (Chengdu shi yinshidian ji chashe qingjie jiancha banfa) to promote the "spirit of the New Life Movement" and improve "working conditions" and the health of citizens in order to "foster good habits" and "strengthen the power of the War of Resistance" in its "struggle for final victory." Thus, the issue of hygiene was linked to the outcome of the ongoing war and the fate of the nation. Guidelines for hygiene, called the "process for inspecting the hygiene of restaurants and teahouses in Chengdu," were required to be publicly displayed in each teahouse.[65]

That same year, as a part of the New Life Movement, the military, government, business organizations, and police at all levels conducted a street-by-street inspection. Furthermore, the Institute of Sanitation Affairs (Weisheng shiwu suo) required that teahouse managers regularly check waiters to ensure that they were "clean," and that men who had pulmonary tuberculosis or fungal infections of the scalp could not be hired. The institute also stipulated that a spittoon be provided for every three tables, and that all utensils, including bowls, saucers, and lids, be kept clean. The Teahouse Guild organized a group to conduct self-checks to preempt the government inspections. The next year, the municipal government's Bureau of Hygiene issued Temporary Hygienic Regulations for Public Places of Recreation, which required all entertainment-related businesses to provide a list of all employees' names, ages, native places, and home addresses, as well as each business's location and number of employees. If a business passed the inspection, the bureau issued an annual, nontransferable license that had to be prominently displayed. The regulations took into consideration the facility's overall quality as well as its emergency exits, windows for air circulation, fire control equipment, spittoons and garbage cans, and related items. It also required that floors be kept clean and free of piles of trash; that toilets be clean and odor free; and that people with contagious diseases such as leprosy, venereal disease, and pulmonary tuberculosis be prohibited from working as waiters. The government did not relax its control of teahouses even when the War of Resistance reached a decisive point in 1945. As part of its overall reform effort, the government issued Regulations on Teahouses in Sichuan (Sichuan sheng guanli chaguan banfa), which demanded that all teahouses meet the standards "absolutely." In 1948 the government reissued these rules.[66]

Examples of Successful Teahouses

Throughout the late Qing and Republican periods, the number of teahouses in Chengdu remained relatively constant at between five hundred and eight hundred. Some teahouses became very successful and famous, and their names often appeared in the local newspapers and in other writings by both local residents and tourists. They served more people than other teahouses. The way they operated, how they were decorated, and the way they treated customers became an important part of teahouse culture. The following examples, chosen from different periods, can help us better understand the teahouse business.

Successful teahouses were usually large and located in prosperous areas. The First Tea Balcony (Diyi lou) on Warm Spring Road was well known in the late Qing. A blackboard advertising that the teahouse used only distilled water was displayed near its entrance. The writer Li Jieren described the teahouse: A few visitors entered the gate and saw that patrons filled every corner and made the place very noisy, but they found a different scene entirely when they went upstairs, where only seven or eight people were scattered among three tables, talking quietly. The room had a dozen mahjong tables covered with white tablecloths, and a big dining table with a vase in the middle, and although there were several new-style armchairs around it, nobody sat there. Tea upstairs was more expensive. As soon as they sat down, "a clean and agile waiter, carrying a huge tea tray, ran up from downstairs and walked directly to the big dining table." He put three porcelain teapots and three tea bowls on the table in front of the patrons and greeted them with a smile, saying "I haven't seen you gentlemen here in quite a while." He then asked if they wanted some snacks. One of the visitors who was there for the first time was surprised at the price, saying, "I am a Chengdu native and did not know there was such an expensive teahouse here!"[67]

Opened in the 1910s, the Sleeping Stream Teahouse (Zhenliu chashe) in the Smaller City Park depended on powerful people, such as police officers, government officials, military officers, and members of the Gowned Brothers, for survival. The proprietor recalled that the teahouse was three hundred square meters and located by the river under a canopy of trees. It had a barbershop, photo shop, and candy booth, all of which were rented out. He tried very hard to establish connections with the local branch of the police by providing officers with free hot water. These officers often "borrowed" chairs and utensils, which the teahouse keeper freely gave. The thinking was that while the police might not be helpful, at least they would not cause trouble. The teahouse lost a lot of tea sets, once as many as fifty in a single day. The thieves were called the "red money gang" (hongqian bang) and had their own organizations. The teahouse also had a connection with gangsters. After a few fights between local thugs that caused massive property damage, friends of the teahouse proprietor contacted a branch of the Gowned Brothers and gave them a payment in exchange for protection. This put an end to the violence. Later, the overseer of the park became envious of the teahouse's prosperity and tried to shut it down. The matter was settled only after the teahouse proprietor sought help from friends in the government.[68]

In the late 1920s, Warm Spring Road (Chunxi lu) emerged as a bustling commercial center in Chengdu, and many different kinds of teahouses opened there. The first well-known one was the Three Sages (Sanyigong), a spacious facility with a courtyard, garden, and balcony, where every seat was filled as long as the weather was good. Most patrons were merchants of all trades. Like the Three Sages, the True Entertainment Garden (Zhengyu huayuan) was also an open-air teahouse, where trees and flowers provided a "pure and clean environment." One source reveals that the teahouse sold two to three thousand bowls of tea daily, mainly to government employees. The Great Wisdom (Yizhi) and the Rinsing Fountain (Shuquan) were also located on Warm Spring Road; their most notable feature was low wooden chairs instead of the bamboo armchairs found at nearly every other teahouse. Although they were not as comfortable as bamboo armchairs, patrons liked to sit in them on the teahouse balcony and watch people pass by on the street below. The teahouse became very profitable.[69] All these teahouses on Warm Spring Road were well known, and are featured prominently throughout this book.

During the war the Prosperity Tea Hall (Huahua chating)—the largest teahouse in Chengdu—opened among many restaurants on East Great Street. It had two courtyards and three large halls, and could serve more than one thousand patrons at once. Its founder was Liao Wenchang, a man with more than thirty years of experience in the teahouse business. Liao brought new ideas of management and enjoyed a good reputation. The Prosperity Tea Hall was the first to use running water, introduced as a strategy to draw customers. On the first day of the first lunar month each year, the teahouse offered free tea from dawn to 10 AM, which brought it even more publicity. Liao organized his fifty to sixty employees into four groups, each in charge of a specific task: management and accounting, boiling water, tending the stove, and providing hot towels. Each group had one person in charge, and each employee had specific responsibilities. Employee guidelines clearly stipulated the behaviors that would bring rewards and punishment. The decor was also elegant, and the teahouse hired a top calligrapher who put many Chinese and foreign phrases on the wall, which were replaced every ten days to two weeks. A huge calendar was hung at the entry of the first hall, reflecting the "modern" style. Like other high-level teahouses, the Prosperity also offered a hot towel service; seven sets of towels with the days of the week printed on them were used on the corresponding days. The utensils were elegant, with specially made tea bowls. This teahouse sold a few thousand bowls of tea during the week, but as many as seven thousand on Sundays, using a few dozen jin of tea leaves. Although its tea leaves were not the best in town, it used more tea leaves per bowl than any other teahouse. In the Prosperity, one jin of tea leaves was used for only one hundred bowls, while other teahouses made one hundred twenty to one hundred sixty bowls with that amount.[70]

The war also created opportunities for some lower-class teahouses. The Japanese bombed Chengdu furiously during 1938 and 1941, and, as many residents moved to the suburbs, crude teahouses emerged on both banks of the Fu River near the New South Gate. The Village on the River (Jiangshangcun) teahouse drew many patrons because of the scenic beauty of the river and the enormous trees and thick bamboo stands that surrounded it. The teahouse had two areas; the front was open air, with square tables and bamboo armchairs, and the rear area was covered and had wooden tables and chairs. In good weather, and when people left the city to escape the Japanese air raids, both areas were crowded with customers.[71]

Conclusion

Through an examination of the issues of size, capital investment, ownership, management, and competition, we can ascertain the source of the teahouse culture's vitality as well as the difficulties teahouses faced. Throughout the late Qing and Republican eras, Chengdu had five hundred to eight hundred teahouses, more than any other city in China. Chengdu's residents also had the closest ties with teahouses, and a large portion of the population were regular patrons. In the 1930s the teahouse offered a livelihood to more than sixty thousand people and became one of the city's most important businesses. The teahouse was central to the city's economy and sustained many ancillary businesses, from restaurants and barbershops to vendors of food and other everyday items. Establishing a teahouse was relatively easy; only a small amount of money was needed. To survive, each teahouse sought to cut costs while providing the best service possible. On the surface, as small shops, teahouses seemed vulnerable to competition, but they could survive and even thrive precisely because their size made them much easier to open and operate and more adaptable to change, and it gave them a faster turnover. The laid-back Chengdu lifestyle and folk traditions provided a steady stream of customers. Even those forced out of business could start again relatively easily. Many teahouses were family businesses, which helped them minimize costs. Even though their marginal return was small, their flexibility meant that they could withstand economic downturns.

Each teahouse had its own story and strategy for dealing with particular situations. Each competed with other teahouses and tried to retain regular customers by offering high-quality tea, a pleasant environment, long hours of operation, skillful service, and colorful performances. Teahouse keepers made an effort to build their social networks and some fostered special relationships with local power brokers. Of course, individual teahouses had their own unique business strategies that they tried—sometimes in vain—to keep secret. These measures improved business operations and became a valuable resource, contributing to Chengdu's unique commercial culture. This culture formed naturally over a long historical period and was enduring and flexible. Some teahouses survived for decades despite wars, political turmoil, and economic slumps; many others failed and have been long forgotten. Any unexpected event, whether property damage resulting from a fire or flood or violence by local bullies, or an unfavorable government policy, could jeopardize business. Almost all large teahouses were big from the time they opened; they had more capital for the initial investment, rented or built large tea rooms, hired more workers, and served more customers. Few small teahouses had a chance to grow into large ones. Proprietors of large teahouses developed special relationships with leaders in the government, military, and commerce, to secure a level of protection not available to ordinary teahouse owners. Few small teahouses were able to expand, because less start-up capital meant limited profits, which prevented them from reinvesting. Most teahouses made just enough money to survive.

Finding a prime location and creating a pleasant environment provided a competitive advantage that also became a part of teahouse culture. Still, most lower-class teahouses did not deal with these issues because they lacked the resources to do so. Sanitation regulations were an example of the state's growing influence over small businesses. Before the twentieth century, government exercised little control over small business, but this situation began to change in the last years of the Qing dynasty. From the government's regulations we find that hygiene was increasingly important to the government, which even addressed the issue in its licensing process. Reformers and the government regarded hygiene not only as a public health issue but also as an important component in Chengdu's image and reputation. From the late Qing period to the end of the Republican era, the local government and police repeatedly issued laws regulating hygiene in teahouses, which may indicate that this effort ultimately was not very successful. To a certain extent, such a failure might also reflect the strong resistance of traditional small businesses to the modernist uniformity that increased their costs and forced them to change the conventional way of conducting business.

CHAPTER 2

The Teahouse Guild

Important Notice, December 24, 1947
Tea prices have been adjusted:
1. Regular jasmine tea: 1,000 yuan/bowl
2. Spring tea and sprout tea: 1,200 yuan/bowl
3. These prices become effective starting tomorrow
These prices will be implemented in all teahouses in all districts.

—Liao Wenchang
President of the Teahouse Guild

THIS "IMPORTANT NOTICE" to teahouses reflects the role of the Chengdu Teahouse Guild (Chengdu shi chashe shangye tongye gonghui): to organize the profession around common interests and to ensure a unified price structure. To achieve these goals, the guild had to deal with the government, and ultimately became an intermediary between teahouses and the local authorities.

In late imperial and Republican China, guilds played a very significant role in urban economic life and society. In Chengdu, all teahouse proprietors were required to join the Teahouse Guild. Study of the Teahouse Guild should give us a better understanding of all such associations and their economic role. In this chapter, we will see that the Teahouse Guild changed from being an autonomous organization to a state-sponsored one, although it still struggled to represent the interests of the profession as a whole and resist increasing state control.

To gain a better understanding of the Teahouse Guild, it is necessary to define the term "guild" and trace its history. Scholars often use the term "guild" to translate *huiguan*.[1] While *huiguan* (literally, "meeting hall"), *gongsuo* (literally, "public office"), and *bang* (gangs) were traditional associations, the *gonghui* (literally, "public society" or "public club") emerged early in the twentieth century.[2] Most studies of Chinese occupational organizations have confirmed that guilds emerged during the late Ming and early Qing eras.

But, in his study of early-Qing guilds, Peter Golas found that native-place associations (*huiguan*) predated guilds. Whereas a *huiguan* came into being because immigrants "often met with discrimination at the hands of the local populace and naturally preferred to associate with others who shared the same hardships," guilds were established for "economic goals" and their members "usually engaged in a single economic activity."[3] Therefore, Golas argues that the *huiguan* is different from the guild, even though they were often combined.

The English term *guild* generally means "an association of persons of the same trade or pursuits, formed to protect mutual interests and maintain standards."[4] From this perspective, the translation of *tongye gonghui* as *guild* is appropriate. As William Rowe points out, "Regardless of their variation in membership criteria and wide range of functions, guilds were basically economic in orientation."[5] While scholars have often used *guild* as a synonym for Chinese associations known as *hanghui*, they have carefully defined the latter in such a way as to avoid any confusion with the European type of guild.[6] As Golas has reminded us, "there is no reason to expect that Chinese guilds were any closer to their European counterparts than Chinese 'feudalism' was to French 'feudalism,' or the Chinese 'gentry' to the English 'gentry.'"[7] In fact, *hanghui* is an exclusively modern Chinese term; in premodern times the terms most often used were *huiguan*, *gongsuo*, and *bang*. It is the *bang*, William Rowe believes, that is "the one most frequently identified with the English 'guild.'" The *hanghui* apparently developed from the traditional *hang*, as Rowe states, and is more like "an autonomous trade association" that is "relatively free from government control."[8] Chinese historians have used the term *hanghui* in their many published works on these traditional social and economic associations apparently without trying to trace the origin of the term.[9]

The relationship between a man's ties to his hometown and his profession is subject to debate. In his study of Hankou in the Qing dynasty, Rowe examines guilds that are categorized by their goals, membership, catchment areas, structures (simple and multiplex), external ties, and functions (cultural, commercial, corporate, and community service). According to his study, *huiguan* and guilds in Hankou actually overlapped. He finds that in Hankou people joined a guild based on three factors: a "common type of work" (*tongye*), "common geographic origin" (*tongxiang*), or "common position within the production or marketing hierarchy—what we may roughly call 'economic class.'" He concludes, however, that shared economic functions were the most basic elements that brought members together. Rowe has also discussed the "rational economy" of self-control in commerce. Usually, guilds were responsible for maintaining an orderly process for commercial trade and setting prices. Rowe points out, however, that self-regulation still left ample room for the development of free markets and free trade.[10] Rowe downplays the role of native place in professional organizations, but Bryna Goodman emphasizes it, although she recognizes that the two often "overlapped," and the boundary often was not clear, because "groups of fellow-provincials often practiced several trades and, moreover, because trades were not always exclusively monopolized by people from one area of China." She comments, "Rowe minimizes native-place organization and sentiment by insisting on fundamental economic primacy" and "overestimates late-nineteenth-century weakening of native-place ties."[11]

The differences between Rowe and Goodman probably spring from the different empirical evidence for the subjects they have studied. In Chongqing, a native-place association was often organized by a *bang* that engaged in a certain trade. For example, in 1801 the *bang* of porcelain makers established the Zhejiang *huiguan*, whose members were from the province of Zhejiang. All of its regulations addressed trade; none pertained to native-place sentiment or charitable affairs, or worship and celebrations that usually concerned native-place associations. This organization seems to have been a combination of a native-place association and guild, more like the model for such associations in Hankou. As in Shanghai and Hankou, the *huiguan* in Chongqing actively participated in urban affairs. The heads of the eight largest *huiguan*, known as the *Basheng shoushi* (Eight heads from eight provinces), played a role in charitable activities as well as in urban administration in matters such as fire control, local militias, and taxation.[12]

As China's economy underwent change, increasingly organizations representing similar lines of work were distinguished from those whose members came from the same region. The separation was partially a result of the state's promotion of *tongye gonghui* (guilds), which functioned solely for economic purposes. Unlike the guilds of nineteenth-century Hankou described by Rowe, the guilds in Republican Chengdu lost their independence from the government. Like other cities, Chengdu had many *huiguan*, *gongsuo*, and *bang*, the various roles of which were complex. While some *huiguan* were only involved in native-place relationships and some *gongsuo* were engaged in only trade, some associations with the name *huiguan* were professional organizations and some with a name of *gongsuo* were native-place associations. Some performed both roles. Therefore, it is difficult to generalize about native-place or professional associations. Different organizations had different features and different ties to a place or profession, and moreover these features could change according to place and time. Whatever their nature, however, in Chengdu it does not appear *huiguan* and *gongsuo* played a role in neighborhood and community activities like the "eight heads" in Chongqing, but were handled by patron deity associations (*tudi hui* or *qingming hui*) organized.[13]

In late Qing Chengdu, all merchants were organized into fifty-one *bang*. One was the *bang* of tea leaf merchants, under which there were fifty-four shops, but no teahouses. Promoted by the Qing government, the Chamber of Commerce was established in 1905, and by 1909 sixty-nine *bang* became branches of the Chamber. It was around this time that the professional organization of teahouses emerged. At first, teahouses were included in the same category of local authorities' statistics as restaurants, and not in the *bang* of tea leaf sellers. Later, during the early Republican and warlord periods, teahouses were placed under the "Water Gang" (*Shuibang*) category together with public bathhouses, but it seems the government had only minimal control over the profession, so that when the local government tried to obtain a complete inventory of teahouses in 1914 and again in 1929, the police took on this responsibility.[14] In 1918, the central government issued Regulations on Professional Organizations in Industry and Commerce, which became China's first law on guilds. The next year, although the Chamber of Commerce in Chengdu still existed, the government demanded all of its branches to change their names back to *bang*. In 1929, after the Nationalist government issued laws on chambers of commerce and *tongye gonghui* (guilds) and ordered a reorganization of these associations, the new Chengdu municipal government required merchants of all professions to set up guilds. By April 1931 eighty-two guilds had been established, including the Teahouse Guild, all of which completed the transformation from *bang* to guilds. A new Chamber of Commerce was established and in 1936 the Teahouse Guild was restructured and registered with the government.[15]

There are few sources on the early activities of the professional organizations of teahouses in Chengdu; thus, this chapter does not attempt to write a complete history of these organizations but rather describes the Teahouse Guild during the 1930s and 1940s and its reorganization under the Nationalist government, which involved immersing the guild in a new political and economic structure while retaining some traditional features of the *bang*. This chapter examines the extent to which the Teahouse Guild changed under the Nationalist government's control. By exploring the guild's structure, leadership, membership, functions, and activities, this chapter reveals the relationship and interactions between the guild and state power and the guild's role in dealing with the issue of government control over pricing, taxation, and the registration of businesses. Although the Teahouse Guild was supervised by the GMD, it was able to represent the interests of the profession as a whole in negotiating for price increases, tax decreases, and the imposition of restrictions on the establishment of new teahouses, essentially becoming an agent between teahouses and the local authorities.

Structure of the Teahouse Guild

The Teahouse Guild was operated by a board of directors made up of a president, four standing members, ten executive members, five alternate executive board members, seven consulting members, and three alternate consulting members, for a total of thirty.[16] The guild had four sections: General Affairs, Organization, Accounting, and Mediation. The Mediation Section warrants special attention. It sought to resolve problems and disputes within the profession. During the war, a section on propaganda was added, reflecting the growing influence of politics. The guild had branches, or groups, called *zu*. The heads of the groups were selected by members, not appointed by the guild leadership. Under guild rules, if the position of group head became vacant, it had to be filled within five days and under board members' supervision. In 1946, the guild established an office in each district and appointed a director and deputy director for each.[17]

Several factors affected the guild's organization and operation. Clearly, the Nationalist Party (GMD) reached the height of its power in the guild. According to the membership list from 1940, among the 610 teahouse proprietors who belonged to the guild were seventeen members of the GMD, all whom held positions on the board. No documentation now exists to explain how these seventeen were selected, but the fact that they constituted the majority of the board might suggest the GMD tried to dominate the guild. It seems that GMD membership was more important than educational background for becoming a board member. Of the thirty board members, only two had middle school educations; the rest had no more than a traditional private school or modern elementary school education. The size of the teahouse was probably another factor in the selection of board members. The teahouses owned by the thirty board members had a total capital of 17,300 yuan, with an average of 577 yuan, which was much higher than the overall average of 373 yuan. Nevertheless, it might not have been a crucial factor; for example, fourteen board members had only 300 yuan of capital each, the lowest level of capital. Guild president Wang Xiushan had only 1,300 yuan of capital, while the owner of the Cry of the Crane Teahouse, an executive member, held 2,500 yuan in capital, the highest amount among the teahouses of Chengdu.[18]

The guild's budget came from membership fees collected from each teahouse every spring and autumn and the income generated by the property it owned. All teahouses were divided into three levels; the maximum fee (Level A) was 0.50 yuan in June 1940, but this was later raised to two yuan, and then to six yuan. The guild began mandatory registration of all teahouses in May 1941, and the membership fee depended on the class of the teahouse: first class was 16 yuan; second, 10; and third, 6. The guild, however, faced constant financial crises. In October 1942, for instance, it was 2,000 yuan in debt and organized a committee to review its accounts and find ways to cut spending.[19] In October 1946, the guild classified the membership fee into four levels—A, B, C, and D—set at 20,000, 15,000, 10,000, and 5,000 yuan, respectively.[20] This was primarily a response to inflation. During almost the same period (from August 1940 to August 1946), the cost of a bowl of tea increased from 10 cents to 60 yuan (600 times) and the price of rice rose from 141 yuan per dan to 48,727 yuan (345 times). This huge increase, however, did not solve the deficit issue.[21]

The guild nevertheless sought to maintain a cohesive membership and took responsibility for maintaining some public facilities that benefited the whole profession. In 1942, the guild collected money to repair the harbor; each teahouse donated from 5 to 50 yuan, but the Society of the King of Water-Carriers (Shuigong wangye hui), which benefited most, donated 100 yuan. The donations totaled 507 yuan, enough to cover the costs of materials and labor. The guild also provided financial support for members who needed immediate assistance. As a representative of the teahouse proprietors, the guild had to deal with the Union of Teahouse Workers. In June 1940, for example, when the union asked for an increase in wages, the guild proposed a process that allowed each teahouse to make its own decision.[22] However, the major issue the guild confronted was pricing, which was determined through a significant and complex relationship among small businesses, their professional organizations, and the local government.

The Issue of Pricing

The Teahouse Guild had various functions, but its biggest job, and the one of most concern to its members, was to stabilize prices and, even more important, to negotiate with the government to keep prices in step with inflation. Prices for a bowl of tea were not determined by individual teahouses, but by the guild. When it appeared that prices needed to be raised, the guild met to decide whether to proceed. Before the decision to increase prices could be enacted, it had to be approved by the local authorities. Because drinking tea was so important in the everyday lives of Chengdu residents, tea prices became a sensitive issue.

One of the major reasons teahouses attracted so many patrons was because they were affordable; a bowl of tea was only a small portion of the daily earnings of even those in the lower class. In the late Qing, a bowl of tea cost only 4 to 6 wen, about as much as a toasted cake or three rice balls. At the same time, a carpenter typically earned 96 wen per day; a mason, 106 wen; and a blacksmith, 200 to 250 wen.[23] In 1924, a bowl of tea cost 20 wen, but the price climbed to 70 wen just a year later.[24] Because record keeping was inconsistent, little detailed documentation exists about prices between the late Qing and the 1930s, but more exists from the 1940s. The cost of a bowl of tea in 1937 was two cents but rose to 15 cents in 1942, and then jumped to 12 yuan in 1945, and then skyrocketed to 1,800 yuan in 1948. To put these prices in context, it is necessary to compare them with the prices of other goods. During the first half of the twentieth century, prices for everyday goods in Chengdu increased dramatically, and especially during the late 1940s they spiraled out of control. A comparison with the price of rice—the most important commodity, the price for which was the foundation for the pricing of all other goods—is helpful (see the Appendix). During the same period, the monetary system was changed several times. In the late Qing, silver and copper yuan were used, while *fabi* ("legal tender") was adopted in 1935; this was replaced by *jinyuanjuan* ("golden yuan") in 1948. These changes make price comparisons difficult. To overcome this problem, I have calculated the price of every hundred bowls of tea and a dan of rice. From the late Qing to the late 1940s, if we only look at the years of 1909 and 1948 (January) and ignore all other years, we find there was little change in the ratio of prices: a hundred bowls of tea in 1909 cost the same as 0.054 dan (16.74 pounds) of rice and 0.057 dan (17.67 pounds) in 1948.[25]

During the war, the government established a Price Evaluation Committee (Pingjia hui), which met regularly to address the issue of price controls and review requests for increases. Any price increase had to be approved by the committee, a policy that continued into the Civil War era. The guild had to be diplomatic, reiterating that it always followed the government's rules. On August 7, 1940, in response to a demand by teahouse owners, the guild decided to raise the minimum price of "regular tea" to 10 cents a bowl, and to allow each teahouse to determine the price for all other kinds of tea. The guild required that "all teahouses raise their prices on August 20," or face a fine "according to the regulation." This statement indicates that some teahouses maintained lower prices to attract customers. To avoid this and to protect the profession's common interests, the guild tried to enforce a single price. The guild increased the price to 15 cents per bowl effective January 1, 1941, then to 20 cents just twenty days later. In May 1941 the price was raised to 25 cents. In August, when the government ordered a price reduction, the guild kept the price at 25 cents while negotiating with the government for another increase. On November 5, 1941, the guild raised the price of regular tea from 25 to 30 cents, but individual teahouses could decide the prices of other blends. On May 17, 1942, the guild increased the price of regular tea from 40 to 50 cents, effective June 1, but this did not apply to higher-quality brands or tea sold in special areas such as Warm Spring Road.[26] Therefore, within two years, the price of tea was increased five times, from 10 cents to 50 cents.

The guild's action was a response to the rising cost of other goods and supplies important to teahouses, such as tea leaves and coal. For instance, the price of coal rose from 0.6 yuan per jin on May 1, 1942, to 1.4 yuan per jin on July 15. All other costs rose comparably. Just a few days later, the guild held an emergency meeting to discuss the issue of rising costs, especially the soaring price of fuel, and planned a dramatic increase in the price of a bowl of tea from 50 cents to 70 cents beginning August 1, although teahouses in specially designated areas could decide their own prices. The government responding by allowing the price of regular tea to go up to 60 cents, 10 cents less than the guild proposed, and it also required that all teahouses display wooden boards listing their prices beginning July 30, 1942. Dissatisfied, the guild appealed and "explained the difficulties of the teahouse business," but the government once again denied the request. While the guild continued to press for a price increase, it had to ask all teahouses to obey the government's decision.[27] During 1942–1945, after constant struggle, the guild managed to increase the price from 60 cents per bowl to 12 yuan to catch up with inflation.[28]

Sometimes disputes between the guild and the local government led the leaders of the guild to protest. For example, in 1942, guild president Wang Xiushan claimed that he had to leave town because of a personal matter, and turned his responsibilities over to an acting president.[29] In fact, the real reason behind his departure—a conflict with the government—was much more complicated and was revealed only later. In October of the same year, the guild approved Wang's leave and organized a committee to handle routine affairs in his absence.[30] Min Ciyuan temporarily assumed Wang's responsibilities. In April 1943, Wang Xiushan submitted a letter of resignation to the municipal government. It is interesting to note that he did not approach the board of directors about this, showing that this position was apparently an appointment made by the government rather than by the board. He wrote that he was resigning because he resented the government's control, which he believed would lead to a crisis because the prices of major supplies, such as tea leaves, coal, and food, had doubled within six months, but teahouses were not allowed to raise their prices. Thus, as president, he found it very difficult to maintain accountability with both the government and teahouses. Although he did not directly criticize the government, he admitted that he was no longer able to "represent the interests of teahouses, resulting in many complaints." He used his resignation to express his anger: "I do not have the ability to carry out government policies while also helping members solve their difficulties." He asked the government "to appoint a member to replace me in this position."[31] As the government-appointed head of the guild, he had to carry out government policies related to the teahouse trade. However, his leadership and authority were based on the trust built among teahouse owners in representing their interests. When the government repeatedly denied his requests, his credibility foundered. His resignation reveals the conflict of interest between the state and social organizations.[32]

The end of World War II did not improve economic conditions, and in fact, made them even worse. In April 1946, Wang Xiushan, who still was president of the guild, once again asked the government to allow a price increase. According to his petition, the price of all supplies—oil, rice, electricity, coal, labor, tea leaves, tea utensils, tables, and chairs—had doubled, and teahouses were sustaining huge losses by charging only 45 yuan per bowl of tea. Under the government's restrictions, teahouses could not set rates based on their costs and were therefore "suffering unbearable pain." The petition clearly expresses growing resentment: "According to the government, all teahouses should obey the order even though it leads to unbearable suffering." The guild, on the one hand, did not dare disobey the restrictions on prices, but on the other hand, it also wanted the government to be aware of the risk that all teahouses could be forced out of business and that those who made their living through teahouses could go hungry. Compounding this, the electric company had doubled its price and cut off service to the teahouses that could not pay their bills. Moreover, the government was promoting the introduction of plumbing, but teahouses still had to hire water-carriers to transport "running water" from water stations, which was more expensive than drawing water directly from the river, resulting in higher costs to produce a bowl of tea. Therefore, "to raise the price was of the utmost urgency," the guild pointed out, adding that teahouses had obeyed the government's decision by not raising prices during the preceding six months, but as a result suffered enormous financial losses and incurred huge debts.[33]

In 1947, the situation worsened and teahouses suffered even greater losses, according to data from the guild. The income generated by the sale of every five hundred bowls of tea was 35,750 yuan, but costs were 53,042 yuan. The guild noted that based on production costs, a bowl of tea should sell for 90 yuan.[34] Liao Wenchang continued to protest low prices when he became guild president in 1947. In September of that year, on behalf of all teahouses, he wrote the government asking for permission to raise prices, giving the same rationale: the price of almost everything else had gone up. Many teahouses went out of business, and unemployment became increasingly serious. If teahouses were not allowed to raise their prices along with other businesses, the situation would become much worse. In his letter, Liao wrote, "Coal is the main fuel for all teahouses, as is electricity, but why do teahouses alone have to bear the higher costs of these commodities?" He pointed out that for a teahouse to survive, a bowl of tea should cost 600 yuan. The guild asked the government to investigate and ease price restrictions to prevent more teahouses from going out of business and workers from losing their jobs, which could jeopardize "social order." Of course, the devastation of teahouses reflected the decline of the overall economy during the Civil War, when inflation skyrocketed and the national economy verged on collapse.[35]

For the guild, this struggle seemed never-ending. In one short period in 1948, the guild asked the government for a price increase five times without a single approval.[36] It is true that inflation had become dangerously high, but the guild seems to have overstated the situation. According to the Appendix, during 1946 and 1947, the price of tea reached its highest point: one hundred bowls of tea were about equal to 0.12 dan of rice (thirty-seven pounds). Therefore, one may be skeptical about the claims of teahouses and the guild, whose survival and economic interest depended on putting forth a worst-case scenario. The Teahouse Guild did its best to fight for the interests of the teahouses while avoiding confrontation with the government. To achieve both missions was not easy.

The Tax Burden and Tax Protests

Although we do not know much about the Teahouse Guild in the early Republican period, we do have relatively plentiful evidence of its opposition to tax increases. Tax records contain a wide range of valuable information, including standard costs of running a teahouse, the basic facilities and supplies needed, how many tables teahouses had, and how many customers could be served, all of which add to our understanding of the conditions facing small businesses in Chengdu. During the early Republican period, the police were responsible for collecting taxes, a task they took very seriously because the revenue generated was an important part of their budget. In order to enforce teahouse taxation, the police demanded that all teahouses report such information as the names and addresses of the owner and manager, the number of tables, the prices charged for various blends of tea, and the amount of tax to be paid. The amount of tax was based on the number of tables, so the police checked this carefully, and required that any changes be reported; these records provide valuable information. Usually, an individual teahouse paid its tax directly to the police but sometimes the Teahouse Guild paid the total tax for the whole profession and was reimbursed.[37]

The earliest detailed tax information available is from 1914, when Chengdu had 681 teahouses, with a total of 9,958 tables. This resulted in 60,302 wen in taxes per day, and 1,749,080 wen monthly, for an average of 176 wen per table per month, or 2,568 wen per teahouse. Large teahouses, such as the Memorial Garden (Huaiyuan) and Hibiscus Pavilion (Furong

Ting), had as many as forty tables and paid 200 wen in taxes per day, but small teahouses, such as Leng Hongfa Teahouse (Leng Hongfa chashe), might have had as few as three tables and paid 15 wen in taxes daily.[38] There are more systematic tax records during the 1920s. In 1924, the police raised the teahouse tax, accusing the smaller teahouses of "taking advantage of and disregarding the rules" and issuing a public notice to enforce the new tax rate. The new rate, like previous ones, was based on the number of tables and classes of teahouses. Those that charged 50 wen per bowl paid tax of 50 wen per table per day; those that charged 20 to 50 wen per bowl paid 30 wen; and those that charged 20 wen paid 20 wen. The tax hike immediately met strong resistance. The *bang* of teahouses (the precursor to the Teahouse Guild, which was established in 1931 and restructured in 1936) presented a petition to the police, "explaining their hardship in great detail" and "asking them to withdraw the new tax." According to the petition, the proprietors were "shocked" when they heard this news because the tax had been increased twice recently and they already had been forced to "reduce their [expenditures on] food and clothing" just to survive. Moreover, a war that lasted more than half of 1923 directly and indirectly affected the teahouse trade, and many other factors also caused teahouses to suffer great, even devastating, losses.[39]

A complete archival record from 1924 documents the new tax on teahouses in the East District (one of five in Chengdu at that time), which was divided into six subdistricts. This record lists the name, location, and number of tables of each teahouse in the East District, as well as the amount of taxes each paid under the old and new tax structure, which provides a basis for estimating the total number of teahouses found there. From this record, we can see that the East District had 117 teahouses, whose total tax at the new rate was 51,010 wen per day, or an average of 389 wen. We find that the taxes were increased 74 to 83 percent over the previous rate. Because this tax was based on the number of tables, the average tax tells us the size of the various teahouses. The record shows that the teahouses in the East Central and East Fifth subdistricts were small, and those in the East First, Second, and Third were larger, but that the East Fourth, where teahouses paid an average of 800 wen in tax, had the largest teahouses in the East District.[40]

Let us look more closely at the East Central subdistrict, where the smallest teahouse had only four square tables while the largest had eighteen. Of the subdistrict's twenty-one teahouses, seven had six tables and eight had seven to ten tables; the majority had fewer than ten tables. Their taxes ranged from 120 to 550 wen. The twenty-one teahouses paid a total of 4,835 wen per day, for an average of 230 wen. Only six sold tea for 20 wen per bowl; most charged between 30 and 40 wen.[41] A few teahouses charged as little as 20 wen per bowl, and some, such as the Hidden Garden (Yangyuan), charged as much as 80 wen. The Hidden Garden paid a fixed rate of 3,500 wen in daily tax because its courtyard, which had many tables, could be used only when the weather was good.[42] However, the new tax was based on the number of tables, and the Hidden Garden agreed to pay an additional 300 wen only. The police investigator assigned to the case said that as soon as the new tax rate was confirmed and the tax paid, the teahouse could add more tables. The Hidden Garden manager offered to pay an additional 500 wen, for a total tax of 4,000 wen per day, which the police accepted. This outcome was favorable to the Hidden Teahouse, because an additional 500 wen in taxes was an increase of only about 10 percent. Most teahouses had much higher percentage increases, on the order of 70 to 80 percent.[43]

Teahouses always tried to find ways to ease their tax burden. As soon as the First Park (Diyi gongyuan) was opened in 1925, the First Teahouse (Diyi chashe) was established there, and although it had many tables and sold tea for 70 to 200 wen per bowl, it never paid taxes. When a policeman went to collect the tax, the manager claimed that the teahouse was owned by a public organization and therefore had no tax obligation. This statement indicates that teahouses that were public property had previously been able to claim a tax exemption. But the police no longer recognized this privilege.[44] That same year, nineteen teahouses in the Green Goat Market (Qingyang chang) appealed to the police for tax relief. According to their petition, although this market had only three streets and no more than two hundred households, there were nineteen teahouses, for an average of one teahouse per ten households. This actually reflects a feature of the economy of marketplaces where people come and go regularly; in this market, the second, fifth, and eighth days of each ten-day cycle were trading days. Therefore, each month had only nine days when business was good; the rest of the time "customers were as sparse as morning stars." Because this situation was "totally different from the teahouses in other areas," these teahouses asked the police to levy tax based on an "average" of 15 wen per table per day for both trading and non-trading days. The police agreed to recognize the differences between the city and its suburbs, but did not adopt the flat tax. Instead, they required the teahouse to pay half the tax during non-trading days and the full amount during trading days.[45]

Although the Police Department tried to maintain a hard-line approach, some police in the districts and subdistricts that directly dealt with teahouses were sympathetic to the plight of the teahouses. The way they dealt with one veteran's teahouse in 1926 is a good example. Li Lieyang, who had been wounded as a soldier, lived in the Home for Disabled Soldiers (Feibing yuan) and opened a teahouse for veterans. He claimed that disabled soldiers had little money and lived an "extremely miserable life." The wounded soldiers in the home could not even afford a bowl of tea at the typical teahouse. Therefore, Li rented half a room with three tables next to the home and opened a teahouse.[46] The teahouse served only soldiers who had been wounded, allowing them to pay on credit; although a bowl of tea cost 50 wen, little cash exchanged hands. Under the new tax rule, Li would have had to pay a "table tax" of 90 wen per day. Li petitioned the subdistrict of the police, asking special consideration for the welfare of the wounded soldiers, who received no pay and had no money. The director of the subdistrict found that what Li described was true, and asked the department to determine whether or not to grant an exemption. The department declined to give an exemption, stating that "opening a teahouse requires the payment of taxes, and therefore the request for an exemption is not granted. The tax should be paid according to the rules to prevent similar requests from other teahouses; if not, the teahouse should not be allowed to stay open." Li appealed, claiming that he barely earned enough to feed himself and could not afford the tax. The director of the subdistrict confirmed his claim and also asked the department to give serious consideration to the request. The department finally approved the petition by saying, "since, as the wounded soldier Li Lieyang repeatedly explains, the teahouse is selling tea only to wounded soldiers, it should be treated differently from regular teahouses."[47]

As this case reveals, the relationships between small businesses and the state was complex. Apparently, Li Lieyang was not a member of the guild because his was not a "regular" teahouse. There might have been many more of these "irregular" teahouses that sought to avoid taxes.[48] These teahouses, usually owned by charitable or social organizations, were tax exempt and thus information about them was not included in the statistics. For example, the Confucian Society (Rujiaohui) ran a teahouse that sponsored lectures and operated without a business license.[49] In fact, the teahouse guild pushed the local government to regulate the number of teahouses in order to limit the number of tax-exempt teahouses that ultimately became their competitors.

Teahouse politics can be seen from an economic angle, especially in the protests against tax increases that constantly threatened to erupt throughout the Republican period. When their tax burden became intolerable, teahouse keepers would unite and fight for relief. One of the most influential strikes occurred in 1928, soon after the establishment of the Chengdu Municipal Government. This strike was probably the first serious conflict between the teahouse trade and the new government. A newspaper, under the headline "Teahouses Strike against Taxes" (Chashe tingye kangjuan), reported that "there is a radical trend combined with a peaceful petition." After the police used force to collect the "tea-table tax" (*chazhuo juan*), the guild of teahouses (known at that time as the teahouse *bang*) held several meetings to ask the police for an exemption and issued several resolutions in an effort to resolve the problem peacefully. When these efforts failed, the guild held an emergency meeting and resolved to strike. On the morning of December 10, 1928, all teahouses in Chengdu, from the smallest to the largest, shut their doors, and their managers pledged they would reopen only if the tax were abolished. On that day, some observers claimed that Chengdu's vitality seemed to slip away. People who depended on teahouses, such as barbers, tobacconists, and water-carriers, supported the strike and organized a public petition to be handed to the police. The guild also issued a declaration:

> The proprietors of teahouses have suffered under exorbitant taxes and levies. The burden is overwhelming, and therefore, we ask for this exemption. The Police Department refuses to consider our miserable situation, and has sent policemen to forcibly collect the tax, illegally arresting and brutally beating teahouse owners, whose suffering is unspeakable. Our weak and powerless merchants never expected this kind of treatment under the Nationalist government. Today, our members have been arrested and jailed, so our teahouses have no option but to close. We hope that all citizens and the notable people in the [Nationalist] party and government will sympathize with our plight and support us. We would rather die in glory than live in dishonor. If we cannot reach the goal of abolishing the tax, we will never reopen for business.[50]

The guild's brazen challenge was unprecedented. The teahouse guild always tried to maintain a good relationship with the government because it often depended on local authorities to regulate the overall teahouse trade (this issue will be discussed later in this chapter). The strike obviously was a last resort in a fight against a tax increase that threatened the entire occupation's very survival.

The strike would also hurt business enormously and was probably just an expression of the proprietors' anger. Teahouse keepers ended up compromising and reopened for business the next day after the guild's board met and resolved to send a telegram asking the Nationalist government for justice. In the meantime, the guild decided it would continue to collect the tax for the police and would negotiate for the release of those who had been arrested. All teahouses were asked to reopen at once.[51] From this, it is apparent that the guild had a very flexible strategy that struck a balance between the need for teahouses to continue to operate and the struggle to serve the interests of the whole trade. The guild never let the situation disintegrate into chaos even as it pushed for a confrontation with the police and government.

The guild had to ensure a true collective action in its fight for the interests of the trade. In early 1931, after the Bureau of Finance took over the tea-table tax from the police, the guild held a general meeting and resolved to ask the Nationalist government for justice based on its order against overly burdensome taxation. The guild organized a committee to request a tax exemption, and asked that no teahouses pay any taxes until the Nationalist government made a decision, and that any teahouse that violated this resolution should be required to pay the tax burden of the entire trade. The guild also held a press conference to publicize its position that the teatable tax was created in the late Qing era to raise funds to build beggars' workhouses and thus was no longer needed, and that this tax violated the Nationalist government's order against unreasonable taxes. The guild sought to use the media to build wider support in the community. The next year, another movement against the tea tax, called the Tea Tax Unrest (*chajuan fengchao*), occurred, in which some of members of the teahouse guild and teahouse workers were arrested. The government released all those who had been arrested as the movement came to an end, but ordered the ouster of guild head Li Yunjie, who had led the movement.[52] Although these two cases make it clear that the teahouse guild sought justice from the central government, it was unlikely to get a positive result because Sichuan was basically under the control of warlords and was highly autonomous until 1936. The Nationalist government, even though it would have sided with the teahouse trade in Chengdu, did not have enough power in Sichuan to address issues of local taxation.

When the municipal government levied a new tax in August 1940, the guild required its members to "never acknowledge this tax and resist it to the end" and decided that all teahouses would strike if the government began arresting its members. The guild emphasized that it would "persuade anyone who resisted with the truth," and that all members would condemn those who continued to ignore its requirements. To encourage participation, the guild promised to pay the living expenses of any members who were arrested. All participants signed the resolution. Under this pressure, the government had to put the new tax on hold; in the meantime, the guild continued to fight and asked the government for an exemption from the onerous burden. The guild achieved victory early the next year when the government decided that the tax would be based on a teahouse's classification rather than on the number of its tables, and that the license fee would be paid quarterly instead of monthly.[53]

Registering a Business

Whereas the Teahouse Guild often fought the government over pricing and taxes, it usually supported local authorities when it came to limiting the establishment of new teahouses. Limiting the opening of new teahouses had been a long-standing policy of the local government. The Teahouse Guild favored this regulation and cooperated with the government in limiting competition. In fact, the guild felt it desperately needed government action to regulate the number of teahouses in the city. More teahouses meant more competition, which brought more difficulties to the whole trade. However, the guild did not have enough power on its own to regulate the entry of new shops into the market and so asked the government to enact regulations requiring the licensing of all teahouses to prevent too great a concentration in any given area. Their goals were the same but their motivations were different: the guild sought to prevent unreasonable competition while the government sought to discourage public gatherings and "wasting time." Thus, during the Republican period, and especially in the 1940s, the policy concerning licensing became more stringent, and the guild and the government enacted more restrictions regarding the opening of new shops, the transfer of ownership, and the relocation, renaming, and reopening of existing shops.

The government, in an attempt to limit the number of teahouses, was very chary about issuing licenses. A teahouse that lost its license or planned to move had to repeat the entire inspection and licensing process. Typically, the proprietor wrote a request to the guild explaining his situation, which the guild forwarded to the municipal government, along with confirmation that the proprietor's claims were true. The responsible office of the government would send one or two clerks to investigate and write a report for the office director, other high-level staff, and the mayor. The office director would send another letter to the staff and mayor to explain his opinion, although his letter often simply repeated the investigator's report. The authorities would make a decision based on the relevant regulations and the individual case. A teahouse had to have a shop as a guarantor to co-sign these documents.[54] In the 1940s such a policy was enforced to an unprecedented degree; in fact, the municipal government basically refused to allow any new teahouses to open. A regulation known as "Restricting Teahouses in Chengdu" (Chengdu shi chaguan ye qudi banfa) issued in 1943 made clear that no new teahouses would be opened; that teahouses in "inappropriate places" and that "harmed public hygiene and traffic" had to be relocated or closed; and that a teahouse "should not be run by a person other than the one named on the license."[55]

This policy was widely encouraged by existing teahouses because it eliminated new competition. There were many allegations of impropriety. In 1947, for example, seventy-eight teahouses co-signed a report accusing the Four Fountains Teahouse (Siquan chashe) on Golden Fountain Street (Jinquan jie) of opening "illegally." This teahouse had been doing business on Lower River Bank Street (Xiaheba jie) before being shut down soon after the owner's death in 1944 and, according to the report, should not be allowed to reopen because this would violate the regulations of the municipal government and the Teahouse Guild. The guild asked the government to investigate.⁵⁶ Those who tried to enter the business naturally resented this restriction. That same year, eighteen people presented a petition to the Chengdu City Council (Chengdu shi canyihui) asking that the restrictions be relaxed. They emphasized that teahouses were a great convenience for both travelers and local residents, and especially merchants, who gained information about local and national markets at teahouses. But, they complained, the government allowed current teahouses to continue in business but prohibited new ones from opening because bad people went to teahouses and because customers wasted time there. They added that the demand for teahouses as a source of drinking water and a place where coolies and water-carriers could take a break had grown along with Chengdu's population, and that some coffeehouses actually sold tea. They also pointed out that the law provided for "freedom to do business" (*yingye ziyou*).⁵⁷ Therefore, they asked that the restriction be abolished and that the market be free to find the balance between supply and demand.

The transfer of ownership also was forbidden, but some people ran teahouses despite this. In 1944, five teahouses were forced to close and their licenses were suspended because of this violation. According to the investigator's report, the proprietors of these teahouses had illegally assumed the licenses held by the previous owners. The government's restrictions made obtaining a license very difficult; when a teahouse was sold, the new owner usually operated under the previous owner's registration. In some cases, the previous owner and new owner formed a bogus joint venture to hide the transfer of ownership.⁵⁸ In 1947, for example, some teahouse owners reported to the government that the Willow River (Liujiang) and Grand Rising (Hongsheng) teahouses were operating under the license that belonged to the previous owner, which violated "commercial codes" (*shanggui*). In general, as soon as the government confirmed that ownership had changed, it forced teahouses to close. Furthermore, *dingda*, tenants subletting space to another tenant, was common in the teahouse business but prohibited by law.⁵⁹

This policy also made it difficult to relocate except under special circumstances. Owners of teahouses in areas where competition was keen resisted this policy. In 1947, thirteen teahouse managers alleged that the purpose of the Central Peace Garden Teahouse (Zhonghe yuan) on Central Green Goat Market Street (Qingyang chang zhengjie) had been changed without permission, "ignoring the guild's regulations." In response, the owner, Luo Chongde, explained that his teahouse, the Southwest Pavilion Teahouse (Xi'nan ge), also on Central Green Goat Street, had been properly registered, but that in 1943, widening of the street made his space too small to be viable. Therefore, Luo entered an agreement with Tuo Zhonghe to run the teahouse together by using Tuo's teahouse on the same street as the new location, with Luo registering equipment such as tables and chairs under his name. He claimed that he and Tuo told the other teahouse owners on the same street about the situation at the grand opening, and "they all agreed." However, Luo Chongde claimed that he never completed the application because he did not know the procedure. The teahouse was reopened on the same street, so it could not be considered a new teahouse and it did not affect the operation of the other teahouses there.[60] This case illustrates how teahouse proprietors sought to eliminate their nearest competitors. When Luo was forced to relocate, his rivals took advantage of the opportunity to put him out of business.

In the cases mentioned above, the government found more success in its efforts to limit the number of teahouses than in its attempts to impose higher standards of hygiene (discussed in Chapter 1). With the cooperation of the Teahouse Guild, the number of teahouses was limited to around six hundred during most of this era, which relieved the pressure of additional competition. The archives for some cases include complete records that allow a more comprehensive discussion and a better understanding of the relationships between teahouses and government control, and illustrate the difficulty small business owners encountered in making a living in the face of severe competition and the government's rigid control. The following cases may address different problems, but they show how and to what extent local authorities could control the teahouse business.

The Co-Prosperity Teahouse and Inn. To open a teahouse, owners had to register and complete paperwork with the government. The archival records contain the complete registration documents of the Co-Prosperity Teahouse and Inn (Tongxing chashe kezhan) from 1942. Among these documents is an "Application for Commercial Registration," which gives a good sense of the registration process and provides useful material, including the name of the owner and the teahouse, its location, its amount of capital, the fact that it was a partnership, and so on. This teahouse was established by Fu Rongqing and Wu Pinrong, whose written partnership agreement reveals some details about this new business. Fu and Wu rented from Zhou a shop with a total of five rooms on Lower Laundry Street, paying a 400 yuan deposit and 40 yuan per month in rent. They also rented all the necessary tea kettles and tea bowls, tables and chairs, quilts, beds, and mosquito nets from Zhou. Fu and Wu each contributed 1,000 yuan for the deposit, rent, tea leaves, fuel, labor, food, and other expenses. Fu Rongqing was responsible for inventory and accounting, while Wu Pinrong was in charge of overall business operations, buying supplies, and preparing meals. They took turns supervising employees and handling other routine affairs. Accounts were settled biweekly, and they split any losses. When profits reached 2,000 yuan, this amount could be withdrawn, but none of the other supplies, such as tea leaves and coal, could be taken. Both partners had to agree on major decisions such as closing or reorganizing the business. In addition to Fu Rongqing and Wu Pinrong, four witnesses also signed the document.[61]

The government posted a public notice when the teahouse opened: "On March 16, 1942, the application for the registration of the Co-Prosperity Teahouse and Inn was submitted. Upon examination, the application was found to meet the regulations, and the license may be issued with public notification." The two owners' names were added at the end of the notice. A license, called a "Registration Card of Commerce," was also issued.[62] One wonders how this teahouse managed to secure a license in an era when the government denied virtually every other request. Moreover, the government discouraged teahouses that also provided overnight accommodations. The available material contains no evidence that this teahouse was one that had relocated or reopened. However, government restrictions were often flexible for those in powerful positions or who had special relationships with government officials.

The Golden Fountain Teahouse. In November 1946, the heads of the tenth police district requested that the municipal government allow the Golden Fountain Teahouse (Jinquan) to reopen upon the demand of the head of the *baojia* (the neighborhood administrative system). The Golden Fountain had opened early in the Republican era, but in 1943 its owner, Qiu Shuyi, rented it to Deng Jinting, and the municipal government closed it in October 1946 for operating without a license. Deng, the letter from the police stated, was "illiterate" and a "fool" who went insane when his teahouse was closed, endangering his family's livelihood and his ability to pay his debts. The head of the *baojia* obviously wanted to help him, asking Deng's family to supervise him to avoid any accidents, and reporting the case to the local authorities. The police asked the government to consider the fact that both Deng and his wife had become ill and bedridden after losing their business. To avoid further tragedy, which could disrupt social order, the government should postpone carrying out the regulation. The request confirmed that Deng "indeed is a rube (*xiangyu*) who knows nothing about laws or regulations" and that postponing the closure would give him a chance to clear out his tea, coal, and other supplies so that he could recoup some of his investment.[63]

The government ordered the Golden Fountain Teahouse to be closed within one week of the discovery of this violation, but the inspector claimed that the teahouse continued to operate for two more weeks. He listed four infractions: (1) the teahouse failed to register with the local government; (2) the teahouse engaged in business although no new teahouses were allowed; (3) Deng had operated this teahouse illegally for several years by not registering; and (4) Deng deliberately disobeyed the government's order to close within one week. Therefore, the official wrote, the teahouse should be closed under the second article of the regulation of teahouses and the appeal to postpone the order was outside the scope of the law. However, he did not offer an opinion on handling the issue and deferred to the mayor. The archives contain a note from the mayor, declining the request to allow the shop to reopen.[64] Ultimately, an outpouring of sympathy by community leaders did not prevent the government from shutting down the teahouse.

This case also illustrates how business rivals manipulated government regulations for their own benefit. It was Qiu Shuyi, the landlord, who had reported Deng for operating without a license. Qiu exposed Deng because of a rent dispute. Qiu rented two rooms and equipment to Deng in February 1943 and claimed that he was entitled to renege on the agreement at any time because there was no written contract. In fact he had tried to renege not long after the deal was finalized and had discussed the issue with Deng several times, but Deng refused to cooperate. In retaliation, Qiu accused Deng of "refusing to register" and "believing that the government has no way to force him" to comply with the 1942 government code that required all teahouses to register. Therefore, "to protect the regulations, such a violator should be punished" and "his teahouse shut down."[65] Obviously, Qiu strategically turned to the government when he could not attain his goal independently, and the situation ended as a tragic example of the hardships faced by small shop owners.

The Three Chinese-Scholar Trees Teahouse and Inn. Some merchants joined with the government to limit competition in the teahouse business. An anonymous letter to Mayor Chen signed by "Law-abiding Businessmen in Chengdu" and dated January 5, 1946, involves one such case. In this letter, the merchants claim that "now that the eight-year war has been won, construction is on the way. Chengdu is the capital of Sichuan, and all illegal businesses should be banned.... The construction of a new Sichuan should start in Chengdu." The letter stated that a former head of a nearby village who was a master in the Gowned Brothers opened the Three Chinese-Scholar Trees Teahouse and Inn (Sanhuaishu chashe kezhan) on Long Fluent Street (Changshun jie). The letter alleged that, "As a civil servant, he dares to conduct an illegal operation and violate the regulations," and asked the government to investigate immediately and close his business.[66]

The investigation found that the Three Chinese-Scholar Trees Teahouse and Inn was formerly the Tung-Tree Shadow Teahouse and Inn, owned by Chen Jiyun. Chen sold the teahouse to Wang Pinsan, who wanted to rename it the Three Chinese-Scholar Trees Tea Garden (Sanhuai chayuan), but the government refused, citing the "regulations of restricting teahouses" and ordering him to cease doing business. In February 1946, Li Qiyi, the former manager of the Tung-Tree Shadow Teahouse, asked to continue to use that name, but the investigator stated that since the original license had been transferred in violation of the regulations, the government should shut the business down. After confirming that the teahouse had been sold, the government ordered Li to surrender the license by a given deadline and issued a public notice signed by Mayor Chen declaring that the license would be invalid beginning March 10. This investigation reveals that the key issue that concerned the government was the license and the infraction that occurred during the transfer of ownership. It is interesting to note that the anonymous letter emphasized that Wang was a master in the Gowned Brothers, but there is no evidence that the government pursued this. It seems that membership in the organization was so common that the government had no interest in it.[67]

The Great Northern Tea Hall. In June 1949, the municipal government investigated an allegation that the Great Northern Tea Hall (Dabei chating) in the New Shopping Mall (Xin shangchang) was a black market for gold and silver. The government revoked the Hall's license and forced it to shut down. The Teahouse Guild represented the Hall in its appeal, in which the two co-managers claimed that the teahouse had been in operation for a long time, and that all of its customers were "legal merchants" of wine, cigarettes, grain, dried vegetables, printing, soap, Western medicine, and paper. The teahouse was the site of "tea meetings" (*chahui*) for these merchants, but it never allowed any illegal trading in gold or silver and even repeatedly refused offers to get involved in these activities.[68]

The guild asked the government to allow the teahouse to reopen and guaranteed that it had operated legally. The mayor, however, denounced the teahouse as "always having provided a place for black market trading, disrupting normal business operations and damaging social stability." The teahouse, he said, had been warned several times but did not obey the law, and therefore its request was denied. On June 28, 1949, the guild again represented the teahouse in its bid to reopen, stating that its own investigation had revealed that the teahouse had repeatedly turned away buyers for black market goods, and that it should not be blamed for the presence of a few merchants engaged in illegal activities. Vendors of legal goods, such as grain and dried vegetables, needed a place for their trade. Under pressure, the government finally relented and allowed the teahouse to reopen, but the managers had to sign a pledge that any illegal trading would be prohibited and that the teahouse would be shut down if any violations occurred.[69]

In the meantime, the government began requiring other teahouse managers to sign this pledge as well, which became another tactic in its control of teahouses. From the case of the Great Northern Tea Hall, it is clear that the government treated prominent teahouses with significant ancillary businesses relatively leniently. Of course, the guild's strategy also was effective. To satisfy the government's requirement, the guild had the Pleasant Garden (Yiyuan), Great Northern Tea Hall, and seventeen other teahouses sign a pledge to adhere to government regulations prohibiting illegal trade and to immediately contact the guild if illegal conduct was discovered. The pledge stated: "We voluntarily obey the government regulations and refuse any illegal activities on the part of merchants. We will also report those activities to the nearest police station or to the municipal government at once in order that criminals be apprehended. We are aware that any violations will result in severe punishment."[70]

Although there was a gap between the government's policies and their enforcement, and although the government often met with resistance from proprietors, managers, and performers, it was still able to exert a measure of control over the teahouse trade. On the one hand, the police insisted that teahouses had to meet their guidelines, and on the other hand, when the teahouses and performers worked very hard to do so, they had to make a living before getting approval. From these cases, it is evident that sometimes a compromise was struck between the government's attempt to exert control and people's struggle to earn a living. These cases also underscore the intense internal strife between teahouse keepers who did not stand together to resist the extension of state power, but tried to take advantage of it eliminate rival businesses. From these cases, we find that newcomers who lacked powerful connections in the government or the guild had a difficult time breaking into the business. In each case, the government sent clerks to investigate and considered the guild's report. However, its decisions were sometimes arbitrary, and often resulted in tougher punishment for smaller teahouses.

A Balance between the State and Teahouses

Although the power relationship between the guild and government was often unbalanced and disputes were inevitable, the two had mutual interests and thus usually addressed conflicts through negotiation or other strategies of accommodation rather than through direct confrontation. While the government forced the guild to obey its orders, it did not want the guild to risk losing its authority over the entire trade. Government agents found that using the guild as an intermediary was much easier than dealing with each member of the trade individually. The guild understood that personal relationships with government officials would greatly benefit its cause. For example, when the guild sought to raise its prices, it was standard practice to give money to the relevant officials under the guise of contributing money for an announcement in the media. The guild recognized that this was "in fact a bribe" and decided that in the future, it would hold a public meeting to discuss the issue and invite members of the GMD, government, and media, in order to avoid this cost.[71]

To raise prices, the guild first had to obtain the support of either the GMD or the government. On October 14, 1942, for example, the guild held a meeting at its members' request to discuss ways of dealing with price issues, and more than two hundred members attended. An official from the local branch of the GMD also participated and said that the party would allow "reasonable" price increases, but that this would be difficult because the government was trying to control price increases overall. Guild president Wang Xiushan emphasized that "this meeting is a legal gathering to seek a solution for prices in the teahouses," and that "since the establishment of the Price Evaluation Committee (Pingjia hui), the prices of all kind of goods, especially grain and clothing, have risen, and therefore, the price of tea should also be increased a reasonable amount." He swore that the guild would try its best to pass along its members' opinions to the committee.[72] The result of this kind of effort often was not good; in this case, it led to Wang Xiushan's resignation as president.

On the one hand, the Teahouse Guild struggled with the local government to protect the interests of its own profession; on the other hand, it got its power and authority from the local government, especially in the area of pricing. If any teahouse was found to violate the rates set by the guild, it would be forced to change its prices or face action against it. Such power was recognized by the government. For example, in September 1941 the guild sent a letter to the Tian Hongxing Teahouse warning that its prices were "too low" and did not conform to the "legal price," and demanded that it obey the guidelines or else face being "reported to the authorities" and possibly shut down. Usually, the proprietors of teahouses that did not follow the guidelines were compelled to meet the guild president to pledge that they would sell tea at the price determined by the guild. The guild also sent people to teahouses to check prices; violators were importuned to correct their "mistakes." If they refused, after a formal warning letter from the guild, the guild would ask the government to close the business.[73] In short, the guild worked with local authorities to enforce uniform pricing.

The guild played a role in communication between the state and teahouse proprietors not only regarding prices, but also concerning issues such as taxation and even political activities. As noted, the guild carried out government regulations while also trying to represent the interests of the trade. The guild also acted as a mediator in disputes between teahouse proprietors and the government and participated in activities promoted by the government. In 1940, for example, the guild participated in the government's Movement to Economize (*Jieyue yundong*). That same year, the government advanced a movement called Saving for Rebuilding the Country (*Jianguo chuxu*), which tried to persuade people to save more money in banks by promising that the principal and interest would be repaid to all depositors after six months. The Chamber of Commerce asked the guild to convince teahouses to save a total of at least 5,000 yuan, and the guild determined "to try its best to persuade the members to save," with the president volunteering to deposit the first 500 yuan. When the Friendship Society of Wounded Soldiers on the Frontlines (Qianfang kangzhan shangbing zhiyou she) put forth a national call for contributions, the Chamber of Commerce asked the guild to donate 300 yuan. During the war, charitable requests for donations of clothing, food, or money, were frequent. The guild always encouraged teahouses' active participation in these activities, especially in "sending people's best wishes to the army" (*laojun*).[74]

Many of these voluntary donations became mandatory. In 1941, for example, in order to "donate" 1,500 yuan requested by the Chamber of Commerce, the guild appointed representatives to collect money from each teahouse. In early 1942, the guild had to "donate" money to the cause of "donating planes to the military." Sometimes, teahouses gave items on hand, such as opera tickets and rice coupons. When a major holiday approached, the guild had to solicit more of these payments, which eventually became taxes. For instance, before the Chinese New Year of 1942, the guild collected funds from each teahouse for four mandatory requests: airplanes (*feijijuan*), fire control (*xiaofangjuan*), music (*yinyuejuan*), and gifts from the Spring Festival for the military (*chunli laojunjuan*). During the war, although the guild made donations to maintain its social reputation and demonstrate its "patriotic zeal," these requests came one right after another and, because "the demands were very huge," they placed a heavy burden on the teahouses' already strained capabilities.[75]

In 1947, the municipal government ordered all teahouses to use running water for the sake of sanitation, a measure that brought resistance from many teahouses. The guild summarized the difficulties this placed on the teahouse trade: plumbing was installed on only a dozen streets, and there were only eight stations that pumped water. Therefore, it was not convenient for every teahouse, especially for those on the outskirts of the city, to get their water from the water stations. For these teahouses, labor costs for having water transported manually were very high. While the guild held a general meeting of all members and encouraged teahouses along the water-pipe route to use running water, it also made several recommendations to the government: to order all teahouses to buy running water, to put a sign about the use of running water in front of each shop, to install more plumbing and to open more water stations, and to reduce the price of running water.[76]

The municipal government basically adopted some of these suggestions with three caveats: the guild was responsible for ensuring that all teahouses along the pipeline route used running water and listing their names; the water company would be responsible for opening more water stations and installing more pipes and for making wooden boards, on which was written "this teahouse uses running water" to be hung on teahouse doors. However, the government let the water company determine the price of this water.[77] Apparently, the most important issue confronting teahouses—their heavy financial burden—would not be mitigated.

Conclusion

The Teahouse Guild originated from a traditional *bang* in the late Qing, and was reorganized in 1931 and again in 1936 under the auspices of the government, and in the process lost many of the features of traditional *huiguan* or *gongsuo*. As Bryna Goodman argues, the reformation of traditional organizations such as guilds and native-place associations was a part of state-building and creating a national identity. Mosea Ballou Morse, in his 1932 book on the guilds of China, emphasizes the function of religion and defines the guild in China as "a solely religious and benevolent fraternity." Morse explained the different origins of guilds in Europe and China; in England, the power of guilds was granted by the king, feudal lord, parliament, or municipal government, but in China, guilds had a "purely democratic origin, without grant or licence from the governing powers."[78] This is true for Qing-era guilds, but in the Republican period, especially during the war and after, guilds increasingly depended on the government to enforce their authority and implement their goals. At the same time, in an example of how the state's power infiltrated the very lowest levels of society during the Republican period, the government increasingly manipulated social organizations like guilds. Also, whereas early native-place associations often overlapped with guilds, during the war they no longer carried any function of *huiguan*; in a word, these two traditional organizations had completely split apart. Thus, the Teahouse Guild came to act solely as a professional organization while it became much less autonomous than its predecessors.

As we have seen, during and after the war, the guild played an important role in the profession. Although routine affairs were handled by representatives elected from the membership, the guild was largely controlled by the local government, to which all decisions had to be submitted for approval. The Teahouse Guild, however, tried very hard to deal collectively with issues of pricing and taxation. It often clashed with the state regarding pricing and taxation. In short, the guild became a complex social organization that tried to balance the needs of the state and the profession. To a certain extent, the guild's struggles underscored the resistance of social organizations to the intrusion of state power.

The government controlled pricing, and individual teahouses in general did not have the right to adjust their prices according to their costs and market demand. The government enforced prices in the name of "market stabilization" during the war, but this practice often hurt teahouses, even forcing some to shut down when costs became too high. The guild cooperated with the local government on local affairs but resisted if the interests of the entire trade were threatened. Although the government emerged the victor in the vast majority of these cases, the guild occasionally prevailed. As we have seen, the Teahouse Guild was a powerful tool of the teahouse trade. Its strategy of conducting unified action to fight for common interests was overt and often effective. Teahouses that united and acted together had a much stronger voice that demanded careful consideration from the government than those that acted individually. Of course, the guild tempered its political activities with its desire to maintain a harmonious relationship with local authorities.

The guild in general did not allow violations of its regulations, and while it lacked the power to punish teahouse proprietors who disobeyed the "principles of the profession," it pushed the government to take action against violators. Most violations were reported by the proprietors of competing teahouses, illustrating the internal strife in the trade. The balance between "principles of the profession" and profit-seeking by teahouses often led to conflict. Of course, the guild often prevailed because it had the authority of the local government behind it. The guild tried very hard to enforce a uniform price structure to prevent competition. Furthermore, with government support, the guild effectively limited the total number of teahouses in Chengdu, which helped the teahouse trade by stabilizing market forces and limiting competition. Of course, these actions met resistance from those who wanted to enter this business, but government regulation helped the Teahouse Guild achieve its goals. On the one hand, the guild struggled for more operational "freedom," such as the right to determine prices. On the other hand, it tried very hard to secure the government's involvement in limiting the number of teahouses, which actually became an obstacle to this freedom. This controversial stance reflected the guild's dilemma. Those who wanted to enter the teahouse trade fought not only the government but also the guild. To a certain extent, this was a result of the controls imposed by both the Teahouse Guild and the government, which created strong resentment among those denied entrée into the business. Although the Western notions of "free competition" and "freedom to do business" were introduced in Chengdu in the late Qing era, by the time of the Republic the city's economic structure had not changed much, and the government and the various guilds associated with different occupations still played an important role. Even though some people struggled to achieve "freedom to do business," this goal was never realized during the Republican period.

The relationship between the government and the guild was often mutually beneficial. The guild fought for the interests of teahouses while striving to maintain a good relationship with the government to ensure its continued support. The guild, however, often faced situations that made it difficult to maintain a balance between these two interests. One of the guild's major missions was to communicate the opinions of teahouse proprietors and to negotiate with the authorities on their behalf. We have seen that while the guild often was unsuccessful—and, in fact, it often failed outright—it still facilitated communication. The guild was a conduit through which both the government quickly distributed its new policies to each teahouse, and the teahouse trade transmitted its requests to the local government. The government's basic policies toward the teahouse from the late Qing to the Communist victory emphasized control, restriction, and punishment. The task of control was not easily implemented, however, within a beloved and thriving cultural institution. From the available evidence, it is clear that some policies were more successful than others, and some measures were more effective when implemented at different times. The success of many government polices depended on the cooperation of the guild. The government and the guild usually tried to address conflicts of interest through negotiation or another strategy of accommodation rather than through direct confrontation. While the government forced the guild to obey its orders, it did not want the guild to risk losing the authority it held on behalf of the entire trade. Government agents found that using the guild as an intermediary was much easier than dealing with each member of the trade individually.

CHAPTER 3

Labor and Workplace Culture

In 1942, when Chinese soldiers were fighting bloody battles on the front lines, people in Chengdu, in the isolated upper Yangzi region known as the Great Rear Area (Dahoufang), still frequented their favorite teahouses as an important part of everyday life. One evening in the fall of that year, war hero General Feng Yuxiang and several other prominent figures went to the Bright Spring Tea Balcony (Jinchun chalou) in Chengdu to drink tea and to watch the well-known waiter nicknamed Pockmarks Zhou (Zhou Mazi) at work. As soon as they sat down, Pockmarks Zhou brought to their table a large purple brass kettle in one hand and a pile of more than twenty sets of tea utensils in the other. He stopped at a distance from the table, placed the saucers precisely in front of each patron, and put a bowl onto each saucer. Although the customers requested many different kinds of tea, Zhou filled their orders without error. He moved two or three feet back from the table and poured boiling water into each bowl. Then he stepped forward and hooked each bowl lid off the table with his little finger and covered each bowl. The process was neatly done in a single step, and not a drop of water was spilled. The observers felt like they were watching a magician's performance. When Zhou received payment, he did not give change back immediately because he was too busy serving others. When the customers were about to leave, however, he gave precise change to each customer without any confusion, regardless of how many he had served. His "extraordinary memory" amazed patrons.
—Li Sizhen and Ma Yansen, "Jinchun lou 'sanjue'—Jia Xiazi, Zhou Mazi, Si Pangzi" [Three Bests in the Bright Spring Tea Balcony: Blind Jia, Pockmarks Zhou, and Fatso Si]

CHENGDU WAS HOME to many teahouse waiters like Pockmarks Zhou who bore the popular informal title of "masters of tea" (*cha boshi*). As the phrase suggests, these waiters personified teahouse culture. They also were called *tangguan* ("officers in charge of the hall"), *chafang* ("teahouse men"), *yaoshi* ("young masters"), *tizhengtang* ("carrying [kettles] at the front hall"), and *tihu gongren* ("workers carrying kettles"), but "masters of tea" became their enduring "elegant name" (*yaming*).[1] Although the term "masters of tea" was meant to be humorous, it nonetheless reflected these workers' great skill and considerable knowledge of tea, as well as their rich social experience. Many men made their living as masters of tea in the various teahouses throughout Chengdu. While there is little literature on small-business-sector workers in general, the relatively rich information that is available on teahouse workers makes it possible for us to determine their working situation, the issues that concerned them as a group, and their interactions with politics. The fact that teahouses were public places made teahouse workers more visible than workers in other small businesses and ensured that anything that happened at a teahouse would draw considerable attention, much of which was recorded (see Figure 3.1).

This chapter explores workplace culture in small businesses by focusing on employees, mainly waiters and waitresses, who labored in Chengdu's teahouses. While previous studies focus mainly on the relationship between teahouses, their patrons, and society, this chapter shifts the focus to internal issues, in particular the relationships among small businesses, the labor force, the workplace, and workplace culture. No study of the waiters and waitresses who worked in restaurants, wine shops, and teahouses has ever

FIGURE 3.1: A skillful waiter, holding a pile of tea bowls in one hand. Photo by Chen Jin, 1980s. Photo courtesy of Chen Jin.

been conducted in the fields of Chinese history and anthropology.[2] Teahouse workers dealt with complexly interwoven social relations and their experiences reflected various social conflicts played out in a public arena. The study of teahouse workers and workplace culture can provide a window through which to observe the small-scale Chinese business workforce and working environment more generally, and to understand workplace culture in Republican Chengdu, more specifically, providing another side of the story of the Chinese working class.

In fact, studies of workers in any type of small-scale service business, such as traditional stores, restaurants, teahouses, and other small shops, are virtually absent from Chinese urban and labor history. Most of the noteworthy publications on the modern Chinese working class focus on factory workers.[3] Yet, in Republican China, workers in small shops accounted for the majority of the workforce. By 1919, for instance, the total number of workers in factories throughout China was only about 1.5 million, while the Ministry of Agriculture, Industry, and Commerce (Nonggongshang bu) in 1912 found that 2.1 million people worked in various workshops in the province of Sichuan alone.[4] Although these workers were a substantial majority, they were little visible in urban history and labor history because they were scattered across many small workplaces. While workers in factories played a prominent role in the transformation of the urban landscape and culture, workers in small-scale businesses also made a great contribution; in fact, to a certain extent, they better represented urban culture because their workplace was in public. To date, we have uncovered little about service workers' working conditions and environment, the issues they faced, their strategies for survival, their relationship with the community, gender conflicts among them, and the roles they played in public life. This chapter explores all of these issues.

The War of Resistance (1937–45) was a turning point for Chengdu's teahouse workforce, a time when workers felt the effects of economic depression, women challenged the exclusively male workforce and brought new workplace culture into teahouses, and workers found a voice in the new Union of Chengdu Teahouse Workers. This chapter explores the following major issues: First, how waiters used their rich social experience and skills to deal with various problems and survive in teahouses. Second, the dramatic change in teahouse culture resulting from the influx of a large number of war refugees—most from the lower Yangzi region—who brought not only more business but also new elements of coastal culture to the teahouse. Women invaded this male domain to become waitresses who, while attracting more patrons, actually faced a hostile working environment; waiters resented the increased competition and local toughs brought sexual harassment. Third, the public perception of teahouse workers as defined by their job performance, criticism from elites, and government intervention. Finally, the Union of Chengdu Teahouse Workers, established in 1939, became teahouse workers' most important representative protecting their rights and interests even though it often suffered internal crises and was supervised by the government. In the past, scholarship has focused on the external relations of unions with forces such as employers, political parties, and governments, but this chapter focuses on the union's internal workings and the relationships among the leaders and between male and female members.[5] These aspects are well documented, which enables us to examine these issues from the perspectives of cultural and social history.

The Teahouse Business and Wage Workers

Large teahouses hired as many as thirty to forty workers, mid-sized ones ten or so, and small ones only three to five.[6] Some teahouses remained family businesses in which the husband served as proprietor and waiter, the wife as dishwasher and maid, and the son as stove keeper and water-carrier.[7] Statistics from 1951—just after the Communists took over China—offer some important insights about teahouse workers. Since the Communist government had not yet launched any major changes, the 1951 statistics reflect Republican-era conditions. In Chengdu, there were 1,404 teahouse wage workers in 1951; of them, 1,368 were male, and only 36 were female. The statistics do not indicate the backgrounds of the 1,783 people—more than the number of the wage workers—listed as "other." I assume that these were family members, who received no pay and for which no labor cost was incurred. The source also tells us that 3,885 people depended on the teahouse trade, for an average of 6.9 people per teahouse. The trade had very few apprentices; of the 3,885 people who worked in teahouses, only ten, or 0.25 percent of the total and 0.7 percent of the total number of hired workers, were apprentices.[8] This suggests that teahouses lacked a well-developed system of training prospective masters of tea. The fact that I have not so far seen any detailed documentation that mentions apprenticeships in teahouses supports this assumption. This might be a result of the nature of the job: a new hand in a teahouse could provide basic service without formal training, but he could become a master of tea only after many years of experience.[9] The First Subdistrict of the East District (Dongyiqu) (see Map 3), for example, had twenty-four teahouses, in which 150 people made a living.[10] Each teahouse had an average of only six employees. Of these 150 people, only forty-eight were paid employees; the rest were family members. The record also indicates the employment practices of these teahouses. Of the twenty-four teahouses, one had no hired workers, eight had only one, and only two teahouses had four workers, the maximum number. Of the forty-eight hired workers, only one was a woman.[11]

To encourage hard work, teahouses paid waiters a daily salary and gave them free meals. Lower-level workers were usually paid by the month and also were given free meals. A teahouse waiter earned an average of 4.47 yuan per month in 1938, when the average salary of all workers in Chengdu was 13.41 yuan. A 1942 record shows the monthly expenses and salaries at the teahouse of Wang Xiushan, president of the Teahouse Guild. That teahouse employed ten workers, and its total monthly labor cost was 4,000 yuan, or about 400 yuan per worker. Counting a month as thirty days, the per-worker daily cost was 13.3 yuan, but the document does not indicate how much went for salaries and how much for meals. A record of the cost of meals at the Cry of the Crane Teahouse (Heming chashe), which also had ten employees, shows a monthly total of 1,800 yuan, or 6 yuan per person per day. If we assume that the cost of meals per person at the first teahouse was the same, then its salaries would have been 7.3 yuan per person per day.[12] Yet this was recorded during the war, when prices fluctuated wildly and rapidly, making it necessary to compare wages with prices to make sense of workers' incomes. In November 1942, when salary figures were recorded, rice cost 444 yuan per dan (one dan was equal to about 310 pounds), or 1.43 yuan per pound.[13] Therefore, a teahouse worker's daily salary could buy about five pounds of rice. Teahouse waiters, however, received some "soft" income; "water money" (*shuiqian*), which was the money earned by selling "plain boiled water," belonged entirely to the waiter, and often amounting to more than his regular wage. Stove keepers could also supplement their daily wages by earning so-called fire money (*huoqian*) by providing extra services like stewing meat and blending medicinal herbs.[14] Nevertheless, waiters and stove keepers found it difficult to support their families.

"Masters of Tea" (Cha boshi)

In Chengdu, "masters of tea"—the highly skilled waiters—were considered the "spirit of a teahouse." Although the proprietors managed the business, their main task was simply to sit behind the counter, weigh tea leaves, receive payment from the waiters, and hand out bowls of tea to waiters. Their role is reflected in a local proverb: "An officer is less important than his adjutants; a teahouse keeper is less important than his waiters" (*zhangguan buru fuguan, zhanggui buru tangguan*).[15] Workers usually did not have any break time, often starting to work right after meals or even working while eating. A folk poem gives an even more vivid description of teahouse waiters: "They never leave the gate though they walk a thousand *li* per day; they do not govern people though they act like an official; they have a pocket full of money by day, but nothing at night."[16] Waiters in a large teahouse came up with a satirical saying: "Being busy from early morning to night, my two legs feel broken. As soon as a call ordering me to add boiled water comes from this corner, another call arises from the other side. I run hither and thither, but cannot earn enough to buy a *sheng* of rice."[17]

Waiters were responsible for taking care of all patrons, greeting and seating new arrivals, maintaining the supply of boiled water, keeping tables clean, giving correct change, and treating all customers equally.[18] They were expected to respond to all calls immediately, listening and looking in all directions at all times. When a customer entered, the waiter would greet him by name—"Master X," "Brother X," or "Mr. X"—lead him to his seat, and ask what kind of tea he wanted. The waiter's response had to be lightning fast. Waiters' speech patterns gradually took on a highly distinctive style. At peak times, patrons could hear the waiters' greetings and answers rising one after another, mingling with the general hubbub. Waiters also had to learn the secret gestures and jargon of any secret societies that met at the teahouse.[19]

Waiters had to understand their patrons. According to some observers, a teahouse waiter had to have both "the skills of carrying a tea kettle and pouring boiled water" and "the ability to make everyone happy," but it was not easy to achieve both, and any slight error could offend customers. Even receiving payment, for example, might not be simple. A waiter often met situations in which a patron entered the teahouse and ran into his friends, who all hurried to the front to buy a bowl of tea for him. Facing so many hands, the waiter would take money from one of them and tell the others to "keep your money for next time," after which everybody went back to their seats, satisfied.[20] But to do this, the waiter had to have considerable knowledge of his customers.

Other teahouse workers also personified the strong local teahouse culture and traditions. Stove keepers probably were second only to waiters in importance in the functioning of the teahouse. While a stove keeper did not have to run around the teahouse and deal with customers directly, his job was not easy, for his day started very early in the morning and did not end until midnight. He boiled water before dawn for the regular early morning tea drinkers.[21] At midnight, when the waiters settled their accounts, the stove keeper had to cover the fire with just enough ash to prevent it from dying before the next morning's opening. He also suffered from tremendous heat in summer and choking dust when adding coal or cleaning ash from the stove. He had to be frugal in using coal while at the same time keeping sufficient boiled and hot water on hand. He had to adjust the temperature of the fire for "peak times" and "slow times" (see Figure 3.2).[22]

FIGURE 3.2: A teahouse stove, commonly used in old-style teahouses. In the foreground are kettles and, to the right, a hot-water vat. Photo by Chen Jin, 1980s. Photo courtesy of Chen Jin.

Waitresses in a Man's World

Most servers in Chengdu were male, but during the war women began to work as waitresses. In Chinese society, women were important contributors to the economy, mainly through home-based handicrafts such as spinning, weaving, and shoemaking, or domestic service as cooks, wet-nurses, nannies, and so on. In rural areas, women also did various chores on farms. Entertainers and prostitutes, considered low-class and indecent, were the only women who earned a living in public places.[23] Therefore, women entering teahouses as waitresses represented, at least in Chengdu, an important change in many areas, from employment patterns and teahouse culture to women's public roles and gender relationships. Teahouse waitresses, called *nü chafang*, emerged in 1937, drawing great attention because this was a new phenomenon in Chengdu.[24] Local newspapers provided much more coverage of the personal and professional lives of waitresses than of their male counterparts. These reports provide valuable information about waitresses' roles and social impact. Yet waitresses, an important segment of the modern female workforce, have hitherto drawn no attention from historians of China.

The flourishing of teahouse waitresses in Chengdu was a direct result of immigration. The Japanese invasion caused a huge number of refugees from the seaboard to move to Chengdu, which, as a conservative and isolated city, placed relatively great restrictions on women in public. Although the attitudes of the people of Chengdu toward women had changed since the late Qing era, no previous transformation was as rapid as this one.[25] These refugees brought to Chengdu the relatively open attitudes found in the coastal areas, and the women from downriver had less hesitation about working in public. Also, at the beginning of the war, at least, people concentrated almost exclusively on the national devastation caused by the war, and followed its progress very closely. The perpetuation of traditional morality was less of a priority for elites and the government, and thus the emergence of women in the public workforce drew relatively little attention. As a result, many upscale teahouses, such as the Great Wisdom Tea Balcony (Yizhi chalou) and Three Sages Teahouse (Sanyi gong) on Warm Spring Road (Chunxi lu), sprang up in the city's most prosperous area. These new teahouses not only provided private rooms to attract customers, but also were the first in the city to hire women as waitresses. The presence of waitresses attracted more male customers, who came to gawk at the novelty of women at work, and often made fun of them.[26] Later, virtually all of Chengdu's teahouses followed this trend until waitresses could be found in even the crudest teahouses. A teahouse without a waitress at that point was considered "out of fashion," and suffered a loss of business.[27] Waitresses quickly learned which behaviors, gestures, and voices were appropriate for a particular clientele and wielded their power to attract male customers.

The waitresses came from a variety of backgrounds, but most were poorly educated married women from poor families. The drastic increase in the cost of living meant that many men who received monthly salaries often could not even support themselves, and their families were thrust into poverty. According to one observer, the husbands of waitresses were usually petty clerks in government offices, laborers, and soldiers who were away fighting the Japanese. Because women had to overcome intense social pressure in order to work in the teahouses, some people called them "pitiful birds" (*kelian de xiaoniao*).[28] Of course, a hierarchy among waitresses soon emerged. In high-class teahouses, the waitresses were prettier and in better physical condition because the proprietors were very selective. Waitresses also preferred to work in prosperous teahouses where they could earn more.[29] These women, who were usually demure eighteen- to twenty-three-year olds, typically sported short hairstyles, minimal makeup, Chinese traditional dresses (*qipao* or *cheongsam*), and white aprons, indicating that they had only recently come from their kitchens into the public arena. They exploited their perceived naiveté and purity to lure patrons. In lower-class teahouses, most waitresses were actually hired by hot-towel men or cigarette sellers, and their main job was selling these items for only 1.5 yuan per day, with hiring on a day-to-day basis. They had to recoup any losses out of their meager salaries, which also were based on customer turnover, although they received free breakfast and lunch. In some simple and crude teahouses, however, waitresses often could not earn enough to survive.[30]

Most of the waitresses in Chengdu's teahouses were married women with families to feed. Their jobs were not stable and they were often alone in handling work-related issues. Teahouses were always crowded, noisy, and exciting places, with little physical space between patrons and waitresses, which made harassment a constant threat. Waitresses faced a dilemma: although their basic role was not to provide entertainment, many patrons expected much more from them than mere service. If waitresses refused to meet the needs of customers through "flirting" and "making jokes," they might upset both their customers and employers; if they behaved as patrons expected, they risked social ostracism for being "indecent" or "like a prostitute." In fact, the image of waitresses was complicated, defined through a combination of job performance and public perception.

The Union of Chengdu Teahouse Workers

There is little information about the early history of the teahouse workers' union in Chengdu. According to the available sources, teahouse workers, including waiters, stove keepers, and water-carriers, had a traditional organization called the Three Officials Society (Sanguan hui). In 1926 they organized the Union of Tea Workers of Chengdu (Chengdu shi minggongye zhiye gonghui), a male-only association that eventually claimed more than two thousand members. The union "registered with the party [GMD] and the government," with the claim that "all members enthusiastically participate in activities to save our nation under the Three Principles of the People and the national flag." The union functioned until 1939, when Japanese bombing raids forced Chengdu residents to flee to the relative safety of the surrounding areas. As soon as it was safe to do so, they returned with other Chengdu residents to the city and their jobs. The union was reorganized by Ling Guozheng, a female "trader in a teahouse," into the Union of Chengdu Teahouse Workers' Livelihood (Chengdu shi chashe minsheng gonghui). She changed the formerly all-male union into one that admitted women.[31]

Soon after, in 1939, this organization was renamed the Union of Chengdu Teahouse Workers (Chengdu shi chashe ye zhiye gonghui). The government-imposed regulations under which the union operated clearly show that it was a state-sponsored organization. On the original copy of the regulations in the Chengdu Municipal Archives the words "Chengdu shi chashe ye zhiye gonghui" (Union of Chengdu Teahouse Workers) were simply written by hand in the blanks on a printed document. All professional unions, we can assume, used the same regulations, which were approved by the authorities. This assumption can be verified by the contents of the regulations. Nowhere in the five chapters and thirty-five items is there specific mention of teahouses except for a few places where the phrase *chashe ye* (teahouse business) was filled in by hand (see Figure 3.3).[32] This suggests that the union did not possess independent power beyond the control of local authorities. We are unable to find, at least from the available sources, evidence of a single strike organized by the union over issues such as workers' rights, wages, or working hours, topics that had precipitated strikes in other major Chinese cities since the 1920s. In fact, the union was a product of the Nationalist government, which twice issued laws on unions, once in 1929 and again in 1943. The major items of the regulations were obviously adopted from the law of 1929.[33]

Even though the regulations were not specific to teahouses, they nonetheless became the foundation for the activities of the Union of Chengdu Teahouse Workers. According to the regulations, the union was created to "enhance relations" between workers, "encourage learning and promote better working skills," "improve production," and "improve working and living conditions."[34] Thus, the union had modest goals; only the last item indicates any potential effect on the rights of workers. These regulations also reveal information about the union's membership and leadership. Under the codes, anyone older than sixteen, including women, could join if he or she worked, or previously had worked, in a teahouse, or for the union. On the other hand, people who were "deprived of the rights of citizens," or were guilty of "counterrevolutionary words or deeds," or had claimed bankruptcy, or were disabled, were not allowed to join. Here, the denial of membership because of so-called counterrevolutionary words or deeds apparently reflected the political control of the Nationalist government over the union.[35]

The regulations reveal the union's internal structure. The union had a board of directors made up of nine members and four alternate members. A standing member of the board, selected by the other members, was in charge. The board had the following responsibilities: managing the union's routine affairs; representing the union; holding assemblies and meetings of members, and carrying out their decisions; and implementing members' suggestions. The union had three departments: one dealt with documentation and routine affairs; one handled education, training, publications, registrations, organization, investigations, and record keeping; and one took care of cooperation, mediation, sanitation, entertainment, job searches, and workers' welfare. Each department had a clerk hired by the board. The union also set up a supervisory board, with five supervisory and two alternate members. A standing member of the supervisory board, selected to a one-year term by all supervisory members, was responsible for routine

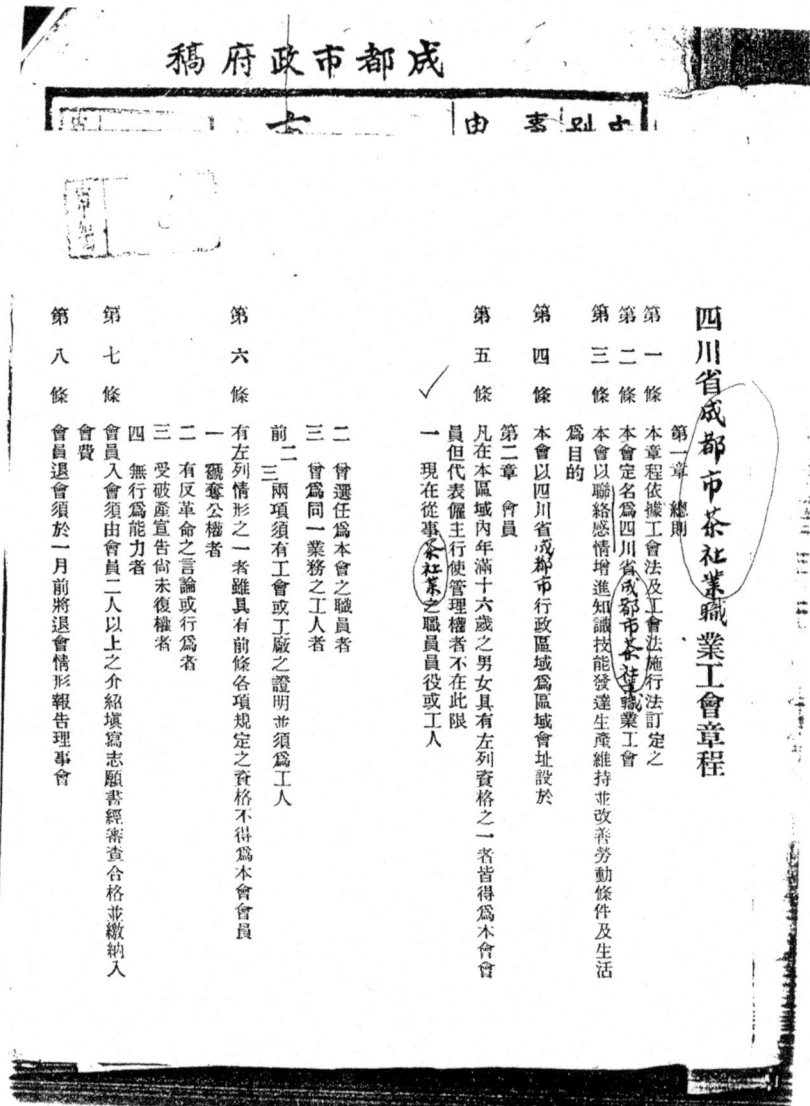

FIGURE 3.3: Regulations of the Union of Chengdu Teahouse Workers. This document has a total of five pages; this is page one. The words *Chengdu shi chashe ye* (Chengdu teahouses) were filled in by hand on the pre-printed template. From CSZGD, 38-11-982.

affairs. The supervisory board had the following responsibilities: auditing accounts; keeping up with all business matters; and overseeing the performance of board members and other members. The positions on these two boards were for one year but board members could be reelected. Meetings of all members or representatives were required every six months, but an emergency meeting could be called if requested by one-third of the members or the board of directors. Meetings were official only when more than half of the membership was in attendance, and decisions required a favorable vote by more than half of the attendees. The union had district branches, under which were groups. One head per group was chosen by the board of directors.[36]

These regulations also give us an opportunity to examine how the government defined labor organizations. As previously noted, the regulations were clearly a standard document used with all labor organizations. The union's responsibilities, as determined by the government, included: signing, revising, and abolishing "collective contracts" (*tuanti xieyue*); establishing a placement office to help locate jobs for members; assisting with financial matters such as savings, insurance, hospital coverage, and day care; setting up collective organizations that provided help in many aspects of working and living; providing education; establishing libraries, plus newspapers and other publications; setting up members' clubs and other recreational facilities; resolving disputes between the union and members and employees and employers; offering suggestions on government regulations and laws and answering members' questions on these matters; investigating workers' families and their livelihoods, and compiling employment statistics; and handling other matters related to working conditions and members' welfare.[37] These "responsibilities" cover a wide range; obviously, the union could hope to carry out only a few of them. But, since the regulations were standardized, the union had to adopt them as its own.

Whereas the regulations were not made by the union, the members' pledge of the union (Chengdu shi chashe yonggongye zhiye gonghui huiyuan gongzuo gongyue), including seventeen items that reveal how the union organized and controlled its members, was specifically written for teahouse workers. The pledge claimed that the union would strive to improve the lives of members and support the War of Resistance. According to the pledge, all teahouse workers were to register with the union and complete all membership procedures before starting work, "in order to keep bad people from sneaking in who could damage security in the rear area and harm the business and the reputation of the union." To register, all applicants had to have a shop as a guarantor or be recommended by two members of the union. Any members who found employment had to report this to the union and fill out an "introduction form," which was intended to prevent disputes between employers and employees. The union also played a role in settling disputes between workers and employers. If a dispute occurred, a union clerk was sent to mediate, but disputes that could not be settled or were potentially "big cases" that could affect existing "laws" had to be reported to the municipal government and GMD party headquarters. Female members were to obey the regulations on teahouse waitresses enacted by the municipal government and the police. All members had to wear membership badges to distinguish themselves from patrons or other workers or tradesmen. The union also established an employment office (zhiye jieshao suo), whose goal was to "relieve the pain of members' unemployment," "to locate jobs for members," and "to stabilize the lives of members." Any member of the union who lost his or her job could ask the office for help in finding a new job. But if a member did not use the office and instead found a job on his or her own, the office would not get involved in any disputes that arose between the employer and employee. Workers hired through the office were not to be fired without a legitimate reason, but the office required employees not to be lazy, or to steal money or other property from the teahouses. Applicants paid a fee of one yuan. Anyone who violated any of these regulations three times was reported to the government and punished.[38]

It appears that not all workers were enthusiastic about joining the union. In fact the union met with furious resistance when it tried to force the issue. Membership was mandatory, and those who did not join faced punishment. In this regard, a June 1943 report is particularly interesting. According to the report, President Wang Rongzhang and other union staff went to the Wei Family Ancestral Temple Teahouse (Weijiaci chashe) to collect membership fees and recruit new members. But Yang Qingrong, a worker there, "not only refused to join the union," but also called on other workers "to disrupt the union's work there." The union staff tried "every way to convince them to join, but failed." Yang also "incited his followers to oppose registration." Finally, the writer of the report rather helplessly added that the union "should have punished them, but we do not have such power." However, the report noted that "if we let them go," others might follow them, and "the consequences would be unthinkable." Therefore, the union requested that the municipal government punish Yang and his coworkers. In response, the municipal government issued an order: "All teahouse workers are required to register. The names of people who refuse to obey will be listed and reported to the government, and they will be punished." This is additional evidence of the state's sponsorship of the union. Later, the union submitted the names of seven recalcitrant waiters and their workplaces. Under one of the names, the union noted that "this man is the resistance leader who incited others not to register." This document also shows that at two teahouses, "all the workers refused to join the union."[39]

This resistance tells us that the union might have represented the interests of only some workers. The main reason that some refused to join, at least from the evidence presented above, was that they did not want to pay the two-yuan membership fee. On the one hand, this amount was not unreasonable (as discussed previously, the average waiter earned about 7.3 yuan per day at the end of 1942; considering the dramatic inflation during the war, this fee represented about one-third of a typical waiter's daily salary). On the other hand, salaries already were barely sufficient to cover basic living expenses and any extra expenditure would be a heavy burden.[40] The fact that some workers refused to pay such an insignificant fee, however, reflects deeper issues. First, teahouse workers did not see a need for the union. They might not have benefited from the union or the union might not have successfully made a connection with them. The union failed to establish solidarity within the organization and among workers. Internal power struggles and inadequate leadership might also have hurt the union's credibility. For example, in early 1944, eighty-three members submitted a petition alleging that the election of union officials at the end of 1943 had not followed regulations, because many members did not know when the election was to be held. As a result, some "troublemakers" (*daoluan fengzi*) and even two nonmembers were elected to the board. Only seventy of the union's two thousand registered members voted, according to the petition, which requested that the government order a re-election under the Labor Movement Code (Gongyun fa).[41]

Another likely reason was that many teahouse workers already were members of the Gowned Brothers (*Paoge*), Sichuan's sworn brotherhood, whose members ranged from government officials and military officers to businessmen, ordinary residents, and low-level workers. For those who lacked the power to seek redress of grievances on their own, the protection offered by Gowned Brothers was attractive. In fact, many teahouses were either built by or used as headquarters by the Gowned Brothers. There they held meetings, conducted routine business, and contacted other branches of the organization. Therefore, workers in such teahouses inevitably also became sworn brothers, and apparently suffered much less harassment from local toughs under their protection.[42] These workers surely believed that they had no need to join the union.

Even though the union had a variety of problems, it was still able to conduct some activities to promote self-discipline and self-protection. For example, the union tried to regulate waitresses by requiring them not to wear makeup, perm their hair, or flirt with patrons, and "to maintain decency." The union demanded that all members wear a membership badge while working, and often sent staff members to check members' behavior. "The rules of the union," it was said, "were seriously enforced."[43] The regulation of waitresses reflects general notions regarding the physical appearance of women in the public workplace, and also shows that the union tried to separate waitresses from women in less acceptable occupations such as entertainment and prostitution, who faced constant discrimination. Wearing badges was intended to create a positive image of the profession and to promote the union, although it was also intended to lead to better service for patrons. The union, however, often acted to give teahouse workers a voice and to protect their interests when dealing with local authorities, as discussed below.

Unions of Other Professions in the Teahouse

Other professions that depended on teahouses for their livelihood also established unions; almost all were organized in the 1930s, including the Union of the Popular Storytelling Profession of Chengdu (Chengdu shi tongsu pinghua ye zhiye gonghui), the Union of the Golden Coin Bamboo Clippers' Popular Lecture and Propaganda Profession of Chengdu (Chengdu shi jinqianban tongsu jiangyan xuanchuan ye zhiye gonghui), and the Union of the Ballad Singing Profession of Chengdu (Chengdu shi qingyin zhiye gonghui). These unions were for performers, and coexisted with the Union of Chengdu Teahouse Workers, which shows that people who worked in the same teahouse might belong to different unions, depending on the nature of their work. Although singers and storytellers worked in the teahouse, they, unlike waiters and waitresses, were not employees of the teahouse. They were more like subcontractors who rented the teahouse as their stage.

The Union of the Popular Storytelling Profession was established in 1936. Its regulations were virtually identical to those of the Union of Chengdu Teahouse Workers issued by the Nationalist government, which again demonstrates the government's control. Its goals, like those of the Union of Teahouse Workers, were to improve workers' relations, enhance learning and working skills, and develop social education, with the addition of several goals specifically related to the occupation, such as "to promote social culture." During the Republican era, storytelling was still a man's profession, and membership was limited to men who were twenty or over who could read, had "good morals," and "understood well the Three Principles of the People." Many sections of the regulations, such as those dealing with members' rights and responsibilities, the organization of the union, the membership assembly (huiyuan dahui), and budget and accounting practices, were similar to those of other unions. The union claimed to offer many services to members, such as finding jobs, providing professional training, setting up a library and reading rooms, providing publications, organizing membership clubs and providing equipment for entertainment, mediating disputes between members or between members and their employers, investigating members' living standards and economic conditions, compiling statistics about its investigations, and various other services designed to improve working conditions and protect the interests of the members. However, there is no evidence the union achieved more than a few of these goals.[44]

In the late 1930s, ten performers co-signed a petition asking the government to allow them to organize a Union of the Golden Coin Bamboo Clippers' Popular Lecture and Propaganda Profession in Chengdu. They claimed that although they did not fight against the Japanese, they had worked very hard to disseminate propaganda and participated in all kinds of other patriotic activities. Their programs, they declared, were simple and easy to understand, which could "arouse the patriotic zeal" of ordinary people. In the past, these actors joined the organization of popular entertainers, but with the growth of their profession, they wanted to establish their own union, which could handle affairs of the whole profession as well as prohibit amateurs from performing "profligate works" that damaged social mores.[45]

We have much more material on the Union of the Pure Singing Profession of Chengdu, including its regulations and information on its leadership, membership, and functions. The regulations consisted of six chapters, dealing with routine business matters, membership, organization and responsibilities, meetings, and budget and accounting. The "general principles" section claimed that the regulations were based on the Law on Unions (Gonghui fa) and the Law on Union Operations (Gonghui shishi fa), the same as the regulations of other unions. The union's headquarters were in the Deity of Tasting Tea Balcony (Pinxian chalou).[46] Based on the membership list of the union, there were eighty-six members; twenty-eight were women, the oldest of whom was fifty-four and the youngest only eleven. Quite a few girls aged eleven to thirteen were members. The board of directors had the following responsibilities: managing the union's affairs; representing the union; holding meetings of all members and of representatives and carrying out their decisions; and implementing members' recommendations. Meetings of the full membership and of the representatives were held every six months, but an emergency meeting could be held if requested by two-thirds of the members or by the board of directors. Decisions were made by simple majority vote. The union generated income from three kinds of membership fees: a fee of one yuan when joining the union; a regular monthly fee of 0.12 yuan per person, which could be reduced or waived for members who had lost their jobs or faced emergencies; and additional membership fees, which were collected only when an emergency was declared and approved by all members or their representatives. A financial report was presented to all members every six months and the accounts were subject to being audited at the request of one-tenth of the members.[47]

These unions, like the Union of Chengdu Teahouse Workers, were obviously under the government's supervision and were strongly influenced by national and local politics. According to the regulations of the Union of the Pure Singing Profession, for example, amendments could only be made by the full assembly of members or a meeting of the representatives and required the approval of the GMD and the municipal government. In addition, almost all union regulations excluded from membership people who were "deprived of the rights of citizens," were guilty of "counterrevolutionary words and deeds" or had claimed bankruptcy, or who "did not have the ability to represent themselves."[48] As discussed earlier, this is strong evidence of state manipulation of these organizations.

Gender Conflict and Sexual Harassment

The introduction of women to the workplace caused resentment by male workers and often led to gender conflict.[49] This issue was fully explored after the Union of Chengdu Teahouse Workers was restructured in 1939. An archival document gives information on the members of the union's board, such as name, position in the union, sex, age, native place, address, and years of experience. Of twenty board members, seventeen were male and three were female, including forty-two-year-old President Ling Guozheng, an enthusiastic activist in the labor movement, who was praised for "her zeal for the public's welfare."[50] But, in the fall of 1940, Ling Guozheng faced a challenge from male teahouse workers. Two groups of waiters presented petitions to the government criticizing Ling for "taking over power illegally." They also accused her of amassing power by "deceiving the Party [GMD] and the government." Before the election, she had negotiated with most of the members so that "the minority who disagreed with her had to accept facts."[51]

From these accounts, it is apparent that Ling depended on the support of waitresses. The evidence shows that Ling was the force behind the transformation of the traditional friendship organization into a union. No matter how she gained power, the fact remains that she successfully integrated an all-male organization and then took control of it, a testament to her remarkable skills as an activist. The waiters' futile struggle to retain their all-male domain is a clear example of the era's prevailing gender conflict. Many waiters who opposed Ling simply could not tolerate her desire to "to put our few thousand proud men together with coquettish female workers." They criticized her apparent obliviousness to job differences, which they compared to "forcing pigs and sheep to stay in the same pen." Therefore, they claimed, "for the sake of teahouse waiters' dignity and rights, we must formally declare the facts and request the government to dissolve the union and reinstate the old union that separated male and female workers."[52] This action of waiters against waitresses was not unique in labor history. In her study of the history of waitresses and unions in the United States, Dorothy Sue Cobble notes that in the 1930s and 1940s "male unionists as well sought the exclusion of women from their trades and the continuation of sex-segregated workplaces in order to secure better jobs and working conditions."[53]

The waiters' group fought not only for segregation by sex, but also for their very livelihood. Ling's power was built on the support of waitresses, and she fought very hard to protect their right to make a living in the teahouse. Waitresses, when they suddenly appeared in this male domain, caused a dramatic change in the employment practices of the teahouses; many teahouses fired waiters in order to hire waitresses, who could be paid less, were more easily controlled, and attracted more patrons. Waiters realized that their very livelihood was in jeopardy. They took their argument to court, where Ling won the case after effectively and passionately convincing the judge of women's right to work in the teahouse. Under her influence, joining the union became a way for the waitresses to protect themselves.[54]

One of the petitions accused Ling of "trying every way possible to collect money" and having more than three hundred members as her followers. She was also accused of arranging for several policemen to force workers to buy badges and of stealing public funds by giving receipts for only one yuan after receiving the two-yuan membership fee. Waiters denounced her as a "tyrant who is no different from the warlords during the warlord era." They claimed she was "exploiting workers for their hard-earned money" and creating a situation in which the "minority is oppressing the majority." In these petitions waiters tried to cultivate an image of Ling as an "imperious and despotic person" in order to expel her from the union. However, a 1942 essay describes a totally different kind of person. I have not found more detailed information about her, but the available evidence indicates that she worked with some women's organizations before becoming president of the union. Although I do not have enough evidence to judge the accuracy of the descriptions and accusations found in these petitions, it seems clear that the "wrongdoing" Ling was accused of was not as serious as alleged, and that sensational terms such as "tyrannical," "exploitative," and "despotic" do not correspond with what is known about her. I do not know if Ling made any effort to ease these tensions, but I found in an undated list of union board members that at some point Ling was replaced by Fan Rongwu, whose name was on the top of one of the petitions against Ling noted previously. The 1942 essay mentions Ling's death, but does not indicate whether she was still in office when she died. Therefore, I am not sure whether the change of leadership resulted from the struggle of waiters against waitresses or from her death. Nevertheless, at least we know that the waiters were unsuccessful in restoring the union's all-male status.[55]

Waitresses were more likely to become targets of sexual harassment and violence in the workplace than most other women because of the nature of their work. Hoodlums, "who disregard the laws and do whatever they like," often gathered in teahouses and caused trouble, which not only "spoiled workers' livelihoods, but also threatened social order."[56] In 1939, two cases drew a great deal of attention. In the first, a waitress was brutally beaten when she refused a man's advances. Tang Bingyun sold hot towels and cigarettes in the Spring Dragon Tea Garden (Longchun chayuan). One day, on her way out to buy a meal, she was stopped by Zhou Ziming, a local hoodlum. When Zhou attempted to molest her, she rebuffed him and ran back inside the teahouse, but Zhou chased her and assaulted her. When she denounced his behavior, he became furious and seriously injured her, causing her to spit blood. When patrons tried to calm him, he continued to shout threats.[57] The other case involved Xie Lizhen, a waitress in the Yuan Garden Teahouse (Yuanyuan chashe). A patron named Ding grabbed her foot as he pretended to pick up a towel from the ground. She asked him politely to stop. Not only did Ding not heed her request, but he savagely bit her, as well as her employer, who tried to intervene.[58] Such incidents became a serious issue that threatened waitresses' livelihood.

Many men regarded women who worked in public places where men gathered as "indecent" and exaggerated their "misbehavior." They assumed that these women were prostitutes in the "floating world." Therefore, hooligans took advantage of waitresses at every turn. As victims, waitresses found little help or sympathy from local authorities or society at large. In the face of workplace violence, the union became a major protector of workers' security. In 1939, after investigating the two cases of bullying of waitresses just described, the union appealed to the municipal government to "protect laborers" and "purify social customs." According to the petition, hooligans often took liberties with waitresses and even became violent when the women resisted. Therefore, the weak had no choice but to be trampled, while women's attempts to maintain their dignity could lead to "tragic results." Such incidents, the petition claimed, "occur one after another," and waitresses had to rely on the union for protection. To generate sympathy, the union pointed out that most waitresses were the wives of officers and soldiers fighting in the bloody front-line battles against the Japanese. These women could barely eke out a living in their husbands' absence, so they went to work in teahouses. The hoodlums were "violating women's rights, attacking decency," and harming the morale of the brave officers and soldiers by causing trouble back home.[59]

The union also appealed to the government and society to hold a positive view of waitresses and to try to understand them: "Now we are experiencing a time when the country depends on the military and the mobilization of all citizens, when even women can go to the front lines if the nation requires." Therefore, the government should support and protect "women's economic independence." The union requested the government issue a public notice banning harassment and promising harsh punishment of violators. Two weeks after receiving the union's request, Mayor Yang passed the letter to the Sichuan Provincial Police. In his memorandum, Mayor Yang pointed out that "such incidents attack decency and disregard human rights" (*youshang fenghua, mieshi renquan*).[60] Although we do not know the outcome of this request, we can see that at least the mayor sought to address this issue as a result of the union's effort.

Of course, the union's ability to respond was limited by several factors. First, as discussed earlier, the union was basically a state-sponsored organization, and although it could represent workers, it had to follow the rules set by the government. Second, it did not have strong leadership and often experienced internal crises that damaged its credibility. Third, it faced competition from guilds and, in particular, the Gowned Brothers. Workers who joined the Gowned Brothers openly opposed some of the measures the union tried to enforce. Finally, the ongoing war hampered the union's efforts. The government constantly issued propaganda urging people to sacrifice their personal interests for the national interest, so that any action the union launched for workers' rights could be criticized as unpatriotic if it contradicted the government's stated position.

The Social Image of Teahouse Workers and Fate of Waitresses

Teahouse workers were more closely scrutinized than workers in most other professions because they served the public. Their social image was based mostly on their job performance, but was also shaped by the opinions of local elites, who tirelessly promoted modern and Western ideas in order to create a new and progressive image for the provincial capital.[61] Because of their high visibility in public, teahouses and their workers naturally became targets of reform. It is not necessarily true that all teahouse workers had a negative social image, but they, like teahouses, had very complex social relationships, which led to many serious criticisms despite their popularity.

Thus, teahouse workers had a variety of images constructed from different perspectives. There is no doubt that waiters, even those who worked in the most elegant teahouses, were of low social status. Although elites enjoyed waiters' skillful service and social interaction with them, they also criticized them for perceived or real misconduct simply because of social prejudice. Waiters did indeed sometimes misbehave on the job; it was not unusual, for example, for a waiter to trick both his customers and his employer to obtain extra money. Often, a waiter might pilfer tea leaves from each of the bowls ordered until there was enough for an additional bowl of tea, which he would sell for his own profit. In other cases, waiters were thieves or pimps, something that drew harsh criticism from elites. These cases underscore not only some waiters' desperation to earn more money, but also their ability to survive. A 1941 newspaper article about how a waiter took advantage of a woman was reported under the headline "Detestable Teahouse Worker!"— words that clearly reflect elites' resentment. A military officer wanted to have sex with a "good-looking" woman who sold books and newspapers in teahouses and restaurants, so he asked the waiter to serve as a go-between. The woman could not resist the lure of 500 yuan, even though she initially hesitated. But the waiter gave her only 50 yuan and kept the rest for himself, resulting in a fight between the pair. The woman went to the authorities, and the waiter ran away, because it was illegal for a teahouse waiter to be a pimp.[62] Such cases of misconduct gave local authorities good opportunities to gain control of teahouses, an area of concern to a government worried about "public order."

There were two prevailing attitudes toward waitresses. Those who sympathized with the waitresses' plight, for example, described teahouses as furnaces in which women were tempered; waitresses had to deal with all sorts of characters, and as a result, their outlook became much broader. The emergence of waitresses, to a certain extent, changed the social mood as well. Bachelors courted and in some cases married waitresses. One observer noted that in most cases the courtship ritual first involved attending local operas, and then, as the relationship progressed, exchanging gifts such as a scarf or a piece of cloth. If the couple decided to spend the rest of their lives together, they would move their belongings to a small rented room and get married without a dowry or a wedding ceremony. Teahouses thus became known as a "place of lovers" (*lian'ai changsuo*). Others who sympathized with waitresses, such as Zhou Zhiying, considered these women pioneers of economic independence who proved that "women could do the same work as men."[63] Considering that this was a time when most women's activities and marriages were strictly controlled by their families, we have to admit that these women forged a path to freedom that directly challenged the customary direction of ordinary women's lives.

Some tried to explain why waitresses were needed in teahouses. "It would be boring if all the people in a teahouse were men," one pointed out, adding that women brought vitality to teahouse life. Responding to the charge that some waitresses flirted with patrons, this observer argued that if the women did not try their best to meet patrons' needs and make them happy, their employers would be irate. Besides, patrons did not like waitresses who were overly serious. Commoners, such as sedan-chair carriers and petty peddlers, loved to go to teahouses after a hard day's work for a brief respite in the company of waitresses.⁶⁴ Moreover, it should be emphasized that the appearance of teahouse waitresses redefined the relationship between men and women in public. Under Chinese tradition, a woman was not supposed to have any direct contact with a man who was not a family member. The connection between waitresses and patrons in the teahouses began to erode this custom, which also became one of the reasons why waitresses suffered such harsh criticism.

The prevalence of criticism is evident in many newspaper reports. A common belief was that "waitresses are degrading and also become a ready source of income for teahouse proprietors." Such strong sentiment gradually spread through society, even though waitresses were being victimized by thugs. One case involved a candy peddler who argued with a waitress in a teahouse. When other teahouse workers intervened, the peddler sought revenge. A few days later he returned with several army "riffraff" (*lanbing*) who beat her badly after she finished her shift. The local newspaper accused the waitress of "having connections with hooligans and riffraff," and being "fat and ugly," making it inevitable "that she fell into trouble."⁶⁵ It was probably true that the waitress had some connection with local toughs, but it would have been very difficult for waitresses to avoid these relationships while working in such a public environment and trying to survive in these jobs.

Some social critics believed that the moral standards of women who became waitresses declined. According to these critics, women who formerly were "pure, innocent, and without social experience," could not resist the seduction of material life and money, and "fell into the abyss of shameful suffering" and "lived like prostitutes." Those who refused to be humiliated had to quit their jobs and return to their kitchens. One critic condemned waitresses in the 1940s for "acting like buffoons" (*choutai baichu*), contrary to those in the 1930s, who had behaved like "good women" (*liangnü*). In the 1940s, a critic stated that waitresses had become "sophisticated" and "indecent," because "they wear red lipstick on their lips, rouge on their faces, permed hair on their heads, and high-heeled shoes on their feet, and laugh loudly and flirt with patrons." As soon as someone enters a teahouse, the critic complained, a waitress would ask him with a cheeky grin, "Would you like to wash your face? Would you like a cigarette?" and tried to make the patron laugh by acting silly. It is clear that society was much more critical of women's public behavior than of men's. We do not find criticism of men "flirting" with waitresses. Only a very few waitresses sold their bodies for money. Often, accusations of prostitution and "indecency" were based on widespread prejudice against waitresses, which is not surprising given the experiences of women entering this traditionally male arena. Women began frequenting teahouses as customers in the late Qing era, but their presence was still an ongoing battle until the 1930s and 1940s.⁶⁶ Critics were mostly elites, who generally opposed women's appearance in public, and often exaggerated these issues.

Given such a social mood, local authorities enacted many restrictions on this occupation. In 1941, the Sichuan Provincial Police ordered the Teahouse Guild to supervise teahouses, out of concern about such issues as waitresses' failure to wear aprons, their "flirtation" with patrons, and disputes over tips. The police issued ten rules on waitresses' clothing and behavior: waitresses were to wear long-sleeved white aprons or blue Chinese traditional dresses (*qipao* or cheongsam) and numbered badges. Furthermore, waitresses were not allowed to be playful with patrons or engage in "indecent behavior," which was to be reported to the police. Waitresses were not to prostitute themselves, or do anything "against decency," and they were not to ask for tips or charge more than the standard price for the products they sold without authorization. Teahouse keepers were to notify the authorities if waitresses had relationships with "traitors" (*hanjian*, people who sided with the Japanese), or stole patrons' belongings; any keeper who failed to do so would be held responsible, and any waitress who violated the rules would be punished.[67] These rules no doubt added to the burden of waitresses.

The "golden age" of the teahouse waitress ended in the early 1940s under the weight of these new regulations, the economic crisis, and relentless social pressure. The ongoing war and deteriorating economy caused prices to soar, and middle- and lower-class people—the majority of teahouse patrons—had difficulty putting food on the table. Furthermore, when the war activity leveled off in China in the early 1940s after the panic earlier, elites and government officials began to restore the old order by targeting and attacking waitressing as an occupation. On the one hand, the decline of the teahouse trade resulted in many waitresses being fired; more than two hundred lost their jobs in 1941 alone. On the other hand, intense social pressure from the many people who regarded waitresses as prostitutes made most women stay away from this occupation, or quit if they were already waitresses. Therefore, the number of the waitresses decreased from more than four hundred in 1937 to fewer than one hundred in 1942.[68]

These women met various fates. Many went back home, but, according to observer Lu Yin, "a few who no longer wanted to live in poverty became prostitutes." Some, however, tried to find another way to maintain economic independence, and gathered in groups of three or five to seek work in teahouses outside the city. In the market towns near Chengdu, according to one report, these women succeeded in attracting more patrons to teahouses, just as they initially had done in Chengdu. Yet, they rarely worked in one place for more than two months and had to move frequently because local governments always expelled them for "frivolous behavior and acting against decency." In Chengdu as elsewhere, the local government increasingly enacted restrictive rules for teahouse waitresses, whose working situation continued to deteriorate. In March 1945, the provincial government dealt the occupation a fatal blow by issuing new regulations on teahouses, which finally banned "young women" from working there.[69] Therefore, we can see that the largest obstacle for waitresses was the government's restrictions, which eventually drove them out of this occupation.

Conclusion

Teahouse workers created special bonds with their customers that exemplified a crucial part of teahouse culture. Good service, an important component of all kinds of small businesses, was fundamental to the very existence of a teahouse. Patrons expected the service provided in teahouses to far exceed that found in most other small businesses. Whereas people went to a restaurant to have a meal, to a store to buy something, or to a handicraft shop to have an item repaired, they went to a teahouse to spend their leisure time, relax, and be entertained. Therefore, they, more than anyone else, cared about how the waiters treated them. Also, teahouse workers developed much closer bonds with their customers than did workers in other shops. Because their work attitude and skills directly affected a teahouse's bottom line and thus their livelihoods, teahouse employees had to make every effort to ensure customer satisfaction. In so doing, they cultivated feelings of humility, warmth, and enthusiasm, and learned to deal with a variety of people. Furthermore, interactions between teahouse workers and their patrons reflected the complex social relations and colorful workplace culture of teahouses.

Studies of teahouse workers reveal workplace conflict between men and women as the War of Resistance and wave of refugees arriving in Chengdu created an environment that temporarily opened the doors of teahouses to women. The invasion of waitresses into the male-only profession caused resentment from the "masters of tea" who were afraid they would lose their jobs to "unskilled" newcomers. Unlike the case with other occupations, it is very difficult to define teahouse workers as "skilled" or "unskilled." To serve patrons did not require the kinds of apprenticeships found in other occupations, but a waiter could aspire to become a "master of tea" only after many years of experience. However, it is important to keep in mind that teahouse proprietors hired women as waitresses, and patrons welcomed them, not because of the women's working skills and experience, but simply because of their sex and appearance. When these unskilled women took jobs away from skilled "masters of tea," they inevitably met furious resistance, which caused gender conflicts in the workplace. Working in public places, waitresses also suffered constant sexual harassment, including outright bullying by thugs, and had to fight for workplace security.

The emergence of waitressing as a profession challenged traditional views and added momentum to the women's struggle for rights, marking the beginning of a new era in the cause of women's economic independence. Individually, however, waitresses had to contend with harsh prejudice from waiters and other male workers. The ultimate demise of the waitressing profession in Chengdu's teahouses resulted in part from this gender-based hostility. Conflict between waiters and waitresses also reveals that workplace struggles were common not only between different social classes but also among members of the lower classes. Furthermore, waitresses also faced extreme pressure from male patrons as well as from government regulations. Chengdu had remained quite conservative until the war, and traditional values still dominated perceptions of women, especially those in public. These conservative views, combined with increasingly strict government rules, made it difficult for waitresses to prevail. The way men regarded teahouse waitresses precisely reflected Chengdu's social and cultural tradition. Of course, we cannot simply blame all discrimination against women on culture; many other elements, including economic and political factors, also influenced attitudes toward waitresses. Because of these and other obstacles, waitresses were vulnerable; when the economy plunged into recession, women workers were the first to be let go.

During the Republican period, major Chinese cities such as Shanghai, Tianjin, and Beijing had a much larger industrial working class than did inland cities, and the workers in these cities were visible as a group and represented by powerful unions. Most teahouse workers in Republican Chengdu, however, came from the countryside, and provided cheap labor in an unfamiliar environment. They were scattered throughout many small workplaces, which made it difficult to become organized. In addition, unlike in the major cities, a worker's place of origin did not play a prominent role in the teahouse trade, even though Chengdu was a city of immigrants.[70] While each trade in Chengdu was often dominated by merchants who came from the same place, this model generally was not followed in the case of hired labor; teahouse workers, for example, could come from anywhere. There was a teahouse guild, but it was for teahouse owners, not workers. Many native-place associations and guilds could be found in Chengdu at that time, but they were aimed mainly at preventing unreasonable competition between shops, protecting their common interests, and establishing networks among people from the same native places.[71] Elites such as shop proprietors and rich merchants controlled these organizations and used them to help their own businesses, and the workers, including teahouse workers, had no voice.

The Union of Chengdu Teahouse Workers was supervised by local authorities and faced many problems in maintaining solidarity but still functioned as a voice for teahouse workers and represented the occupation's common interests. The most visible role of the union was clearly not to organize workers to fight for better working conditions or wage increases, but to act as liaison between the government and workers, in clear contrast to the situation in other cities. Before the establishment of the union, workers had no venue for communicating with the government, and no organization represented them or fought for their interests. One of the union's early achievements was to fight for women's right to work in teahouses. Even though it lacked the power to provide comprehensive protection, the union represented victims of violence before the local government, thereby drawing attention to workers' rights and cultivating public sympathy. There is no evidence, however, that the union ever amassed the power necessary to confront either proprietors or local authorities.

This chapter has examined the various relationships between teahouse workers and patrons, the conflicts between male and female workers, and the general public's perceptions of teahouse workers, and has given an overview of how the Union of Chengdu Teahouse Workers tried to protect its members and resolve internal power struggles. The furious resistance to the changes was brought on by the introduction of the coastal culture into Chengdu, with the relocation of China's capital from Nanjing to Chongqing and with the flood of refugees from East to West China, when the modernized state extended its power into the teahouse, the most basic unit of society. The results of this resistance differed; sometimes it succeeded while other times it failed. The fact that waitresses were driven out of the teahouse reflected the strength of local conservative culture and customs. Ironically, the government seemed to use the uniformity of modernity to transform inland culture under the banner of nationalism, under which, at least in theory, the government should have supported women entering the workforce. The establishment of unions symbolized a new relationship among the workers themselves and between laborers and the state. All of these changes represented an important transformation in the workplace environment and workplace culture in small businesses in China. Studying teahouse workers and their workplace culture gives us a good opportunity to examine the life and livelihood of the urban poor and to see how their fate connected with that of the larger society, the economy, and politics.

PART TWO

Teahouse Life

CHAPTER 4

Public Life

> In Beiping [Beijing], at every crossroads there is a grocery store (that also sells vegetables), a grain shop, and a coal store, but Chengdu is different; there, a large teahouse substitutes for all of these. We know that for Chengdu people, going to the teahouse is more important than getting oil, salt, vegetables, rice, and coal. The teahouse looks like an antique, with eaves that are not very high, walls that are gray, and columns that are flimsy. At night, lights are faint (electric lights are as dim as oil lamps), and there are low black unpainted wooden tables and big old yellow bamboo chairs; the whole setting appears aged. People who like modern coffeehouses will leave after a glance, but we have seen that from very early morning to late at night, people lounge in chairs, a bowl of tea in front of them, looking leisurely and relaxed, and in good spirits. Sometimes, a teahouse does not even have a single empty seat, and it seems that it is the scene of a huge party, but in fact, each person there has nothing but a bowl of tea.
> —Zhang Henshui, "Rongxing zagan"
> [Random thoughts on a trip to Chengdu]

ZHANG HENSHUI, a famous novelist, wrote this passage in the 1940s when he visited Chengdu. Despite being an outsider, he drew an accurate and vivid picture of Chengdu and caught the most prominent aspects of everyday life there. From this passage, we can imagine the atmosphere of the teahouse, a simple, even crude, setting crowded with patrons. Frequenting the teahouse became a lifestyle for Chengdu's men, and therefore, teahouses were best known "as places where one could relax and have a good time," where friends met and conducted a variety of activities, such as chatting, playing chess, discussing business, and socializing. The teahouse had an allure that made men want to spend as much time as possible there every day.[1] This chapter explores where this power came from and how it attracted people, and what people did once they got into the teahouse. The teahouse was not only a space for everyday life, but also a stage on which all kinds of people performed roles.

In Chengdu, teahouses provided the kind of crowded, bustling atmosphere that was compelling to those who sought public life. As Han Suyin, a descendant of a missionary, wrote in her family history about the late Qing teahouses:

> The copper kettles jetted steam, on lacquered tables the teacups shone their flowered porcelain, on the bamboo chairs waiters slapped embroidered cushions. Beggars dragged their sores and drowned our talk in sing-song lamentations, wizened children somersaulted and twisted their hands backwards between their feet among the tables, shooed away they returned, pertinacious as flies, hungry and mangy like the dogs about our feet with which they fought for scraps.[2]

Of course, this is only a single scene; reality was much more complicated and colorful. The teahouse was not merely a place for relaxing, but was a multifunctional public space. People usually went to the teahouse to conduct business, find a job, meet friends, and so on. If two friends had a dispute, they would go to the teahouse; after having tea and cigarettes, their friendship was restored.[3] However, some people also went to teahouses to plot conspiracies and illegal actions; therefore, "the teahouse also is a place that produces vice."[4]

A 1938 guidebook by Hu Tian and a 1943 travel note by Yi Junzuo give two very useful terms regarding the clientele of teahouses: the "idle class" (*youxian jieji*) and the "busy class" (*youmang jieji*).[5] These terms could describe almost everyone in the multitudes of people who regularly frequented teahouses. The "leisure class" could include local scholars, the literary intelligentsia, absentee landlords and other property owners, and retired officials, while the "busy class" could be classified into three groups: those who used the teahouse as a stage, such as storytellers and performers of local operas and folk songs; those who used it as their business office, such as merchants and doctors of traditional medicine; and those who used it as their workplace and market, such as peddlers and craftsmen. Of course, these terms are not restrictive definitions of social classifications. For example, "idle" people might not always be rich, and a poor man who did not have a job and was spending time in a teahouse might be an "idler," just as a rich man who was conducting business in the teahouse might be "busy." This chapter will examine how all sorts of people used the teahouse as sites of relaxation and socialization to create teahouse culture.

Although teahouse life, like all other aspects of life in Chengdu, was influenced by social, political, and economic transformations throughout the late Qing and Republican periods, the basic form of teahouse life remained, providing a continuity of culture. This chapter describes how the teahouse became a hub of the street or neighborhood. News always spread first in the teahouse; for a man in old Chengdu, going to a teahouse was comparable to getting news from newspapers, or the radio or television today. At the teahouse, people met formally—to resolve neighborhood disputes, for example—or informally to gossip with acquaintances and friends, and children gathered for fun. This chapter also examines how residents interacted and built their social and professional networks in this public place, especially through the custom of "calling for tea money." The reason people liked to use the teahouse for socializing was also related to living conditions. Rich people went to the teahouse to find excitement while poor people had small living quarters that could not accommodate guests. Furthermore, poor people could not afford expensive forms of entertainment, so the teahouse became their only option. During social turmoil, the teahouse was a sanctuary that provided an escape from misery, albeit temporarily. The teahouse created an environment where people could linger for as long as they liked, where people did not have to worry about how they looked or behaved; to a certain extent, it was a genuinely "free world." We can be certain that the atmosphere of Chengdu and the lives of its individual citizens would have been vastly different without the institution of the teahouse.

Seeking Leisure

The deepest impression Chengdu made on visitors was of its relaxed atmosphere and lifestyle as embodied by the teahouse. Chengdu residents fully embraced their "leisurely" lifestyle lived out in the teahouse, which remained virtually unchanged during the first half of the twentieth century even as virtually every other aspect of political and social life changed around them. People from all walks of life went to teahouses whenever possible (see Figure 4.1). The elderly were a large portion of regular teahouse-goers and became the most loyal customers of the teahouses near their homes. If the teahouse had a storyteller, they would go there every night. Chengdu had many offspring of rich families, absentee landlords, and property owners, called "sojourner masters" (*yugong*), who came from other places but enjoyed lives of leisure in the city. They became regular customers of teahouses too. However, many others who worked very hard for their livelihood, such as sedan-chair carriers, rickshaw pullers, and peddlers, also frequented teahouses, as did scholars and teachers. All were welcomed. Some teahouse-goers were "addicts," who would "lose their souls if they do not go to the teahouse on any given day."[6]

116   Teahouse Life

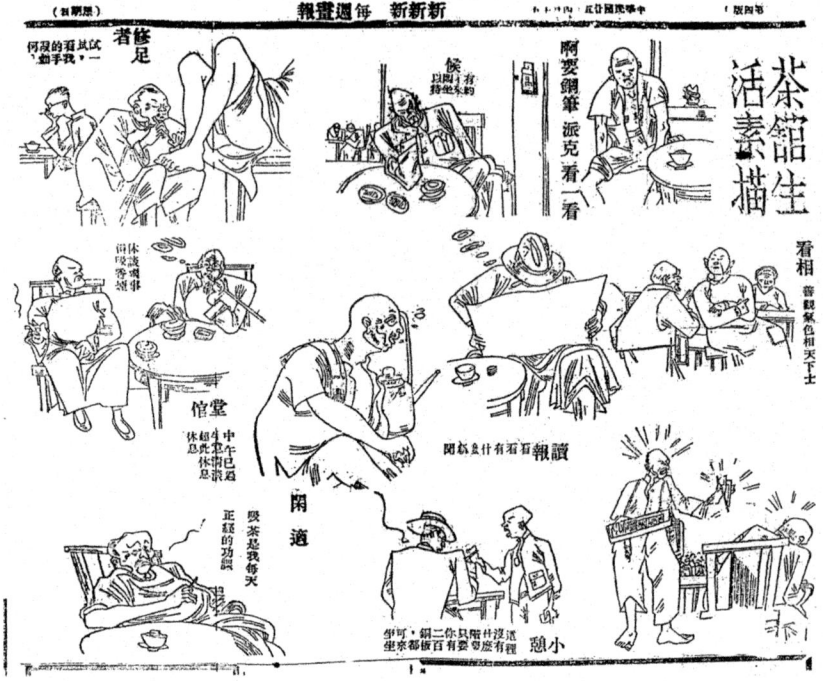

FIGURE 4.1: Sketches of teahouse life. *Left to right, top to bottom*: (1) A pedicurist: "Try and see my skill." (2) "Waiting quietly for an appointment." (3) I Buy Pens: "Show me if you have a Parker." (4) "Don't talk about national affairs but smoke freely." (5) A waiter: "When business slows down in the afternoon, the waiter takes a moment to rest." (6) Reading the newspaper: "Take a look and see what's in the news." (7) A fortune-teller: "Inspecting people's faces and complexions." (8) Leisure: "Drinking tea is my daily routine." (9) Taking a break: "There is no class system here, and you can sit as long as you have 200 coppers." (10) A peddler. From XXXW, April 19, 1936.

Li Jieren's historical novel *Great Wave* (Dabo) describes the leisurely life of young elites in late Qing Chengdu. When a few educated young men got together and discussed how to spend their time, one of them made the following recommendation:

Each of us had only twenty-five cents—five cents less than the cheapest ticket for a local opera. So first, we should go to the teahouse in the Center for Promoting Industry and Commerce (Quanye chang), which is bustling with activity and is better than the Smaller City Park (Shaocheng gongyuan), to feast our eyes on the many women. Then we should go watch Li Shaowei and Jia Peizhi's shows in the Theater of Pure Ballad Singing and Shadow Plays (Qingyin dengying xiyuan) on New Jade Sandy Street (Xin yusha jie). Their singing is good and the gongs and drums are not so loud that we need to protect our ears; also, the room is spacious. After that, we should go to the Common Prosperity Restaurant (Guangxinglong) near Brocade Bridge for dinner; we could have wine, entrees, and noodle dishes, getting drunk and filling of our stomachs.[7]

These young men were not rich, but were educated elites and wanted to find a suitable way to spend their time; going to a teahouse to watch folk performances was affordable. In this novel, Li Jieren paints a vivid picture of teahouses in parks and temples before the 1911 Revolution. His protagonist, Chu Yong, looking for a teahouse in which to kill time early one hot summer afternoon when "it is not a good time to see the Sichuan opera or shadow plays," went to the Wuhou Temple, which was heavily shaded by trees, where there was a teahouse run by Daoist priests. Under the huge trees, there were both square tables and "eight-deity tables" (*baxian zhuo*), a kind of large round table. Chu Yong found that all the square tables were occupied. The patrons seemed not to be visitors who would leave when they finished their tea, but mainly elderly peddlers or craftsmen, wearing cotton shirts and smoking tobacco, who were seeking relief from the heat. Some played cards or Chinese chess, while others worked on handcrafts. This teahouse was quieter than most, and people kept their voices down when chatting. "There were two seats left at a square table, but the two craftsmen who occupied the other two seats were making something; he could sit there but he didn't want to."[8]

Ordinary people, however, used the teahouse even more frequently. According to Li Jieren, until the late Qing, Chengdu did not have large modern factories where workers had to keep strict working hours, but instead had many handicraft workshops, retail shops, restaurants, and other service establishments where people had very flexible working hours. Craftsmen who worked in the small shops along the streets, for instance, often went to the teahouse when they took a break, but their apprentices did not share this privilege. The teahouses on street corners served all kinds of people, such as the bricklayers, carpenters, stonemasons, water-carriers, tailors, cart pushers, and others who lived on both sides of the street that was also their workplace. Even factory workers who had to follow a strict work schedule took advantage of every opportunity to visit the teahouse.[9]

Even the collapse of the empire had little impact on this lifestyle. A satirical novella in the *Citizens' Daily* (Guomin gongbao) in 1918 describes how people in rural areas longed for Chengdu's city life, where people were happy to spend all their time drinking tea in the crowded and exciting teahouses.[10] The well-known educator Shu Xincheng recorded his observation of teahouse life in 1920s Chengdu:

Many men and women spend their days in teahouses and opera gardens, so one might pity them for wasting time and money! Those who do are very stupid. One should know that money is for circulating, and money becomes most valuable when it can satisfy desires. People desire to drink tea, so the money is going where it should. If one stays in the teahouse for a whole day and buys only one pot of tea, the total cost is only 100 to 200 wen—about 3 or 4 cents in silver yuan (*dayang*). If he pays 300 to 400 wen and has a bowl of noodles, plus 100 to 200 wen for snacks, the total is just 20 cents in silver yuan. First-class tickets cost just 600 wen; second-class, 400; and third-class, 300. Even someone who buys a first-class ticket every day pays just 5 silver yuan, less than workers in Shanghai pay for cigarettes. Therefore, it is hard to say that going to the teahouse is a waste of money. As for being a waste of time, people do not need to spend money on time. Even those who have stable jobs in the military, government, and education are often two to three hours late for their appointments, but nobody accuses them of "wasting time." Therefore, we do not need to be bothered by the issue of going to the teahouse.[11]

Shu apparently admired and tried to defend the lifestyle that Westernized elites had criticized for wasting money and time. Such a defense of teahouse life, made by a famous educator and new intellectual, was unique, especially during the New Cultural Movement, when attacking tradition and embracing the West became fashionable.

There are many more sources about teahouse life in the 1930s and after. Hai Su recalled that in the early 1930s his father took him to the First Fountain Teahouse (Diyiquan), a block from their home, every evening after dinner. His father would buy a single bowl of tea but occupy two seats. While he drank, the child ate handfuls of peanuts. "After finishing the peanuts," Hai Su remembered, "I felt sleepy. While he enjoyed himself to the fullest, I was dreaming, so he had to carry me on his back on the way home. As time passed, I was subconsciously influenced by what I heard and saw, and became a regular teahouse-goer."[12] Hai Su's experience reveals the centrality of the teahouse to ordinary people's daily lives. The overall environment and culture, as well as the conversations and behavior of individual patrons, taught people about society, helped them build their social networks, and even cultivated their personalities. As already noted, even those who worked during the day stopped by the teahouse whenever possible. For example, in the 1930s, a group of workers in a factory near the East Gate went to a teahouse at the end of East Gate Bridge every day during their lunch break to fish in the river and sip tea. The teahouse keeper also enjoyed fishing, so they became friends and he kept their fishing equipment and cooked their fish for them. Similarly, government workers liked to go to the Farm Garden Teahouse (Nongyuan) and the United China Teahouse (Lianhua) during their lunch break. Some even risked going there during working hours; one police officer who did so was caught by his boss and punished.[13]

The war could not stop residents from going to the teahouse. Zhou Wen, a war refugee, recalled a teahouse scene in October 1937, just after the war broke out: When an incident occurred on the street below, "a row of heads appeared from the balcony railing to watch." Just as he entered the teahouse and began going up the stairs, a crowd swarmed by, shoulder to shoulder. As soon as he reached the second floor, he saw that the room was crowded with people, "their heads like apples in a basket and their noise like the roar of a vast and mighty river." The smoke from water tobacco pipes and cigarettes formed a thick fog above people's heads. He felt dizzy and when he was about to leave, he heard someone who was looking at the street from the railing yell, "Look, look! The stupid woman!" and many heads immediately peeped out to watch. The noise, smoke, and crowds were part of the allure of teahouse life, and the author blamed patrons for being insensitive to the nation's fate during wartime.[14] A 1938 guidebook to Chengdu noted that people's devotion to leisure could be clearly seen in the large number of teahouses that were "full of people every day." People came to the teahouse from very early in the morning until 9 PM to "read newspapers, chat, and eat snacks, which easily kills their whole day." This lifestyle was said to be something that outsiders fantasized about.[15]

In 1944, a local writer identified four kinds of teahouse-goers. The first was people who "drank leisure tea" (*chi xiancha*), usually at the large teahouses such as those on Warm Spring Road, the Commercial Center, the Smaller City, and the area outside Revival Gate. The first two areas in particular were lined with shops that drew many middle- and upper-class women shoppers. Many patrons came to these teahouses not to drink tea, the article mocked, but to feast their eyes on the women. A bowl of tea was inexpensive, and customers spent much more on cigarettes and snacks such as fried seeds and fruits, plus hot towels, and tips. In teahouses that hired waitresses, many patrons were more interested in having fun with the waitresses than in drinking tea. Therefore, the customers in these places were considered "frivolous young people" (*fulang zidi*).[16] This might not be a fair judgment, however. In fact, as discussed in Chapter 3, waitresses could be found in all kinds of teahouses and served all kinds of customers.

From the Civil War until the collapse of the Nationalist government, teahouse life remained very active. An editorial in a 1947 issue of the *West China Daily* (Huaxi ribao) pointed out that many shop workers regarded the teahouse as a "semi-home." Their small, dim, and simple living quarters were cramped and boring; those who could not stand being cooped up for long hours after dark went to the teahouse for entertainment. In the past, many artisans and apprentices who came from other places lived in their shops, many of which lacked a means of heating water. They spent most of their time in the teahouses, from the time they washed their faces early in the morning until they washed their feet at night.[17] On the eve of the Communist victory, local elites still accused Chengdu residents of not taking anything seriously, and one of their major examples was teahouse life. "Because of their leisurely and carefree character," an article stated, "Chengdu people have fostered the habit of frequenting the teahouse." As soon as they get up early in the morning, they carry their birdcages to a teahouse and stay for hours. This came to be known as "sitting in the teahouse" (*zuo chaguan*) because many patrons simply sat for hours doing nothing. "Regardless of whether they have anything to do or not, sitting in the teahouse occupies a portion of their life."[18]

Socializing at the Teahouse

The teahouse was used for far more than leisure activities. In the words of Li Jieren,

> The teahouse is a parlor or a place for rest for middle and lower-class families. . . . Lower-class families do not have a drawing room and they, of course, use teahouses a lot. Although middle-class families have a front room with tables and chairs, or have a drawing room, and teapots and tea bowls, and even a servant, as a custom, after a few words when a guest arrives, if the host regards him as a friend, he will ask him to go a teahouse to have tea.[19]

A folk poet also noted: "When friends or relatives run into each other on the street, it is only polite to extend an invitation to a teahouse." In Chengdu, when people greeted each other on the street, they always said, "Let's have tea at the corner of the street, my treat." Although this was merely a "courteous gesture," this greeting reflects the importance of the custom of meeting friends and socializing at the teahouse. A writer said, "It is joyful to be free," and the invitation "Let's meet at the so-and-so teahouse" became a customary greeting among the middle and lower classes in Chengdu.[20] Interestingly, elites also adopted teahouses as their drawing room. In a diary entry from March 1915, Wu Yu wrote that he hired a sedan chair to take him to Dragon Bridge (Longqiao), a market town near Chengdu, and stayed there overnight. The next morning after breakfast, he went to the Xiong Dingshan Teahouse to wait for the market to open. Then he went to the Peng Daqi Teahouse with his friend, where he had an appointment with one of his tenants regarding the payment of rent.[21] This itinerary shows how a scholar might spend his day and provides clues to his general lifestyle of moving from one teahouse to another to meet friends or conduct business.

A teahouse often became a customary gathering place where people could meet friends without making plans in advance. Many decisions concerning daily life were made in teahouses. William Sewell's memoir from the 1920s tells how when one of his friends got into trouble they met in a teahouse to discuss a solution. Another writer said there were three reasons why people liked to meet friends in the teahouse. First, Chengdu was a big city, and it was often more convenient for both parties to meet in a teahouse halfway between their homes. Second, entertaining guests at home required the preparation of elaborate meals, which might be too time consuming and difficult. And finally, Chengdu was a capital city that drew many outsiders, but because it was inconvenient as well as uncomfortable to conduct business in lodges, the teahouse became a good place to meet.[22] Frequenting the teahouse often became a lifelong daily habit. The first thing many people, especially senior citizens, did after waking up was to go to the teahouse to "drink early tea" (*chi zaocha*) when the streets were still dark, the whole city was still asleep, and restaurants were closed. After that, they would go home to wash their face, brush their teeth, and eat breakfast. These people went to the teahouse not only to drink tea, but also to share the latest news and gossip. If a resident did not go out for a couple of days and wanted to find out what had happened during his absence, he would go to the teahouse. As a result, the word "teahouse" always connoted "public opinion." In Chengdu, it was common to hear phrases such as "Why did I not hear about this in the teahouse?" or, "I heard this in the teahouse the day I came to the city."[23] Indeed, the teahouse played a role as a neighborhood or community information center.

The teahouse was a place for everyday interactions. As Agnes Heller pointed out, "Everyday contact takes place in its own space.... It is [one's] everyday life that articulates [one's] space, in which experience of space and perception of space are indissolubly fused together." In the teahouse, conversations were the most basic form of everyday contact, "another basic component in everyday life."[24] Most conversations were spontaneous and without purpose; as a saying put it, "Conversation in the teahouse flows wherever it wishes." One teahouse near the West Gate was simply called *geshuo ge* (random talks). Joining the conversation required no preparation or qualifications. Men could express any opinion without being held responsible as long as they did not offend anyone and nobody took what they said seriously. In a teahouse, people could join conversations with strangers or simply listen if they preferred. People from all walks of life visited teahouses and shared all kinds of stories and personal experiences. For example, the teahouses in the Smaller City Park were popular with retired military officers, out-of-office politicians, government clerks, teachers, students, members of the literary class, chess players, prostitutes, old and young property owners, and so forth. "By sitting in the teahouses in the Smaller City for a day, you can learn more than from reading books for ten years," was a popular saying in Chengdu. Although this is an exaggeration, teahouses were indeed good places to learn about society. If a teahouse-goer did not want to chat, he could read a book or newspaper. During the 1930s, customers could rent newspapers for a few cents from peddlers. After they finished, they could exchange the newspaper for another.[25]

In a teahouse, people discussed topics ranging from daily life to politics, often revealing information about social customs and culture.[26] One writer recorded a dialogue depicting the contrasts between city residents and rural dwellers:

Man A: Rural people consider it wasteful to wear good clothes during the day, but they wear good clothes at night when they sleep.

Man B: People in the capital city always try to wear nice clothes, but they take them off to sleep under a quilt.

Man A: Rural people are afraid that bandits will kidnap their children, so they are too scared to sleep but carry their children on their backs all night.

Man B: Townspeople are not afraid; they put their children aside to embrace their wives.

Man A: When rural people hear gunfire, they stay awake all night.

Man B: Townspeople know they are surrounded by a high city wall, so they sleep well and do not get up before noon for breakfast.[27]

Although the report did not mention the speakers' backgrounds, from this conversation I assume that Man A lived in the city and Man B lived in the country. Chengdu residents had a tradition of disparaging rural people and developed proverbs that mocked them as filthy, stupid, and mean. Although the dialogue between these two superficially deals with lifestyle differences, the undercurrent reflects different life experiences and issues. The urban dweller seems to feel superior and mocks his companion for treasuring nice clothes and fearing that his children will be kidnapped. The rural dweller concedes that residents in Chengdu enjoy a higher standard of living and are safer, but states that they have their own problems, and ridicules city dwellers who would prefer to embrace their wives (perhaps an allusion to sex) than care for their children, and get up late in the morning, suggesting laziness, both traits that traditional values disparaged.

Elites as well as commoners cultivated social lives at the teahouse. Scholars who discussed poetry and literature at the teahouse were known as "people who like to show off their literary pursuits" (*fengya zhishi*). Some brought books to the teahouse, where, a writer commented, "they find real pleasure in reading romantic stories while sipping tea." Some local scholars liked to "play the poem game" (*bai shitiaozi*). To play this game, they put two or three tables together and placed on them two or three pieces of large paper, on which many squares were drawn, each containing a Tang or Song poem. They deliberately wrote one wrong word in each poem, and encouraged patrons to find the mistakes. Patrons who gave the right answers would be rewarded and ones who gave wrong answers would have to pay

10 wen. For some scholars, the teahouse became a place to display or share their writings. Wu Yu had his poems printed out and posted at the teahouse for the public to read and purchase. In a 1915 entry in his dairy, Wu asked somebody to send his printed poems to the Fragrant Taste Teahouse (Pinxiang). The entry for the next day describes how Wu Yu found many of his poems posted at the Hidden Garden Teahouse (Yangyuan) when he went there with friends. Scholars had their favorite teahouses. Wu Yu often went to the Fragrant Taste Teahouse, where his favorite actor, Chen Bixiu, who always played the role of a young female, performed. It seems that during the Republican era, Chengdu scholars never sought to hide their relationships with actors. Wu even wrote and sold poems about Chen at the teahouse. According to his diary, he once went with a friend to the Fragrant Taste to watch Chen perform in the morning and returned with more friends that afternoon. Wu Yu said that Chen was so pleased to have him as a fan that "Chen always kept his eyes on me in public"; Wu also seems to have enjoyed being the object of his attention.[28]

People in Chengdu liked to bet on bird fights in the teahouse. *An Investigation of Chengdu* (Chengdu tonglan), an eight-volume work published during 1909 and 1910, indicated that this activity was popular in the late Qing. During the Republican period, bird fights often were held on the outskirts of the city, such as in the Mouth Hole (Dongzi kou) outside the West Gate and the Emperor Returns Town (Tianhui zhen) outside the North Gate (see Figure 4.2). Therefore, feeding birds was not merely a hobby, but also became "a tool for earning money." This was an overt activity, heavily promoted to attract huge crowds, and was institutionalized through standardized procedures and rules. The fights were judged, and the winners were awarded a piece of red cloth to wear. Bird fighting was only one of many forms of teahouse gambling; people also placed bets on games of mahjong, cards, and chess, and played the lottery. Mahjong was forbidden in teahouses during the late Qing because it was often used for gambling, but in the early Republic, gambling flourished again after the restrictions were relaxed. In 1928, the lottery was introduced in Chengdu and lottery shops were opened throughout the city's prosperous areas. The lottery headquarters, the Guild of Lottery Shops, was located in the Peace and Quiet Teahouse (Jing'an chashe) in the North City Park. People crowded into the teahouse on the sixth day of every lunar month to hear the winning lottery numbers. The grand prize winner would wear a red cloth and be paraded through the streets on horseback in a ceremony sponsored by the guild.[29]

The novelist Sha Ting vividly described life in the teahouses in the market towns near Chengdu, which were comparable to the lower-class teahouses in the city or to the teahouses of old Chengdu. His long novel, *Digging Gold*

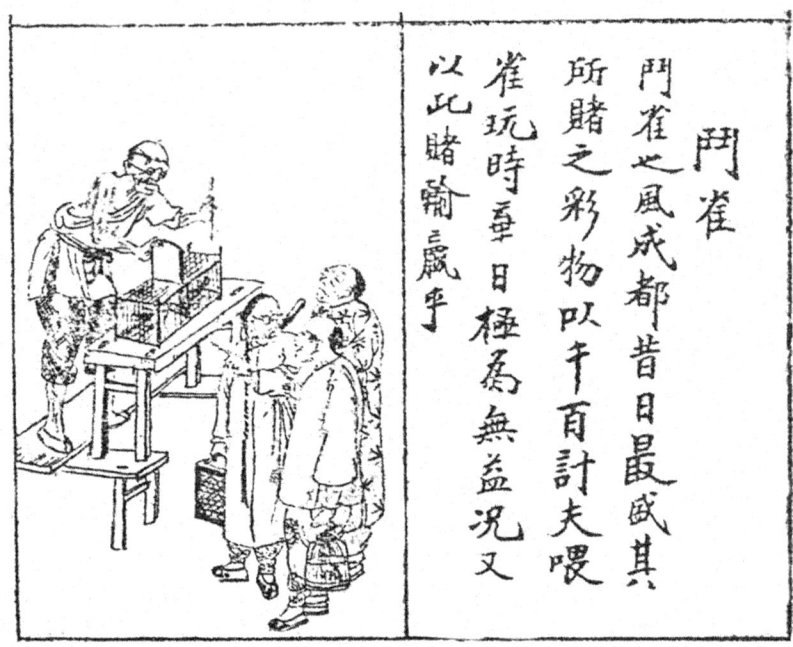

FIGURE 4.2: A bird fight in the late Qing era. Bird fights have long been a popular form of gambling. From CDTL, 3: 116.

(Taojin ji) was set in 1939 and was written in 1941. The first scene takes place in a teahouse:

> The first significant matter for people, whether they have a decent job or make their own work schedule, is to go to the teahouse to talk about business matters, exchange ideas, and try to find out the latest news. To an outsider, it might sometimes seem that they are just talking, with no purpose and in a way that is boring and meaningless, but to them, the feeling is different; they use teahouses to meet their spiritual needs and for their practical interests in real life.

The Big Dipper Market Town (Beidou zhen) he describes was small, with only one main street and two alleys called "urinal alleys" that were lined with open-air toilets and urine buckets and vats. But even such a small market had eight or nine regular teahouses; when the market was open, the number increased to more than ten, because some teahouses opened for business only during trading days. These teahouses were very similar to those in the Green Goat Market described in Chapter 1. Each teahouse had its own regular clientele, determined by social status, personal relations, and other interests. Each day, "when it is time, everyone finds his own familiar place to have tea just like a person finds his seat at the theater by following the number on the ticket." When a man felt depressed, he usually went to a teahouse. As Sha Ting described a local elite in his novel: "He walks with heavy steps into the Pleasant and Peaceful Chamber (Changhe xuan) teahouse while slowly and carelessly greeting the guests there. After he is seated, he seems deliberately to avoid conversing, but in fact he wants to forget his unhappiness, so he asks the waiter to find Lao Luo to pick his earwax to relieve his anger."[30] (See Figure 4.3.)

The teahouse was the most affordable place for relaxing and socializing, and shows performed there attracted all sorts of people. Folk performances were cheap; if a young man did not have enough money to see a movie, he could go a teahouse to have "a reasonably priced and pleasant time." A man could go alone to the teahouse and lounge for several hours in the bamboo chairs, reading a book and eating fried melon seeds. Although the price of a bowl of tea constantly rose, drinking tea remained relatively affordable. For example, listening to a storyteller with tea combined cost just about one yuan in 1943. As a newspaper essay in 1949 stated, "In this bad year, people suffered enormously from spiritual depression," but in this "detestable time" (*kewu de shidai*) if "you want relief for a moment," the author suggested,

FIGURE 4.3: An earwax picker serving a customer. The way earwax pickers serve their customers and the devices they use have barely changed after more than half a century. Photo by the author, spring 2003.

"you should go sit in a teahouse. When lounging on a bamboo chair and stretching, you forget all the troubles that were bothering you and feel like you are in another world."[31] Thus, according to the author, the teahouse was a sanctuary where people found temporary peace and satisfaction.

Culture and Customs

The teahouses of Chengdu fostered customs that became an important part of the broader popular culture. Teahouse culture was reflected in everything from the utensils used, how tea was drunk, the jargon used, and how patrons behaved. The utensils were a part of teahouse culture as well as the material culture of society, reflecting the ecology, environment, and overall level of available material resources. Tea settings in Sichuan teahouses were known as "the three pieces": *chawan* (tea bowls, because they looked like bowls), *chagai* (tea lids), and *chachuan* (saucers, literally, "tea boats," because of their shape). Tea drinking in teahouses was called *he gaiwan cha* (drinking lidded-bowl tea). The *chachuan*, or saucer, was used to hold the bowl and prevent spills. The lid that covers the bowl was used to keep the water hot but also to stir the water to accelerate the blending of the hot water and tea leaves. In addition, drinking from the gap between the bowl and the lid prevented tea leaves from being drunk. Tea utensils were relatively expensive, and lower-class teahouses would use the bowls as long as possible. According to Li Jieren's satirical description, there were probably only "ten good bowls among one hundred," the rest having been repaired. Repairers made pieces of broken porcelain from different bowls into a complete bowl. They were so skillful, William Sewell said, that when the pieces were put together, "it was difficult to see" that the bowl "had ever been broken" unless one inspected the bottom of the bowl.[32] Tables and chairs were also indictors of teahouse culture. Bamboo for the chairs came from the abundant bamboo stands in Sichuan. Bamboo, which played a major role in people's daily lives, was often used as building material for homes and for making everyday items such as chopsticks, tool handles, and furniture. In Chengdu's parks or suburbs, teahouses were usually located in bamboo stands, where people could enjoy cool breezes under the shadow of bamboo trees during the summer. Most chairs in the teahouses had both backs and armrests, which matched the tables, and were comfortable to sit in or lie on. The bronze-colored and glossy surface of well-worn chairs revealed the tremendous appreciation residents had for these establishments.[33]

The emerging material culture also caused concern among some teahouse lovers. For example, the author of a short essay in the *Chengdu Evening News* (*Chengdu wanbao*) complained in a humorous tone: "After thermos bottles came out, the art of tea began dying" (*wenping chu, chadao wang*). The essay concerned the trend of tea drinkers to use insulated thermos bottles to carry boiled water so that they did not have to constantly boil water. The hot water from the thermos, the author stated, could not match the quality of freshly boiled water and affected the taste of both tea and water. Without the high quality of freshly boiled water, tea drinking was no longer an "art," so the thermos bottle was actually "destroying" the "art of tea." Despite this criticism, the author claimed, "I do not reject the thermos bottle."[34] This conclusion reflected the complex attitudes toward the new consumer culture. On the one hand, innovations brought great convenience to daily life, but on the other hand, they were responsible for changing the proud and highly treasured traditional lifestyle. Another result, which the essay did not mention, was that the use of thermos bottles might keep some people at home for tea drinking. Teahouses were the only source of freshly boiled water for many in Chengdu; the introduction of the thermos, to a certain extent, solved this problem. I do not find any evidence suggesting that any teahouses at this time replaced the waiters who served boiled water to customers with thermos bottles.

The items used in the teahouse also were indicators of how proprietors ran the day-to-day business and what supplies were needed. Little documentation about the everyday items used in small shops has been found, so little is known about what items were considered necessities. Although these items might not have much significance, they could provide clues about the operation of small businesses and material culture. I have found a list of items used in a teahouse that was made for the purpose of getting compensation after a violent incident.[35] Although some supplies might not be on the list, the list at least tells us of the basic equipment a teahouse should have. Interestingly, besides tea bowls, kettles, chairs, tables, and tea leaves, some everyday medicines were considered necessary, which may suggest that teahouses also sold some medicines. The teahouse also provided supplies for smokers, ranging from traditional tobacco and smoking pipes to cigarettes.

The teahouse also cultivated a special vernacular. Not only did waiters use their unique sing-song calls to welcome and send off customers, to energize the atmosphere, and to attract the attention of passersby, but they also used jargon found only in teahouses, which patrons readily understood. On the night before a new teahouse opened for business, for instance, it would hold a ceremony called "washing tea bowls" (*xi chawan*) or "lighting the hall" (*liangtang*). On that evening, it provided free tea for guests, most of whom were friends or relatives of the proprietor or prominent residents in the neighborhood. The ceremony not only was intended to promote the business, but also to help secure protection from local powerful men. As mentioned in Chapter 1, busy times of the day in the teahouse were called *dayongtang*, (literally, "rushing into the hall"), and slow times were called *diaotang* (literally, "hanging around the hall"). Some poor people who could not afford a bowl of tea would buy a bowl of plain boiled water, called *miandi* (literally, "no bottom") or *boli* (literally, "glass"). Teahouses allowed patrons who could not afford tea or did not like the tea leaves sold there to bring their own tea leaves, so they needed to buy only plain boiled water. Teahouses also sold boiled and hot water, *chutangshui* (literally, "out-of-hall water"), to the residents in the neighborhood.[36]

Teahouses in Chengdu usually allowed truly destitute people to drink the tea left by departed customers, a practice called *he jiabancha* (literally, "drinking overtime tea"). Some older residents of Chengdu have vivid memories of drinking overtime tea. Liu Zhenyao recalled that as a child he often went the Quieting Waves Teahouse (Anlan chaguan), which had three rooms on two floors. The proprietor was very nice; he never chased away young boys who wanted to drink overtime tea. Liu would walk up to any table in the teahouse and say, "Grandpa (or uncle), let me drink overtime tea." Before they could respond, he would take away their bowl. He would leave without even saying "thank you" as soon as he put the bowl back down on the table. The patron whose tea it was would continue his conversation and smoking without acknowledging the incident. Of course, this may be an extreme example of how well children were treated, but adults who drank overtime tea followed some customary rules: they drank only tea that was uncovered, which indicated that the patron had left, and they did not drink directly from the bowl, but used the lid to ladle the tea from the bowl.[37]

Some teahouses established mutual-trust relationships with patrons by offering credit. In the early 1940s, for instance, a big hole was made in the south side of the city wall and a wooden bridge was built over the South Fu River (Funan he) in order to disperse residents during Japanese air raids. During that time, the South Fu River was very clean and full of fish. Outside the South Gate was a field covered with fragrant yellow rapeseed flowers and the butterflies that were attracted to them. At the south end of the bridge, a small teahouse with three or four tables and fewer than twenty chairs was opened in a thatched cottage. Although it was small, the location was excellent, with a beautiful and broad view of the river, bridge, field, and trees, and business was brisk. The teahouse also served noodles, so people could linger all day. It soon became the favorite of high school and college students. The proprietor treated poor students very well, letting them pay on credit if needed. The accounts were listed on a small blackboard on the wall, which had each debtor's name followed by the Chinese character *zheng*, which is written in five strokes, represented five bowls of tea. The customer's name was erased when the debt was paid.[38]

Distinct customs emerged from teahouses, which often hosted informal social organizations, called "tea rotations" (*chalun*), that were organized by twenty to thirty friends or people of the same occupation. They had regular meetings in the same teahouse and took turns hosting, and paying for the tea. These teahouses, especially in market towns outside the city, would often hang a board on the wall that listed the names of all the people who participated in the tea rotation. Members of these groups often established tight social networks, which could help them in business, in their social life, and even in politics. Members exchanged information about business issues, government policies, and local news. When confronted with an issue or problem, they might first turn to the group for help. Some groups in the teahouse were based on common hobbies. "Beating on drums" (*daweigu*) or "sitting operas" was a popular amusement for local opera lovers, who gathered in the teahouse to sing local operas using simple instruments and without make-up or costumes; because of this, it was also called "stool opera" (*bandeng xi*). An illustration in *An Investigation of Chengdu* depicts this activity (see Figure 4.4). "Sitting operas" often drew large audiences and also helped nurture some professional performers who practiced singing month after month, and even year after year, without growing bored.[39] Some teahouses functioned like social clubs. For example, the Optimistic Tea Garden (Leguan chayuan) in Sun Yat-sen Park (Zhongshan gongyuan) was located in a dove market. Dove

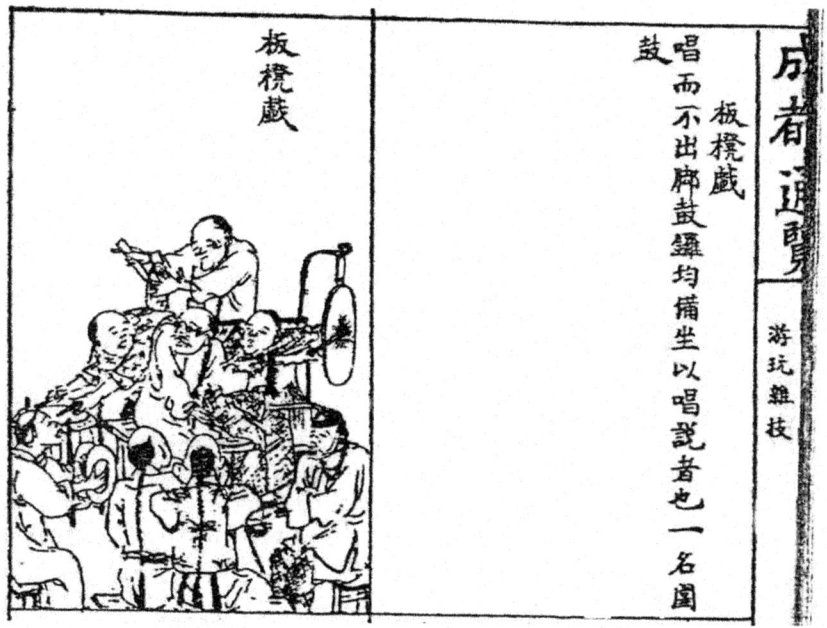

FIGURE 4.4: "Sitting operas." From CDTL, 3: 120.

lovers often gathered there to trade and exchange information about doves, and thus it became known as a "dove lovers' club."⁴⁰

Teahouses usually provided a toilet. As a popular saying put it, "Look for a teahouse if you want to use the toilet" (*Yao jieshou, chaguan zou*). Most toilets were very simple and well below the common standard of hygiene. They were usually not separate from the teahouse and the stench attacked customers' noses. Often, the toilet simply consisted of a hole near the stove or in a dark corner at the rear of the teahouse, covered with a shed. Or toilets could also be built with broken bricks, bamboo strips, or wooden boards. The crudest toilet was simply a wooden bucket in the corner. These became public lavatories that passersby and residents in the neighborhood could use freely. Farmers used the waste as fertilizer, paying after the fall harvest with a bag of dried broad beans known as "urinal broad beans" (*niaoshui hudou*), which symbolized payment and gratitude.⁴¹ Thus, the teahouse was the site of standard business practices as well as special relationships unique to the teahouse.

"Calling for Tea Money"

The most noteworthy and popular custom that demonstrates the complex relationships between people in the teahouse was the so-called calling for tea money (*han chaqian*). In Chengdu, it was a social custom that when a man entered a teahouse, his friends or acquaintances who were already there would call out to the waiter "Mr. X's tea is on me." Such a call could come from every corner if Mr. X had many friends or acquaintances. This scene was repeated in almost every teahouse at all times of the day or night. In some cases, however, the newcomer would offer to pay for his friends' tea. In this case, his friends usually replied, *huanguo* (literally, "replaced") with a smile, which meant, "Okay, I will ask for a new bowl of tea that you will pay for," although the saying was seldom taken literally. Sometimes, if the recipient did not want a fresh bowl or had to leave, he would uncover the bowl and take a single sip to show his politeness in a process known as *jie gaizi* (uncovering the lid).⁴²

People's eagerness to buy tea for others was part of the important social custom in Chengdu, and throughout Sichuan, of "saving face." People in Chengdu felt they had to offer the gesture of being willing to pay for tea for their friends or acquaintances even though they did not want to. A man who failed to make this gesture would "lose face." The more people who showed a willingness to pay for the recipient's tea, the more flattered he would feel. Whose money was taken was a serious matter. The waiter could easily offend a patron if he did not handle the matter tactfully, and could even drive patrons away or lose his job if his boss received many complaints. Chengdu's residents, according to some critics, liked "pretending" to be wealthy or generous, which made it difficult for a waiter to read his patrons' minds. Li Jieren, for example, described a scene of "calling for tea money": A man went to the First Balcony. After he paid for his tea, he saw two acquaintances coming up the stairs, and immediately looked away. He later pretended that he just then saw them and said with a smile: "Just arrived? Your tea is on me!" He waved bills at the waiter. But they called the waiter and said, "Take our money to pay for the tea at that table [pointing to him]." The waiter knew both gestures were only symbolic, and announced, "Both sides thank each other." He did not bother to take money from either of them, which is precisely what was expected.[43] In this case, the waiter handled the situation very well. This paying for others, like giving gifts, was a way of building a social network, and the monetary value could be converted to emotional credit that could be collected in the future. In the city, people lived according to the social rules of various relationships, which were very important to daily life. Paying for others' tea was a common practice in obeying these unwritten rules.[44] The milieu of gestures, the waiters' ability to respond and their ways of handling the complicated situation indeed embodied a very strong feature of local culture. The waiters' experience in the teahouse reflected their relationship with teahouse-goers.

Waiters' skill and deftness in handling various unexpected social situations became the basis for their survival. An experienced waiter knew very well the "art of receiving payment" and had his own principles. The decision regarding whose money to accept depended on various factors, such as the patrons' social status, age, whether they were residents of the city or visitors, regular or infrequent customers, and so on. Usually, a waiter would take money from a stranger rather than from a regular customer in an effort to avoid inadvertently displeasing a regular patron and causing him to choose another teahouse due to the waiter's "naiveté." For the same reason, a waiter usually took money from a young person rather than from an elder, because elders usually were regular customers. A waiter also preferred to take money from a rich person who was unconcerned about paying for a bowl of tea. In addition to these factors, a waiter generally would take money from a person who really wanted to pay rather than from one who seemed to be merely pretending. But, how could intent be divined? An experienced waiter knew to look for gestures typical of those who were merely pretending: acting preoccupied rather than taking money from their pocket while yelling, "Don't take anyone else's! Take mine!" This gesture was known satirically as "two hands capturing a king" (*shuangshou qinwang*), a term used in the martial arts. Or, customers carrying a bill and waving it around while yelling, "Take mine!" This was satirically called "playing *taiji*" because the gesture was like practicing slow-motion Chinese boxing. Or, customers calling for their money to be taken but standing in place far from the waiter; this gesture was satirically called "joining in the fun" (*huodao nao*). Of course, waiters acted according to the general principles behind these behaviors except under some special circumstances. For example, waiters generally preferred to take money from earnest payers who often gave a small bill and told them not to bother with the change. At the end of the night, however, when they wanted to get rid of many small coins and bills and thus make settling accounts easier, they might take money from a "*taiji* player" who held a big bill. Therefore, a savvy "*taiji* player" knew the trick of "using big bills in the morning but small ones at night."[45]

Interestingly, a custom similar to "calling for tea money" developed in the saloons of America's cities. This custom was called "treating," which was "the most important drink custom" for fostering the "traditional reaffirmation of solidarity and equality among males." This custom became "a social law": "If a man happens to be in an inn or public-house alone, and if any of his acquaintances come in, no matter how many, it is his duty to 'stand,' that is, to invite them to drink and pay for all they take." It was "a deadly insult to refuse to take a drink from a man, unless an elaborate explanation and apology be given and accepted."[46] Roy Rosenzweig found that this custom emerged from the Irish countryside, where "local social and economic relations were often based on a system of mutual rights and obligations rather than a rationalized market of monetary exchange." Country dwellers in Ireland had a social custom of helping neighbors, part of a "local system of mutual obligation" that reflected "one's acceptance of the mutuality, friendliness, and communality on which it was based."[47] The nature of people's relations in traditional Ireland, in some ways, was like that in Chengdu, although the two did not share a geographical or cultural background. This similarity between the Chinese and Irish tells us that people who lived in different worlds could create a similar social practice based on mutual obligation and a desire to establish social protocols. Regardless of race, culture, and nationality, people seem to have a need to bond, and although the means of building such a bond might differ, sometimes they were similar, as seen in cases of "calling for tea money" in Chengdu and "treating" in American cities.

Conclusion

According to sociologist Joffre Dumazedier, "Leisure is not idleness, since it presupposes a job as its polar opposite, whereas idleness negates employment." However, he defines leisure as "freedom from household tasks as well as from work." He believes that the "sociology of leisure" should "distinguish between leisure and spare time." Therefore, "leisure is more and more conceived for its own sake, to satisfy new personality needs at whatever cultural level." By Dumazedier's definition, a teahouse-goer could be one who was an idler, or who sought leisure, or who was filling his spare time, but these three characteristics could change and overlap. In the teahouse, an idler could also be a leisure-seeker, and a leisure-seeker could also be killing time. As sociologist Sebastian de Grazia points out, in China people intended not to distinguish leisure-seeking from idleness, so the Chinese "must translate the phrase *leisure class* into 'having-idleness class.'"[48] Indeed, in China, the concepts of "leisure," "idleness," and "relaxation" are never clearly distinguished; all three can translated as *youxian* (idle or relaxed) or *youxian* (leisure or pastime). These two Chinese terms are, like their pronunciations, often used interchangeably although their original meanings differ slightly. Therefore, a person who sat in the teahouse was often categorized as one who sought "leisure," or was "idle," or was trying to relax, or had spare time.

The teahouse was a place where people pursued leisure activities and where they had equal rights to access a public space and to pursue public life. Each street or neighborhood had a teahouse that served as a kind of "community center" where people went to meet friends, get information, converse, or simply kill time. Although tea is not addictive like alcohol, teahouse life often became a habit. For many people, going to the teahouse became a routine that they dared not disrupt for even a single day. The teahouse was always the top destination, both for the elite class and the lower class. We have seen that customers included prominent scholars, students, workers, coolies, and farmers, none of whom had to spend much money in order to pass time at a teahouse. The teahouses in Chengdu generally did not have an obvious pattern of discrimination based on social stratification, a factor that encouraged the patronage of people of all social backgrounds.[49]

We should be aware that the public roles of people in the teahouses were changeable. A man could act as a peddler at certain times, but be a patron like any other at different times. A peddler, for example, might use a teahouse as a market for his wares during the day but as a place for socializing at night. Folk performers used the teahouse as a stage, while vagrants used it as temporary shelter. For the same reason, the relationship between an individual and the teahouse shifted to reflect the complicated interactions between ordinary people and public spaces. The shifting of public roles indicates that the teahouse served all kinds of people, who could play different roles at different times or dual roles at the same time. To return to the previous example, a peddler could buy tea and drink it while waiting for customers, especially when he did not have many patrons.

People used teahouses for public life and gradually created a unique culture that became an important part of the larger folk tradition. In a teahouse, we can find relationships between customers and between patrons and culture. The teahouse provides a window through which to observe people of all backgrounds. People who did not have any previous connections might come together because they shared the same public space, while people who had connections gathered in the teahouse for shared personal, social, and economic activities. People generally were respectful, at least superficially, to each other and to the proprietors, waiters, peddlers, and others who tried their best to satisfy them. At the same time, customers also tried to build an environment where they would like to linger. All of these people contributed to the rich, colorful, and appealing teahouse culture.

Frequenting teahouses in Chengdu became a lifestyle that boosted the trade. This popularity, to a great extent, was based on the teahouse's ability to address social, cultural, and economic life and to meet the needs of people from all walks of life. Although in the West the bar, tavern, café, coffeehouse, and saloon became a social hub, none of these played as many roles as did teahouses.[50] The basic functions of the teahouse remained although they were influenced by the larger society and its political transformation. Teahouse life provides a fine example of how local everyday culture could maintain its unique identity while resisting the wave of modernist uniformity and the growing role of the state in public life. This chapter has concentrated on the aspects of daily life experienced by teahouse goers themselves. Through this perspective, less is seen of the role of the state, conflicts, and politics, but in fact, the state made every effort to infiltrate teahouse life, and the teahouse was also a place where social conflicts took place, as will be discussed in later chapters.

CHAPTER 5

Entertainment

> My habit of frequenting the teahouse began with listening to storytellers. It was during the 1920s, when I was only a little over ten years old. After dinner one day, an elder member of my family took me to a teahouse. For the first time, I saw how under the dim light of an oil lamp, customers filled the room; the smell of tobacco and sweat attacked my nose. The noise of conversations and the waiter's response to the calls of customers mixed with the sound of the brass saucers the waiter threw on the table. I also heard the customers' calls to "pay for tea here," to which the waiter responded, "So-and-so has already paid for your tea." The voices made the teahouse noisy like a busy street, indicating good business. As soon as the storyteller hit the table with his "awakening board," the room immediately became quiet. This was the starting point of my connection with cultural life.
> —Ba Bo, "Zuo chaguan" [Sitting in the teahouse]

THIS VIVID PICTURE of teahouse life, which conveys the power of the storyteller to turn all patrons into an audience, is in Ba Bo's memoir about his childhood in the 1920s. Although people went to teahouses for socializing, as discussed in the preceding chapter, entertainment, including storytelling, was also a major attraction. Entertainment brought prosperity to the teahouse. An elderly Chengdu resident recalled his childhood in Republican Chengdu, a city of consumers, not producers, with few modern factories, a relatively small population, and primitive transportation. The pace of life was very slow, "giving people an impression of leisureliness and laziness." Especially between two and three o'clock in the afternoon, "it seemed the whole city entered a state of semi-wakefulness and semi-sleep, when the melodious sound of dulcimers (*yangqin*) and sweet songs wafted out of the teahouse widows, just like the sound of the tender, melancholy rain in autumn paints the city in somber colors."[1] Although the city probably was not as tranquil as he describes it, and many changes were taking place, as my study of street culture has shown, Chengdu gave an overall impression of idle leisure.[2] The teahouse became a symbol of this way of life.

The teahouse and the entertainment it sponsored were mutually dependent. In Chengdu, the earliest theaters were found in teahouses—the opposite of the experience in Beijing, where the earliest teahouses were found in Peking opera theaters.[3] Before the advent of professional theaters, itinerant troupes of opera performers, acrobats, folksingers, and puppeteers moved constantly between rural markets, market towns, and cities. In the city, they went from street to street or square to square, often hired by rich families or clans to perform in residential compounds in a practice called "singing for the event in the hall" (*chang tanghui*). These troupes usually performed on temporary stages built for special occasions. Permanent stages, called "forever stages" (*wannian tai*), were used during temple fairs at some temples. The itinerant troupes, however, preferred to perform in teahouses, where the rent was low, schedules were flexible, and options were numerous. If attendance dropped at one teahouse, the troupe could easily move to another; it could also negotiate the terms of rent and search out the best deal.

Some troupes preferred the stability of long-term arrangements, and some teahouses chose to keep a troupe for a longer time to cultivate a loyal audience. Gradually, these teahouses became specialized stages. Folksingers and puppeteers generally performed in smaller teahouses, but local operas were performed in larger ones because they could accommodate the many actors and sets required, and because the stages in larger teahouses usually were in better condition. Therefore, during the early years, there was no distinction between teahouses and theaters; performances were usually offered as part of the teahouse service. In 1906, the Reciting (Yongni) Teahouse was remodeled and reopened as the Elegant Tea Garden (Keyuan), the first teahouse theater in Chengdu (see Figure 5.1). Other teahouses soon followed suit and focused more on local operas than on serving tea, becoming pioneers in the theater business. The Joy Tea Garden (Yuelai), a new-style teahouse cum theater, was built shortly after the Elegant. Next came the Pleasure Spring (Yichun) and the First Tea Garden (Diyi chayuan). These were across the street from each other, and the booming sounds of gongs and drums often clashed during competing performances.[4] However, not all folk performances required specialized theaters; in fact, ballad singing, comic dialogue, and storytelling still used the stages of traditional teahouses.

Almost all of the teahouses that showed local operas were called *yuan* (gardens). These teahouses required a larger financial investment because they were of higher-quality construction and had more elegant decor, furniture, and utensils than conventional teahouses. Beginning in the 1910s, tea gardens came to dominate the performance stages of Chengdu, with advertisements appearing in nearly all the major local newspapers that listed such

FIGURE 5.1: A local opera performance in the Elegant Garden. The inscription reads, "The performances in the Elegant Garden have been gradually reformed. The performers here are more famous, and it is a convenient place to drink and eat." From *Tongsu ribao*, no. 4, 1909.

programs. Reporters often reviewed the performances and covered nearly everything else that happened as well. A few modern theaters opened during the 1920s, a turning point when theaters began the process of separating from teahouses. Still, the combination of teahouse and theater predominated in Chengdu, and throughout the Republican era teahouses and theaters never completely separated.

This chapter examines the teahouse as a place of recreation, the major forms of entertainment it offered, and the audiences it attracted. It describes what kinds of entertainment were available and how patrons took advantage of them, the means and strategies performers used to make a living, and how people behaved in teahouse theaters. Popular entertainment was a powerful educational tool; many people, especially those who had little or no formal instruction, learned about history, literature, and traditional value and virtues from local operas and storytellers. Reformist elites and government officials believed operas could provide enlightenment, enhance civilized discourse, and boost morale. The government used this forum for public entertainment to spread orthodox ideologies and influence the minds of ordinary people, while enacting regulations to control what people watched. These performances promoted different values at different levels; some were orthodox and some were heterodox, revealing the boundaries between elite culture and popular culture. But some boundaries were not clear and often overlapped. Therefore, the teahouse offers us a space in which to observe interactions between elites and commoners and between elite culture and popular culture.

Folk Performances

It is not an exaggeration to say that teahouses were responsible for the emergence of all kinds of folk performances in Chengdu. Most folk entertainers preferred the smaller teahouses that mainly served ordinary people because the rent at the more elegant tea gardens was very high. Sought-after entertainers usually performed at a single location, while lesser-known actors were itinerants who carried their instruments to different streets, smoking dens, and teahouses to make a living, in a process locally called "running on the beach" (*paotan*) or "going through booths" (*chuan gezi*). Many even performed in open-air settings, called "singing under the water shed" (*chang shuipeng*). They usually performed a dozen pieces, each only a few minutes long, and their earnings hardly supported a decent living. Patrons did not buy separate tickets for these shows but could watch if they purchased a bowl of tea. Therefore, actors had to depend on tips or donations from customers who sympathized with these "vagrant 'artists'" (*liuluo de yishujia*). In contrast to theaters where audiences paid three to five yuan, these performances were "the cheapest." Low-income laborers could spend twenty to thirty cents to watch a show in a teahouse and "relieve their fatigue" while sipping tea.[5]

All kinds of folk arts were popular in the middle- and lower-class teahouses: cross talking, golden-coin-clipper chatting (*jinqian ban*), storytelling, folksinging, juggling, and ventriloquism. In the late Qing and early Republican periods, for example, Magician Gao hung a wooden sign advertising his program outside a teahouse in Rising Dragon Alley (Xinglong xiang). He also performed at birthday celebrations and weddings, which was called *tangcai*. *Liulianliu* (literally, "willow and willow"), also called "beating continuous tinkles" (*da lianxiang*), was regarded as the lowest form of entertainment. Performers, usually a duo, carried a bamboo stick and copper coins, singing vulgar and slang-filled songs while tapping the stick against their bodies to keep the rhythm. They usually performed in front of teahouses because of the large amount of space required for their movements. "Beating the Daoist drum" (*da daoqin*), involving a bamboo and leather drum also called a *yugu* (fish drum), was a popular form of performance by itinerant Daoist priests who traveled from one teahouse to another to perform. They always got permission from the teahouse proprietor, and members of the audience who enjoyed their shows would give tips (see Figure 5.2).[6]

FIGURE 5.2: "Beating the Daoist drum." From CDTL, 3: 120.

Storytelling was probably the most popular art teahouses used to boost patronage (see Figure 5.3). During the Republican era, storytelling stages were called "storytelling arenas" (*shuchang*) because, while they were originally used for storytelling, they were adopted for other types of folk performances as well. While both the teahouse and the performers benefited, it was generally believed that "folk performers depended more on the teahouses than teahouses relied on them." Every decision a teahouse proprietor made regarding genres, performers, and programs was made to attract more customers. In so doing, teahouses had to consider factors such as location and the nature of the neighborhood and of the nearby residents. Success in one teahouse did not guarantee success in another; a storyteller could be a hit in the East Gate area but fail in the West Gate area, for example. The teahouses in prosperous areas or commercial centers such as Warm Spring Road and East Great Street did not need storytelling to boost business, and performances were rarely seen there. An observer pointed out that one reason big teahouses did not sponsor storytelling was that it attracted children, who did not buy tea.[7]

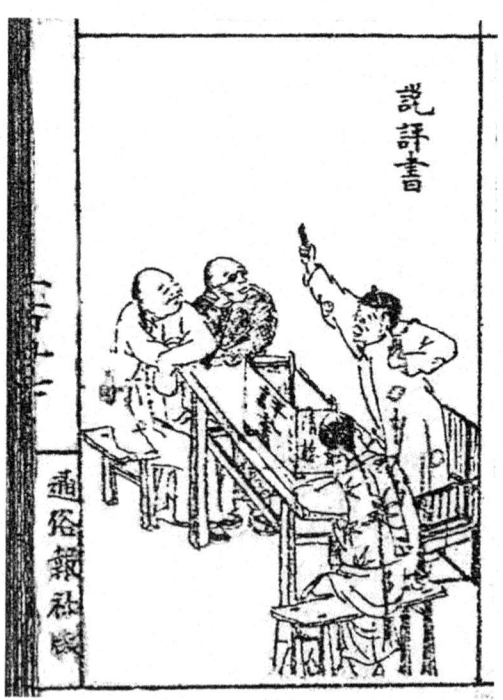

FIGURE 5.3: A storyteller. From CDTL, 3: 117.

Storytellers did not sell tickets; either the teahouse paid performers or performers solicited money directly from the audience, usually twice per night. Both means generated fees only from adult, paying customers but not from children or the crowds who listened for free from the street. If the storyteller collected directly from the audience during intermission, he always made sure he ended the story on a cliffhanger.[8] Every night, people flocked to the bright, crowded teahouses—which stood in stark contrast to the dark and quiet streets—to listen to storytellers for a very low price, for example, in 1942 and 1943 usually only about one yuan for both tea and entertainment. Hai Su recalls listening to storytellers when he was a child. Every afternoon and night, the small teahouse, which was quiet all other times, became crowded and noisy. A table and a high-legged chair were set up for the storyteller. When the room was nearly full, the storyteller would clear his throat and tap a wooden cube three times, and then the waiter would yell: "Please be quiet! Storytelling is beginning!" Immediately, a hush would fall over the whole room.[9]

Since upper-class teahouses did not host storytellers, the rich or the elite had to go to ordinary teahouses to hear storytellers. When a teahouse on Cotton Street hosted the well-known storyteller Zhang Xijiu, it was packed every evening, but the front row was always reserved for a few respected members of the local gentry known as the "Five Seniors and Seven Sages" (*wulao qixian*). Zhang would begin his story as soon as these old men were seated. One evening, after Guizhou warlord Dai Kan became governor of Sichuan in 1916 and implemented a curfew, these old men were stopped by soldiers while on their way to the teahouse. They launched an action against martial law and forced Dai to eliminate the curfew. Class distinctions were blurred with other forms of folk entertainment as well. In his recent historical novel based on his own experiences in Republican-era Chengdu, Che Fu describes how a ballad singer drew acclaim from all levels of Chengdu society.[10]

Yangqin (dulcimer singing) was one of the most popular acts in Chengdu. During the late Qing and early Republican periods, this genre became a favorite of many scholars and retired officials because of its elegant melodies and lyrics. Dulcimer singing flourished after being promoted by the Charitable and Benevolent Hall (Cihui tang) in the early Republican era. The Hall taught dulcimer singing to more than one hundred blind children who developed a style of performing known as the School of the Hall (*tangpai*), which became important in the history of this type of performance.[11] Dulcimer singers performed in teahouses (*baiguan*) and in the homes of wealthy families (*tangchang*). They usually played in the New World Tea Garden (Xinshijie chayuan), the Sacred and Pure Tea Garden (Shengqing chayuan), the Cooperation Tea Balcony (Xieji chalou), and the Hibiscus Tea Balcony

(Furong chalou). Typically, four to six performers sang and played the dulcimer and drum, or sang to the accompaniment of a *huqin* (a two-string instrument), or performed with a three-stringed instrument (*sanxian*). Dulcimer singing was not as loud as Sichuan opera; people from other provinces preferred softer music.[12] The Four Springs Teahouse (Sichun chashe) and the Quieting Waves Teahouse (Anlan chaguan) were the main locations for these performances. They both had one hundred twenty to one hundred fifty seats but had to add more than one hundred bamboo stools to meet the demand.[13]

Many entertainers built a following by performing on street corners, at the ends of bridges, and in public squares. After they became well known, they would move to teahouse stages. An example is Jia Shusan, a master of bamboo dulcimer (*zhuqin*) singing, who had an extremely hard life when he was young, becoming blind when he was only three and growing up in a poor family. He began performing at fourteen and for twenty years performed on the streets and open-air stages and in lower-class teahouses. He took his highly skilled "melody of the dulcimer" act to the Brocade Spring Tea Balcony when it opened in 1930 and performed there for more than ten years. When he performed, the streets surrounding the teahouse became crowded with rickshaws and other private vehicles that brought people from all directions. On the second floor of the Quieting Waves Teahouse, dulcimer singing began at 3 PM every afternoon and ended at 5 PM. The performers were five or six blind men who entered the stage walking in single file, each with his right hand on the shoulder of the person in front of him and carrying an urheen (*erhu*, a two-string instrument) in his left hand. One performer sat in the middle of the foot-high wooden stage and played the dulcimer, while the others sat either beside or behind him. A waiter would be assigned to serve the audience, and brass kettles filled with boiled water would be lifted to the second floor by pulleys. As a customer recalls more than half a century later: "Even today, when I think of the sound of dulcimer playing at the Quieting Waves Teahouse, it's like I have entered an old dream and gone back my childhood."[14]

"Reformed" historical stories also became popular. For example, the dulcimer singing programs at the Quieting Waves Teahouse displayed promotional materials on a board at the entrance to the stairs about stories that praised loyal and righteous government officials, pious sons, and chaste women, such as *Three Sacrifices at the River* (Sanjijiang) and *Pure Wind Pavilion* (Qingfengting). The former is about the wife of Liu Bei, the king of the state of Shu during the Three Kingdoms (AD 220–65), who committed suicide after Liu died in Baidicheng by the Yangzi River. The latter is about an elderly couple who adopted an abandoned baby boy and returned him to his biological mother after he was grown. When Jia Shusan performed in the Brocade Spring Tea Balcony, audiences, including many prominent people, poured into the teahouse every night. Local scholars posted matched couplets praising his act and its social impact. One reads: "He beats drums and sings, looking to the northeast; we hope heroes stand tall. He tells stories about Sichuan and cries from the heart; we cannot sing only about the river and wind." This couplet praises his performance for inspiring opposition to the Japanese occupation in the northeast, and for its concern with the lives of local people. People enjoyed watching him in all the roles he played, and were astonished at his rich language and touched by his stories of loyalty, filial piety, chastity, and righteousness that helped "civilize and educate people." He poured his sorrow at the nation's misfortunes into his songs.[15]

Many folk entertainers performed regularly at the same teahouses. Audiences went to the New World (Xinshijie) Teahouse for Li Decai's dulcimer concerts and to the teahouse near the New South Gate for Li Yueqiu's ballad singing. Some performers juggled acts at different teahouses on the same day. For example, a large bamboo-shed teahouse was built on the empty beach by the river near the New South Gate Bridge, and this became an ideal place for customers to enjoy the cool breeze during summer. Famous folk performers, such as Blind Jia (bamboo dulcimer), Li Decai (dulcimer), Zeng Binkun (vocal mimicry), Li Yueqiu (ballad singing), and Dai Zhizai and Cao Baoyi (comic dialogue), rotated their acts there. Zeng Binkun performed ventriloquism at the teahouse near the New South Gate in the morning and at the Sacred and Pure Tea Garden (Shengqing chayuan) outside the North Gate in the afternoon. In his act, he hid in a covered cage and told humorous stories while imitating the voices of various people, birds, animals, and other sounds. Zeng also performed in the Coming and Going Tea Balcony (Guiqulai chalou), where he had a stage called the Storytelling Arena for Bosom Buddies (Zhiyin shuchang). Blind Jia, Pockmarks Zhou (the skillful waiter mentioned in Chapter 3), and Fatso Si (a peanut peddler) were known as the "three bests" of the Bright Spring Tea Balcony (*Jinchunlou sanjue*).[16]

After the war broke out, many refugees from the lower Yangzi region, called *xiajiangren* (literally, "down-river people"), including many folk performers, arrived in Chengdu. These actors and actresses continued to sing for a living, or as it was called, "singing stories with drums" (*dagu* or *dagushu*). In early 1939, the owner of the Pleasant Wind Teahouse (Huifeng chashe) in Sun Yat-sen Park asked the government to allow "ballad singing" to supplement his income because it was insufficient from selling tea alone. In his request, he complained that he was earning no profit, and the teahouse would suffer even greater losses if he could not find a way to attract more customers. He claimed that the voices of the refugee performers he invited were "pure and elegant" and that they would be singing "new" songs, which would please his customers. In fact, the Pleasant Wind Teahouse was not the first to try this strategy. The Capital Best Tea Hall (Duyi chating) on South Warm Spring Road and the Summer Palace Tea Garden (Yihe chayuan) on North Warm Spring Road had presented "singing stories with drums" that "would not only not hurt social customs, but would educate people about the future of the war." To convince the government, the owner made the point that hiring refugees would help them survive. He was granted permission to build a stage in his teahouse. A screen of thin bamboo strips separated male audience members, who sat on the left, from females, who sat on the right.[17]

Programs and Local Opera Reform

Local opera could be regarded as the most influential and powerful means of educating ordinary people. Typical programs indicate what people liked to watch and what they learned.[18] Before the late Qing reform, stories about romance, legends, historical figures, and deities dominated local operas and other folk performances, although reformers and local authorities criticized these traditional plays as "obscene" and "superstitious." The first regulations on teahouses, issued in 1903, defined what kinds of stories storytellers could and could not perform. Public entertainment, especially local opera, was a powerful venue for leading the masses in the "right" direction. As a government official wrote in 1910, "Performing local operas is a form of education because it depicts the sum of people's experiences: sadness or happiness, and failure or success. People can clearly tell which characters are good and which are evil.... Audiences hate villains... and praise and love heroes."[19] Local elites focused on local opera reform and the government focused on increasing its control of entertainment.

Those who supported local opera reform had two objectives: to revise existing programs and to create new ones. Social reformers also tried to "civilize" individual performers. They believed that a performer's behavior offstage influenced audiences. This reform was part of a larger trend against popular culture during the early twentieth century. The article "On the Relationship between Operas and Society," published by the *Popular Daily* (Tongsu ribao) in 1909, tried to explain the theater's popularity. Unlike many elites who criticized local operas, the author looks at theaters from a positive angle. He first briefly reviews the history of Chinese opera, saying that it originated in the Tang dynasty. During the period of Tang Minghuang (685–762), when "the situation was stable and the country enjoyed peace," the emperor created opera for entertainment and leisure. Its centuries-old appeal was widespread. After many years, all aspects of Chinese operas, from the lyrics, music, and singing, to the costumes, had become very elegant and sophisticated, and an increasing number of people made a living from this art. The opera's stories of joy, anger, sadness, and happiness inspired thousands. To attend the opera cost considerable money and time, so why did people go? The author gave three good reasons: to get rid of depression, to be inspired, and to become morally elevated. Regarding the last reason, the author explained:

> Operas often confuse one thing with another, and the plots are often ridiculous. But if the story is full of emotion, and is rational and passionate, it can touch people's hearts and persuade them to think differently. Furthermore, not everyone in the audience is wise; half of them are foolish or children. These people often believe the stories, whether they are true or not. They are touched by benevolence and loyalty and angered at evil and dishonor. . . . Therefore, letting them often watch the reformed and new operas supplements efforts to improve people's minds.[20]

The author was right to recognize the function of popular education. Through entertainment, uneducated people learned traditional values and history, even though the versions were often inaccurate. He believed that if elites could adopt this tool wisely, it could become a force for social reform. Of course, there was considerable debate about the functions of local opera, and some viewed it in a decidedly more negative light. These diverse approaches help us understand how elites valued popular culture.

In 1910, the *Popular Daily* published an essay titled "In Promoting New Operas the Priority Must Be Reforming Actors' Morality."

> To reform local operas is to enlighten and inspire people, which is also a good tool for shaping social customs. Its function is as beneficial as the newspapers that are written using plain language. Everyone knows the merits of the reformed local operas, so why is the matter controversial? The reason is because people look down on actors, and therefore the literati do not want to have anything to do with performing. You can easily understand why wise and educated people refuse to perform on the stage, because performers are seen as prostitutes. Indeed, some young boy actors behave like prostitutes. As men, they work as prostitutes, not only losing their moral qualities but also becoming shameless. Because of some actors' bad conduct, it is no surprise that people scorn all performers.[21]

To some extent, these criticisms were accurate. In traditional China, rich and powerful men often pursued handsome young actors, a phenomenon described in many prominent literary works, such as the *Dream of Red Chambers* (Honglou meng). As a group, actors occupied the lower level of society; many men became actors involuntarily or because they saw acting as their only means for survival. Reformist elites considered this a moral issue, and the first activity of their opera reform was to turn actors into "decent" people.

In his *An Investigation of Chengdu* (Chengdu tonglan) published during 1909 and 1910, Fu Chongju listed three hundred and sixty operas shown and notes that to avoid charges of obscenity, some troupes changed the names of the plays they performed. For example, the *Nemesis of the Murderous Son* (Shazi bao) was changed to *Heavenly Temple* (Tianqi miao).²² This "obscene" and "violent" play was forbidden by the police, but was popular nevertheless. In fact, throughout the Republican era, "most theatrical troupes could show this play." Why was the play embraced by audiences? Let us first look at the plot:

After petty trader Wang became ill and died, his widow, Xu, hired a monk to hold a ritual ceremony at her home. Xu and the monk flirted during the event and had sex afterwards, but were discovered by her ten-year-old son when he returned home from school. The enraged son drove out the monk. Xu beat him until her daughter fell to her knees, begging her to stop. To teach the monk a lesson and to warn him never to see his mother again, the son gathered his classmates at the Heavenly Temple to beat up the monk. Xu did not see the monk for a few days until she went to the temple with her daughter to meet the monk privately under the pretense of burning incense. The monk told her why he was afraid to go to her home, and Xu became furious with her son. She plotted with the monk to kill her son, but her daughter overheard and rushed to school to tell her brother. After school, the teacher found the son alone and crying, and escorted the child home after learning why he was upset. Once the teacher left, Xu killed her son with a kitchen knife, cut his body into pieces, and put them in an oil vat under the bed. A few days later, the teacher went to Xu's home to inquire about the child, but Xu lied. That night, the son's soul entered the teacher's dream and the teacher woke up, frightened. He was certain that his student had been murdered and immediately went to the local magistrate's office to bang the drum for justice, but was jailed for making a false accusation. The teacher's wife went to the office to protest, which motivated the magistrate to launch a secret investigation. The child's body was found, and Xu and the monk had to confess their crime in the face of the material evidence and the daughter's testimony. Xu and the monk were executed and the name of the teacher was cleared. Justice finally prevailed.²³

This plot was similar to that of many stories of the Bao legal cases (*Baogong an*) and classical traditional dramas, such as *The Injustice of Dou E* (Dou E yuan). In them, injustice was always overturned after the intervention of righteous people and government officials. Affairs between widows and monks were a common plot that audiences found intriguing. Plays involving murder, adultery, and licentious widows and monks attracted large audiences. Although an evil-hearted mother who murdered her son was not a common theme, many plots were similar. What was unique was that this play deliberately depicted blood and the horror of killing, especially in the scene when the audience watched the woman cutting her son to pieces. The play used realistic props, such as the bloodied kitchen knife, the sliced body, and the oil vat, which heightened the audience's sensory experience. Therefore, many social reformers considered this play too bloody, cruel, violent, and frightening. During the late Qing and Republican periods, dramas such as this were often restricted or even forbidden. When teahouses suffered a slump in business, however, they might ignore the restrictions and show these plays. For example, a local newspaper criticized the reformed teahouse theater Elegant Tea Garden (Keyuan) for performing lecherous (*yindang*) plays, calling it "a strange phenomenon." In the 1920s, some struggling teahouses resorted to the old strategy of presenting deity plays. As a member of the local literati mocked, "Teahouses whose business is in trouble try to find a way out, and their challenge is to attract more patrons. The strategy is to show deity plays, and sometimes three troupes end up competing with each other."[24]

An essay in 1917 points out that "songs can touch people deeply," and therefore, reformed local operas could be used as an instrument for social change. The author wrote that fewer than ten percent of the plays in Chengdu were "decent and elegant" and fewer than one percent were "righteous." He also condemned performances for being full of "indecent language," "lecherous behavior," "ridiculous words," and "plots involving ghosts." An incident at the Joy Tea Garden was reported under the headline "Opera Performers Not Allowed to Watch Opera." A *xiaodan* (a young actor who played female roles) who mingled with patrons watching the show behaved in a way that "was different." This incident led to the reissuing of the regulation banning actors from watching shows and underscores the public's perception that actors were not "normal."[25] Reformers doubtless discriminated against actors in many ways, based on everything from their appearance to their behavior, and refused to treat them as equals. An example of the reformers' and new intellectuals' efforts to change the attitudes toward performers was the establishment of new troupes that performed only reformed plays, including the Establishing Peace Society (Jianping she), the Reforming Mind Theater (Gexin yuan), the New Play Society for the Public Interest (Qunyi xinjushe), and the New Play Society for Strengthening China (Qianghua xinjushe), which were established in quick succession in 1916 and 1917.[26]

The local government was a driving force behind opera reform. In 1913, the Department of Internal Affairs noted that local operas and folk performances were "the most popular means of social education" because ordinary people, including children and uneducated manual laborers, enjoyed them and could memorize the lyrics of the songs performed. If the government could "adroitly guide the action according to circumstances" and have performers use "pure language," "encouraging voices," and "touching tunes," then people's minds would be filled with positive knowledge. What should the government do? The department stated that the elimination of "lecherous plays" would only "bring about a temporary solution." To get at the root of the problem, the government should first review popular scripts, approving the good ones and rejecting the bad, and also convene experts to collect stories to use as a basis for writing new operas, novels, and songs that would inspire people and revive good social customs. The old styles of performances such as shadow plays and puppet shows could also be venues for these new programs. When these programs became popular, people would "forget the old lecherous and radical plays." The department basically adopted a strategy of "channeling off," because it believed that "prohibition could only increase their popularity" and "the regulations might be effective on paper only."[27]

In the early Republican era, the popularity of the Eternal Spring Tea Garden (Wanchun chayuan) and the Fragrant Taste Tea Garden (Pinxiang chayuan) increased until they became the major theaters in Chengdu, while the Joy Tea Garden and the Elegant Tea Garden continued to be regarded as the best. Their advertisements appeared more frequently in local newspapers, which could offer as many as twenty titles per day for a single theater.[28] From these advertisements, we find that well-known performers were a major draw; in fact, more people went to a theater to watch their favorite actors than the plays themselves. Most regular audiences had seen the same plays repeatedly, knew every detail, and remembered every word of the script as well as every move by the performers. A troupe's reputation also was crucial in attracting customers. In the major theaters of the late Qing era, people most often saw performances by the Happy Troupe (Yileban), the Imperial Banner Troupe (Cuihua ban), the Long Happiness Troupe (Changle ban), the Revival Troupe (Fuxing ban), the Culture Troupe (Wenhua ban), the Splendid Troupe (Caihua ban), and the Civilization Troupe (Wenming ban), which regularly performed in the major teahouse theaters, such as the Joy, Elegant, Eternal Spring, and Fragrant Taste.[29] Basically, theaters did not host new plays to draw audiences, but relied on the star power of the actors and actresses. Traditional dramas were shown repeatedly everywhere, the major difference being the style and quality of the performances.

At the same time, social reformers wrote new operas. After the 1911 Revolution, political dramas become popular, and in 1912 an adaptation of the famous American novel *Uncle Tom's Cabin* was performed in the Joy Tea Garden. Elites wanted to use the plight of African Americans in the United States to teach the principle of survival of the fittest.[30] Another new play shown in the Joy Tea Garden was the story of the Taiping Rebellion, which was a combination of a traditional religious story and history. After Zeng Guofan seized Nanjing, all of Hong Xiuquan's family was executed except for one of his sons, crown prince Hong Shaoquan, who escaped. He had no place to hide and became a Buddhist monk at the Shaolin Temple while waiting for an opportunity to revive the movement. The opera, performed by the Three Celebrations Society (Sanqinghui), had forty scenes that involved Buddhist deities, combining the human and supernatural worlds. The play clearly praised the Taiping Rebellion, a peasant uprising, unlike the condemnation it received during the Qing era and later during the Nationalist period. This change was made because anti-Manchu sentiment was regarded as positive as revolutionary stories gradually began occupying a portion of the stage in teahouses. In 1929, the Joy Tea Garden presented the *Western Empress Dowager* (Xitaihou), a new play that explained the "reasons why China's people were poor and weak, and the harm of dictatorships." The purpose of the play was to serve "citizens' education." The script, setting, and performances were reportedly "all elegant."[31]

Reformers also wrote plays that dealt with social issues, one of which was the murder story *The Fallen Calyx Canthus* (Luomei), performed in 1917. Chen, a young doctor, is asked to treat a very ill elderly woman. During his visits he falls in love with the woman's daughter, Huifang, and they became engaged. The patient's condition worsens, and Chen examines her. Before he leaves, Huifang puts a calyx canthus on his chest and asks him to try his best to cure her mother. Chen sees a gold box containing a great deal of money by the mother's bed. Chen, worried about getting married without having much money, poisons his future mother-in-law and takes the funds. The elderly woman sees Chen and realizes what has happened. She uses her barrette to scratch "Chen killed me for money" on the floor before dying. Huifang arrives later and sees a calyx canthus by the box, and her mother's words. She reports the murder to the police, and Chen is arrested.[32] What is the message of this "new" play as an instrument of "social education"? Chen talked about "morality" and "civil behavior" (*wenming*), but his true character was greedy and shameless. This play was intended to unmask "hypocrites" (*weijunzi*). However, this "new" drama still promoted traditional values. What Huifang says when she confronts Chen in the courtroom is very interesting: "If I did not put you on trial for justice's sake, then I would not be a dutiful daughter. But if I marry another man, I would not be righteous; therefore, I swear that I will never marry in my lifetime." She tries to prove her righteousness as "a good woman who loves only one man" by sacrificing the prospect of marriage for the man who killed her mother. From a moral perspective, this play espouses traditional values using characters that were true to reality and plot devices guaranteed to attract audiences: love, money, and murder.

During the late Qing opera reform, Zhou Shanpei, a social reformer and police chief, promoted the establishment of the Joy Tea Garden as a forum for reformed plays and new operas, where the authorities could oversee the performers' skills and ethics.[33] Zhou hired Huang Ji'an, who helped transform Sichuan opera, to write and compose new operas, which were formally printed and circulated. When Huang died in 1924, he had written more than eighty Sichuan operas and more than twenty titles for dulcimer singers. He donated almost all of his Sichuan operas to the Three Celebrations Society, the first and most prestigious professional organization that produced

Sichuan opera. Almost all of his plays were based on ancient Chinese history and promoted righteousness, loyalty, trust, and patriotism, thus providing a social education. In his *Moral Integrity at the Firewood Market* (Chaishijie), *Three Loyalties* (Sanjinzhong), *Red Deity Town* (Zhuxianzhen), *Yellow Heaven Lake* (Huangtiandang), and *Lin Zexu*, Huang praised the patriotic national heroes Wen Tianxiang, Zhang Shijie, Lu Xiufu, Yue Fei, Liang Hongyu, and Lin Zexu, who had fought foreign invaders. These stories were used to inspire people when China was confronted with the invasion of Western imperialism. *Moral Integrity at the Firewood Market* told the story of Wen Tianxiang, the chief minister of the Southern Song, who was executed at the Firewood Market after refusing to surrender to the Mongols. Huang tried to humiliate those who betrayed their country by surrendering to the enemy. In *Jiangyou Pass* (Jiangyou guan), he deliberately created a plot in which Ma Miao was decapitated and his head publicly displayed.[34] When some audiences pointed out that this contradicted the historical facts, he answered, "If I let him live, how can we make a distinction between loyalists and traitors?"[35]

The emergence of modern drama (*huaju*) added momentum to local opera reform. In the early 1920s, some local intellectuals sponsored modern dramas at the Joy Tea Garden. In December 1920, the Sichuan Student Association (Sichuan quansheng xueshengt lianhehui) used the Eternal Spring Tea Garden as a theater for "new operas" to unite all the new-opera troupes in all the schools in Chengdu in performing "reformed operas" to promote social education for both men and women. The association asked the police for help in keeping order during "this time of martial law" and explained that its intention was to "enlighten the masses," not to operate a business. Since the income would be used for the "public good," the association requested exemption from the mandatory "donation for wounded soldiers" and the "fee for keeping order." In 1931, the Modern Drama Society (Modeng jushe) performed a "good patriotic play" (*aiguo jiaju*) called *Tears of Mountains and Rivers* (Shanhe lei) at the Grand Stage (Dawutai), which attracted a large audience and had a significant social impact. The society believed the play could inspire the audience to "share in a bitter hatred of the enemy," the Japanese, who had invaded after the Manchurian Incident of September 18, 1931.[36]

Therefore, opera reform became part of the political agenda of the government, elites, and other social groups. As noted earlier, watching performances in teahouses and theaters was no longer merely an amusement, but a link to enlightenment and local and national politics.[37] Local opera, the most powerful form of popular entertainment, influenced the way people thought, and thus could be used as a political tool. It is clear that the elites found a crucial way to influence and persuade ordinary people. Though traditional operas, which had deep roots in everyday culture, were not easily replaced, they were inevitably altered, based to a large extent on the design of local elites. However, the zenith of the intrusion of politics into teahouse culture came during the War of Resistance, which had an even larger impact on public life, a subject discussed in Chapter 8.

Theaters

In the late Qing and early Republican eras, some large teahouses began to concentrate on performances of local operas rather than on selling tea. These became the sites of the earliest theatrical stages in Chengdu. The Joy Tea Garden (Yuelai chayuan), one of the city's oldest teahouse theaters, which opened in 1906, was multifunctional; besides serving tea, it had two restaurants—the Joy Garden Chinese and Western Restaurant (Yuelai Zhongxi canguan) and the One Family's Spring (Yijia chun)—and a theater. Both restaurants claimed to welcome "scholars, officials, gentry, and merchants." During the late Qing era, at least three teahouse theaters—which became serious rivals—were crowded into the small area around the Center for Promoting Industry and Commerce (Quanye chang, later called Shangye chang): the Joy, the First Balcony (Diyilou), and the Pleasant Spring Balcony (Yichunlou).[38]

Local operas and other forms of folk entertainment were suspended during the 1911 Revolution but were restored soon after. The *Citizens' Daily* (Guomin gongbao) of July 19, 1912, alone published four advertisements for plays. These ads indicate that daily life gradually returned to normal after the turmoil of the revolution. In the early Republican period, other teahouse theaters, often called "dancing stages" (*wutai*), were established. Although these new facilities still served tea, their major function was to showcase performances; these became the earliest form of specialized theaters in Chengdu. The East Asian Theater (Dongya wutai) opened in 1913 and quickly became popular. The theater at the Fragrant Taste Tea Garden (Pinxiang chayuan) also was popular, and Wu Yu went there often in 1915. Later, the Fragrant Taste Tea Garden was established in the Heart of Reform Theater (Gexin juyuan), which became known for elegant performances by well-known actors.[39] The Grand View Tea Garden, Eternal Spring Tea Garden, and Brocade River Tea Garden (Jinjiang chayuan) were also major teahouse theaters during this period.

Each teahouse theater generally had routine shows, called "sitting arena operas" (*zuochang xi*) or "night operas" (*yexi*) because they usually were performed at night. If there was no regular show during the day, some teahouses scheduled actors to perform skits at the audience's request. Although theaters in Chengdu mainly performed Sichuan operas, they did not exclude others types as long as they could attract audiences. The Joy Tea

Garden, for example, gave performances of Shaanxi opera (*qinqiang*) and the Elegant invited famous actors from Shaanxi. This became a good strategy to win more patrons in the face of severe competition. New immigrants also brought their culture to the city. In 1939, the Heaven's Ping Opera Theater (Guanghan pingju yuan) opened and provided a place for seventeen or eighteen refugees who made their living performing Ping operas and folk songs. At the same time, many other theaters also opened their doors to refugee performers.[40] Among these, the Joy Tea Garden (also the Joy Theater) had the longest history and was the most influential.

The Joy Tea Garden was the first teahouse to offer "reformed operas" as an important part of the "New Policies" promoted by reformer Zhou Shanpei in late Qing Chengdu. These became a model for the new entertainment. Because of its reputation, the Joy could attract good troupes and actors. The Three Celebrations Society was established in the Joy Tea Garden, where many old-generation artists had built their reputation (see Figures 5.4 and 5.5). The Joy was still one of the most prosperous theaters in Chengdu when the Communists took over in 1949. In 1950, theater

FIGURE 5.4: The Joy Tea Garden today. The board at the entrance reads: "This is the old site of the Three Celebrations Society, a well-known Sichuan opera organization." Photo by the author, summer 2003.

FIGURE 5.5: The Joy Tea Garden and its stage. Photo by the author, summer 2003.

workers were required to register with the government. According to the registration forms, the Joy Theater alone had 126 employees. These forms give us information about their backgrounds, including their place of origin, age, sex, the nature of their jobs, home address, level of education, working experience, relatives, membership in social organizations, other occupations, and other data.[41]

The registration forms make clear that men were the main workforce in the theater; only a few employees were women. The division of labor in the Joy was very specific, with jobs including door keepers, ticket sellers, accountants, managers, tickets printers, communications personnel, program-board painters, set designers, musicians, actors, and actresses. The résumé portion of the forms provides information about prior work experience. For example, Feng Jiyou studied in an old-style private school from the age of seven to fourteen, and lost his father and mother when he was twelve and fourteen, respectively. At the age of fifteen, he went to work as a low-level clerk in a government office and stayed there until he was thirty-one. Then he became a "tradesman with little capital" until age sixty-seven, for a total of thirty-five years in petty trade before coming to the Joy. Chen Kongrong studied the "old learning" from the age of eight to sixteen, then worked in small shops for a few years. Leng Qianmo studied the "old learning" when he was eight years old and worked in the fields from the age of ten to twenty. While he worked for the Joy, his wife and two daughters made handicrafts at home to "make a living." Zhang Mingxuan was disabled; his left leg was crippled when he was eight years old, but he was still able to go to a traditional private school to study the "old learning" for eight years. Then he was an apprentice in a salt shop before going back home at eighteen to get married. After that, he studied Chinese medicine for five years and then ran a sedan-chair shop for five years. He had eight years of "doing nothing at home" before going to work at the Joy at thirty-seven. This background information indicates that most workers received at least some education, especially from old-style private schools, and had a higher level of literacy than we generally recognize.[42] Some were failed peddlers, and some were former shop workers or soldiers. Some still had to supplement their low salaries by growing vegetables or selling handicrafts. Many of the actors and actresses had relatively simple backgrounds, studying Sichuan opera under their masters when they were young, some at ten years of age, some at thirteen, and some at seventeen. All were members of the Three Celebrations Society and almost all were from lower-class families.[43]

Audiences praised the performances in the Joy. Tickets to shows featuring famous performers sold out well in advance. Once, a man was so touched by a show that he donated twenty yuan to the performers, though this expression of generosity "was unique," according to a newspaper report.[44] Some local literati wrote their impression of the programs, such as this poem in a local newspaper:

Musical instruments are playing every day in the Brocade City,
And one new song is like a piece of splendid silk.
The view at the Center for Promoting Industry and Commerce is pleasant,
And let me try to describe my visit to the Joy Tea Garden with the pen.
The Joy Theater looks so magnificent,
Its balcony and pavilion are small and exquisite, as if they are floating in the clouds.
Rich and noble people stop their carts here,
And people seem to be in a world of colorful glazes.
Actors are desperate to display their best skills,
Singing songs melodiously and dancing elegantly.

. . .

Following the flow of people into the theater,
I feel like I am standing on a high tower.
I never tire of watching the spectacular displays of prosperity,
Ah!
Sichuan has been called a "State of Heaven" since ancient times,
Where many notable clans and rich merchants have lived.

This is a sign of achievement,
Celebrated by instruments and dancing by all animals.
Since visiting the Joy Tea Garden,
I love only this place.
Just like watching goddesses dance on the moon,
It could never be found on earth.⁴⁵

This poem gives a colorful description of the Joy Theater's pleasant environment, elegant architecture, and lively atmosphere. It also states that many audience members arrived in vehicles (horse carts, rickshaws, or sedan chairs), indicating that they were rich and of a high social class. Of course, this poet devoted more words to describing the performances, how the actors desperately showed their skills and how beautiful their dances were. The plays attracted so many people that the audience seemed to "flow." Audiences were never bored by those wonderful shows, which became an important part of everyday life in Chengdu, and where people felt like they were living in heaven. Using the language of poetry, such a description certainly was an exaggeration, but from it we can see the author's feelings about the Joy Tea Garden and the Sichuan operas shown there, and how much he appreciated the performances.

The teahouse was the precursor of not only the theater but also of the cinema. Moving pictures arrived in China "only months after the Lumière brothers' show in the basement of the Grand Café in Paris on December 28, 1895." The first movie in China was shown at the Xu Yuan teahouse in Shanghai in August 1896.⁴⁶ Movies arrived in Chengdu a few years later and became known as "electric-light operas" (*dianguang xi*) or "electric operas" (*dianxi*) (see Figure 5.6). Social reformers used movies as a tool for social change and development because movies realistically depicted powerful heroes, loyal officials, dutiful sons, and the tragedies found on the battlefield, which "could touch people and improve social customs."⁴⁷ In the early Republican era, the owner of the Fragrant Taste Tea Garden asked the police to allow "electric operas" to compensate for the "huge loss" incurred by the "new operas." The shareholders met and decided to show movies during the day, with men and women in the audience segregated, to make up this loss.⁴⁸ This suggests movies were more popular than the "new operas." In 1919, Liu Jun rented the Eternal Spring Tea Garden for 3,500 wen per night to show films. Equipment, films, and a "professional technician" were brought from Shanghai. Liu claimed that showing movies "provides better social education, unlike opera performances," and could more effectively "change customs and open people's minds." Obviously, the movies introduced from the West represented the "new" during this period, and local operas were regarded as "old." This notion fit the trend of Westernization during the New Cultural Movement.⁴⁹ Most movies were foreign, such as "short American love films" and *Gangsters in Black* (Heiyi dang), a detective series, which, according to the ads in a local newspaper, "were great movies with an unprecedented and adventurous spirit." Prices ranged from 1,000 wen to half a silver yuan depending on the location of the seats, similar to opera shows; servants who were brought by their masters paid 600 wen per ticket.[50]

The early cinema was actually a combination teahouse and movie theater. Audience members placed their bowls of tea in a holder fashioned out of a strip of iron installed on the back of each chair. Waiters walked up and down the aisles pouring boiled water into the bowls as the films were shown. During the early Republican period, few women attended movies, because they were vulnerable to men's advances while sitting in a dark theater. In the crowded and dark cinemas, it was difficult for patrons to go to the toilet, and they also did not want to miss any part of the film by being absent. As a result, a new business emerged: little boys and old women from poor families provided "moving toilets" consisting of two bamboo tubes that they carried up and down the aisles while calling out in a low voice, "Peeing tubes, peeing tubes." Men could urinate without leaving their seats. Using these "moving night pots" (*huodong yehu*) cost about as much as a

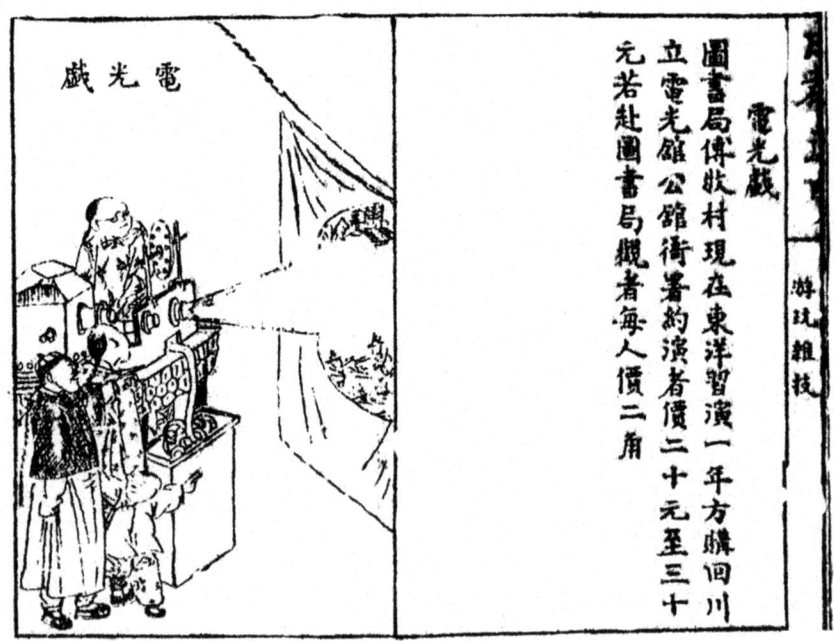

FIGURE 5.6: "Electric-light operas." From CDTL, 3: 114.

single pancake. This example tells us that major new businesses also spawned peripheral businesses created by people who found a way to earn a living by meeting people's needs. Of course, "moving night pots" were offered only to all-male audiences. As women began patronizing movie theaters, this service was not only deemed socially inappropriate, but also prohibited by the police for the purpose of "defending the eyes."[51]

The Audience

Watching Sichuan operas became a part of everyday life for many in Chengdu, and attracting customers was a constant effort of the teahouse theaters. Larger teahouses used local operas as a marketing strategy. Although we do not have a complete record of how people depended on the theater in their everyday lives, some documentation exists that provides a relatively clear picture. In 1916, the local government controlled teahouse theaters by issuing audience quotas. The quotas for several well-known teahouses were as follows: the Deities Gathering Tea Garden (Qunxian), 400; the Joy Tea Garden, 200; the New Sichuan Stage (Shuxin wutai), 200; the Sichuan Stage (Shuwutai), 150; the Elegant Tea Garden, 120; the Fragrant Taste (Pinxiang), 120; and the Eternal Spring Tea Garden (Wanchun chayuan), 100.[52] These seven theaters had a total of 1,290 seats. Although this source does not reveal how many shows were given per day, it seems likely that theaters had at least two, and often three, shows a day. Theaters usually ignored government regulations against adding more seats in order to boost their bottom line and they sold many more tickets than the number allowed by the government.

Daily sales at the Eternal Spring Tea Garden in 1920 ranged from 514 to 870 tickets. From June 14 to June 16, the average sale was 607. After night performances were added, 1,076 tickets were sold on June 19 and 1,584 tickets on June 21. Sales data are available for four theaters in 1933: the Grand Stage of Warm Spring (Chunxi dawutai), Newest Grand Stage (Xinyouxin dawutai), Joy Tea Garden, and Yu Garden (Yuyuan) (see Figure 5.7). Each theater hosted one show each morning and another in the afternoon, with an average of about four hundred customers per show, or a total of 3,200 for eight shows. Each ticket cost an average of 0.6 yuan, for a total box office of 1,920 yuan per day, 57,600 yuan per month, and 691,200 yuan per year. As an observer said, this was enough money to buy 49,371 dan of rice or cover one month's pay for an army of 385,600 men.[53] Chengdu had far more than four theaters in the early 1930s, so the actual number of theater-goers was much higher than this estimate. The writer was trying to "prove" that people in Chengdu "wasted" time and money in teahouses, but his estimate also gives us useful information about how many people routinely went to the theater and how much they spent there.

FIGURE 5.7: The Grand Stage of the Warm Spring. Detail from the scroll painting *Old Chengdu* (Lao Chengdu) by Sun Bin, Zhang Youlin, Li Wanchun, Liu Shifu, Xiong Xiaoxiong, Pan Peide, and Xie Kexin (2000). Courtesy of the artists.

A scholar wrote an essay in 1929 describing a day he spent at the theater, revealing a great deal about the involvement of the elite with the theater in Republican-era Chengdu. He met two friends at the Eternal Spring Tea Garden at 9 AM, earlier than most other patrons. He paid 1,000 wen for a ticket, and wrote that the ticket seller had a very nice attitude. More audience members arrived after 9:30 and the show began just after 10. They were very satisfied with the actors' skillful performances. After the show, they took rickshaws to Warm Spring Road for lunch, after which they drank tea for an hour. They then went to the All Joy Theater (Junle juyuan) on Hunan and Hubei Guild Street because they wanted to see a performance by actress Cui Xia. As soon as they saw Cui Xia's name written on the program board, they bought tickets at 1,600 wen per person. The scholar wrote that he was made uncomfortable by the ticket seller's bad attitude and mocking of those who believed the tickets were too expensive. Despite the price, people flocked to see Cui Xia. The show started at 6 PM, but Cui Xia was absent. The incensed audience demanded refunds, but no one ever came out to give an explanation. The author believed that many in the audience would never return. The author wrote this essay to show how two theaters handled business differently, with praise for the honest theater and condemnation for the one that used false advertising. However, the essay also reveals how people used the theater in their daily lives.[54]

The teahouse theater, as a public place, was always crowded, and disputes and even fights were not uncommon. To keep order, the police required that teahouses have policemen on duty and pay for their uniforms and salaries. It seems some teahouses also requested additional policemen at their own expense. According to a police report, the manager of the First Park Teahouse (Diyi gongyuan chashe) hired a policeman at a salary of 4.9 yuan per month plus the cost of his uniform. The police chief in the district endorsed this request, but said that the policemen there were "extremely poor" because they "received little salary," so instead of sending a single police officer, he arranged for off-duty officers to rotate patrols of the teahouse. The 4.9 yuan salary was divided equally as supplementary income. This means of earning extra money was considered a "good deal." However, the police department denied this request and ordered the teahouse to hire a single policeman to "take on this special responsibility."[55]

People went to the theater not only to watch the shows but also because they enjoyed the atmosphere of frivolity and excitement. The theater never was completely quiet, even while a show was being performed. The voices of singers, clang of drums and gongs, yells of waiters, calls of peddlers, and cheering of the audience created a nonstop cacophony. Boys walked the aisles, selling cigarettes, candy, nuts, and fried melon seeds from a box that hung around their necks. Hot-towel men flung towels to patrons in every corner who wanted to wipe their faces or hands. "Human-powered fans," made of thin wooden boards and connected to a wheel by a long rope, were provided during the summer. A theater might have several fans. While the audience enjoyed the cool breeze, the fan pullers worked very hard. Many people—usually shabbily dressed laborers or young boys—also gathered outside the teahouse to watch the acts for free. They scattered during intermission when the entertainers collected donations and returned as soon as the show resumed. During the summer, paying patrons were not happy when these vagrants blocked the fresh, cool breezes, but welcomed them during the winter when they became a human wall that blocked the cold wind. Of course, this was the case only at teahouses that opened onto the street. Most stages were enclosed, and could not be seen from the street.[56]

The audience represented all occupations and social classes, but we lack detailed documentation on this topic. However, some material does reveal useful information. In 1938, a mob of soldiers threw two grenades onto a stage, killing eight people seated in the front rows. A local newspaper reported the names, sexes, addresses, and occupations of the five victims whose identities were confirmed. Three were women: one was the wife of a clerk in the Bureau of Telegrams; another was the wife of a low-level official; the identity of the third is unknown. One of the men owned the theater's candy store, and the other was in the "second-hand goods business."[57] All were common people. The one who sold used goods might have been from the lower class, unless he owned the shop. Front-row seats were the most desirable and often the more expensive. This case may imply that even ordinary families could afford to go to the theater.

Policing Entertainment

From early in the twentieth century, the government made a great effort to control entertainment, which became part of the movement toward reining in and attacking popular culture. Examples from this era indicate how the government sought to control popular culture and the nature of the relationship between teahouses, entertainment, and state power. Supported by the government, elites had worked very hard to reform and control public entertainment in the late Qing. In the early Republican era, the new government began enacting more concrete policies that expanded its control of local operas. In 1913, the governor of Sichuan used the theater as a form of popular education and ordered troupes to perform only historical stories that promoted virtue and courage. The governor condemned "lecherous plays" that were "reformed" literally in name only, as troupes performed familiar works that "damaged social customs and people's minds" under different titles. The governor ordered the police and the Department of Internal Affairs to enforce the regulations and punish managers of theaters where "lecherous plays" were performed. The department enacted measures to "educate people about good customs" and to "squelch this evil."[58]

One measure was to issue Regulations on Local Operas and Folk Performances (Qudi xiqu guize), which had the goal of "rectifying social customs." These regulations were applied to local operas performed in ceremonies and festivals at guilds, temples, and theaters, as well as to shadow plays, puppet shows, and all other folk performances. The regulations required all troupes, theaters, and teahouses to submit their programs to the department in advance, which would approve only those deemed "beneficial to society" and "not offensive to decency." Actors who were found to be performing with "a lecherous voice and in a lecherous manner" were subject to punishment even though the government had approved the program. Actors could wear colorful clothes only while performing. The government also required a report listing the promoter's name, native place, and home address; the source of funds; the location of the theater; and the number of actors. Actors were required to tell the government their age, place of origin, and number of years in the business, and trainees in the troupe had to show a "voluntary letter" that confirmed that their involvement was voluntary. In addition, the regulations stipulated that theaters could not be close to schools, government offices, workshops, temples, or key transportation hubs. The new rules restricted the hours of performances to between 9 AM and 9 PM.[59]

Also in 1913 the Sichuan Police Department (Sichuan jingcha zongting) prohibited all so-called lecherous plays, claiming that the police had "repeatedly" banned licentious operas, but that theaters "have tried every way to attract bigger audiences" by adding "immoral" content. A police investigation found that even some upper-class teahouse theaters, including the Deities Gathering Tea Garden (Qunxian chayuan), Grand View Tea Garden (Daguan chayuan), and Joy Tea Garden, had allowed forbidden plays.[60] These theaters disobeyed the regulations, "hurting social customs and people's minds." The police also accused the Deities Gathering Tea Garden of letting actresses perform in a "shameless" manner and resorting to "ugly gestures that actors should not make," claiming that social customs would be seriously damaged if these shows continued, and threatening harsh punishment if theaters continued performing such plays. The police carried out a much tougher policy than the Department of Internal Affairs. The so-called lecherous plays were often actually love stories or romantic comedies. Elites defined these plots, which revolve around misunderstandings, miracles, and the foolhardy courage of young lovers, as "indecent" and "licentious."[61]

That same year, the Sichuan Provincial Administration issued a list of all the problems involving local operas, stating that since the 1911 Revolution, "people have experienced many difficulties," but "theaters have expanded greatly." This document also blames the Grand View, Joy, Eternal Spring, and Deities Gathering teahouses for "struggling against each other in every way" and criticizes Chengdu residents for "acting like they're going mad" when watching local operas. The Sichuan Provincial Administration considered opera a "backward" custom and "a critical issue for internal affairs" because it did not fit the era of "survival of the fittest." This document compares the Chinese opera with its counterparts in Japan and the West. In Japan, the singing and dancing of geishas were based on scripts written mostly by "scholars and experts in literature," and in France, "most performers are educated at universities and take responsibility for preserving traditional music and language."[62] Apparently, the government discriminated against its own folk tradition, but praised foreign ones. Elites might not know much about geisha and French entertainers, but they admired them because they were from Japan and the West, reflecting the increasing influence of Westernization.

The document states that theaters in Chengdu had three major problems. First, they were not good for education. Theaters depended on "folk songs," "heavy makeup," and "attractive looks and seductive manners" to attract audiences but did not "preserve any language or music." Many people, the document's writer declared, were degraded by such shows. The second problem was that "Sichuan is in an isolated place," and its abundant natural resources were being squandered. Now, when Sichuan sought to promote industry and commerce to boycott foreign goods, Chengdu, as the capital, "should set a good example," but "the booming of its theaters has fostered idleness and laziness, and resulted in people's lack of work skills." Therefore, theaters hurt commerce and industry. The third negative impact was that the majority of people "wasted their limited income in the theaters." Chengdu had been in financial crisis since the looting of 1911, but generating income through higher taxes was difficult when people spent too much money in teahouses, and prices increased dramatically.[63] If this situation deteriorated further, "officials would become corrupt, soldiers and policemen would lose their sense of responsibility, students would be no longer be interested in knowledge, merchants would fail to conduct business, and ordinary people would get money through illegal means to pursue a life of leisure." To solve these problems, the government adopted a restrictive policy "related to the people's future," even though it was difficult to uproot this entrenched social custom. To carry out its goal, the government tried to reform existing theaters and allowed no new ones to open.[64] This was probably one of the government's most sophisticated strategies; it dredged up all sorts of "vices" by repeating the same old accusations.

The year 1916 was crucial in national politics because Yuan Shikai declared his intention to restore the imperial system, a move opposed by the National Protection Movement. In December, after the war against Yuan, the police issued Regulations for Restricting Theaters (Qudi xiyuan fa), which governed every aspect of teahouse management, from seating and tea bowls to tickets and patrons. For example, government officials determined the number of seats a theater could have; more tickets than that could not be sold. There had to be a certain amount of space between seats, and stools could not be added as additional seating. Seats were first-come, first-served; no one could hold a seat for someone else. When the quota of tickets assigned by the government was sold, a sign was to be hung in front of the door. A patron who left but kept his tea bowl on the table was considered the seat's occupant, and another customer could not sit there. Lost items had to be turned over to the police. Teahouse employees had to be polite to customers.[65] This regulation is the most comprehensive and detailed that I have found, and gives a clear idea of how the police tried to control theaters and audiences.

Under such a restrictive policy, entertainers doubtless had a very difficult time making a living. Furthermore, the policy also harmed the teahouse trade. Since performances could lure customers, when the government segregated men from women in the audiences, business plummeted.⁶⁶ Although I have not seen any new regulations that specially targeted performances and local operas between 1917 and the War of Resistance, I have found some concrete cases that provide insight into how the local authorities implemented their policies. For example, in 1936 the Society of the Hall of Righteousness and Morality (Mingde tang), a performing troupe, tried to bring its show to the Lotus Pavilion Teahouse, claiming that it had never shown any "licentious," "evil," or "bizarre" programs in the many years it performed across eastern Sichuan. It also claimed that its "elegant" and "pure" songs could "elevate people's spirits" and "help social education." The troupe, established more than twenty years earlier, arrived in Chengdu in the early spring of 1936 and performed for over a month at the Flower Festival, with police permission, and was "praised by scholars and officials." After the festival, the troupe members had to make their living somewhere else, and ended up at the Lotus Pavilion Teahouse.⁶⁷

A policeman who investigated the troupe found no immoral content in its program. He also found that four of the performers, three of whom were women ranging in age from twenty-one to forty, were disabled, three with vision problems and one who was crippled. The police responded that, "Women performers influence social customs and order. If they were scattered in teahouses across Chengdu, it would cause problems. But, so that they can make a living, these women should be allowed to work in an out-of-the-way and enclosed place that is easily controlled by the police so as to prevent any problems." The police opted to let the troupe perform as long as it did not become too prominent. The police generally discouraged female performers and likely would have denied the request if the women had not been disabled. The troupe could perform only in enclosed places away from the main streets and any passersby. The Righteousness and Morality Hall did not find an "out-of-way place," however, but went to the Hibiscus Pavilion Teahouse, which presented a petition, co-signed by a shop guarantor, to again ask the government for permission to allow performances, stating that the troupe members had not earned money in a long time and could not even afford food. But the police continued to insist that the troupe find a location that was not "close to a street."

The troupe, forging ahead through the bureaucracy but without formal approval, began performing in the Hibiscus Pavilion Teahouse, emphasizing that its members "did not sell their bodies in the name of singing," which may indicate that some singers were also prostitutes. According to the petition, a police officer had confirmed that the teahouse was on the second floor of an out-of-the-way place. After a two-week run, "there has been no damage at all to social customs and social order, which can be confirmed by the heads of the street." The police, however, once again denied permission and forced the troupe to cancel its show. The troupe and the teahouse immediately presented another petition, explaining that they could not find a place to perform despite many attempts. If the show were closed, the troupe members would face starvation. Furthermore, the teahouse and the troupe were mutually dependent; without performances, there would be few patrons, and the teahouse would face tremendous losses. The manager begged that performances be allowed to resume while the troupe looked for a new place. If allowed, "the requirements of the police would be met and the people's livelihood would be protected." In August of that year, the troupe finally relocated to the Citing Fragrant Poems Tea Balcony (Yinxiang chalou) on Shaanxi Street, a moderately prosperous area, and the police finally granted permission.[68] The experience of the Society of the Hall of Righteousness and Morality reflected the state's tight control over popular entertainment, ranging from the content of performances to the location of shows, which made it difficulty for troupes struggling to survive. This control peaked during the War of Resistance, as discussed in Chapter 8.

Conclusion

Entertainment in Chengdu was mainly concentrated in teahouses, where people could watch folk performances and local operas while sipping tea. Indeed, teahouses became the most important location for leisurely pursuits, although they were also multifunctional. To some extent, the relationship between teahouse theaters, performances, and audience members was the relationship between public spaces, entertainers, and commoners. Entertainers and commoners interacted in this public space; the former provided services that enriched teahouse life, and the latter took advantage of these services and also supported the entertainers who worked there. The taste and judgment of commoners became the most important factors in a performer's ability to survive or become famous. Because entertainers depended on their audiences, they had to perform to the best of their abilities. This relationship was scarcely influenced by external social changes and political developments—including the war—in a pattern that lasted from the late Qing era until the mid-twentieth century.

Other forms of folk entertainment, such as storytelling and ballad singing, were also tightly connected with daily life. Actors and actresses made urban life, especially nightlife, bright and exciting. Most performed on teahouse stages, although some low-level troupes and entertainers still earned their living on the streets. Teahouses depended on performers to boost their bottom line. The evidence shows that folk entertainment and local operas coexisted because they served different functions and appealed to different audiences. Folk entertainers usually performed where Sichuan operas were not available, and folk performances provided alternatives to local operas; people who could not afford the opera could still find entertainment. Whereas Sichuan opera was the predominant form of entertainment in teahouse theaters, storytelling became the most popular entertainment in street-corner teahouses, followed by other folk acts.

As a part of their effort to control entertainment, reformist elites and local government sought to reform local opera by imposing a political agenda onto popular entertainment. They tried to introduce new operas and new plots to existing operas that contained "positive," "civilized," and "progressive" messages that could "educate" people. This movement began in the late Qing and continued throughout the Republican period. The programs and people's tastes changed according to social and political developments. Themes and trends reflected external social transformations and political revolutions, whether romantic, "obscene," and "violent," or reformist, revolutionary, and patriotic. The rise of movie theaters brought an end to puppet and shadow shows but had little impact on traditional Sichuan operas. Of course, the reasons behind the demise of some genres were complex, but the local opera was a better developed and more sophisticated art form. Storytellers could still present very complicated and fascinating stories without elaborate settings or costumes; interesting plots kept audiences coming back. The teahouse also chose the acts it believed would be best for business, helped develop some genres of folk entertainment, and transformed the spaces required for these performances accordingly. In the beginning, the acts were secondary to tea drinking, but this changed as certain actors and programs became popular, until the performances became the primary function. This led to the emergence of new forums for public entertainment, such as theaters.

Local operas and other forms of popular entertainment became a powerful tool for social education. The role of elites in the creation of popular amusements can be clearly seen from the fact that elites wrote many scripts of Sichuan operas and other genres of folk performance to promote their orthodox thoughts and values. As a result, popular dramas and stories inculcated Confucian ideals in the common people. Of course, elites were unable to control every message, and many plays, stories, and folk songs were out of their reach. Some programs, despite being steeped in traditional values, were used to criticize social inequities and to express the feelings and thoughts of ordinary people. In addition, the historical legends that were the most popular genre hardly reflected real life. Commoners enjoyed watching a romanticized version of the past that let them forget their own harsh circumstances, at least temporarily.

As movies, a symbol of Western culture, were introduced into Chengdu, teahouses became pioneers of this new form of public entertainment. Movies were never a serious threat to local operas or storytellers, and instead coexisted with them, although they appealed to a wide audience, especially younger viewers. During the late Qing and Republican eras, the films shown in Chengdu were almost always made in the West, and therefore gave viewers a better understanding of Western culture. Feature films opened people's minds and became a driving force of the pro-Westernization movement. Therefore, the teahouse, as a traditional public place where people sought leisure, successfully became a proponent of modern and Western culture, which once again reveals its flexibility in transforming the environment through the adoption of new cultural influences.

The reform of teahouse theaters and the regulations imposed on them reveal the struggles between popular culture and elite culture, and between the uniqueness of local culture and the uniformity sought by the national government. Under the pressure of state power and cultural hegemony, popular entertainment inevitably changed, but the traditional forms of performances and many old programs nonetheless persisted. Though the state enforced new regulations, it had difficulties implementing them or ensuring their effectiveness. Bastions of local culture and customs in Chengdu persevered from the late Qing reform to the collapse of the Nationalist government. During the War of Resistance, however, by using the national crisis to wave the flag of "patriotism," the state was finally able to extend its power into the teahouse and thus control popular entertainment, as discussed in Chapter 8.

CHAPTER 6

All Walks of Life

The teahouse has three functions in the daily lives of people in Chengdu. The first is as a market for all trades. You do not need to bring your goods to the teahouse; as long as you stay there, buyers or brokers will come to you to trade. A certain street, a certain teahouse, and often certain times are set aside for this purpose.... The second function is as a place for gathering and settling disputes. Whenever a religious society, a charitable group, or one or two dozen people need to hold a meeting to discuss matters, they will choose a teahouse, where they can openly discuss, negotiate, and argue with each other. If they do not want others to understand what they are talking about, they can use jargon to avoid interference. If you have a dispute with someone and want to get justice and recover your "face" but do not want to file a lawsuit, or if the problem does not warrant a lawsuit, you can invite your supporters, as many as possible—but of course, your opponent will do the same—to a teahouse for settlement.... The third function of the teahouse is as a parlor or place for rest for middle- and lower-class families. However, the teahouse allows only men; any woman who enters a teahouse—except those who go just to buy boiled water for tea and then leave—would not be considered a good woman but like one who would go to an opium den.
—Li Jieren, *Baofeng yuqian* [Before the storm]

LI JIEREN, a local writer who understood Chengdu very well, found that the teahouse was not only a place for relaxation and entertainment, but also functioned as a market, a meeting place, and a reception room. The teahouse thus became a small business that provided space for other small businesses. Using the teahouse as a place for trade was convenient for both sellers and buyers. In a teahouse, if a merchant failed to make a sale, he could easily move on to the next customer. If he wanted to collect information about supply and demand, transportation, government policies, or financial matters such as pricing, interest rates, profit margins, or taxes, he would first go the teahouse. Some occupations and guilds established their own teahouses, which became true markets and the perfect place for professional gatherings.

This chapter, by examining how people from all walks of life and various social groups used the teahouse and how and in what way the teahouse was connected with people's public lives, supports the idea that the teahouse functioned as a community center, contributing to neighborhood solidarity and community life. Indeed, life in Chengdu without this institution is difficult to imagine. As Li Jieren noted, the teahouse was the ideal meeting place, open to all social groups and organizations, most of which did not have another suitable place to meet. Using a public place also saved members in a social or professional organization the trouble of having to make separate logistical arrangements such as reserving a meeting place, paying rent, or hiring someone to prepare the boiled water and tea. All they needed to do was show up at the teahouse without necessarily even having to be punctual. People who arrived early simply sipped tea until the meeting started.

The Sworn Brotherhood Society, which in Sichuan was known as the Gowned Brothers, also favored the teahouse as their meeting place, and often as their headquarters. Although gangs were illegal, teahouses, teahouse-goers, and policemen ignored them as long as they did not cause trouble. The fact that local people formed their own means of enforcing justice without the involvement of the government or other officials reflects a strong sense of social autonomy. Residents often used the teahouse for settling arguments or disputes, which provides valuable information about how members of a local community handled mundane conflicts without official intervention. This tradition originated in the late imperial period, when state power scarcely reached into local communities and neighborhoods. "Drinking settlement tea" became a popular means of giving local elites an opportunity to establish their influence and leadership. Gender was always a sensitive issue in the teahouse; as mentioned by Li Jieren in the epigraph above, women were generally not admitted. Like the larger society that gradually changed its attitude toward women in public life, teahouse proprietors came to have no objection to female patrons, because their presence improved business. This chapter discusses the process by which the teahouse opened its doors to women.

Social organizations played an active role in the teahouse in a variety of ways, whether economic, social, or political. The teahouse, as a microcosm, contained and reflected all of the elements of the larger society. In a limited space, all sorts of people acted individually and collectively, reflecting the city's vibrant social life and the power of its local culture. Social groups and organizations dominated teahouse life, but the state still tried to regulate their activities, creating different results in different aspects of teahouse life.

Merchants and Peddlers

In addition to the workers and folk performers who made a living in teahouses, others adopted the teahouse as a place for business deals. A local writer pointed out, "It is not right that idlers stay in the teahouse from morning to night." However, he also noted the economic function of the teahouse and acknowledged that "the number of idlers is not greater than the number of people who have business in a teahouse." He remarked that unlike the major cities along the Yangzi River, Chengdu did not have large business sites, and the various occupations also lacked the financial power to build their own markets. The teahouse became an ideal location for conducting business. Each profession had its own gathering place where petty vendors sold their goods or food. The close relationship between the teahouse and the business world is described in a matched couplet: "Merchants from all corners of the world talk trade while members of the gentry chat about ancient legends."[1] In the history of her missionary family, Han Suyin said, "The call: 'I buy tea,' is uttered frequently in the teahouses." Such a call "prefaced amicable talk of business, respect to an elder, demand for a favor, or any of those transactions of land or merchandise which are normally done in a teahouse or a restaurant because the home is no place for such mundane matters." On the streets of Chengdu, geographer George Hubbard saw that "merchants [are] busy [meeting] prospective buyers or sellers at their shops or in a tea room. And the peddler is always there, hawking his wares with an intonation, whistle, gong or clapper, everywhere characteristic of his trade."[2] Although both petty peddlers and merchants conducted business in the teahouse, their means were different. The former sold items on site, while the latter dealt in larger quantities and brought with them a few samples for examination rather than their entire inventory. After a deal was made, the goods would be moved to a different location, usually to storage areas near the four (later, seven) city gates or harbors.

Almost every occupation conducted business in teahouses, and, as mentioned, some had their own teahouses where their professional associations met. As a source noted, "Silk merchants have a teahouse for silk merchants, yarn merchants have a teahouse for yarn merchants, and even rickshaw pullers, second-hand goods traders, and human excrement cleaners have their own teahouses." Some people even went so far as to believe that "there was no occupation that could separate its business from the teahouse."[3] This might overstate the case, but it shows the importance of teahouses to the local business world. Some trades had more than one teahouse, while some teahouses served several occupations. For example, the Peace and Joy Temple Teahouse (Anleci chashe) was used by merchants of Western medicine, soy sauce, oil and grains, and stationery, while the Fragrant Taste Tea Garden in the Joy Commercial Center was used by people involved with lumber and construction, as well as by the Gowned Brothers, who oversaw opium smuggling. The Prosperity Tea Hall (Huahua chating) was a tea leaf market that also became a market for foreign yarn. Generally, merchants liked to meet in teahouses located in transportation hubs, such as harbors, and near the city gates, because they did not want to travel far to conduct business. Also, workers preferred teahouses near their guildhall, workshops, or shops. Teahouses in specialized markets automatically became gathering places. Rice merchants, for example, adopted the teahouses near the rice markets outside the East, West, South, and North Gates. Restaurant workers and other service workers found throughout the city usually met in teahouses where these businesses were highly concentrated. Most transactions for these businesses took place between 8 and 11 in the morning, although some took place in the afternoon and others at night.[4]

The teahouse was also a market where laborers gathered in hope of finding a job. Generally, people in the same occupation gathered at the same teahouse, so employers knew where to find workers.[5] Many casual laborers, seasonal workers, and skilled craftsmen, especially from rural areas, waited at the teahouse for employment. If someone needed a carpenter, for example, he knew which teahouse to go to. Any household that needed workers for home repairs, moving heavy items, or preparing for an important event such as a wedding or funeral could easily find workers in the teahouse. Some craftsmen even used the teahouse as their workplace, repairing shoes, fans, and umbrellas on the spot.[6] Others took their work with them to the teahouse, which allowed them to be productive even while they were taking a break. Teahouse proprietors and customers did not mind the paper, dust, and debris that these workers left behind because their presence was an added convenience to everyday life.

The teahouse was the primary market for many peddlers. Teahouse proprietors usually did not refuse them because they provided a convenience to patrons and ultimately contributed to the bottom line. Some peddlers even helped the waiters when needed, without the expectation of payment. Most peddlers were cigarette sellers, who sold both packs of ready-made cigarettes and paper rolls. The second-largest group was candy peddlers. Others sold everyday items such as brushes, fans, straw sandals, and straw caps. These peddlers boosted business at the teahouse because they met customers' needs. Peddlers entertained patrons by showing off their special skills. A girl who sold seeds was popular because she was able to pick up the exact number of seeds a customer requested, for example. There were so many food peddlers that a member of the literary intelligentsia complained, "As soon as a customer enters a teahouse and calls for a bowl of tea, he is surrounded by a swarm of food peddlers who pester him to buy cigarettes, fried seeds, and peanuts." In fact, customers lingered longer if they had something to eat when hungry and did not have to leave to buy everyday necessities. Many small shops, such as butcher shops, restaurants, and barbershops, had a close relationship with teahouses, either through a financial investment or because they set up booths, stalls, or tables to sell their goods or provide their services outside.[7] Therefore, teahouses and peddlers were partners in a sense, providing conveniences to customers through mutually beneficial arrangements.

People in other professions who were neither employees nor subcontractors of the teahouses also depended on teahouses to make a living. These included hot-towel men, tobacconists, craftsmen of various types, shoe polishers, pedicurists, earwax pickers, barbers, and fortune-tellers. Like waiters, they established special relationships with teahouses and teahouse-goers not only through the services they provided, but because they also became an integral part of teahouse culture and the larger folk tradition, some of which was unique to Chengdu or to Sichuan in general. Their mere presence added excitement to teahouse life. Because pedicurists raised issues of hygiene, local authorities often prohibited them from plying their trade in teahouses. Traditionally, earwax pickers, providers of a service unique to Sichuan, depended on teahouses to make a living. They held their tools in one hand and a metal clipper that made a distinctive sound to attract customers in the other, moving between the seats to announce their service. One observer mockingly said that these pickers performed a kind of art, making people comfortable so that they forgot that these instruments could spread diseases.[8]

Another profession unique to the teahouse was hot-towel service. So-called hot-towel men (*yandai pazi*) served patrons hot towels for wiping their faces, skillfully flinging towels precisely to any customer in the room while catching the towels that customers threw back, even when several towels were thrown simultaneously from different directions. They sometimes deliberately showed off their skills by catching the towels in their mouths, and were rewarded with more tips.[9] The hot-towel man was not a formal employee but a subcontractor who paid for access to hot water and was responsible for helping the waiter and stove keeper as needed. The hot-towel business originated in response to demand from the multitude of teahouse patrons who worked in stores and workshops. Most such patrons were not Chengdu natives, but came from all over Sichuan and even other provinces and often lived alone; thus, the teahouse became their "semi-home" or "part-time hotel," where they went to drink "early tea" and wash their faces before going to work every morning. They returned after work and stayed until closing time, washing their feet before leaving. They went to bed as soon as they reached their living quarters, which typically were simple, crude, and dark. They became regular customers of hot-towel men and brought good business to this profession.[10]

Another common profession was the selling of tobacco by people who were locally known as "water-pipe tobacco servants" (*zhuang shuiyan*) or "serving tobacco boys" (*zhuangyan war*), and as "tobacconists" by foreigners. A tobacconist had two bags, one for tobacco and the other for a few brass pipes and a band of paper rolls. He usually carried a big brass water pipe in his left hand and a burning roll of paper in his right. The tobacconist's water pipe was very long, often more than two meters, which enabled him to easily reach a client from a distance. If the pipe was not long enough, he added extra pieces. Therefore, in a crowded teahouse, a water-pipe man did not need to move much to serve patrons.[11] The development of this method of service indicates that most teahouses were overcrowded, and that people who worked there developed innovative strategies to ply their trades. In his investigation of the teahouses on the Chengdu Plain, Wang Qingyuan found that many tobacconists followed the market days from town to town, as did the traders described by William Skinner. Their main customers were the farmers who went to town on certain days for trading and relaxation, to whom they sold a dozen draws on the pipe for one yuan.[12]

Fortune-tellers usually worked out of a few specific teahouses (see Figure 6.1). As soon as a fortune-teller established a reputation, he enjoyed a steady flow of customers. Thus, fortune-tellers brought business to the teahouse, and they were generally welcome to conduct business there. As an observer wrote, "A teahouse has to have a fortune-teller." An example is the fortune-teller nicknamed Divine Boy (Shentongzi), who usually worked in the teahouses in the Smaller City Park. His arrival excited patrons, who enthusiastically asked him to tell their fortune. Most fortune-tellers were physiognomists (*xiangmian xiansheng*), who told a customer's fortune by reading his facial structure. Fortune-tellers had an incredible knack for giving customers a positive interpretation. For example, they would tell a crippled man that he would be "walking like a dragon or tiger" (*longxing hubu*) and tell customers that they were likely to become high-ranking officials. Or, they would tell someone whose face was scarred from acne that "the number of stars on your face is just perfect," which guaranteed good luck. Customers would take these prognostications seriously and gain confidence. A member of the elite class ridiculed physiognomists, saying that they should be invited to inspire young people to be sent to the front lines during the war because their words were much more powerful and persuasive than government propaganda.[13] Of course, those who advocated modern Western ideas criticized people who believed in so-called superstitions, but it is interesting

FIGURE 6.1: A fortune-teller. Photograph by Harrison S. Elliott, 1906 or 1907. Photo courtesy of Jean Elliott Johnson.

to see that some of their peers viewed this issue differently. Not only did this author praise the flexible and charming language of fortune-tellers, which others derided as fraudulent, but also he revealed his dissatisfaction with government propaganda through his mockery.

Social Organizations

In addition to its business function, the teahouse had an even broader social role as the headquarters or meeting place for various social groups. As a commentator stated, "It is a reality that people go to the teahouse for their own group gatherings."[14] Many social organizations that did not have a budget or a permanent address used the teahouse as a business office. They usually hung a sign with the name of the association in front of the teahouse.[15] Cultural and charitable organizations also used teahouses for fundraising and other activities. In 1914 and 1915, the Constructive Peace Society (Jianping she) was established in the Eternal Spring Tea Garden (Wanchun chayuan) to perform new plays. The government permitted it to pay only half the regular rent because the shows provided "social education." Later, when the Huayang branch of the Chinese Red Cross (Zhongguo hongshizihui Huayang fenhui) tried to raise money to build a hospital, it was granted permission to use the Eternal Spring Tea Garden rent-free for the first two months to organize performances and for half the regular rent after that. The Min River University used the same strategy when raising money to build houses when it held a three-day "party" (*youyi hui*) in the Joy Tea Garden. The programs included some well-known operas, such as *Zhuo Wenjun* and *Tears of Mountains and Rivers* (Shanhe lei), music, dancing, and an exhibition of paintings.[16]

Some social organizations had their own teahouses. In 1921, for instance, some local elites, called "scholars of the old learning," who were dissatisfied with the "social degradation" and "moral decline" of the times, delivered lectures on the classics to "save people's morality." They chose the Three Way Guild (Sandao huiguan) as their headquarters, where they organized the Divine Military Society for Public Lectures (Wusheng jiangyan hui), funded by donations from local gentry and merchants. The society opened a teahouse, called the Teahouse of the Divine Military Society for Public Lectures, at its headquarters. This attracted a great deal of attention, and many elites believed that "lectures are a good tonic for saving the world" and expected the society to become a model for other cities and rural areas. To avoid harassment by local thugs, the society sought protection from the local government and municipal offices and also received a tax exemption from the police, which issued the following public notice: "The Divine Military Society for Public Lectures gives lectures on all matters of life and tries to enlighten the uneducated. It is registered with the police. Audiences there should not make loud noises. This public notice is made especially to protect the society, and all people should obey it."[17] It is noteworthy that the New Cultural Movement was at its peak at this time, and some "old" style scholars tried to use this to resist the "new" intellectuals' attack on Chinese tradition and the intrusion of Western culture. By comparing this with the opera reform mentioned in the last chapter, it is apparent that the teahouse had become the site of the struggle between the "old" and "new" cultures.

Students who came from outside Chengdu organized native-place associations that met in the teahouse. During the war, as large numbers of refugees arrived in the city, such activities became prominent. Students at Sichuan University, for instance, met in the Four Dimensions Teahouse (Siwei chashe) near the East Gate, and students at the West China Medical University and Jinling University gathered in the Little India Teahouse (Xiao Tianzhu chashe). Middle school and high school students went to smaller and simpler teahouses, called "wild shops" (*yedian*), on Lime Street (Shihui jie) and at the rear of West China Square (Huaxi ba). In 1949, professors at Sichuan University held a strike to protest their low pay and poor living standards. According to a newspaper report, many students went to teahouses—notably the Sleeping Stream Teahouse (Zhenliu chashe)—during the strike. The Sleeping Stream also was popular with high school students who came from better-off families outside Chengdu.[18]

Writers, scholars, and other intellectuals had their favorite teahouses, such as the Thick Shadow (Nongyin) and Green Sky (Lütian) in the Smaller City Park. The former was quiet and people went there to play chess, so it was nicknamed the Chess Art Teahouse (Qiyi chashe). School principals and teachers went to the Cry of the Crane Teahouse (Heming chashe) in the same park. Teachers looking for jobs went there during the sixth and twelfth lunar months. The competition for teaching contracts became so fierce that the teahouse was regarded as a "battlefield," where there were "fights every sixth and twelfth lunar month" (*liula zhizhan*). The Two Fountains Tea Balcony (Erquan chalou) in the Commercial Center was popular with those who worked in cultural and political institutions. He Manzi recalled that when he was an editor of a literary supplement for a newspaper in Chengdu, he met authors in a teahouse in order to save time and the cost of postage. Movie stars liked to go the Three Sages (Sanyigong) and journalists gathered in the Playing River (Zhuojiang). The Small Garden Teahouse (Xiaohuayuan chashe) and the Three Sages were popular with Sichuan opera performers. Peking opera actors went to the First Tea Balcony (Diyi chalou) on Warm Spring Road, but amateur performers of Peking operas met in the Lucky Light Teahouse (Xiangguang) on Horse Walking Street (Zouma jie). Teahouses also had ethnic divisions. Muslims frequented the teahouses in their neighborhoods, such as the Reciting and Whistling Balcony (Yinxiao lou) on Examination Yuan Street (Gongyuan jie), Dongpo Pavilion (Dongpo ting) on East Imperial Street (Dongyu jie), and Prosperous and Happy Chamber (Ronglu xuan) on South Three Bridges Street (Sanqiao nanjie).[19]

"Drinking Settlement Tea" (Chi jiangcha)

Teahouses in Chengdu became a place for settling disputes in a process known as "drinking settlement tea" (*chi jiangcha*). In seeking a resolution, the two parties would invite a mediator, who usually occupied a high social position, to a teahouse. Typically, each person would first make a statement, and the mediator would then determine who was at fault. That person would pay for the tea and publicly apologize. Liu Zhenyao recalled that the Quieting Waves Teahouse (Anlan chaguan) on West Imperial Street (Xiyu jie) became a major site for "drinking settlement tea" because most customers were elites who had high standing in the neighborhood. People would tell those involved in a dispute to "go to the Quieiting Waves for settlement," then ask a respected person to serve as mediator. This shows that elites also used teahouses as a place for social involvement and that they became neighborhood hubs. Therefore, some people regarded the teahouse as "the office" of the community and the *baojia*. According to one writer, disputes between neighbors, family members, and even children could be settled in the teahouse, and he praised this function, saying that "the merit and virtue of the teahouse are immeasurable," although there were some cases of injustice.[20]

This practice underscores the relative autonomy of citizens, who sought to settle conflicts without official involvement. It also indicates the existence of a social force that was based on the reputation of the mediators. Of course, mediators were members of the elite class—usually they were masters in the Gowned Brothers or heads of the *baojia* or militia—and had considerable influence. A newspaper article claims that the teahouse "was the most democratic court for the masses" (*zui minzhu de minzhong fating*). Those involved in a conflict would say, "Let's have tea [in the teahouse] on the corner" (*kouzishang chicha*). Heads of *baojia* and even neighbors were invited, and the party judged to be at fault would "be completely convinced." This might be an overstatement, but it shows that these judgments were considered authoritative even if some were not persuaded, and the parties "never overturned the verdict," according to the writer. Therefore, the article concluded, "'Let's have tea at the corner' is the best representation of democracy (*minzhu*) in Chengdu."[21] The author's repeated emphasis of the term *minzhu* might reflect the notion that ordinary citizens, not government authorities, were responsible for dispensing justice, although the word probably was not used accurately.

The successful resolution of disputes at teahouses in Chengdu became so commonplace that newspapers rarely covered these events. Newspapers did report the times when the practice ended violently or sensationally. An example in 1929 involved a cook for the military who sought to settle a dispute on the second floor of a teahouse. Both parties brought supporters and the discussion broke down into yelling and verbal abuse. The cook's followers started a fight and before long, tea bowls, tables, and chairs were hurled through the air. The violence caused the floor beams to break, plunging people and furniture downward and injuring more than half a dozen customers on the first floor. This did not stop the cook's supporters, however, who continued to beat their prostrate and bleeding opponents. The owner of the teahouse immediately reported the incident to the police. Another case in 1941 involved a dispute over a factory worker's debt to a shopkeeper. They tried to settle the issue at the Four Springs Teahouse (Sichun chashe). When the shopkeeper saw the worker frantically calling more than one hundred supporters into the teahouse, he went to the police. The worker's supporters followed him, eventually attacking and wounding several policemen. One policeman was even taken to the factory and beaten severely. The local newspaper called incidents such as this "performing violent opera" (*yanwuju*).[22] Although the first case occurred in the warlord period and the second during the War of Resistance, when Chengdu was under the tight control of the Nationalist government, the causes and style of the mass violence were similar.

Members of the Gowned Brothers played an important role in "drinking settlement tea." In addition to often being asked to serve as mediators, they also used teahouses to settle their own internal disputes. Because of the nature of this organization, violence was ever-present. In 1947, for instance, Wu Jiecheng, a member of the Gowned Brothers, owed 10,000 yuan to

Tang Bingnan, a member of another branch of the gang. One afternoon, Tang went to Wu's home to ask for the money and they ended up fighting. They immediately brought followers to the Era Teahouse (Shidai chashe) on One Heart Bridge (Yixin qiao) for "drinking settlement tea." Tang brought more than thirty soldiers and Wu brought more than ten. As soon as the mediator saw the situation, he tried to get the two parties to calm down and choose another day for settlement. Fortunately, this forestalled any immediate violence. This case motivated the police to implement severe measures to prevent violence in the belief that liaisons between the Gowned Brothers and soldiers were very dangerous.[23]

The practice, however, sometimes ended in disaster. In 1949, for instance, Xie Zhendong, the proprietor of the Moral and Prosperous Teahouse (Derong chashe), appealed to the government after being bullied by the head of the Gowned Brothers because of a dispute caused by "drinking settlement tea." According to his petition, he was a "good man whose neighbors know of no illegal behavior." Xia Zhongkang, who was head of a *bao*, captain in the militia, and head of a branch of the Sworn Brotherhood Society, had many followers and was responsible for security in the area, but "abused his power and disrupted peace and freedom." The problem began a week earlier, when a nearby resident asked Xia to mediate a dispute between his family members in Xie's teahouse. The mediation began in the morning and ended at 5 PM without success, at which point Xia left without saying a word. Xie had to clean the tables before the storyteller took the stage. However, when Xia came back after drinking wine he became angry because his tea bowls had been taken away and struck one of the teahouse workers, injuring him. After that, Xia and twenty to thirty members of his militia began drinking at the teahouse every day without paying. They also smashed tables and threw chairs, disrupting business. Xia even tried to have Xie arrested "by making up stories." Xie petitioned the government to investigate and clear his name.[24] This conflict took place on the eve of the Communist victory, when "drinking settlement tea" was still common. Although the purpose of "drinking settlement tea" was to solve a problem between two parties, in this case it caused a feud between the mediator and the teahouse owner. Xia was invited to settle a dispute among family members, which indicates that this custom was used to resolve internal as well as external disputes. Xia's identity as head of a *bao*, a captain in the militia, and a head of a branch of the Gowned Brothers, is significant. This gives us one more example regarding the background of mediators. When a teahouse keeper, such as Xie in this case, offended such an influential man, he found it difficult to defend himself and protect his business interests.

Although "drinking settlement tea" was accepted by the residents of Chengdu, it could not handle all cases fairly, and the many violent conflicts were reflections of this limitation. Some resolutions reflected the mediators' bias. Also, some mediators rendered a verdict based on the number and power of the supporters present. Hai Su witnessed a case of "drinking settlement tea" when a shop owner raped a girl from his neighborhood, and the girl's parents asked him to drink settlement tea. Because the shop owner gathered more people and had greater power, the mediator judged that the victim was at fault, blaming her parents for not disciplining their daughter and making them pay for the tea.[25] Of course, this may not be a typical case; if a majority of the settlements were unjust, the practice would have dwindled as people found other methods for resolving disputes.

In the late Qing era, the local government banned "drinking settlement tea" because it was thought to incite violence. In 1914, the police reissued the prohibition, which seemed to affect the bottom line of teahouses, and the *bang* of teahouses—the predecessor of the guild—pointed out that when several people drinking tea in a teahouse suddenly began arguing, it would "look like drinking settlement tea." This confusion could result in the government punishing the teahouse. To avoid these perceptions, the *bang*, representing all teahouses, appealed to the police to distinguish these actions from legitimate cases of "drinking settlement tea." But this practice never disappeared, so that in 1946 local authorities issued still another public notice that prohibited gatherings in the teahouse for "drinking settlement tea" and disturbing the public order. The government was unsuccessful in eliminating this activity because Chengdu's residents considered the teahouse their "civil court," where disputes were resolved before escalating into lawsuits, reflecting the community's self-control and autonomy, even though these had been continuously weakened since the late Qing era.[26]

The Gowned Brothers

The Gowned Brothers (*Paoge*)—the Sworn Brotherhood Society in Sichuan—adopted teahouses as their headquarters.[27] Prohibited during the Qing era, the Gowned Brothers acted openly during the 1911 Revolution, when they worked with the Association of Railroad Protection, whose flags flew in the teahouses where the Gowned Brothers had its headquarters (*matou*). The presence of the Gowned Brothers made these teahouses ideal locations for political activity at that time because it was easy to call for collective action. The Gowned Brothers were banned immediately after the 1911 Revolution, so they took their activities underground. Common sense would dictate that they would choose places that drew little attention, but the reality was different. In fact, most Gowned Brothers set up their turf in teahouses, many of which they established and owned, even though any activity that took place there was subject to scrutiny by the public or even agents of the government. Why did the Gowned Brothers choose such a public place? First, the government was never able to control them effectively; its regulations were implemented loosely, if at all. Second, teahouses were the most convenient place to have a meeting or make contact. Third, although the teahouse was public, its crowds and noise provided good cover for surreptitious activities. A covert action would not attract undue attention in a crowded teahouse. Therefore, the Gowned Brothers felt safe mingling with patrons. Also, communication with colleagues in a public space would not implicate the participants' family members if things went wrong. Fourth, the government and police often chose to ignore the Gowned Brothers as long as they did not cause major problems.

Local authorities recognized the importance of teahouses as the headquarters of the Gowned Brothers and the site of their illegal "black markets." For example, the Gowned Brothers smuggled gold, silver, U.S. dollars, and cigarettes into the Peace and Happiness Temple Teahouse (Anlesi chashe) during the day and into the teahouse of the New Commercial Center (Xin shangchang) at night (see Figure 6.2).[28] The government occasionally tried to cut the ties between teahouses and the Gowned Brothers. In the early

FIGURE 6.2: The Peace and Happiness Temple Teahouse. Detail from the scroll painting *Old Chengdu* (Lao Chengdu) by Sun Bin, Zhang Youlin, Li Wanchun, Liu Shifu, Xiong Xiaoxiong, Pan Peide, and Xie Kexin (2000). Courtesy of the artists.

Republican period, the police required all teahouses to pledge that they had no contact with the Sworn Brotherhood and bandits. The archival records from 1912 to 1914 contain more than two hundred of these pledges, all using the same language: "I pledge not to allow any members of the Sworn Brotherhood or other criminals to gather and conduct any activities there. I recognize that I will be punished if I violate this pledge."[29]

The Gowned Brothers developed unique gestures and argot, and often wore special clothing and carried special weapons, so they were not difficult to identify. Xiong Zhuoyun, a former member of the Gowned Brothers, said that when any member entered a teahouse, waiters immediately recognized his identity from his gestures and the way he carried and set down his tea. When members from different branches wanted to contact each other, they often showed their "red and black boards" (*hongfei heipian*) as a means of identification. The Gowned Brothers' method of communication in the teahouses was also called "showing secrets" (*liangdi*, literally, "showing the bottom"). An urgent and important letter would have a hole in it with a feather attached. Xiong was also the manager of the Quiet Orchid Chamber Teahouse (Jinglanxuan), which was opened by a branch of the Gowned Brothers. A common means by which members of the Gowned Brothers contacted other members was to play "tea bowl formations" (*chawan zhen*), which was an alternative to their secret language (Figure 6.3). The Regulations for the Inspection of Gambling, Thieves' Dens, the Sworn Brotherhood,

---

FIGURE 6.3 (right): "Tea bowl formations." Each of the formations (except the first and the last) is accompanied by a poem that gives the meaning or explanation of a formation. *From top right*: Seven Star Formation: "Usually used in drinking tea on ordinary occasions"; One Dragon Formation: "A lotus flower floating in the water / I use it to clean my cutter. / I swallow the Qing empire into my stomach / And blow it out as the blue smoke"; Two Dragon Formation: "Two dragons are happily playing in the water / Like Han Xin joyfully visiting Zhang Liang. / Today brothers meet here / Drinking tea before talking things over"; Peach Garden Formation: "Three deities came from noble families / Looking carefree. / Three swore as brothers in the Peach Garden / And sacrificed the black cow and white horse to heaven and earth"; Dragon Palace Formation: "Four oceans become pure and peaceful / Because our kingdom has many sages. / Crowned Prince Ne Zha goes to disturb the sea / Which makes the dragon king suffer." *From bottom right*: Conflict Formation: "Gold, wood, fire, earth, and water / These five elements are Rulai's power. / If you understand what happens in space / You will be a wise man in this place"; Six Kingdom Formation: "It was Su Qin who persuaded six kingdoms to unite / So everyone knew this feudal master. / If you have traveled many places / Come to the Hong family to recite poems and essays"; Treasure Sword Formation (without a poem). The names in the poems are historical or fictional figures. From Hirayama, 1911: 64.

All Walks of Life 181

and Heterodox Sects (Qingcha wodu, wodao, shaoxiang jiemeng, chuanxi xiejiao guize) enacted in the late Qing stated that police were to stop and question men who were in groups of three to five, wore strange clothing, had angry expressions, and acted violently. This description gives us an idea of how local authorities identified members of the Gowned Brothers.[30]

Li Ying, an "old teahouse-goer," claims that all of the teahouses in Chengdu's suburbs were the "turf of the Gowned Brothers." This might be an exaggeration, but it reflects a significant social phenomenon. Teahouses were where "dragon head masters" (*longtou daye*) held regular meetings of members

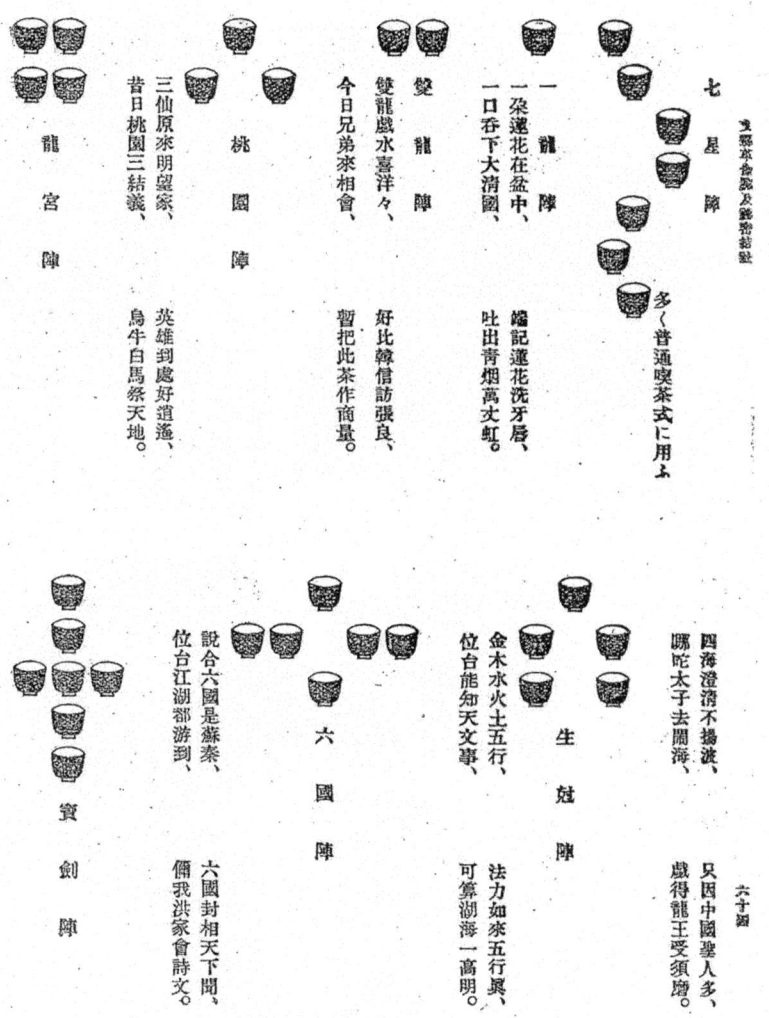

and ceremonies for important visitors, and discussed punishment for members who broke the gang's rules. The First Fountain Teahouse (Diyiquan) was the headquarters of a branch of the Gowned Brothers. Early every morning and at night, it bustled with noisy patrons who filled the room with a fog of tobacco smoke. When an important person entered, everyone who knew him would nod or bow while simultaneously yelling at the waiter to pay for his tea, which sometimes led to disputes. Fortunately, experienced waiters knew which patron should pay for the tea, and the situation would be resolved to everyone's satisfaction. Then everything went back to normal, with the cacophony of coughing, chatting, and calling for boiled water mingling with the calls of petty peddlers who sold fried melon seeds, peanuts, and cigarettes.[31]

As mere small business owners, teahouse proprietors were often targets of local toughs and powerful people who refused to pay, never returned chairs they "borrowed," damaged property, disrupted business, or even forced some teahouses to shut down. Therefore, teahouse keepers sought protection wherever it could be found, including from officials, policemen, military officers, and gangs. During the Republican period, the Gowned Brothers became the most popular source of protection. Many teahouses were established and owned by the Gowned Brothers, and most proprietors of other teahouses joined the Gowned Brothers for the purpose of security. In return, they had to supply a never-ending stream of gifts and special banquets to their protectors. The Prosperity Tea Hall (Huahua chating), for example, set aside money for Gowned Brothers and secret agents who helped prevent harassment and thefts by local toughs. Some teahouses, however, were immune to these difficulties because they belonged to powerful people, such as a few large teahouses on Warm Spring Road that were owned by military officers, policemen, or special agents.[32]

On the eve of the Communist Party's victory, the Gowned Brothers' power had reached into the government, the police, and even the military, resulting in a mutually dependent relationship with local authorities. According to one estimate, more than 90 percent of the Gowned Brothers chose teahouses as their headquarters or turf. Signs announcing "So-and-So's Turf" hung outside teahouses. As an investigation shows, of 119 headquarters identified, 36 were clearly located in teahouses and all others were identified as being located on specific streets, which were most likely also in teahouses. By 1949 there were total of 176 generals (zongshe) and branches (zhishe), many of which did not have specific meeting locations. Of these, 72 identified their headquarters as being in teahouses.[33] Sometimes a teahouse could house several branches of the Gowned Brothers. For example, a teahouse outside the New South Gate was the headquarters of the Fourth and Fifth Branches of the General Mass Benevolent Society (Qunyi zongshe). The Fourth Branch had more than one hundred soldiers as members, headed by a colonel under warlord Yang Sen, while the Fifth Branch had more than one hundred secret police agents.[34]

Mass violence in teahouses often involved the Gowned Brothers. In a case in 1946, four secret agents were sent to investigate a report that people were causing trouble in the Brocade River Teahouse (Jinjiang chashe) on Eight Treasures Street (Babao jie). About 4:30 PM, a fight over a debt broke out between two groups of Gowned Brothers, who wielded batons as weapons. More policemen arrived but were "overwhelmed by the number and strength" of the fighters. One officer saw that the situation was out of control and shot his gun twice into the air. The policemen finally arrested five of the primary fighters and five suspects. A total of eight people were wounded and sent to the hospital, including the mother and son of the teahouse owner. In the meantime, the security army sent a force to the area to maintain order and direct traffic.[35]

Because the police closely scrutinized teahouses, some of their reports include detailed information about the activities of gangsters. Private citizens also were encouraged to report suspicious activities. One of these reports, written in 1946 by shop owners on Long Fluent Street (Changshun jie), claims that the Tung-Tree Shadow Teahouse and Inn (Tongyin chalüdian) was a haven for smugglers of opium and guns where many "evil bullies" and hooligans used knives and guns and conducted illegal activities. The government had not responded to previous allegations. The situation had deteriorated since Wang Pinsan purchased the teahouse in the previous winter. The report charged that Wang illegally amassed "tens of millions" in wealth during the war. Wang had established his turf in Jianyang County and was said to have had more than ten thousand followers. Local gentry feared his power while ordinary citizens suffered from his bullying. His teahouse in Chengdu was his hub of operations and a gathering place for his followers. He also bought influence in the government and claimed that he received support from many prominent figures in the provincial and municipal governments, and thus was not afraid. The shop owners pointed out that Wang Pinsan ran the teahouse unlawfully because under municipal regulations a business license could only be used by the person to whom it was issued. The previous owner, Chen, had not returned the license to the government after he sold the teahouse, so Wang was operating the teahouse illegally. The government demanded that Wang submit his license and close the business within three days. But Wang Pinsan ignored the demand. His teahouse remained open and nobody else dared intervene. The biggest cause for concern for most residents was the "open turf time" (*kaili matou*) in the middle of every month, when thugs and criminals of every sort crowded into the teahouse. Shopkeepers and merchants were afraid that this would affect their businesses, but dared not confront them openly and instead reported it covertly to the government. They appealed to the government to close the teahouse and force Wang into supervised exile in his hometown in Jianyang County. They also asked the government to take away his license and punish the officials who took Wang's bribes.[36]

This case reveals that the Gowned Brothers sometimes had a very tense relationship with the neighborhoods they inhabited because of their illegal activities. Owners of nearby shops wanted to avoid direct confrontation and went to the government for help. Of course, this is just one side of the story. In fact, as we have mentioned many shops depended on the Gowned Brothers for protection and other services. On the one hand, the Gowned Brothers challenged the government's authority by conducting illegal activities, but on the other hand, the local government relied on the Gowned Brothers' extensive networks, which reached much deeper into the community than its own influence, to maintain social order. At any rate, this case reveals both how the Gowned Brothers openly used the teahouse for their illegal activities and the power of their influence in the community.

Class Distinctions

People of different classes mingled freely in the common space of Chengdu's teahouses. Therefore, some observers believed, one of the "virtues" of Chengdu teahouses was that they were "relatively equal." Indeed, teahouses were accessible to both the "idle class" (*youxian jieji*) and the "busy class" (*youmang jieji*); people who had nothing to do and those who had plenty to do went to teahouses to meet friends, conduct business, chat with other patrons, take a break, watch passersby, and seek other amusements, as discussed previously. In fact, teahouses were not as egalitarian as generally thought. Various accounts underscore that class distinctions were observed, although not as prominently as in other regions. Hu Tian, who wrote a guidebook to Chengdu, found that teahouses there were stratified according to the social status of their patrons. Another guidebook writer, Zhou Zhiying, also stated that the teahouses "where high society goes" were neater, with cleaner tables and fresher air; these included the teahouses in the Smaller City Park and the True Entertainment Garden (Zhengyu huayuan) on Warm Spring Road.[37] An essay in a local newspaper further confirmed the presence of class distinctions, stating that the crude and simple teahouses for the lower classes were usually located in poor areas away from the main streets and had only a few hundred yuan in capital. They had only a dozen tables and a few dozen bamboo chairs. By contrast, the teahouses on the main streets and scenic areas that served middle- and upper-class patrons were more elaborately decorated, with intricately painted tables and glass table-tops, and with "horse-shape chairs" (*mazhayi*) on which customers could lie comfortably. These teahouses had much more capital, ranging from 3,000 to 4,000 yuan up to 20,000 yuan, and could afford better and more expensive settings and utensils; their tea bowls, for instance, usually came from Jingdezhen, the source of the finest porcelain in China.[38]

During the late 1940s the Teahouse Guild classified all 618 teahouses into four groups: 33 were Class A; 348 were Class B; 150 were Class C; and 87 were Class D. From the list, it is clear that second-tier teahouses accounted for more than half of the total number; if Class C is included, these account for 81 percent (498) of the total. Both the highest and lowest levels were only a small proportion of the total number, while the middle tier that served many different kinds of customers was the most prevalent. This is probably why some people hardly recognized class distinctions. Class A teahouses were usually located in parks and prosperous areas. For example, there were six Class A teahouses in the Smaller City Park and three in Sun Yat-sen Park. The commercial area of Warm Spring Road, Main Mission Street, and the Commercial Center had ten such teahouses. Information on how teahouses were classified no longer exists. However, from the 1940 membership list of the Teahouse Guild, I have found that the amount of capital could have been one of the criteria. Other factors probably were the number of employees, the number of tables and chairs, total sales, and the amount of taxes paid.[39]

Class distinctions were also found in writings about teahouses. In his novel about late Qing Chengdu, *Before the Storm* (Baofeng yuqian), Li Jieren wrote that a few elites went to the Spring Tea Balcony (Tongchun chalou), but were given special seats in an area where tea was much more expensive. They sat around big dining tables that had tablecloths and vases. When Yi Junzuo visited Chengdu for the first time in the 1930s, he went to have a bowl of jasmine tea at the famous Two Fountains Tea Balcony (Erquan chalou) and saw that all patrons there were well dressed. In his memoir, Hai Su wrote that although Chengdu had many teahouses, people "went to the ones where they belonged" (*gejiu gewei*). Lower-class people "would never enter the huge teahouses while the wealthy would not even glance at small ones."[40] In Republican-era Chengdu, larger teahouses were usually high class, while small ones were lower class. Class distinctions were found even within a single teahouse. In Chengdu, some teahouses provided "elegant seats" (*yazuo*), usually in private rooms or separated by screens from regular seats. Because teahouses could provide different levels of service to different customers, they seemed "egalitarian," thus maximizing their business capacity.

An author wrote an essay about his own experience with how teahouse waiters treated customers based on their appearance. In Chengdu, there were two major distinctions in men's attire: those who did not depend on their physical strength to make a living wore long gowns, while those who did wore jackets. The author once wore a jacket to watch a local opera at the Joy Tea Garden, and the waiter did not greet him. When he humbly asked to buy a ticket, the waiter looked him over from the head to toe and replied that the tickets were sold out. However, just a moment later, some men in long silk gowns, accompanied by ladies who had permed hair and wore traditional Chinese dresses and makeup, entered the teahouse and went directly to the most exclusive seats on the front row. The waiter greeted them immediately and gave them tickets that he had in his pocket.[41] This case demonstrates the existence of class distinctions from another angle, although we have also found that most waiters tried to provide every customer the best service possible, as discussed in Chapter 3.

How patrons spent money in teahouses also reflected their economic situation. Once, a man "put on quite a show" by buying eight bowls of tea for others, to the surprise of everyone there because such displays of wealth were rare at that time. When Shu Xincheng visited Chengdu in 1925, he found that the city not only had a great many teahouses, but that the teahouses were large. Small ones occupied three to four rooms, while big ones could serve hundreds of customers in several dozen large rooms. I believe that Shu is describing the elegant teahouses found on the main streets, where customers were well dressed and clearly from the middle and upper class. Shu saw a few women wearing modern attire, but most were middle-aged men who wore long gowns. They, Shu guessed, "do not have to worry about earning a living, are not school aged, and have no occupation, so therefore they spend their time in teahouses." They usually went to the teahouses in groups.[42] Shu Xincheng probably never had a chance to visit lower-class teahouses in poor neighborhoods; however, he gives a lively description of teahouse-goers:

After being seated, the waiter will come up to take your order for tea and snacks. People who have money drink there, eat there, and even nap there. In addition, they buy newspapers to read, or discuss all kinds of news, both domestic and foreign, or recite poems. They also watch women and exchange stories about chasing them. When their stomachs are full and they feel tired, they lie back on the bamboo chairs and put all their hopes into wonderful dreams. When they wake up, it is sunset, so they continue their routine and go back home for dinner. After dinner, they begin their nighttime routine by going to theaters to watch local operas. Those who do not have enough money cannot do everything rich people do, but they can still stay in teahouses day and night for many hours and take naps there. They linger in teahouses much longer than do people in Nanjing.[43]

Shu Xincheng found that Nanjing had far fewer teahouses than Chengdu, and they served only middle- or lower-class people, who usually went there only during morning hours. Shu's description indicates that Chengdu's teahouse lifestyle was not dependent on class, but was universal.

Many small teahouses that served the lower classes were found on out-of-the-way streets and small alleys. Although these teahouses were not as profitable or desirable as those in better locations, they were sufficient for making a living. A teahouse, for example, was even opened under the stage of the Temple of the City God.[44] We can imagine that patrons who tolerated this cramped and noisy setting probably were not well-dressed gentlemen. The teahouses on the streets and alleys behind the main roads were very simple and crude, usually consisting of nothing more than a room that opened onto the street and had a few low tables and stools (Figure 6.4). They primarily served wheelbarrow pullers, sedan-chair carriers, and other manual laborers. Lower-class people felt more comfortable mingling with their own kind. The weavers who worked at the many workshops concentrated in the area of Half Side Street (Banbian jie) and Tobacco Bag Lane (Yandai xiang) during the 1910s frequented the teahouses on these streets. During the 1920s,

FIGURE 6.4: A street-corner teahouse. Detail from the scroll painting *Old Chengdu* (Lao Chengdu) by Sun Bin, Zhang Youlin, Li Wanchun, Liu Shifu, Xiong Xiaoxiong, Pan Peide, and Xie Kexin (2000). Courtesy of the artists.

Shaanxi Street (Shaanxi jie), Junping Street (Junping jie), and Wang Family Corner (Wangjiaguai) became a hub for weavers, and almost all patrons of the nearby teahouses were craftsmen who worked in weaving shops. Teahouses were also resting places for sedan-chair carriers, cart pullers, and other coolies; itinerant peddlers often stopped by a teahouse when they were thirsty or tired. When lower-class people could not find a job, a teahouse was the only place for them to kill time, adjust to life, and rest. The author of *New Chengdu* (Xin Chengdu) complained that people wasted time in the teahouse, but acknowledges that "it would not be reasonable to criticize laborers for staying in the teahouse."[45] Furthermore, as discussed previously in this chapter, many laborers found employment through the teahouses; for them, the teahouse was not a place of leisure, but a place of struggle for their livelihood.

Teahouses were always crowded, making them an ideal place for panhandlers, which indicates class distinctions from another angle. There were various styles of begging in the teahouse. A popular way was to "sell cool wind" by fanning a patron during the hot summer. This was actually another form of begging; if the recipient was pleased, he would give the beggar some coins. Some beggars simply extended their hands without saying a word, while some dropped to their knees before a potential donor. The majority sang and played instruments in the middle of the teahouse, and solicited donations when finished.[46] A local writer stated in "Observing Beggars in the Teahouse" (Chaguan guan'gai) that there were several forms of begging: forcing (*qiangpo shi*), piteously entreating (*aiqiu shi*), and silently entreating. He wrote, however, that one old man made the deepest impression on him by "telling lies with humor" (*huaji chehuang shi*), saying "Sir! I am a folksinger, but my throat is sore, so I have to beg. But this is my first time." This beggar also cleverly called everyone "boss." "Boss!" he would say, "Since you have such a successful business, wouldn't you care to give a few yuan?" He also told an obvious lie to amuse the person he was begging from: "I have never been a greedy beggar; for example, I didn't ask you for money the last time I saw you in the True Entertainment Garden (Zhengyu huayuan)." The writer admired the beggar's charm, even though he clearly was lying.[47] This story shows that beggars could make a person happy without resorting to obvious flattery. In this case, the beggar implied that his customer had high social status by saying that he saw him in the swanky True Entertainment Garden. Even though this was not true, the beggar would not risk offending the patron.[48]

Women

Women's experiences in the teahouses of Chengdu were vastly different than those in coastal cities, especially Shanghai. Restrictions against women were loosened much earlier in the coastal areas.[49] Women who appeared in public were treated differently in different parts of the country; for example, there were more restrictions in Beijing, where prostitutes were the only female customers in teahouses, but "it was common to find women in Shanghai teahouses" beginning in the 1870s. By the late Qing era, both men and women in Shanghai could attend shows, "though the seating was sometimes segregated." Audiences in theaters were seated around tables; women "chatted and gossiped" in what was often described "as a hotbed of women's freedom and sexual desire."[50] Women's frequenting of the teahouses in Chengdu was restricted by social custom before the late Qing reform and by the police after the emergence of the police force in 1902. Under the new rules, "women of good families" (*liangjia funü*) stayed away from teahouses. Of course, women were not excluded absolutely; they typically went to their neighborhood teahouse to buy boiled or hot water or to ask the stove keeper to boil meat for stew or to blend Chinese medicines. Elderly women faced fewer restrictions, because society paid more attention to unmarried and young married women. In addition, people paid more attention to middle- and upper-class women than the lower-class ones, who often worked outside their homes and appeared more often in public.[51]

In 1906, the Elegant Tea Garden (Keyuan) became the first teahouse to admit female patrons, but so many curious people stood at the gates to watch the middle- and upper-class women that overcrowding and fighting became a problem, and the police soon forbade the practice. Later, the Joy Tea Garden admitted women, but they had to use an entrance on another street. Women and men were segregated, with men occupying the main floor and women in the curtained balcony. The shadows women cast onto the curtain still attracted men's attention.[52] Both the Elegant and the Joy were reformed teahouses that became models of the new form of public leisure in Chengdu, but they were primarily for the middle and upper classes. The admission of women was an important milestone in Chengdu's culture. At first, women who entered the teahouses had to have enough courage to deal with gossip and stares, but the presence of elite women watching local operas in teahouses was common by 1911. Li Jieren, in his novel *Great Wave*, described how the protagonist, Chu Yong, a young educated man, went to the Joy Tea Garden with the wife of a member of the local gentry:

That day Chu Yong invited Mrs. Huang to the Joy Tea Garden to watch Peking opera. During the show, Chu, who was in the male area downstairs, wrote a note and asked a little boy who worked for the theater to take it to Huang upstairs. The neatly written note asked her not to eat any snacks, because after the show, he would wait for her at the exit for female guests on West Chinese Catalpa Bridge Street (Zitongqiao xijie) and they would go eat dumplings together at the entrance of the Center for Promoting Industry and Commerce. She read the note, then smiled and nodded at Chu from the balcony, which attracted the attention of a few men and one old woman, a worker who served female guests at the teahouse. She ingratiated herself with Mrs. Huang and asked her if she was sending a token of love. The old women even told her stories of how several others, including a concubine of a prefect, a mistress of a magistrate, and a few female students, wooed their boyfriends by depending on her and the little boy to carry letters and souvenirs.[53]

Although this episode is from a novel, it provides a vivid account of how people behaved in the theater on the eve of the Revolution. The scene takes place before Chu and Mrs. Huang begin their affair. They were relatives, so they had opportunities to go to the theater together, where, despite being seated in different areas, men and women could still see each other and communicate through servants. This passage also indicates that the theater became a place where elite men and women could socialize while watching shows, drinking tea, and eating snacks. The Joy also was in a good location, very close to the newest shopping mall, the Center for Promoting Industry and Commerce, where people could easily continue their nightlife after the show. Teahouses became a good place for socializing between the sexes, and some even played a matchmaking role for young lovers. This scene also shows how teahouse workers acted as go-betweens for "teahouse lovers." This phenomenon was written about extensively, which attracted more social attention. One essay described how teahouses became places for brokering marriages (*pitiao ke*) and "one-night stands" (*lushui fuqi*), and where, the article claims, "many men who had a bright future are led down the wrong track" and even "fall into the pit of hell."[54] Obviously, the author regarded public interactions between men and women as a vice and viewed them negatively.

The late Qing and early Republican era was a transitional period when the teahouse moved from being a male-only sanctuary to being open to both men and women. Li Jieren's novel depicted the situation in this transition; when Chu Yong walked with his lover, Mrs. Huang, to the gate of the Pleasant Spring Balcony (Yichunlou) in the Center for Promoting Industry and Commerce, he asked her join him inside to drink tea. Li Jieren then wrote:

It has become common for women from middle-class families to go to the Pleasant Spring Balcony and the teahouses in the Smaller City Park. However, high-society ladies who wear lots of makeup and splendid clothes do not want to lower their status by going to teahouses. Mrs. Huang, who is more open-minded and bolder than most, has visited the teahouses in the Smaller City Park a few times, but she did not have the courage to enter the Pleasant Spring Balcony and Memorial Garden (Huaiyuan) in the Center for Promoting Industry and Commerce, or the First Balcony (Diyilou), even though she had passed their gates several times. "It is not appropriate to go to the special seats (*tebie zuo*). You see, all of them are for men. Also, the window is wide open, with people coming and going." "Okay, let's go to the regular seats (*putong zuo*); there are some women there." Chu Yong looked across the big, crowded room and said with a little surprise, "Ah, there are quite a few women here!"[55]

The teahouse theaters were the first to admit women, but other teahouses soon followed. Although women still hesitated to enter teahouses where they would mingle with men, they seized the opportunity to enjoy more freedom in public. Teahouses encouraged women's patronage because the presence of women brought more male customers. When the Riverside Shadow Play Tea Garden (Linjiang yingxi chayuan) suffered a decline in business, for instance, it submitted a request to the police to allow women customers, but the request was denied. Business was good after the Game Stage Teahouse (Saiwutai) introduced an acrobatic act, but after female patrons were banned, patronage dropped dramatically and the show was cancelled. An article in the *Popular Daily* (Tongsu ribao) in 1911 reported that business was good at the Joy Tea Garden, although it did not mention if this resulted from the admittance of female customers. The article emphasized that the Eternal Spring Tea Garden would have doubled its profit if it had allowed women, which suggests a close relationship between women customers and profits.[56]

Women experienced many obstacles in their efforts to venture into public and enjoy teahouse life, and these came not only from the conservative tradition that forbade women to appear in public but also from the social reformers. A 1910 essay in the *Popular Daily*, titled "Women Should Not Go to the Theater" (Funü buke tingxi), articulates this notion. The writer expressed disappointment that "the social mood has been increasingly degraded" and criticized performers for trying to satisfy people's tastes in "unhealthy" programs. According to the author, audience members should enjoy the costumes, actions, gestures, and singing, but the atmosphere of teahouse theaters was unsuitable for such pursuits as people interrupted the performances by pounding on tables and shouting "bravo." The plots of these plays were "lecherous"; for example, the actor carried his pants in his hands, bit into a handkerchief (a common gesture by women when they were facing men), spoke with a sexy voice, made movements behind the bedroom curtain, unbuttoned his garment, smiled with a sexually expressive look in his eyes, and kissed and held the hands of an actor performing a female role. The author called these behaviors "real pictures of pornography" (*huo chungong*) and claimed that equality between men and women and free marriage were "evil ideas" that he was afraid might spread. The author worried about women's apparent dislike of "reformed," "civilized," and "healthy" operas. The presence of women in a theater attracted male patrons who came not to watch the play, but the women (see Figure 6.5). During the show, women and men cheered and made flirtatious gestures. The author urged "women who come from good families" and lacked social experience not to go to

FIGURE 6.5: "Local opera craze: Watching the show or watching women?" This illustration mocks those who go to the theater to watch women instead of watching the performance. The poem reads, "Women in the balcony, / don't turn your head. / Hurry to the front / and take big steps. / If no woman appears, / why do I bother to come here? / The reason I am here / is to watch beautiful women. / To say I come here to watch local opera / is wrong." From *Tongsu huabao*, no. 35, 1912.

the theater in order to avoid the bad influence of prostitutes there, and that their families should be held responsible for enforcing this. The author went on to complain that troupes ignored the law requiring government approval and performed many licentious plays, some even adding sexual content to attract patrons. If these plays were banned in Chengdu, women could go to the theaters outside the city. Therefore, the author called on men to exert authority over their wives: "Gentlemen who are literate, understand ritual, and care about morality and their reputations should control their wives and never allow them to go to any theater."[57] (See Figure 6.6.) As mentioned previously, women were first admitted to teahouse theaters in 1906, but this right was repeatedly abrogated. The conservative views of the new elites were a major obstacle to women's pursuit of public life. The reformist elites promoted other Western ideas, but not this one.

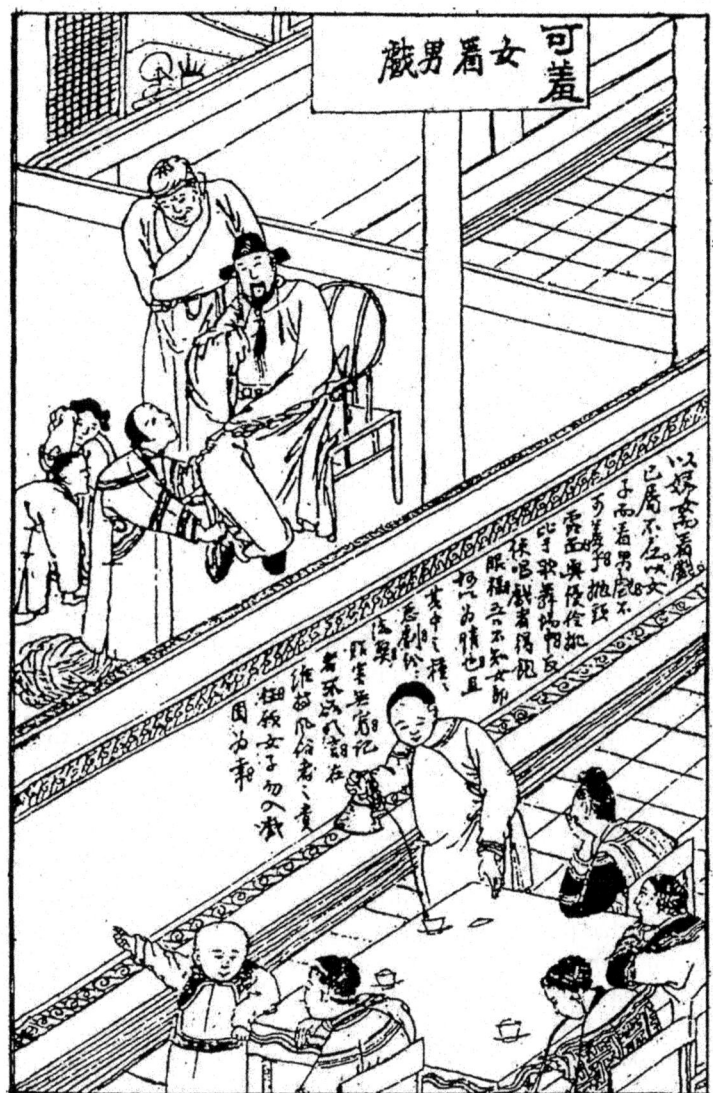

FIGURE 6.6: "Shameful! Women watching male performers." The inscription at the edge of the stage reads, "It is not right for women to watch local opera, but it is even more shameful for women to watch performances by men. Showing up in the theater, letting male performers have the opportunity to feast their eyes on women. There are many kinds of maladies in the theater, which entail untold troubles. Decent people should tell women not to enter the theater." In this picture, we can also see three-piece sets of teacups and how a waiter pours boiled water into a bowl. From *Tongsu huabao*, no. 5, 1912.

The police prohibited mixed-sex audiences after the 1911 Revolution, so some teahouses specified different times of the day, or different days of the week, for men and women customers. The Elegant Tea Garden (Keyuan), for instance, had "men's days" and "women's days." It sold tickets to women on the second, fifth, and eighth days of every ten-day cycle (so that women would be admitted on the second, fifth, eighth, twelfth, fifteenth, eighteenth, twenty-second, twenty-fifth, and twenty-eighth of each month, for example) and admitted men only on all other days. However, when the day for women fell on a Sunday, the teahouse would admit only men and the next day would be designated for women. Obviously, this arrangement was still for the convenience of men. Ads for the Eternal Spring Tea Garden in 1912 show that on September 22 and 24, day tickets would be sold to female patrons only, for 0.30 yuan each, and 0.10 yuan for servants who came with their mistresses, while tickets for children were half-price. The show lasted from 8 AM to 4 PM. Tickets for night performances were sold to male patrons only at 0.20 yuan, and the show started at 5:30 PM and ended at 9 PM. Apparently, this system did not encourage men whose main motivation was to watch the females in the audience. Although some teahouses admitted women customers, this custom was not common even by the mid-1910s. Mixed audiences seemed to generate energy and excitement, even if they were segregated. When an opera reached its climax, men often stood to watch the women, and women "tantalized the men with loud laughter," causing "disorder in the teahouse."[58] This disruption became another reason that social reformers opposed the mixing of women and men at the theater.

Women's gaining equal access to public spaces, including teahouses, was a long process in Chengdu. By the 1920s, the mingling of male and female patrons in teahouses was still not popular, but some teahouses provided segregated places for men and women.[59] In 1932, women were banned from the teahouses in Sun Yat-sen Park (Zhongshan gongyuan) because the government alleged that prostitutes had seduced "uneducated young men" and led them in the "wrong direction." Hooligans made trouble and caused fights when they harassed female guests. The park had to hire special guards to regularly check each teahouse, and violators were sent to the police. The park even asked the municipal government and the police to issue a public notice prohibiting women from patronizing the teahouses there "in order to keep public order." Of course, this ban hurt business, but "public order" was a greater concern. By the time the war broke out in 1937, teahouses were still basically a man's domain, and "more than 90 percent of patrons were male." Women customers, especially in suburban teahouses, were "as sparse as morning stars."[60]

Unlike most women, prostitutes were not reluctant to visit teahouses.[61] Prostitutes were forbidden in teahouses, but some challenged this law, risking public humiliation and punishment from the police. An account from 1914 shows how people dealt with the presence of prostitutes. Chen Yueqiu, a famous prostitute nicknamed Juicy Red Peach (Shuihong taozi), was once identified as she mingled with patrons at an opera in the Joy Tea Garden. Her identifier tried to ridicule her by writing on a blackboard that someone was looking for Chen Yueqiu. A teahouse worker carried the blackboard around the theater, which was a common way to find someone during a show. A policeman asked who wanted to see Chen Yueqiu, and the man answered. The surprised policeman asked, "Chen is a prostitute, so why did you come here to look for her?" The man replied, "She is here." The policeman finally found Chen on the balcony and took her to the police station. The man was fined two yuan for not reporting her to the police and for "frivolous and immoral behavior." Prostitutes nonetheless continued to frequent teahouses, and some teahouses turned a blind eye. This was the subject of an essay in the *Chengdu Bulletin* (Chengdu kuaibao) in 1938, which claimed that prostitutes sat by their customers, who were locally called "old masters" (gongye), "talking licentiously and laughing" (yanxiao yinlang) and "behaving frivolously" (judong qingfu). If the waiter refused to serve them, he risked being slapped on the face. The author of the essay concluded, "This is a serious issue, which cannot be solved only by displaying a public notice," and asked the government to intervene.[62]

People often regarded singers, in particular those from Yangzhou, as a kind of prostitute. During the war, many prostitutes from the eastern coast flocked to Chengdu as refugees and called themselves "refugee singing girls" (liuwang genü). They often appeared at the Three Sages Teahouse, the Two Fountains Teahouse, and other teahouses in prosperous districts. A few dozen singing girls performed at the Great Heavenly Singing Theater (Daguanghan gechang) when it opened in the Pure and Harmonious Tea Balcony (Qinghe chalou) in 1940. At night, on the bright stage, the girls sang songs at patrons' request for twenty yuan; the singers' share was eight yuan, with the balance going to the proprietor. Girls who never were called on to sing received five yuan. As soon as the Grand Heavenly Hall Singing Theater opened, according to one report, "many prostitutes went and registered as professional singing girls" (zhiye genü) to ensure their livelihood and prevent expulsion. During the war, the government forbade prostitution in public places such as restaurants and hotels, but, according to a critic, people who took "advantage of the national disaster" frequented the theater and mingled with prostitutes who claimed to be "a member of a singing girls' group" (peng genü). A bowl of tea that cost thirty cents in other teahouses cost three yuan in the Grand Heavenly Hall Singing Theater. When the show started at 6 PM, many "members of the group" (pengke) gathered to forget the ongoing bloody battles at the front lines as they watched splendidly dressed girls perform one song after another. One writer sighed with emotion: "During this national emergency, people still engaged in such a lifestyle, as if the war were happening only in a dream."[63] Although the commentator was expressing dissatisfaction, he also revealed that people continued to enjoy teahouse life even after the war.

The war was a turning point for women's appearance in the teahouse. While waitresses made a living there, as discussed in Chapter 3, female entertainers and customers found more space for their activities in the teahouse. For example, the New Deity Forest Teahouse (Xinxianlin), located on Main Mansion Street, in the central part of the city, sold "leisure tea" (*xiancha*) on the first floor and "performance tea" (*shucha*) upstairs. The teahouse hired female entertainers who came to Chengdu in 1937 as war refugees to sing selections from Peking opera. They wore colorful clothing and the programs announcing their performances were written with white ink on red paper. Customers paid extra to hear them sing, and many went there specifically for that purpose.[64] In the teahouses on the outskirts that especially served the people who had fled the city to avoid the Japanese air raids, many fashionable young women sat and mingled with men while drinking tea, chatting, reading, or playing cards. These female customers were treated as equals and attracted more men customers, who wanted to see the well-dressed women.[65] It seems that people tolerated the presence of women who had come to the city to save their lives, and that opportunities for women in public were one of the contributions of the downriver culture to the upper Yangzi region.

Conclusion

The teahouse was an arena that served different purposes for different individuals and groups. As we have seen, the teahouse was often a place for business by those in a specific trade. Chengdu did not have a trade center in the late Qing and Republican era, and teahouses filled this need even though they were scattered throughout the city. This plying of trades benefited not only the individual merchant, but also brought good business to the teahouse. Peddlers used the teahouse as much as merchants, but in a different way. Whereas merchants made deals through conversations, negotiations, and official documents, peddlers dealt at a more basic level by bringing their goods to sell. Therefore, it is not an exaggeration to call the teahouse a "market." Many people besides the entertainers discussed in Chapter 5 also depended on the teahouses to make a living. These included hot-towel men, tobacconists, fortune-tellers, barbers, earwax pickers, and pedicurists. We cannot find another public space that housed so many trades under one roof, especially in such a mutually beneficial and noncompetitive environment.

Social organizations adopted the teahouse as their office, which was the cheapest method of operation. Most did not have regular sources of income, and renting an office that might not be used every day was too expensive. The teahouse also was the most convenient meeting place for people who did not have a formal association or who shared common interests. Some merchants had the financial ability to build a guildhall for their native-place associations, but the majority who were not wealthy used a teahouse as their center of activities. As has been noted, people in the same occupations gathered in teahouses regularly to exchange information or just to chat. Teachers, students, scholars, actors, and laborers systematically organized themselves into their own groups when they chose a teahouse. These categorizations often had a practical basis; people often went to the teahouse for purposes other than leisure. For example, teachers gathered at the teahouse in the Smaller City Park to seek teaching contracts. The teahouse provided a place where all of the complicated processes of employment, including announcing vacancies, reviewing applications, conducting interviews and presentations, and undertaking negotiations could be carried out in one spot, like today's job fairs, but apparently more cheaply and efficiently.

The teahouse was not only an economic center but also a place for building a sense of community, strongly shown in the activity of "drinking settlement tea." One of the reasons this practice was so widely accepted was that judgments were rendered under public scrutiny, and mediators tried to be fair or risked damaging their reputations. Furthermore, violence in the event that a settlement could not be reached was thought to be less likely because the players were in a public place. Fights that did break out were often limited as bystanders stepped in to intervene. The activity of "drinking settlement tea" might also indicate that people did not trust the government and preferred to put their fate into the hands of mediators of their own choosing. Such a practice, of course, was not supported by the state. Whereas the state recognized social autonomy and did not disrupt this quasi "civil court" in traditional Chengdu, the modern state machine made this practice illegal, one of the measures by which it extended its power into the community and restricted local autonomy.

The government, however, was never able to completely control this practice. Through the late Qing and Republican periods, "drinking settlement tea" was common and played an important role in people's daily lives. Although this unofficial practice did not develop to a level that could challenge or jeopardize state power, its existence and social influence diminished the state's official power to some degree. In addition, this unsanctioned form of civil justice had only limited power, did not guarantee that outcomes would be fair or verdicts implemented, and was prohibited by the government. There is no question that this social force was very fragile compared with state power. However, cynicism might have been one of the reasons that these unofficial forces was ignored or downplayed. In fact, it is unrealistic to expect absolute justice from any source of mediation or to expect nonofficial sources to develop to the point that they can threaten state power. Given the nature of its activity and the environment where it was found, it is surprising that "drinking settlement tea" lasted so long and had such deep roots in society. It survived when many other social practices disappeared one by one under dramatic political and economic changes, attacks by the state, and radical ideological and cultural shifts.

The teahouse, as a public place, was adopted by the Gowned Brothers in another example of how teahouses welcomed all kinds of people. To a certain extent, it can be said that the Gowned Brothers helped teahouses prosper because they not only opened many of their own teahouses, but they also provided protection to numerous teahouse proprietors, and brought a large number of their members into teahouses for the organization's activities, in effect making them customers. The fact that teahouses became the headquarters of the Gowned Brothers complicated their role in society, and brought covert and surreptitious activities to a public place. Teahouses, for ordinary residents, were full of curiosities that added excitement and new observations to everyday life. The teahouse, of course, also popularized the Gowned Brothers and their activities by offering a place where they could coexist under the same roof. Although everyone knew that the organization was illegal, most people did not care. Ordinary people who sought protection from the Gowned Brothers, of course, easily found contacts for the organization at the teahouse. They, as teahouse-goers, might have already established ties with the society through waiters and other patrons. Thus, the teahouse became an important part of the Gowned Brothers' social network.

The process through which women earned the freedom to enter public places in Chengdu was long. During the Qing era, women were denied admission to teahouses under an unwritten law, but the restriction was gradually relaxed, symbolizing a new stage in the teahouse business. The appearance of women in the teahouse resulted from both social developments and women's struggle for equality. Ironically, social reformers set up more obstacles for women's rights in the teahouse. The stories in this chapter underscore how many decades this process took. Women were first admitted to a teahouse in 1906 but by the 1940s there were still obstacles to women patronizing teahouses. We have actually seen that two tracks coexisted in Chengdu through the Republican period: on the one hand, women earned some rights in the teahouse after years of struggle and as the attitudes of society at large changed; on the other hand, both elites and the government continued to discourage women from going to teahouses.

Prostitutes, of course, were pioneers of sorts because they defied conventions by entering teahouses, but when it came to women at large gaining free access they did more harm than good. Prostitutes went to teahouses at least as early as the Song and Ming periods. Many women hesitated to enter teahouses for fear of being mistaken for prostitutes. The government and police banned women from the teahouse by citing "immoral activity." Elites and local authorities used prostitution to justify the continued exclusion of women from teahouses. Prohibitions against prostitutes, which made it more difficult for them to earn a living, actually created a better environment for women customers of teahouses. Although prostitutes did not challenge the police directly, they adopted a strategy of "daily resistance," mingling with patrons despite the risk of humiliation and punishment. In fact, as a small business that struggled to attract customers, the teahouse welcomed all patrons, regardless of sex, and encouraged the admission of women, who always attracted male customers.

Teahouse life, in short, involved more than ordinary residents; it also included social associations and organizations. The teahouse thus served both individuals and groups. The teahouse, as a public space, became a fortification against modernist uniformity launched by the Westernized elites and the state. People who depended on teahouses for their livelihood dealt with the government regulations, forming alliances with individual patrons and other teahouses so that their operations could continue in the face of official restrictions. To a great extent, teahouses embodied a strong local culture that survived the reforms and radical changes of this time. The state, however, paid more attention to public collective activities than to the activities of individuals in consideration of the powerful social influence of the former. The residents of Chengdu succeeded in protecting their own interests, especially the use of the teahouse as a "civil court" by communities and as a "headquarters" by the Gowned Brothers. Although all kinds of regulations were enacted by the government during these years, the Gowned Brothers continued their activities in the teahouse and even flourished. Scholars have conventionally called these "secret societies," but in fact they acted almost brazenly, especially during the late Republican era, clearly indicating that their power far exceeded the government's ability to control them. The imposition of the uniformity of modernity and Western culture, however, did have an impact, as seen in the increasing presence of women in public nationwide. The inland city of Chengdu became more open toward women just as the state experienced significant achievements in terms of imposing its politics on the teahouses, as seen in Part Three of this book.

PART THREE

Teahouse Politics

CHAPTER 7

Conflicts in Public

The Oriental Tea Balcony on Warm Spring Road was managed by You Kangcheng, who rented from Yang Fenru, a rich silk merchant. You had rented the shop cum house two years earlier from Yang for five silver yuan per day. However, after a slump in business You owed Yang 54 yuan in rent. The week before, Yang went to the teahouse to demand payment, and struck the manager, Xia. When a patron tried to intervene and calm him down, Yang hit the patron, breaking his watch, and shouted, "This is none of your business! I don't care if I'm executed if I kill him." You was afraid of causing more trouble and begged Yang to extend the debt for another week. But a week later, You was still unable to pay it off. Yang arrived in the teahouse to collect the money and saw that Tang Hongxing, one of the teahouse workers, was taking down the wooden wallboards to get ready to open. Yang claimed that the door could not be opened until all debts were paid and tried to stop Tang, resulting in a fight. Yang beat Tang brutally, not stopping until Tang lay dying on the ground. Tang died, leaving his elderly mother, wife, and son, who suffered greatly and lost their main source of income.
 —*Guomin gongbao,* July 27, 1929

THE EPIGRAPH from the *Guomin gongbao* (Citizens' Daily) summarizes a well-known 1929 case, "Murder at the Oriental Tea Balcony" (*Dongfang chalou ming'an*). The savage public murder attracted a great deal of attention. Local newspapers covered developments in the case in a series of reports describing how the case was taken to the "heads of the neighborhood and community" instead of the police. Apparently, those involved initially tried to settle the case without involving the police by asking Yang to pay the costs of the funeral and burial, but Yang refused. This indicates that social mediation still played an important role in neighborhood and community life at this time, but it is surprising to see that a murder case, far beyond the scope of the "civil disputes" that social mediation usually handled, was still resolved internally. This obviously criminal case should have been reported to the police, but community leaders attempted as much as possible to prevent official intervention. If Yang had accepted the settlement, the case probably would never have attracted public notice. People were shocked and resented Yang's attitude, which resulted in a great deal of publicity.

According to follow-up reports, teahouse keeper You and Tang's family took Yang to the local court and asked for an autopsy. More than one thousand angry people turned up demanding justice when the court held an open hearing.[1] If this case had happened somewhere besides a teahouse and before the eyes of the public, it might not have drawn as much attention. People probably were furious for several reasons: they sympathized with the powerless teahouse worker whose sole focus was on serving customers; they were shocked by the brutality of the murder and the murderer's callousness; and they were concerned that the court would side with the party that was rich and powerful instead of delivering justice. Because the teahouse was a public place, anything that happened there could be reported in great detail, which provides useful material for historians studying public conflict. This case alone underscores the complicated relationships between waiters, teahouses, landlords, and the local community.

The full spectrum of social relationships and interactions, however harmonious or contentious, could be found in the teahouse. This chapter, however, deals with all levels of conflict, arguments, fights, and even mass violence. All sorts of people gathered in teahouses, for all sorts of purposes, making conflict inevitable. Conflicts could occur between patrons or between patrons and teahouse workers or even between teahouse workers and local authorities, but most were between patrons or teahouse workers and local toughs. These incidents took different forms, for various reasons, between various people, and had different outcomes. As a public place used by all kinds of people, the teahouse often was the scene of unexpected incidents. Also, most teahouses were small, and people crowded together without the physical separation that could help "cool down" a dispute. Furthermore, people sought solutions to their problems at the teahouse, such as through "drinking settlement tea"; when an agreement or solution could not be found, conflict or even violence often resulted.[2]

The teahouse, although mainly a place for leisure, business, and public life, thus also became an arena for the struggles associated everyday life. The teahouse was a microcosm of Chengdu, and anything undertaken there reflected the larger society. Conflicts in the teahouse, to a large extent, reflected current social issues. Fights broke out when people found it difficult to solve their problems or to make a living, or when they faced threats to their very survival, or when they were anxious or unhappy in the face of injustice, the deteriorating economy, hunger, insecurity, and war. On the other hand, conflicts also arose from the abuse of power and privilege and the tyrannical response to social turmoil by thugs, unruly soldiers, and outlaws. The first half of the twentieth century presented several such unfortunate periods. On the one hand, disputes usually reflected political turmoil, economic deterioration, or social dislocation—factors prevalent at the time but which lacked a direct connection to broader political, social, and cultural realities. Also, a majority of the conflicts involved civil disputes, but did not lead to violence. Some, but not all, of the examples in this chapter are cases reported to the government; their resolution ultimately depended on the will of the government or community. An examination of the types of conflict and the processes for addressing them provides a specific perspective on society and its problems. The government used the excuse of keeping public order to enforce various regulations that increased its control of the teahouse, part of urban reform since the late Qing and an effort to limit the use of such places or to ensure they could operate only under government supervision. These regulations resulted in a deeper penetration of the state into the city's social life, creating greater resistance from residents.

Daily Conflict between Patrons

Newspaper reports on conflict in teahouses were common in the late Qing era and even more prevalent during the Republican period. Some disputes resulted from minor issues such as gossip, which could be harmful as well as innocent. Gossiping satisfied curiosity about other people, adding novelty to the lives of the gossipers and bringing attention to the subject of the gossip. In some cases, gossip led to arguments or even violence. Some sociologists believe that "to be able to gossip together, individuals must know one another," and although gossipers do not have to be friends, "they must be familiar enough with one another to minimize intervening social distance," because gossip among strangers could be risky and might cause "dissatisfaction or misunderstandings which can make the further development of a social relationship difficult."[3] However, this was not exactly true in the teahouse, where strangers freely gossiped; verbal conflicts sometimes arose when the object of gossip was well known or a relative or friend of someone sitting nearby. In an article titled "Conflict while Drinking Tea," the *Popular Daily* (Tongsu ribao) in 1910 reported that gossip resulted in a fight among more than ten people in a teahouse on Square Street (Fangzheng jie), which required the intervention of the police.[4]

Even a minor dispute could escalate into violence. In the Joy Tea Garden, overcrowding caused fights over seats; a local newspaper mocked, "It was another drama played off stage accompanied by the deafening sound of songs and drums onstage." A similar incident happened at the Grand View Tea Garden (Daguan chayuan) when a late-arriving customer carrying a stool brushed against someone as he tried to pass through the crowd watching the show. Their argument ended in a fight during which they were injured and later arrested. Gambling on bird fights, which as has been mentioned in Chapter 4 was very popular in teahouses, also caused disputes, sometimes violent, over language, money, and behavior. Mere curiosity could also end in trouble in a teahouse. For example, when an actor who usually played young female characters (*xiaodan*) drank tea in the Pleasant Spring Balcony (Yichunlou) without first washing off his makeup, "a group of uneducated people" watched him through the window, blocking the sidewalk until policemen came. The *Popular Daily* reported this under the headline "Drinking Tea with a Powdered Face" (Fenlian chicha), noting that "both the actor and onlookers were shameless."[5] Apparently, elites took this opportunity to criticize people's public behavior but did not understand that because of the restrictions on actors in public places during the late Qing and early Republic, when they appeared in public they drew a great deal of attention and aroused tremendous curiosity. The case had nothing to do with social morality.

In 1913, Wu Longqu, a law student, wrote a letter to the Provincial Police Department to complain about mistreatment by the police at the Fragrant Taste Tea Garden (Pinxiang chayuan) that reveals some interesting information about the relationships between teahouse patrons, theaters, and the police. At the beginning of his letter, Wu wrote, "Local opera is one way of supplementing social education and also one way to enlighten uneducated people. Therefore, theaters should be regulated, and policemen should follow the law. Otherwise, theaters may be a bad influence." He then told his story. One evening, he and his friends went to the Fragrant Taste Tea Garden to see a play. After they were seated, they felt someone spitting on them from the balcony. Wu stood up and found six women sitting in the balcony. As soon as a policeman showed up, Wu asked why women had been allowed in the theater at night, when only men were permitted. The policeman denied that women were present, but Wu insisted that he investigate. They went to the balcony and found the women. Wu asked the policeman for his branch and badge number. The policeman and manager told him that he, as a student, had no right to ask these questions, and demanded that he show his ticket. Wu thought it unfair that the policeman not only did not investigate the allegation, but deliberately made the situation more difficult for him. Later, Wu went to the district branch of the police to file a report, but the officials there claimed that all the women were family members of shareholders, not regular patrons. Then the chief asked Wu to get a guarantor. Surprised, Wu asked why this was needed since he had not violated any laws. Wu wrote, "Such an ignorant chief did not know the meaning of the term *republic* and encroached on people's freedom. He did not fulfill his duty and hindered the enforcement of the Republic's laws." Wu insisted the police should enforce the law prohibiting women customers—even those related to shareholders—at night and that the theater's only interest was profits. "If the police let this situation go without taking it seriously, other teahouses in the city will follow and the damage to society will be severe," Wu wrote.[6] It is interesting that the policemen did not take the regulation seriously and were challenged by a young student. As discussed in Chapter 6, there was a period immediately after the 1911 Revolution when male and female audiences were admitted to shows at different times. For some reason, the police ignored this violation and accused the student of causing trouble; they probably had a special relationship with the teahouse or received favors. The student's motivation is unclear, but there are at least two possibilities: he might have been conservative and opposed the presence of women in the teahouse, or, as a student of the law, he might have sincerely believed that regulations should be enforced.

Such important social groups as workers and students also contributed to the turmoil. The workers of Chengdu's few modern factories, like almost everyone else, frequented teahouses although they, unlike those whose work schedules were flexible, tended to go to the teahouses after work and during weekends and holidays. Like other residents, they also preferred to hold their meetings and social gathering in teahouses, which also occasionally led to conflict. In January 1941, for example, the proprietor of the East Garden Teahouse (Dongyuan chashe) reported to the Teahouse Guild damage by a group of factory workers. Late one afternoon, a few hundred workers from a nearby factory rushed into the teahouse and ordered 365 bowls of tea. For reasons unknown, an argument escalated into violence as the workers threw bowls and broke chairs before running away. The teahouse suffered extensive damage for which it was not compensated. The proprietor asked the guild to seek reimbursement from the people involved.[7]

Students also could be troublemakers. In December 1946, several dozen students from Sichuan University, described by the teahouse manager as a "mob," destroyed the Chinese Flowering Crabapple Teahouse (Tangyuan chashe). The manager listed his losses for the court and the police in a document co-signed by the head and assistant head of the *bao*, the head of the *jia*, and six neighbors, to sue the students for compensation. The Provincial Police Department ordered the local police "to settle the dispute and, in order to maintain security, make sure that the students no longer have any conflicts with merchants and residents."[8] Another case involved a college student at the Violet (Ziluolan) Teahouse who expressed his disappointment at "students' moral degradation" when he saw two groups of students arguing. Some of the students followed him after he left and beat him, injuring his face, tearing his shirt, and stealing a gold ring. The police arrested one of the culprits, a middle-school student.[9] In Chengdu, students were considered well-educated, model citizens, but these cases indicate that this cohort was not as peaceful as people expected, and had conflicts not only among themselves but with others. Although the record does not provide detailed information about these students, it would not have been unusual for spoiled upper-class students to misbehave in public, causing conflict with other groups and their own kind. During the late 1940s, students organized one protest after another in the face of political instability and the stress of the Civil War. The Communist movement was widespread among students, who increasingly turned to the left politically. The government, concerned that mundane nonpolitical conflicts might escalate, watched students closely. After the incident in the Chinese Flowering Crabapple Teahouse, the Provincial Police Department issued the following statement: "Students occasionally have disputes with merchants and residents, which are inevitable. Sometimes, because we did not handle these disputes very well, they became huge problems. Therefore, it is very important that the police address issues quickly to reduce the likelihood that a situation will escalate."[10]

At the same time, when people desperately struggled to survive, thefts in the teahouse rose dramatically. Petty thieves constantly stole tea bowls and other utensils, which they usually sold. The better teahouses used bowls made in Jingdezhen, which produced the best porcelain in the country. Saucers ("tea boats") also were stolen, most likely because they were made of brass, which was prized by second-hand dealers. With the deterioration of the economy in the 1940s, thefts became more frequent. Xiong Zhuoyun, former manager of the Cry of the Crane Teahouse (Heming chashe) in the Smaller City Park, recalls that the teahouse lost around ten thousand saucers when he worked there. In 1947, the Teahouse Guild reported to the police that "teahouses suffer an enormous loss" from theft and requested that anyone caught stealing be sent to a labor camp. Of course, thefts increased as the economy declined, but the teahouse environment might also have given thieves more opportunities. For example, electric lights were relatively new and the power supply was often unstable; during power outages, thieves had an opportunity to steal under the cover of darkness. In 1949, the guild represented the Prosperity Tea Hall (Huahua chating) in asking the government for protection against theft, pointing out that items were most often stolen during power outages.[11]

Teahouses implemented many strategies to prevent theft, including assigning more employees to watch over the property, but without great success. As a result, some created novel ways of preventing property loss. In

1948, for instance, the Pleasant Wind (Huifeng) Teahouse became a market for silver yuan, which attracted many thieves. The teahouse trained a parrot to yell, "Stop thief!" repeatedly, which was said to have been successful in scaring away many thieves. In 1949, some high-level teahouses began using bowls engraved with the names of the teahouses and announced in the local newspapers that anyone caught selling them would be reported to the police. The Teahouse Guild asked every authority in Chengdu, including the court, the municipal government, the police, the security army, the army police, and the Chamber of Commerce, to support this plan and issued a public announcement asking people and teahouses not to buy contraband bowls and lids and to report those in possession of these items to the police.[12]

When teahouse managers got their hands on thieves, they demanded reimbursement of their loses or turned the thieves over to the police. But sometimes they treated them especially harshly, subjecting them to physical torture and public humiliation. It appears that would-be thieves who were tied to a pillar and cursed at and humiliated by teahouse workers and patrons received very little sympathy. However, there were exceptions. The manager of the New Tea Garden (Xin chayuan) on Great Peace Street (Daan jie) caught a man who had stolen more than twenty sets of tea bowls. Surprisingly, the manager did not punish him but instead treated him to a meal and cigarette. This exercise in reverse psychology was effective; the thief not only apologized and offered to pay a fine but also said that he wanted to return more than thirty sets of bowls that he had stolen previously. The newspaper called this action "using goodness to dissolve badness."[13] The teahouse keeper was a wise man. Most people stole because they were poor and desperate, driven by hunger and cold. They created far fewer headaches than the pervasive violence of tyrannical rogues and soldiers.

The Struggle to Make a Living

Many people, from proprietors and waiters and waitresses to water-carriers and performers, struggled to make a living in the teahouse. Teahouse managers were wise to encourage peddlers, barbers, earwax pickers, shoe polishers, fortunetellers, folk performers, and others to do business there because they not only received a deposit, but also because these peddlers provided services that the teahouse was otherwise unable to offer. Teahouses usually gave the privilege of providing these services to more than one man—often to a few or even more—but limited space led to intense competition for business. In addition, the teahouse manager had to deal with other aspects of running the business, such as debt service, supplies, customers, local toughs, and so on. Many conflicts in the teahouse, however, resulted from minor matters between people who made a living there, or between peddlers and the teahouse management, between teahouses and nearby residents, or between teahouses and other institutions, such as the local authorities, over regulations and rights.

Teahouses often fell prey to internal disputes regarding issues such as management and profit distribution.[14] Individuals who wanted to open a teahouse typically raised money from various sources, and disputes arose between teahouse owners and shareholders.[15] Some conflicts erupted between proprietors and contractors, such as an incident that took place in the Wind and Cloud Pavilion Teahouse (Fengyunting chashe) in 1928. Woman Wu, who owned the teahouse, accused Ma Shaoqing of stealing tea bowls. Ma in turn claimed that Wu made a false allegation because she wanted to terminate the agreement that allowed him to sell tobacco in her teahouse so that she could offer the privilege to someone else. Wu reported the case to the heads of the streets, also accusing Jin Huazhang, Ma's guarantor, who was owner of the Moist Soil Tea Garden (Runyu chayuan), of helping Ma sell the booty while asking Jin to settle the dispute. The militia of Fragrant Herb and Fountain Street (Chaiquan jie) arrested Jin, but Jin argued that he had nothing to do with Ma's actions and as a guarantor was not responsible for his conduct. The militia beat Jin with heavy rods and chained his feet to force him to reimburse Woman Wu. When Ma saw that his guarantor had been implicated and attacked, he agreed to pay for fifty sets of tea bowls. Jin, severely injured, was released after Ma and Wu reached this agreement. Jin later accused Wu of plotting a trap and the militia of arresting and torturing innocent people. The police ordered the militia head to punish Jin's attackers, but the head refused, causing "public resentment" among the militia on Jin's street. Jin's local militia and the street head petitioned local authorities for justice.[16]

There is no way to know if Ma Shaoqing actually stole the tea bowls or if Woman Wu deliberately made a false allegation, but this case underscores the conflict that was typical among those who worked in teahouses, as well as some general business practices. Ma said that he paid rent in exchange for selling tobacco, but another tobacco peddler became jealous and tricked Wu into breaking this agreement. Ma refused to go along on the grounds that he paid his rent on time and the agreement was still in effect, which led Wu to accuse Ma of theft. Although there is no way to confirm the accuracy of Ma's claims, from his statement it is clear that Ma paid Wu for the right to sell tobacco in the teahouse. We also learn that selling tobacco was competitive; when one peddler found a teahouse where business was good, others might try to force their way in. However, there was an unwritten law in which the teahouse proprietor established an agreement that gave a peddler exclusive rights to the teahouse, and as long as the peddler paid his fees on time, the manager would honor the agreement. To conduct business, a peddler had to have a shopkeeper as his guarantor to be held responsible for his actions. This general practice in traditional Chinese cities helped shops build a bond of mutual security and made control by the guilds and local authorities much easier. In this case, we learn that women could run teahouses and that gender was not necessarily an issue when disputes arose.

The militia's involvement in the community is another notable phenomenon. This example involves conflict between two militias in different areas, which would have generated more attention. Even the *Citizens' Daily* (Guomin gongbao) reported this incident under the headline "The Wind and Cloud Pavilion Teahouse Loses Tea Bowls and Two Branches of the Militia Lose the Peace." The newspaper probably considered the "lost peace" between the two militia groups more important than the theft or accusations. This case is also a good example of how the teahouse, as a microcosm, reflected the problems of the larger society. In addition to the general business practices this case illustrates, it also gives us a sense of the local militia, its role in the community, and how the local community handled conflicts between neighborhoods. Such social organizations, which changed constantly with the political situation, provided security in neighborhoods.[17] In traditional Chengdu, local security was often provided by street or neighborhood organizations headed by elites. During the early Republican era, these organizations became less influential as the state extended its power to the local level, but they continued to play a role, especially during chaotic times. The local government's relationship with these voluntary associations was complex; when it did not have enough resources, it encouraged citizens to organize for their collective defense. But when the political and social situation stabilized, the government tried to weaken or even disband such groups. From this case, we find that these organizations were still in place in March 1928, when the incident at the Wind and Cloud Pavilion Teahouse took place, a few months before the municipal government of Chengdu was established and formally took over this function. Although Chengdu's residents had a strong collective identity, they still sought to continue to protect the interests of their own streets or neighborhoods when necessary, which is why Jin's fate caused the two militia branches to "lose the peace."[18]

Teahouses, Their Neighbors, and Local Authorities

A teahouse not only faced competition from other teahouses but also had to deal with social forces. Disputes often arose between the teahouse and its employees or local authorities, especially the police. The police used every means possible to get money from teahouses, which caused resentment and resistance.[19] Teahouses paid their fees in different ways, including providing free tickets to the police. For example, the Joy Tea Garden presented a popular play in which the character of a prostitute sings a song that was very well known because the 1930s movie star Zhou Xuan had sung it in a movie. Typically, the police chief would send someone to the theater before the show to pick up the tickets. Once, when the theater did not provide enough free tickets, policemen went back and stopped the performance, claiming that the role of a prostitute was harmful to social values. The actress was already onstage and the audience was eager to see what would happen next. The manager then walked on stage and apologized, saying that the show had just been banned by the police. Several policemen jumped onto the stage and beat him, and the theater fell into chaos.[20]

Although teahouses and nearby residents were mutually dependent and maintained close ties, conflicts could arise. In 1937, several residents of Ningxia Street, concerned about the fire risk, reported to the municipal government that a teahouse on their street was violating the rules. They claimed that the teahouse, which was between a school and a residential complex, was small, with walls of thin bamboo strips. Furthermore, every morning and evening, tables and chairs were placed on the sidewalk and in the road, blocking traffic. The residents worried that a fire during the hot summer would be catastrophic because people would not be able to evacuate quickly. They also complained that "good and bad men intermingled" at the teahouse, and that robbers used the teahouse to gain access to the school and homes. They urged the government to regulate the teahouse. This case was not unique. In another example, from 1949, a resident accused the Near Sage Tea Garden (Jinsheng chayuan) of "illegal trade," including gold smuggling and gambling. Many people gambled on mahjong there, which led to frequent conflicts. The resident who complained, a woman identified by name, asked the government to investigate and suppress these activities.[21] The fact that her letter was not only signed but also sealed suggests that this woman was free to express her opinions. These two cases indicate that some residents feared that they would be affected by the misconduct that took place in teahouses.

In March 1946, a teahouse proprietor and a resident got into a violent dispute over a loan. We know two versions of their story. Xu Shaoqi claimed that Liu Fujian, owner of the Cold Winter Teahouse (Suihan chashe) on North East Street (Beidong jie), owed him 6,200 yuan, which resulted in constant arguments between the two. One day, Liu asked Xu to go to his teahouse to get the money. Liu, however, had gathered more than a hundred "corrupt soldiers" and hoodlums there. Liu pistol-whipped Xu, took 56,000 yuan from him, and ran away. Xu immediately complained to the police, saying that "teahouse owner Liu Fujian brazenly gathered people to do violence and stole other people's money, disregarding the law." The police apprehended Liu and closed his teahouse. At this crucial moment, the Teahouse Guild intervened. Guild president Wang Xiushan provided a different story in his letter to the government. Based on the guild's investigation, Wang said, Liu, Xu, and a friend of Xu's drank wine in a wine shop without incident before the alleged attack and agreed that Liu would pay the debt as soon as possible. After they left the wine shop, Xu's friend suddenly claimed that he was the real originator of the loan, and demanded that Liu pay the money that very day, which was impossible. This resulted in an argument between Liu and Xu and Xu's friend that turned violent until passersby separated them. The guild also denied the charge that Liu had assembled a crowd in the teahouse, claiming that the fight took place quite a distance away. Moreover, the letter said that Liu's teahouse was too small to hold that many people and that if this event had been premeditated, it is unlikely they would have met earlier in the wine shop. The guild also claimed that Liu had not stolen Xu's money, based on reports by neighbors who saw Liu at home after the incident and saw him later leave with his friends to buy supplies for the teahouse, not to escape from the scene of a crime. The guild accused the police of arresting Liu and closing his teahouse to prevent him, his family, and his employees, from being able to make a living. The guild asked the municipal government to order the police to allow the teahouse to reopen, noting that Liu would not be able to pay off the debt without an income.[22] As is often the case, it is now impossible to know which version of events was true and how the issue was resolved, but this case at least reveals the unfortunate situations that teahouses and their keepers sometimes faced. Also, from this case, it is clear that the guild, which was clearly more powerful than a single individual, could provide assistance. At least the guild put forth an explanation that favored the proprietor.

Some well-known teahouses, such as the Joy Tea Garden, also had tense relationships with certain residents at certain times. In May 1945, a letter signed simply "some residents of the street" was sent to the municipal government, describing in detail "all sorts of illegal conduct" at the Joy, including a "secret opium-smoking den." The letter claimed that several workers at the Joy were addicted to opium, and that the manager, Leng Yuanfeng, had set up a secret area for them in the employees' room. The letter also claimed that gamblers—including Joy employees, opera lovers, and local thugs—used a "secret gambling room" day and night and paid kickbacks to the Joy. The letter also claimed that a gambler's cigarette once caused a fire, which did not lead to serious damage only because the fire brigade responded quickly. The anonymous residents worried about the enormous damage a fire could wreak on the concentration of shops in the area. The residents also claimed that the teahouse likely would collapse due to poor maintenance if a fire broke out, and patrons would not be able to escape through the narrow exists. The writers rebuked the Joy for "loving money more than anything else." Another charge was tax evasion. The letter claimed that business at the Joy "was better than others in the same trade," but that the manager reported much less than the actual profits. Finally, the letter asked the government to "severely punish the Joy to send a message to other violators." The government sent a few officials to investigate, but they found no evidence of gambling or opium smoking, even after conducting both "open and secret investigations." In addition, the head of the *baojia* and neighbors wrote a statement that no fire had occurred there. The manager of the Joy also signed a pledge that he would be willing to be punished if any of these charges were proven to be true. The investigators checked all the accounting records from January to April but found no evidence of tax evasion. However, the investigators did find that the facility, built during the reign of the Guangxu Emperor (1875–1909), had structural problems, including a balcony that was in poor condition and might collapse under certain conditions. Furthermore, the alley outside the theater—which provided the only entrance and exit—was long, narrow, and tortuous, and crowded with vendor stalls on both sides, creating a serious traffic impediment. The report recommended major improvements in these areas.[23]

From the existing archival materials, it is difficult to determine the truth, or why residents lodged such serious accusations against the Joy. It is impossible to determine if the Joy gave favors to or otherwise bribed investigators. However, this case at least provides an example of a tense relationship between a theater and nearby residents. If the anonymous charges were not true, then the letter illustrates the desperation of someone, perhaps a business rival, a revenge-seeker, or someone jealous of the Joy's success, who wanted to force the teahouse out of business. The language used in the letter suggests that envy was the primary motivation; for example, the writer requested severe punishment and an end to the Joy's "haughtiness and arrogance" (*jiaojin ziman, mukong yiqie*). As the most prestigious theater, the Joy might well have been thought of as "haughty and arrogant," which could offend some people. Finally, how many people contributed to this letter is unknown; it is signed "some residents of the street," but it could have had a single author.

Teahouse Life under the Shadow of Violence

Bullying and other such behavior by local toughs—such as members of the Gowned Brothers, hooligans, and soldiers—were a constant threat in teahouse life. Thugs often drank tea without paying or damaged teahouse property. Actors and actresses, as well as waiters and teahouse proprietors, were often badly treated by these local toughs. Such incidents were increasingly reported in the local newspapers and also appear in the archival records.

As seen in the case of the Oriental Tea Balcony mentioned in the epigraph to this chapter, teahouses were sometimes the scenes of murders, which reflected social turmoil and reminded residents of the country's deteriorating social and political condition. Periods of political turmoil usually weakened the government's ability to maintain public order, which encouraged illegal activity. Hoodlums, prostitutes, and others often gathered in the teahouses near theaters or on streets away from the main roads, and provoked many disputes, ranging from fighting for a man's favors to showing off with guns, which sometimes ended tragically (see Figure 7.1).

The following are just two examples of routine news reports in the late 1920s and early 1930s, a period of warlord domination in Sichuan. One evening, when a teahouse inside the Prefectural City God Temple (Fu chenghuang miao) was most crowded, someone stabbed a man in the chest without warning, killing him instantly, but managed to escape. In another case, a man ran into the teahouse on the corner of Date Tree Street (Guaizaoshu jie) and shot another man, who ran madly after him out onto the street. The assailant fired two more shots and the victim died, his blood spread everywhere on the street.[24] These two cases inform us that guns and knives were used in crowded teahouses. These two murders were not random or crimes of passion, but the deliberate acts of killers who sought out their victims. It appears that the murderers did not care that their actions were conducted under the eyes of the public or that their violence could harm other patrons. Newspapers often did not have information regarding motives, and usually reported that the crime was a "hate killing" or a "revenge killing" (*chousha*). Violence most often resulted from conflicts between branches of the Gowned Brothers or between others fighting over women, property, or money.

One day in August 1943, several ruffians (*liupi*) ordered tea at the Confirmative Tea Balcony (Buer chalou), telling waiter Lü Qingrong that they would pay later, but then they sneaked out while Lü was serving others. Lü had to pay for this loss from his own pocket. The next day, the same group returned and Lü chased them when they tried to sneak out. But the thieves claimed that Lü made them lose face in public, so they not only refused to pay, but they savagely pistol-whipped Lü until he was black and blue, and one of them fired a shot into the air to intimidate bystanders. Those who knew Lü said he was "a trusting and kind man" who "has never had any trouble with his customers" since going to work in this teahouse many years earlier.[25] This incident reveals the vulnerability of waiters. They could not afford to lose money, but if they tried to protect their interests, as Lü did, they risked being assaulted or even killed. The huge number of refugees and veterans who flooded into Chengdu during the war contributed to social disorder, which the police failed to control. Workers had to depend on their own organizations such as the union or secret societies for protection.[26]

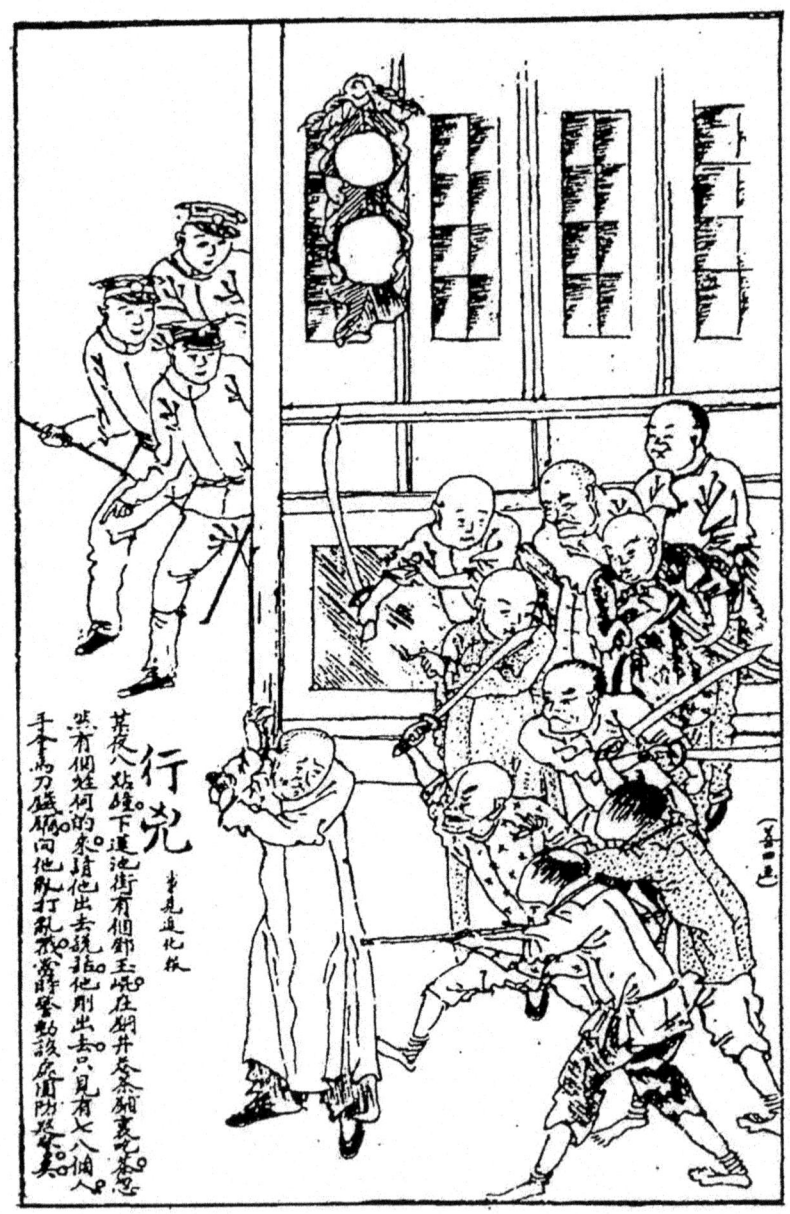

FIGURE 7.1: "Doing violence." The inscription reads, "When Deng Yukun was drinking tea in a teahouse on Copper Well Alley (Tongjing xiang) one evening, a man named He called him out for a talk. As soon as he went out, seven to eight people beat him viciously with sabers and iron rods. The police rushed in to stop them." From *Tongsu huabao*, no. 29, 1912.

Mass violence also took place in teahouses, and mobs even dared to fight policemen. For example, a fight once broke out during a performance at the Grand View Tea Garden (Daguan chayuan), immediately plunging the theater into chaos. The police, overpowered by the mob, retreated. Some audience members were wounded, some tried to hide, some ran for help, and some remained frozen in shock as tea bowls, tables, chairs, and other items were destroyed. Some violent incidents took place during failed attempts to "drink settlement tea." One afternoon in 1946, for example, Yang Jinglu, a master of the Gowned Brothers, led more than two hundred people to the Dragon Friends Teahouse (Longyou chashe) to drink settlement tea. When the parties could not reach an agreement, Yang and his followers savagely attacked their opponents, killing two. They then robbed the teahouse, resulting in significant property loss.[27] In April 1948, the Teahouse Guild asked the municipal government to punish and demand restitution from the ruffians who severely damaged the Great Northern Tea Hall (Dabei chating). The guild reported that several dozen ruffians rushed into the teahouse one evening, brandishing pistols and hand grenades. They guarded the front and back doors and did not allow anyone in or out while they beat their intended victims. Later, a large number of policemen arrived and arrested the troublemakers. The guild pointed out that "the teahouse is a public arena," where "order should be maintained by the government." If a similar incident happened again, "the consequences would be unthinkable." Therefore, the guild asked the government to protect the business so that it could continue to operate.[28]

Although the government tried to maintain public order, it seems to have found only limited success in combating violence, from bullying to murder, by both individuals and groups, in teahouses. However, the threat of violence never kept residents from going to the teahouse and customers learned to deal with occasional chaos. Teahouses persisted in doing business despite the constant risk of property damage and loss. But these examples reflect just a portion of the magnitude of trouble the teahouse had to cope with, and in fact, the teahouses in Republican Chengdu faced another, much tougher enemy: corrupt soldiers.

Corrupt Soldiers and Wartime Turmoil

Beginning in the 1911 Revolution, when rioting Qing soldiers looted the city and burned down its most prosperous areas, corrupt soldiers had became the most dangerous threat to security in Chengdu. During the chaotic warlord period, Chengdu experienced one disaster after another as the result of wars and the actions of warlords and out-of-control soldiers.[29] These soldiers, locally called "corrupt soldiers" (*lanbing*) or "hoodlum soldiers" (*qiuba*), became residents' worst nightmare. The volatile situation improved slightly after the GMD unified China in 1927 and the Chengdu Municipal Government was established in 1928, but teahouses and teahouse life never escaped the reach of the criminals and brutal soldiers who tyrannized even the local government and police. Teahouses were intimidated into giving soldiers special treatment, but favorable treatment from the government and police did not entirely prevent trouble.[30]

Soldiers on leave often invaded teahouses, gambling and arguing, hurting business and scaring customers. According to a newspaper report in 1930, five verbal conflicts occurred on one morning alone in a teahouse, and a violent fight in which tables and chairs were used as weapons took place that afternoon, but the culprits fled when military policemen arrived. The soldiers caused significant damage to the teahouse and threatened nearby residents and businesses.[31] "Hoodlum soldiers" harassed women and fought each other for power and revenge in teahouses. For example, He Yingfa, a low-level officer, and several soldiers chased a young woman in Sun Yat-sen Park one afternoon in 1932. She ran into a teahouse to escape, but the men followed and sat beside her, relentlessly harassing the embarrassed and frightened woman. Another man ran outside for help. A moment later, several soldiers, led by a man in civilian clothes, arrived and caught He and two soldiers, but He managed to get free. The man in civilian clothes fired at He three times as he ran to the back door. He died instantly but his assailant ran out of the park and disappeared after getting in a rickshaw. The people still in the park tried to escape and a police squadron searched the park in vain.[32] This case remained a mystery because the shooter's identity was unknown; was he a secret agent of the local or military police, or just a man feuding with He, or a stranger who sought to defend the woman? Regardless of the facts behind this incident, it illustrates the chaos that permeated society and teahouse life.

During the war, when the nation depended on soldiers fighting the Japanese on the frontlines, some of the armed men in the rear area took advantage of their special role and behaved horrifically. In 1938, the *Chengdu Daily Bulletin* (Chengdu kuaibao) reported that soldiers seated in the balcony of the People's Theater (Pingmin juyuan) on South Private Academy Street (Shuyuan nanjie) threw two grenades onto the stage, killing eight people seated in the front rows and injuring thirty or forty others. The scene was described as "flesh and blood flying everywhere." Such an incident, the newspaper stated, "has not been seen for many years." An investigation revealed that the conflict started when four soldiers forced their way into the theater with just three tickets. When the gatekeeper stopped them, they argued and a fight broke out until military police arrived. The police held two of the soldiers but the other two escaped, gathering eighty to ninety more soldiers and returning to the theater as the night show was under way.

The mob beat up several military policemen who were trying to maintain order and took their weapons. A soldier lobbed the two grenades as people tried to flee in the ensuing panic. The authorities tried to arrest and punish the culprits, but also blamed the theater managers for mishandling the matter. Based on a report issued the next day, when the four soldiers presented the three tickets at the gate, they told the gatekeeper that they were "officers and soldiers who had fought in battles" and asked for special treatment. The gatekeeper not only rudely refused the request, but also injured one of the soldiers.[33] It is doubtful this report is true, because it is unimaginable that a lowly gatekeeper would dare initiate a fight with a soldier. The War of Resistance was just beginning, and although the government pledged to punish the murderers, it apparently did not want to damage the reputation of those who were asked to sacrifice their lives in battle. The government may also have wanted to send a message to all theaters that they were to accommodate soldiers under any circumstances.

The situation did not improve after the war, and the Civil War that followed also unleashed much turbulence on daily life. Multiple murders continued to take place in teahouses. For instance in 1947, when more than two dozen soldiers gathered in the Beneficial and Prosperous (Yihua) Teahouse to "drink settlement tea" with a young man, a fight broke out, and they damaged nearly two dozen sets of tea utensils and other items. The owner of the teahouse asked them to pay for the damage, which they promised to do the next day. Instead, more than one hundred soldiers showed up the next morning, demanding that the teahouse keeper tell them where they could find the young man. The teahouse keeper told them repeatedly that he did not know where the young man was, but the mob destroyed everything in the teahouse: sixty-four sets of tea bowls, more than ten tables, more than forty bamboo chairs, two wooden boards, five stools, and five electric light bulbs, as well as windows and doors, for a loss of about 640,000 yuan. After the incident, the heads of the *baojia* and neighbors gave eyewitness accounts, and the police verified their claims. But it seems that the police had no real power and could only report the case and ask the military and the governor of Sichuan Province to "investigate and punish the responsible people in order to protect security and enforce the law."[34]

After the Civil War broke out, a large number of soldiers moved into the city and many of them were lodged in teahouses, causing business to decline sharply. In 1946, Wang Xiushan, president of the Teahouse Guild, complained to the government about the business downturn caused by soldiers' occupation of teahouses. His petition claimed that soldiers were billeted in 523 of the 623 teahouses in Chengdu. The teahouses asked the guild to inform the government about their losses and request relief. The guild claimed that all the teahouses that housed soldiers had suffered a loss in business and some even had to close; teahouses had to pay the costs of electricity, lighting oil, water, and coal that the soldiers used, and for the chairs, tables, windows, tea bowls, and kettles they damaged or stole. Damages totaled 35.6 million yuan, or an average of 300,000 yuan per teahouse. This occurred just after the Japanese surrendered and civil war had broken out. The petition said, "Although it is a time of catastrophe and national emergency, the guild cannot let the suffering of 523 teahouses continue unknown. So, it has to report the truth and ask for government relief and action to remove the soldiers."[35]

Maintaining Public Order

Facing the serious issue of public security, maintaining public order, especially in the teahouse as a public place for relaxation and entertainment, was one of the government's major concerns. In 1932, the government banned beggars and peddlers from the parks because they "go to teahouses in the parks and disrupt the environment and public order." However, this prohibition inconvenienced customers who depended on peddlers to provide a wide array of food, toys, and other everyday items. The government later compromised by issuing an "entrance card," limited to ninety peddlers in Sun Yat-sen Park, and renewable biannually. But in 1937 the government refused to renew the cards, using the excuse that public order should be maintained because the New Life Promotion Association (Xinshenghuo cujinhui) gave public lectures at the teahouse there. Park officials as well as representatives of the vendors asked that the cards be renewed so that peddlers could continue making a living and adding to the area's local color and vitality. The park manager appealed to the municipal government by pointing out that peddlers were "the poorest of the poor" and to prohibit them was to end "their way of making a living."[36] Although there is no record of the outcome, a policy that ran counter to this popular and centuries-old tradition would have been virtually impossible to enforce.

The government sometimes cited concerns over security in its regulation of teahouses. In June 1939, the Chengdu Garrison Headquarters (Chengdu jingbei silingbu), the Chengdu Municipal Government, and the Provincial Police Department issued a public notice prohibiting teahouses along the riverbanks outside Revival Gate (Fuxing men). The notice stated that the tea booths (chapeng), which included tile-roofed structures, thatched cottages, and mat sheds, were illegal, that many people had been killed or injured there during recent Japanese air raids, and that they were likely to become future targets as well. To prevent a repeat tragedy, the public notice ordered the dismantling of the thatched cottages and mat sheds within two days and of the tile-roofed teahouses within five days. The police would use force if these deadlines were not met.[37] That same year, several universities, including Qilu, Jinling, Jinling Woman's (Jinling nüzi), and West China (Huaxi), were relocated from the coastal areas to a space by the river outside Chengdu's South Gate because of the war. Their presidents petitioned the provincial government to restrict the nearby teahouses, claiming that they harbored "lawless brigands" (*bufa zhitu*) and threatened security.[38] In July 1945, Huang Jilu, president of Sichuan University, asked the municipal government to remove all teahouses and wine shops on the sides of the road near the student dormitories, because "all sorts of people gather there and make noise, interrupting the students' study." Also, he emphasized that "bad people" often hid in such places and thefts were common.[39] In short, teahouses near universities faced resistance.

The government also tried to eliminate the common practice of teahouses occupying public spaces such as sidewalks, the ends of bridges, land in front of temples, public squares, or public spots in the shade of nearby trees. The teahouse's use of space in parks was an unwritten law, and when a teahouse opened in a park, it counted on using the surrounding property to maximize its capacity to serve customers. But police control over these spaces had increased since the late Qing era, although this met with resistance from teahouse keepers.[40] The use of public space became a never-ending battle. A new regulation would be enforced rigorously at the beginning, then relaxed, and later the government would start its campaign all over again. In 1929, the municipal government enacted a new regulation that prohibited teahouses from occupying public space beyond their own property. The teahouses in the Smaller City Park, Sun Yat-sen Park, and Zhiji Temple Park asked the government to reconsider the prohibition, which would significantly reduce their business. They claimed that during the summer teahouses provided much-sought respite from the heat. The city was crowded and polluted, especially during the summer, when people went to teahouses in the parks to enjoy the cool air. Teahouses had to move tables and chairs outside to accommodate these crowds, a practice that had been carried out for many years without affecting security. Teahouses would hardly be able to stay in business in this era of small profits if this practice were ended, and without this service, parks would be much less appealing.[41]

Sometimes, the expansion of teahouses in a park caused disputes between teahouses, and the government was asked to intervene. In 1946, for instance, the Green Shadow Pavilion Teahouse (Lüyin ge chashe) requested the municipal government to issue a public notice confining teahouses to their own property to avoid disputes. The manager of the Green Shadow said that a teahouse rented a spot inside the Smaller City Park years earlier without incident until recently, when some customers moved tables and chairs outside without authorization. Tables and chairs were often damaged when moved, and tea bowls often went missing. Waiters who asked customers not to move tables and chairs were often yelled at or beaten, and tea bowls, tables, and chairs were often damaged in the process. Customers seemed to care only about their own comfort and paid no attention to the trouble that resulted when the government blamed the teahouse for not following the regulation. In response to this request, the municipal government issued a public notice that reaffirmed the prohibition against moving tables and chairs outside:

> The teahouses in the park are meant to provide visitors a place for temporary rest. The areas of business have already been clearly defined. No teahouse is allowed to move tables and chairs beyond its walls, blocking pedestrians. Now, during the heat of summer, sanitation should be specially emphasized. Therefore, no tea is to be served and no tables and chairs are to be moved beyond property lines. Any violation will be punished.[42]

In this example the public notice emphasized the ban on the expansion of teahouses rather than the conflict and property loss that were the subjects of the Green Shadow's original petition. This case is unique in that a teahouse voluntarily asked the government to limit its scope of business.

Conclusion

The teahouse, a small public arena, was the scene of a variety of conflicts, from verbal disputes and fights over simply trying to make a living to violence and murder. These conflicts reflected larger social issues, from struggles to make a living, relationships between small shops and their neighbors and local authorities, and everyday disputes between customers in public places. They also convey how people lived in the shadow of war. But the most serious threat came from rogues and soldiers, who disrupted business by harassing or bullying customers or even by engaging in mass violence. These incidents devastated teahouses and caused an enormous amount of property damage. Most teahouses operated with very little capital; they barely survived even under normal conditions, and such an incident could drive them out of business entirely.

The conflicts described in this chapter took place at the lowest levels of society, reflecting the contention between social groups, classes, and occupations over making a living in a public space and the right to use that space. Teahouses were the site of more conflict than other places because they were highly visible public arenas with a high concentration of many different kinds of people, from common people to gangsters, criminals, and soldiers. Furthermore, the teahouse was an open forum for all kinds of activities, legal or otherwise. Even though most teahouses did not welcome illegal conduct, managers did not have the power to prevent it, and had to deal with criminals very carefully to avoid trouble. Disputes and conflicts reflected the current political, economic, social, and cultural situation. Taking soldiers as an example, after the 1911 Revolution, the military became deeply entrenched in national and local politics, so that the number of soldiers increased and their political power and interests grew increasingly complex. The local government and police were often overpowered by these groups. The relationship between the military and local residents was constantly demonstrated in the teahouse, which became a kind of indicator of the larger political scene.

The teahouse also functioned as a stage where all kinds of people performed roles that were both good and evil and an intrinsic part of teahouse culture. While "drinking settlement tea" was a practice through which people mediated disputes in teahouses, it was one that occasionally broke down into fighting and violence. Thus, an activity intended to make peace ironically resulted in the loss of peace, becoming one of the sources of teahouse violence. Chengdu had five hundred to eight hundred teahouses from the late Qing era to the collapse of the Nationalist government. Even though incidents took place daily in some teahouses, teahouse life could still be described as normal for the most part. While this chapter explores the "dark side" of teahouses, it is not intended to convey the idea that they were hotbeds of danger and vice. All cases of disputes, conflicts, violence, and murders were collected and consolidated from sources from the 1910s to the 1940s, which can lead to an erroneous impression of reality, just as is found when a single germ is examined under a microscope. Also, it is true that "no news is good news," and that newspapers report and archival sources keep only material on the most sensational events.

Conflicts gave local authorities an opportunity to seek control of the teahouse. The government always paid more attention public spaces than private places. Since the introduction of the New Policies in the late Qing, local authorities and reformist elites, like those in other Chinese cities, launched a campaign to improve the city's image by restructuring the city's appearance and landscape and to enforce their power by regulating public areas. The teahouses of Chengdu, as important public places, became major targets in this campaign. The government enacted many restrictions over teahouses concerning security and order throughout the Republican period, extending its social manipulation that enabled state power to penetrate all aspects of society. Although mundane disputes or violence or increased government control could bring a temporary disruption, they could not destroy teahouse life and everyday culture. Teahouse culture proved to be tenacious. After the war broke out, however, the national crisis gave the state the opportunity it needed to finally expand into the teahouse just as the central government also moved inland.

CHAPTER 8

A Political Site

The night breeze is blowing dry air,
And the teahouse is full of frivolity.
Patrons throng upstairs and downstairs,
Where the waiter is calling out and bringing boiled water.
Bowls and plates are jingling,
While fried melon seeds are crackling.
Some customers are chatting and some are arguing;
And some are in trouble, but some are laughing.
Some are discussing national affairs,
And some are airing their complaints.
The teahouse keeper is so afraid
That he comes to ask in a low voice:
"Sir, please, out of concern for my business,
Never discuss your opinions about politics.
Or national affairs.
It is difficult not to complain.
But you and I will suffer
If your conversation causes a problem.
You may lose your job,
And my teahouse may be shut down.
But losing your job is not the worst,
You might be put in jail.
What you should talk about is the weather,
And then go home and sleep well after drinking tea here."
"Ha ha . . . ," everybody is laughing.
"The teahouse keeper is talking nonsense,
Because we have had too much sleep.
More sleep,
Makes us more stupid,
And more frustrated.
Instead, let's talk without taboos.
Get rid of the bastards who oppress us, exploit us, and don't let us speak freely."
—Wen Yiduo, "Chaguan xiaodiao"
[A canzonet of the teahouse]

WEN YIDUO, the popular left-wing writer who was assassinated in 1946 after delivering a speech condemning the GMD at a public meeting in Kunming, wrote the song "Chaguan xiaodao," which became popular all across Sichuan, when he was a professor at Southwest Union University. Although the teahouse he describes was probably not in Chengdu, the teahouse politics he describes were universal. Wen Yiduo's choice of the teahouse as a setting for the expression of political ideas was not coincidental. He might have believed that setting the conversation in a teahouse would have the maximum impact on the populace because it typified the Nationalist government's suppression of free speech. The teahouse he described was crowded, with windows and the door opened wide to allow the cool air in, or, more likely, patrons were sitting at tables on the sidewalk. All kinds of noise could be heard, from the sound of bowls hitting saucers to conversations and the calls of waiters. Some people laughed and talked while others sighed or complained. The teahouse keeper was afraid of political discussions because he knew secret agents of the police might be mingling with patrons to collect intelligence. Political talk could result not only in people losing their jobs or being arrested but also in the teahouse being closed down.

This chapter discusses how the teahouse became a political arena and how elites, ordinary people, and the state used it to further their various political agendas. We can see the growing role of the state in the teahouse, which reflected the political transformation of the nation, the province, and the city. As the capital of Sichuan Province, Chengdu experienced almost all of political, economic, social, and cultural transformations that were current in China from the late Qing reform to the Communist victory. I generalize these changes into four historical periods. Each period was quite different from the others. Although the city was inevitably influenced by national politics and the national economy, it retained its unique characteristics during the first half of the twentieth century.[1] In premodern Chengdu community life was basically organized by local elites,[2] but this began to change when the police force was established in 1902. In 1910, the City Council of Chengdu and Huayang (Chenghua cheng yishihui) was formed as a part of the self-government movement, with its members being selected by elections. Both the police and the council became the early foundation of the Chengdu municipal government but the former played a much more important role. The collapse of the Qing brought more chaos to the city but did not result in a fundamental change in its administration. In 1913, by order of the central government, a new City Council was set up to handle public affairs. As part of the national trend of organizing municipal governments, the provincial government approved the creation of the Public Office of Chengdu Municipal Affairs (Chengdu shi shizheng gongsuo) in 1922, which was restructured in 1928 into the Chengdu Municipal Government, the first formal city administration. From the 1920s to the 1940s, the City Council coexisted with the municipal government. The members of the City Council were elected from among residents, who often had disputes with the municipal government. In December 1949, the establishment of the Communist government brought Chengdu into an entirely new system of municipal administration.[3] This administrative evolution inevitably influenced the development and control of the teahouse trade and culture.

Because teahouses were public, many conflicts and unexpected incidents took place there. In addition, teahouses, as the most popular public space in Chengdu, often reflected the city's image. Therefore, local authorities were greatly concerned with public order and attempted to control teahouses. In so doing, the local government implemented many regulations during the late Qing and Republican periods. To date, I have collected fifteen: one was enacted before the 1911 Revolution, three were enacted in the 1910s, one in the 1920s, two in the 1930s, four during the War of Resistance, and four in 1948.[4] These regulations covered almost every aspect of teahouse operation, including registration, gambling, suppression of gangsters, entertainment, hours of operation, police supervision, and so on. Some were general and some addressed a single issue. Of the fifteen regulations, nine were comprehensive; two dealt with hygiene; three concerned teahouse theaters and performances; and one sought to limit the number of teahouses in Chengdu and their hours of operation. There are no obvious differences in their approach to the issues, which may suggest that the authorities implemented consistent policies regarding the control of teahouses. There is no question that the government increased its control over teahouses during the late 1940s.

The teahouse was doubtless full of conversations about politics, ranging from discussions of class conflict and complaints about the social situation to talk of current policies and the government. The teahouse was a true witness of China's political transformation, a place where people discussed social reform in the late Qing era, the Railroad Protection Movement, the 1911 Revolution, warlords and wars in the early Republican period, the GMD and the Chinese Communist Party (CCP), the War of Resistance (1937–45), and the Civil War (1945–49). Even the rumors that circulated might have been a response to social, economic, and political turmoil.[5] As Wen Yiduo's lyrics indicate, the teahouse became a space where people expressed their anger over social and political developments. Politics in the teahouse, of course, often took the form of power struggles between elites and commoners, between the state and elites, between the state and commoners, and between the members of each of these groups. They often struggled to promote their own personal interests, the interests of the small groups they associated with, or the interests of their own class. Although teahouses filled people's needs in terms of leisure, business, and public life, they often became an arena of political struggle or were forced into the political orbit. In fact, local and national political developments were always in evidence in the teahouse and teahouse life. From this point of view, the teahouse could be considered a political stage, where all kinds of people and powers played roles in the ongoing drama of politics.

During the war, the national crisis increased the state's opportunities to engage with teahouses and use them as a tool for political propaganda. Remarkably, the teahouse also created a kind of amateur politician, known as a "teahouse politician" (*chaguan zhengzhijia*), whose opinions and behavior became an indicator of trends in local and national politics. This chapter discusses how public space, leisure activities, and entertainment were always connected with politics and closely associated with changes in the economy, social inequality, and political movements, and how various political forces struggled to exert their influence in these domains. The government was intent on suppressing the spread of any political ideology or activity that could jeopardize the GMD's rule. As seen in Wen Yiduo's lyrics, teahouse owners did their best to stay away from politics, but often failed because both the government and patrons engaged in politics there.

From Reform to Revolution (1900–1916): Reshaping the Teahouse

The first decade of the twentieth century saw urban reform under the influence of the New Policies promoted by the Qing government and the self-government movement advanced by reformist elites. The city became a center and model of industrial, commercial, educational, and social reforms. During this period, local elites, supported by state power, enthusiastically participated in reforms that expanded their influence over ordinary people and built their social reputation.[6] The evidence indicates that the attitudes regarding popular culture held by elites and the government consistently guided the issue of how to deal with teahouse life. The influence of pro-Western values had grown since the late Qing era, and the teahouse was often criticized as a symbol of a "decadent" or "backward" lifestyle as opposed to the "civilized" and "modern" Western lifestyle.[7] All formal and informal sources of authority regarded the teahouse as a facilitator of a wide range of social ills: poor sanitation, gossip, gambling and other vices, disreputable entertainment, and so on. Therefore, the teahouse was a constant target of social reformers and those wielding state power who imposed rigid control and enforcement as the first step in their social manipulation that ultimately enabled state power to penetrate all aspects of society. Although some elites tried to promote the virtues embodied in the teahouse and convince people of the teahouse's central role in society, many Westernized elites, joining forces with the government, held a negative attitude, which, of course, provided legitimacy for the government to restrict, control, and even attack teahouse culture. These measures varied from moderate to severe, shifting with trends in politics, the economy, and society at large.

Under the anti-popular-culture trend, the Regulations on Teahouses enacted in 1903 were part of urban reform efforts, as was the establishment of the police force, indicating that the government was paying close attention to teahouses even in these early years. The regulations stated that all teahouses had to register with the police and obey the following rules: No gambling, bird fighting, or secret society rituals (*bai matou*) were allowed in any teahouse; storytellers had to notify the police before performing, and those who told "obscene," "evil," or "bizarre" stories were to be expelled; tables in teahouses were not be put too close together or placed in the street; the police had to be notified of all disputes; all teahouses had to close by 11 PM; and all teahouses had to allow policemen to enter for investigations but were not permitted to sell them tea. A teahouse that violated any of these rules would be fined or even shut down. Police officers always scrutinized teahouse patrons. The Rules for Watching and Patrolling for policemen enacted in the late Qing era required policemen to pay special attention to teahouses and a few other places. Teahouses were required to turn their lights off by 1 AM or the police would investigate.[8] The hours of operation were not as restrictive as during the Republican era, when teahouses were required to close much earlier, sometimes by 9 PM.

Between 1911 and 1916 Chengdu became a center of patriotic revolution and experienced unprecedented political turmoil. Many residents joined the Railroad Protection Movement, which opposed the policy of nationalizing railways. In late November 1911, Sichuan declared independence from the Qing empire and organized the Great Han Sichuan Military Government (Dahan Sichuan junzhengfu).[9] In 1913 Governor Yin Changheng was replaced by Hu Jingyi, a protégé of President Yuan Shikai. That same year, some revolutionaries responded to Sun Yat-sen's call for a Second Revolution, but this failed. Sichuan was a major battlefield during the National Protection War of 1915 and 1916, which sought to oust Yuan Shikai, and the entrance of the Yunnan and Guizhou armies into Sichuan at that time became a direct catalyst of the catastrophes that followed.[10]

Since the teahouse was a hub for conversation about politics, its employees also inevitably were involved in political activities and participated in protests against tax increases and government restrictions as well as in national charitable relief activities. The teahouse's role as a political stage was obvious during the Railroad Protection Movement of 1911, when residents of almost every neighborhood gathered in teahouses to discuss the latest developments, and, as Li Jieren notes, "stood on stools and yelled in excitement" when good news arrived. In her memoir of her English missionary family, Han Suyin wrote that at the end of May 1911, Chengdu "was uneasy, irritable, anxious, the teahouse in the public gardens and on the streets exuding unease. An anxious city, poised for rioting." Teahouses no longer were places for idle chitchat, but full of political debates and activities; as Han described it, "The call 'I buy tea' was now practically a clarion call for an immediate drift of diverse loiterers, small groups coalescing into larger ones, some even standing to listen as debates went on concerning the nationalization question and the railway loan; and silently they would drift apart again, then on to another teahouse, to hear another man expound" (see Figures 8.1 and 8.2).[11]

Some teahouses took advantage of political change to engage in public affairs and improve their social reputation. In the late Qing era, some teahouses took on more charitable activities, nationally as well as locally. For example, the Elegant Tea Garden in 1909 invited several famous actors to perform and donated two days' worth of the income to famine relief in Gansu Province. The next year, the Joy Tea Garden organized a performance for famine relief in Hunan, for which more than fourteen hundred people

FIGURE 8.1: Policemen and residents on a commercial street. Policemen have gathered to keep public order. Photo by Luther Knight, 1911. Photo courtesy of John E. Knight.

FIGURE 8.2: A crowd in the Imperial City. During the 1911 Revolution, the Imperial City became one of the most popular public gathering places for political meetings. This photo was taken by Luther Knight on November 27, 1911, the day of the establishment of Great Han Sichuan Military Government. The Bright and Distant Hall (Mingyuan lou) can be seen in the background. No trace of the Imperial City remains today. Photo courtesy of John E. Knight.

bought tickets at one yuan each. In 1912, the Eternal Spring Tea Garden (Wanchun chayuan) announced that it would contribute two days' worth of income from opera performances to the "citizens' tax" (guomin juan) and encouraged people to buy tickets. Of course, teahouses used charitable activities to publicize their programs, enhance their reputation, and boost business, but these activities also helped them connect with the local and national political scene. Teahouses were often used for political celebrations, such as when the One and One Tea Garden (Yiyi chayuan) hired the best troupe of puppet masters in Chengdu for a celebration of National Day.[12]

Under the Warlords (1917–1936): The Teahouse in Political Chaos

From 1917 to 1936 Chengdu experienced wars, destruction, and reconstruction. During this period, almost all of the highest positions in the provincial government were held by warlords, who constantly fought for power. The city was also a target of various warlords' relentless attacks, especially by military forces from other provinces. In 1917 residents' worst nightmare became reality when the Sichuan army battled the Yunnan army and later the Guizhou army on the streets of Chengdu. Many innocent civilians were killed and injured and thousands became refugees when part of the city was destroyed and countless homes ruined.[13] During the "alley battles," frightened residents hid in their homes and most shops were closed. During fighting, teahouses were always the first public place to open and the last to close. In his diary, Wu Yu wrote that he sent his servant out to check on the situation every time the sound of guns and canons faded. If the servant reported that the neighborhood teahouses had opened, he felt safe enough to venture out, even if all other shops were still closed. Therefore, the teahouse, to a certain extent, became a barometer of security and normalcy in the city. The police regarded teahouses as places where spies collected information and spread rumors that could cause further turmoil and issued an order requiring the managers of teahouses to report anyone who had a non-Sichuan accent or discussed military issues or otherwise behaved like a "spy for the enemy." If the suspect turned out to be a spy, the police gave the informant a reward of 10 silver yuan.[14] In this case, police used the excuse of identifying so-called spies to suppress anyone who dared to publicly challenge the government's authority.

In 1921, the rapid growth of the self-government movement resulted in a declaration of independence by the Provincial Assembly. By 1926, Sichuan's military leaders were able to expel the Yunnan army and then the Guizhou army from the province under the slogan "Sichuan people govern Sichuan" (*Chuanren zhi Chuan*). After warlord Yang Sen became governor in 1924, he launched large-scale urban reconstruction in Chengdu, opening new commercial districts and widening the main streets, changing the landscape of the city.[15] Between 1928 and 1936, Sichuan was virtually autonomous but warlord power was strongest, although the rest of China was largely united under the Nationalist Party (GMD). In 1928 the Chengdu Municipal Government was established. During this period, as mentioned, the central government exercised little control over Sichuan, which was in the hands of five warlords who shared power under a "system of Defense Districts" (*Fangqu zhi*).[16] During 1932 and 1933, the Red Army entered Sichuan and established a base in the northern part of the province. As a result, the warlords shifted their focus to fighting the Communists and thus were forced to seek support from Chiang Kai-shek; the central government took this opportunity between 1935 to 1937 to finally extend its power into Sichuan.[17]

The political uncertainty during this period was clearly reflected in teahouse life, and especially in the daily conversations found there. Although talk on any topic imaginable flowed freely every moment that every teahouse was open, there are few records of specific conversations. However, journalists recorded what they heard in the teahouse in a few newspaper accounts. Some teahouse conversations might have political implications even if they were not overtly political. Here is a random conversation between two people in 1917:

Man A: The Chinese people and the imperial court respected chastity for thousands of years. Therefore, people everywhere praised chastity. However, after the Republic was established, chastity was no longer emphasized, and social customs and people's minds became degraded.

Man B: I disagree. In the past, people paid attention to chastity, but now they respect native places. For example, in 1913, nearly everyone claimed to be from Sichuan on their business cards, while in 1914 everyone denied having Sichuan origins. In 1916, though, after the Republic was restored, their business cards again showed that they were Sichuan natives. But, today they all say they are from outside Sichuan. This is a proof that scholars and officials emphasize native places, but which one constantly changes, depending on what is more advantageous.

Man A: A person's native place constantly changes, and nobody knows his real native place. As you have just said, no scholars or officials have a true native place. Our country has scorned liars for thousands of years.[18]

Here the discussion was ostensibly about native places, but it implied that politicians were dishonest. During the early Republican era, people in Sichuan played a more active role on the national political stage. When politicians from Sichuan had power in the central government, the province was highly regarded; otherwise, people ignored it. These conversationalists also believed that values had been degraded, because society had abandoned its reverence for chastity. As we know, in traditional China a woman without chastity was considered a "disgrace," but this conversation implied that politicians had lost their "chastity" and become shameless "liars."

The more important information we may get from this conversation is the anxiety of losing a cultural identity in the face of constant political struggle and the transition of power. One's native place was a crucial factor for Chengdu's residents, underscoring virtually every aspect of society, economics, and politics and tying people to their cultural roots. This legacy could bring people together to survive in a new environment and help them resist other cultures. After the fall of the Qing, however, the politicians and elites found that the native place could be used as a tool for political gain. The notion of native place began to change although it was still important. This conversation in the teahouse regarding native place reveals people's bewilderment and dissatisfaction regarding the chaotic situation in the early Republican period.

Teahouse-goers not only chatted and gossiped about the minutiae of daily life but also complained about their hardships and expressed anger at the endless political power struggles and corrupt government, along with their opinions about what should be done. Here is a snippet of a conversation between two elderly men:

Man A: Have you noticed recently how everything is new: a new world, new trends, new knowledge, and a new vocabulary? Although we will not follow these new things, we do not have the old ones, either.

Man B: In my opinion, they're just boasting wildly. They are only fooling inexperienced youngsters. Any person who has a mind will know they are boasting and cheating. Haven't people as old as you and I seen enough? The happiness promised in 1911 has not reached us. Do you remember the idea of no taxes? Now taxes have to be paid several years in advance. As for freedom, you were scared when you lived in your big house in the country and moved to the capital city. You do not dare to go back home. Are you free? I am tired of the wonderful promises.[19]

It is necessary to look at the historical context of this conversation. This dialogue took place in 1922, when the New Cultural Movement was under way and many new ideas and new consumer goods had recently appeared, including burgeoning new material culture, which caused a rift between Westernized elites and conservatives. Obviously, this conversation was between two conservatives who disliked new things. From this snippet, we find that they opposed the new because in their experience new things brought false promises; they looked good on the outside, but were rotten inside. They remembered the disappointment and hardships of their own experience after the 1911 Revolution and did not feel secure. The promise of the revolution was never realized and the situation only worsened. People lived in a more dangerous world, paid more in taxes, and were not free. Therefore, these men simply blamed their suffering on the advent of the new. Their conversation also hints at their feelings of hopelessness; on the one hand, they resisted the new, but on the other hand, they could not rely on the old traditions either, because the revolution and the New Cultural Movement had destroyed that way of life. At the same time, they expressed their feelings of superiority and their scorn for people who admired the new by emphasizing their social experiences, akin to the so-called spiritual (or psychological) victory that Lu Xun ridicules in his novella *The True Story of Ah Q*.[20]

The warlord government also sought to control the teahouse. The regulations issued in the early Republican era dealt only with teahouse theaters and performances (see Chapter 5); the first comprehensive regulations were not issued until 1932.[21] In the late spring of that year, the municipal government issued "five restrictions," which addressed sanitation in particular but also dealt with gambling. In 1935, the local government issued so-called restrictions for "preventing incidents that endanger the public." The new rules allowed only one teahouse in each park, leading to the closure of some teahouses in high-density areas; the remaining teahouses could be open only six hours per day, and only during the morning and at night, and had to close during weekends.²² These new rules were a reflection of the government's radical and growing concern about the social issues embodied in teahouse culture. There is no evidence that these new regulations were completely enforced. Enforcement would have been disastrous for teahouse workers who faced losing their jobs or who would no longer have been able to make a living. There is also no evidence of a significant decrease in the hours of operation; teahouses still were usually open fifteen to sixteen hours a day. Also, as seen in Table 1.1, the number of teahouses in Chengdu not only did not decrease in 1936, but actually increased from 599 to 640. The fact that the regulations were ineffective reveals the tenacity of local customs and teahouse culture in resisting attacks by the state.

The Politics of Resistance (1937–1945): "The Fate of the Nation and Tea Drinking"

The War of Resistance (1937–45) brought Sichuan and Chengdu onto the central stage in national politics. The Nationalist government's move to Chongqing had a profound impact on Chengdu and the relationship between Sichuan and the central government.²³ Many offices of the central government and other provincial governments, social and cultural organizations, schools, and factories moved to Chengdu. A huge number of refugees flooded the city, bringing many new cultural elements with them.²⁴ The War of Resistance brought politics into teahouses to an unprecedented degree. Social groups and government officials used teahouses to spread propaganda, displaying slogans, posters, and public notices, and overseeing performances and public meetings related to the resistance effort and patriotism. Teahouses actually became a stage for "saving the country." Discussions focused on the war, where people could learn the latest news from the frontlines, as well as stories about the resistance, the ruthlessness of the Japanese invaders, and wartime tragedies. Although people still went to the teahouse, an activity still criticized by elites and the government, they could not escape the impact of the war there and were inevitably drawn onto a political stage.

In a letter to a friend, Zhou Wen described what he saw when he arrived in Chengdu in the late 1930s, when the "movement for saving the country from crisis" was at its highest point. He describes a group of students in a teahouse carrying flags, with one intensely emotional student standing on a chair and giving a speech as all of the patrons listened. Yet Zhou also found that the war did not seem to change daily life much; just a few days later, he saw people passing through the streets beating drums to advertise performances, and noted that the theaters were still crowded. Zhou was not the only one to comment on this phenomenon. A report titled "Chengdu under the Microscope" (Xianweijing xia zhi Chengdu shi) criticized residents for living lives of leisure at teahouses and theaters when the whole nation was caught up in bloody battles with the Japanese. It condemned Chengdu as a "grotesque and gaudy society" (*guangguai luli de shehui*). For a period, the government tried to "regulate wartime life" and generated a discussion that linked the "fate of the nation to tea drinking" (*chicha yu guoyun*).[25] Zhou and the author of the report might have seen only the surface of Chengdu society; in fact, the war inevitably affected many aspects of daily life. Although people still frequented teahouses and theaters, the kinds of performances they watched might have already changed. For example, the editor of the publication *New Chengdu* (Xin Chengdu) said that "in the past, storytellers' language was licentious and plots were bizarre, which unconsciously corrupted the thoughts and behaviors of the masses." After the Japanese aggression, storytellers still used well-known materials as the basis for their stories, but inserted patriotic and anti-Japanese themes.[26]

In 1941 a critic condemned the so-called Chengdu phenomenon (*Chengdu xianxiang*) in which central areas such as Warm Spring Road and Main Mansion Street had more than ten teahouses, all crowded day and night. The author criticized some "bored and idle people" (*baixiang de ren*) for sitting in a teahouse all day "without rhyme or reason." The writer observed that "teahouses have recently become an unusual place, where waitresses publicly flirt with customers and even charge four to five times more for tea served in private rooms." Another article also condemned the prosperous entertainment trade during an era of rampant inflation; people wasted time and money on entertainment when they should be frugal.[27] In 1942, the article "Chatting about Chengdu" (Xianhua Rongcheng) described the city as not appearing to be in a country at war; people still flocked to the splendid shops, entertainment venues, and teahouses. The population increase meant that these places emerged like "bamboo shoots after a spring rain," which elites lamented during the national crisis. Another article quoted Chiang Kai-shek as saying that "the Chinese revolution would have been successful if people had used the time they spent in the teahouse to pursue the goals of the revolution." Many elites thought that teahouses reflected the "inertia" of people "who have nothing to do and stay at the teahouse for the entire day." *New Chengdu* claimed that these patrons "kill time in the teahouse, telling stories from ancient and modern times, commenting on society, playing chess, gambling, criticizing public figures, and gossiping about private matters and secrets of the boudoir." The author wondered, "How could there be so many idlers in this land who spend their money while doing nothing?"[28] As discussed in Chapter 6, the teahouse was multifunctional, and these criticisms focus only on the pursuit of leisure in an effort to make life in the teahouse seem diametrically opposed to patriotic pursuits.

The government tightly controlled public entertainment and tried to shape public perceptions during the war by seeking to use teahouses as places of wartime education, bringing innovations to storytelling, providing new books and newspapers, putting new pictures and slogans on the wall, and facilitating "patriotic" forms of entertainment. The government required plays to include some patriotic and anti-Japanese terms and content even though the old genres and materials could be still used.[29] A new organization called the Temporary Instruction Committee of the Chinese Nationalist Party for People's Organizations in Chengdu (Zhongguo Guomindang Chengdu shi renmin tuanti linshi zhidao weiyuanhui) was responsible for examining scripts, some of which are still available in the archives and reveal how politics entered this facet of public life. I have found twelve scripts, all of which focus on the war. Some recall the history of Japanese aggression against China; some praise the brave resistance movement; some commemorate the heroes who lost their lives on the battlefield; some express yearning for the lost motherland; some list Japanese crimes committed in China; some bemoan the nation's sad situation; and some recount bloody battles. The kinds of performances varied, and included storytelling and folk songs. The powerful contents and language were intended to wake up and mobilize audience members.[30]

For example, "Recovering the Motherland" (Huan wo heshan) describes China's beauty, vast territory, rich natural resources, long history, and wonderful culture. The calligraphy of the four characters *huan wo he shan* written by the Chinese national hero Yue Fei during the Song era was well-known and could be found throughout the country. The use of these characters in the title had a powerful influence on people's hearts and minds.[31] "Exposing Traitors" (Hanjian timing) denounced the crimes of the Japanese invaders and named eight traitors, exposing them to public shame and adding that there were too many traitors to name individually. This program also tells how they became traitors. Another script with a similar topic, titled "The Fate of Traitors" (Hanjian de xiachang), warned that "the heads and bodies of traitors would fall apart if they are caught" and their families would be implicated in their crimes, not only losing their property but also permanently tarnishing their reputation. It cautioned people to avoid such a tragic fate.[32] These scripts used rhymes and lyrics full of political ideas, unlike the traditional style of popular entertainment. These materials targeting the Japanese or traitors obviously met the government's need for a powerful tool of propaganda, which became part of the wartime political culture. Without question, they played an active role in mobilizing people to join the movement to save the country.

Of course, one of the motivations behind these patriotic programs was to promote business, and the theaters and entertainers knew how to deal with the government for survival. In 1939, folksinger Wang Qingyun applied for a permit to perform folk songs in the Pleasant Wind (Huifeng) Teahouse. He claimed that he wanted to "spread propaganda to support the government" in the War of Resistance. He promised not to perform any "lecherous songs" but to "wake people up to mobilize the nation." He said that "the final victory must be ours, and we must strongly support Chiang Kai-shek and struggle until the end." In 1941, three people from Jiangsu requested permission to perform operas, claiming that the Nanjing National Opera Theater (Nanjing guoju shuchang) promoted "noble entertainment" and helped "change social customs." They said that they had witnessed the Japanese invasion and the killing of Chinese, and that it was imperative that anyone who had "blood and breath" should fight the invaders and recover the stolen land, and that their performance could inspire patriotism and mobilize the masses behind the frontlines.[33]

In 1941, the government ordered all teahouses to purchase portraits of Sun Yat-sen and other GMD leaders and to prepare space for a lectern, blackboard, GMD party flag, and national flag. The Teahouse Guild issued a deadline for satisfying this new rule "in order to avoid investigations by the municipal government and trouble for teahouses that do not have these items."[34] The military was also involved in wartime propaganda. The military's division headquarters inspected the eleven teahouses on the six streets that made up the Imperial City district for these items. When it was found that none of the teahouses was in compliance, Mayor Yu issued an order to the president of the Teahouse Guild that this equipment was mandatory and that the guild should require all teahouses to meet the regulation.[35] The executive committee of the GMD in Sichuan enacted a Plan of Propaganda in Teahouses (Chaguan xuanchuan shishi jihua), issued by the mayor of Chengdu, which stated that the authorities regarded teahouses as an important arena for propaganda. Under the plan, the 640 or so teahouses in Chengdu were divided into three classes, each of which had different requirements for propaganda.[36]

The government even dictated the messages to be put on the blackboards in each teahouse. A Provincial Mobilization Committee (Sheng dongyuan weiyuanhui) was established and issued a weekly "summary of current news" for display. An example of these summaries had three pieces of news: a two-line update on the war in Europe; a longer description of the Chinese victory in battles in southern Hubei and northern Hunan, which told how many Japanese were killed and wounded; and an item about diplomacy, such as that China had signed an agreement for a loan of five million pounds from Britain. This example also included one sentence about diplomatic problems caused by the United States' refusal to sign a treaty of nonaggression with Japan.[37] From these passages, we see that the government focused on positive news to promote patriotism and inspire optimism.

The government also asked each police district to set up a large, well financed, and centrally located "model" teahouse as an example for all teahouses in the district. These teahouses had a simple platform for propaganda, which included newspapers and posters, a radio or record player, and maps of Sichuan and the world. The rule also gave nine categories of slogans to be put on the wall: uprooting traitors, military service, transportation, air defense, economizing and saving, raising money, "general spiritual mobilization," the New Life Movement, and the "Citizens' Pledge." In the category of "uprooting traitors," the government wanted people to follow the government's policies, carry out the orders of the military, and destroy Wang Jingwei's puppet regime. Through propaganda the government encouraged people to support military service and accept that "avoiding military service is the most shameful action." It wanted people to believe that "the War of Resistance can be won if everyone joins the army," and that giving favorable treatment to servicemen's families and serving in the military were "citizens' obligations."[38]

In the category of slogans, the government gave specific guidelines about what people should know and do.[39] While the government mobilized people, it also tried diligently to control people's thoughts and ideas in the name of the national interest. A so-called general spiritual mobilization was conducted to promote ideas such as the state and nation should be supreme, "selfishness" and "different and wrong thoughts" should be overcome, and so on. Whereas the "general spiritual mobilization" was aimed at mind control, the New Life Movement targeted behavior. It applied Confucian doctrines such as "the rite is a serious principle," "the righteous face death bravely," and "a sense of honor is a struggle on a grand and spectacular scale."[40] Thus, the government used traditional values to connect daily life with national current affairs. The government required all teahouses to post a "Citizens' Pledge" (Guomin gongyue) as part of wartime propaganda. The pledge had twelve items, requiring citizens to never: violate the Three Principles of the People; violate government regulations; violate the interests of the country and the nation; surrender to the enemy; join traitorous organizations; serve in the armies of enemies and traitors; help enemies and traitors; collect information for enemies and traitors; work for enemies and traitors; use the currencies of the banks of enemies and traitors; buy goods from enemies and traitors; and sell grain or other goods to enemies and traitors. In addition, government regulations required all teahouses to provide government-selected books and newspapers. These books covered many topics, such as praise of war heroes and members of the resistance, condemnation of traitors, mobilization, and the ideology of the GMD, as well as anti-CCP sentiments.[41]

As the war became a major focus, the government adopted a policy of suppressing all criticism of state power and its representatives. In 1940, for example, the government asked the Teahouse Guild to "stay on high alert" for 120 students from the Resistance University of Northern Shaanxi (Shaanbei kangda) who were coming to Chengdu and Chongqing.[42] The Chinese Communist Party established the university to cultivate leaders. Therefore, the students' arrival concerned the local government, which tried to limit their activities. In the political atmosphere of that time, teahouse employees had to work with the police to enforce local "security." In the same year, the police claimed that some traitors and hooligans plotted their activities in teahouses and demanded that the Teahouse Guild provide "secret reports" on them. The guild had no choice but to cooperate. The government used the term "traitors" loosely during wartime, frequently applying it to anyone who spoke out against the government. For example, the government defined "anyone who damages government regulations" as "a traitor" and demanded "cleaning out traitors and strengthening the rear area of defense."[43]

It is obvious that government control over the teahouse caused tremendous resentment. In 1942, the *West China Evening News* (Huaxi wanbao) published a satirical essay by Ju Ge describing a so-called ideal teahouse (*lixiang chaguan*) as a "municipal teahouse" in the heart of the city. The teahouse should have a director and associate director, and all customers should follow their instructions. The teahouse was to serve only Chinese tea, and the quantity of tea leaves in each bowl should be standardized: two millimeters per bowl of green tea, five millimeters for red tea, and three pieces for chrysanthemum tea. There was no limitation on the number of times a bowl could be refilled, but the quantity of water should not exceed 0.5 *sheng* (about 0.56 quart); customers who weighed more than sixty kilograms or had walked more than two kilometers under the hot sun could request 0.75 *sheng*. The teahouse should be open from 6 to 7 AM, from noon to 1 PM, from 4 to 5 PM, and from 9 to 10 PM. Patrons who stayed longer than two hours would be punished for wasting time. A teahouse-goer had to get a "card for drinking tea in the teahouse" (*yincha zheng*) that certified that he was at least twenty years old and employed, and had received approval from the authorities to patronize the teahouse, including for the reason that his home was too small to accommodate tea drinking. Patrons would be required to dress formally, to "straighten their clothes and sit properly," and to sip tea slowly. "Bizarre clothes," "exposing the neck and shoulders," "whispering," "yelling," and especially "loud talking" would be prohibited. All patrons would be required to be at the teahouse at a certain time, and would not be allowed to enter late or leave early. Before drinking, all patrons would be required to stand up and then be seated. Reading newspapers and playing chess would be forbidden. The teahouse should have a radio, which would be tuned only to certain programs of the Central Broadcasting Station, such as news and market information. All patrons would be required to exit the teahouse by marching in single file.⁴⁴ The author is deliberately mocking the teahouse regulations, such as basing the quantity of boiled water on a patron's weight and requiring patrons to enter and leave at the same time, and so on. The "ideal teahouse" he described is more like a military camp, which reflected people's dissatisfaction with increasing government control.

Never before had there been such large-scale distribution of government propaganda. This movement was well organized and highly controlled. Obviously, teahouses became a "battlefield" in the government's "war" for control. In teahouses, patrons could see and hear only what the government wanted them to see and to hear. We can only imagine the political environment and atmosphere created by those new dramas and the portraits, slogans, and pledges that were posted on the walls. Thus, under its wartime propaganda, the GMD successfully extended its political control into public space and public life. On the surface, teahouse life did not appear much changed, but to a great extent the core of teahouse life was altered by the domination of the national crisis and political orientation.⁴⁵

In March 1945, on the eve of victory against the Japanese, the provincial government enacted the Regulations on Teahouses in Sichuan (Sichuan sheng guanli chaguan banfa), which covered eleven issues ranging from the location of teahouses to hygiene. Under these rules, all teahouses had to be registered, and the number of teahouses was to be gradually reduced in areas where supply exceeded demand. Furthermore, the new rules prohibited the hiring of waitresses, bringing an abrupt end to the short history of women employees (see Chapter 3 for more details). The regulations forbade some services that had been offered for decades, including haircuts and pedicures, for reasons of hygiene. The regulations also brought new force to bear on the ban on certain activities, such as gambling and the singing of "licentious" songs, that had been long been ignored. Some trends, including the private "family tearooms" that emerged in the late Qing era, were also outlawed.⁴⁶

The opportunity to speak freely was an attraction of the teahouse but this freedom was often challenged by the government, which used its power to suppress people who expressed political ideas and criticized the authorities. Discussing politics in a teahouse was risky. The police and the government could use whatever was said in public against the speaker; some people were imprisoned for expressing their political views. The government commonly planted secret agents in teahouses to eavesdrop. Those who dared publicly criticize the government were harshly punished, which became a means of suppressing dissent. The teahouse also was implicated, even to the point of being forced to close. That is why the teahouse proprietor in Wen Yiduo's song in the epigraph to this chapter begged patrons not to discuss sensitive topics. People were afraid to speak freely.

"Do Not Talk about National Affairs"

According to Yu Xi's essay "Teahouse Politicians," "in the past, a public notice stating 'Do not talk about national affairs' (*Xiutan guoshi*) was posted in many teahouses."[47] A drawing of Chengdu teahouses has the caption, "Don't talk about national affairs but smoke freely" (see Figure 4.1), visual evidence of the existence of such a public notice. It is difficult to trace the origin of this public notice. In his novels about late Qing Chengdu, Li Jieren did not mention such a notice in his detailed accounts of teahouses. Yu Xi's article was published in 1943, when he regarded the notice as a relic of the "past," meaning that at least in 1943 it was no longer common.

Another account from 1942, however, indicates that such posters were still publicly displayed although in the form of humorous couplets: "If someone asks your opinion, do not talk about national affairs, just drink your tea" (*Pangren ruowen qizhong yi, guoshi xiutan qie chicha*).[48] In March 1945, when the war was almost over, Bai Yuhua wrote an article titled "A Chat on 'Do Not Talk about National Affairs'" about this phenomenon. According to the author, "In the teahouses off the main roads of Chengdu and those in the market towns and settlements outside the city, a public notice 'Do Not Talk about National Affairs' can often be seen." He in fact suggested that such posters could still be found in some out-of-way teahouses in wartime Chengdu, which caused him to comment:

> This is a backward, not progressive phenomenon. A strong democratic country should not have such a shortcoming, especially during a war that is crucial for the survival of the nation. People's involvement in national politics, the military, and the economy can give the greatest and most effective aid in the War of Resistance. A country's success in political, military, and economic affairs cannot be based simply on reading the outlines and principles of a few books. What can we not discuss? It should be all right as long as there is a limitation. Folks with conservative ideas should open their minds. Here, I hope that the local authorities can tolerate the following three topics: the war that is deciding the fate of the nation, current affairs, and the resistance movement. As long as we act under the government's leadership and guidance, what national affairs can we not talk about?[49]

The author thus expressed his dissatisfaction with governmental control although he was not overtly critical. Here, the author did not risk calling for true freedom of speech but simply asked for permission to discuss the war and its progress.

Posting such a public notice sparked criticism of Chengdu residents' lack of courage to speak out against authority. This blame seems unfair; notices could be found at teahouses in other regions as well. In Lao She's drama *Teahouse* (Chaguan), a similar public notice—*motan guoshi*—was also posted in teahouses in late Qing and Republican-era Beijing. Although the wording differed slightly (*xiutan*, or *motan*, or *wutan*), these notices had the same meaning.⁵⁰ From a certain angle, a sign that read "Do not talk about national affairs" itself was evidence of people's anger and desire to complain about the dictatorship under which they lived, which might serve a similar function as the message sent by those who tape their mouths shut in demonstrations for free speech.

Ultimately, the government could not suppress the topic of politics in wartime conversations. Patrons who frequently discussed politics in teahouses and whose opinions drew attention were humorously known as "teahouse politicians" (*chaguan zhengzhijia*) in Chengdu. In his 1943 article, Yu Xi stated that after the war broke out, people talked about politics more than ever before. It seems that Yu was uncomfortable hearing political talk. "National affairs," he wrote, "do not concern us." He claimed his attitude was not one of indifference but of exasperation with the stupidity of those who claimed to be "concerned with the nation" and "having a political mind" in their loud, daily arguments over politics in the teahouses. For example, those who often proclaimed that "So-and-so is a great man" or "So-and-so is covering up a conspiracy" irritated him. People who "thought of themselves as having political insight" often deliberately and mysteriously revealed one or two pieces of "important news," which they immediately emphasized would never be reported in the newspaper. His essay mocked ignorant "teahouse politicians" who liked to show off by telling "important news" and name-dropping.⁵¹

"Teahouse politicians" were usually those who read newspapers and liked to discuss politics. They lingered for hours each day in the teahouse, and what they heard became fodder for future discussions. They usually believed they were superior to those who did not understand politics and they always wanted to be the center of teahouse discussions. They spoke loudly and disliked opinions that differed from theirs. They wanted others to believe they were always right. Of course, some teahouse politicians earned a positive reputation while others became objects of ridicule. They behaved like actors on a stage and often gave their speeches in public. To a certain extent, they could influence public opinion. Although most public talk was not taken seriously, the teahouse did provide an informal forum in which people could express political views. The government, however, used force to put an end to any remarks it considered negative. In fact, talking about national affairs went on every day and in every teahouse; the notice "Do not talk about national affairs" was more a means for teahouse managers to deal with the government than with patrons because through it they could avoid responsibility for conversations the government did not like.

Yu's article reveals some interesting things "between the lines." The author disliked "teahouse politicians" probably because he resented the government's treatment of patriotic people and because the authorities punished those who expressed unpopular ideas. So, from the author's point of view, "teahouse politicians" were very stupid to get involved in politics, which the government never allowed. Or, the author probably was unhappy at the teahouse politicians' irresponsible claims, or resentful of their allegiance to a broader cause. Some elites thought that only they were qualified to talk about politics and became uncomfortable and even felt threatened when someone they considered inferior engaged in political talk. They did not want these people to be in the spotlight. In fact, although some political views seemed "unprofessional" or "silly," these discussions were the only outlet available to most people. Some people who talked about politics might know little about the subject, resulting in derision from others. Still, the teahouse was an important venue for making their voices heard, and certain factions always shared their opinions.

The End of an Era (1945–1950): Surviving the Civil War

After the War of Resistance, political talk again became taboo as the Civil War deepened and the pro-democracy and anti-despotism movement gained momentum. Most of the posters were replaced by the GMD party flag, the national flag, portraits of Sun Yat-sen and Chiang Kai-shek, and the Citizens' Pledge. The GMD did not tolerate public criticism. In the late 1940s, as resentment grew against corruption in the Nationalist government, inflation, and social disorder, the teahouse became commoners' only outlet for their frustration. When people became angry and started shouting, the teahouse keeper would say, "Be careful! The walls may have ears," meaning secret agents might be listening in.[52] The GMD suppressed the pro-democracy movement but on December 27, 1949, nearly three months after the establishment of the People's Republic of China, the People's Liberation Army captured Chengdu.[53]

Political turmoil not only had an impact on the teahouse trade but also created new teahouse politics. Soon after the war ended, three major authorities in Chengdu—the Chengdu Security Army, the Military Police, and the municipal government—issued a public notice that contained five rules: (1) People who served in the military or who were members of illegal organizations were strictly prohibited from gathering and holding any meeting in lodges or teahouses. (2) "Unworthy people" (*buxiao zhitu*) were strictly prohibited from mingling with prostitutes or gambling. (3) "Law breakers" (*feifa fenzi*) were strictly prohibited from gathering in the teahouse to drink settlement tea or disturb public order. (4) Anyone who damaged the property of lodges or teahouses had to reimburse the exact amount of the damage. (5) Anyone who violated any of these restrictions was to be severely punished.[54]

This public notice, like the many other regulations regarding the teahouse enacted during the late Qing and Republican periods, reflected the government's two major concerns: political gatherings and public order. Regarding the former, the government tried to restrict the exercise of political rights, including those of soldiers and Communists and their supporters, by prohibiting public activities that could develop into a political threat. Regarding the latter, the government was motivated by the need to maintain public security, but often also used ambiguous terms such as "unworthy people" and "law breakers" to attack political opponents rather than simply to maintain social order.

Although the government paid attention to the conversations held in teahouses, it scrutinized the public meetings held there even more carefully. The police and local government sent covert agents to spy on meetings of soldiers in an effort to learn about and squelch any rebellious action. As we have noted, the authorities also tried to control what people read and watched in the teahouse. Such supervision reached its zenith during the war, but the government also continued this tough policy after the war. In 1946, for example, the police sent a secret agent to the Sleeping Stream Teahouse to investigate a gathering of former military school classmates. The investigator reported that one Liang Qinghui organized the meeting to discuss how they could earn a living after being discharged from the military following their service on the frontlines. The group established an alumni association and elected Liang president to seek relief from the government and request that memorials be built in various places for their classmates who had been killed in the war.[55] That same year, the local government issued a public notice restricting such gatherings:

> Under the order of the Sichuan Provincial Capital Police on October 21, 1946, because some soldiers recently organized gatherings without permission and held meetings in inns and teahouses, the Military Security Committee has ruled that such activities be restricted in an effort to cut social disorder off at its roots. The professional guilds must hereby notify all shopkeepers of inns and teahouses that they should immediately report any meetings of military people in their inn or teahouse to the Bureau of the Military Police. Otherwise, they will be punished harshly.[56]

Government officials not only enacted regulations to control gatherings of military personnel but also required professional guilds and their members to act as informants to report any meeting in a teahouse to the government. The available sources indicate that most of these meetings were social and did not have a political agenda. Still, the government sought to eliminate this potential threat. That the government overreacted is reflected in the crises it faced as the democracy movement gathered momentum after the Civil War broke out.

One excuse the government gave as it sought to control teahouses was to change so-called backward social customs in the name of the "national emergency." In 1948, the governor of Sichuan issued an order, called "correcting the bad habits of gambling and idleness in the teahouse," claiming that it was "time for mobilizing, controlling turmoil, and building the state," and "for people to take responsibility and work hard."[57] But "bad habits" persisted, and the "rise in gambling" and the "prosperity of teahouses" continued unabated, which greatly affected people's peace of mind, sense of security, and the national economy. The governor also accused teahouses of being unhygienic and responsible for the spread of infectious diseases. Furthermore, because gossip, "licentious songs," and "evil plays" contributed to superstitious beliefs and immoral behavior, the governor supported teahouse reform for "popular and social education," to "turn uselessness into usefulness," to "regulate people who do not follow rules," and to "improve the city's appearance and sanitation." Under this order, no new teahouses would be allowed to open, a move the governor believed was an "important procedure for changing customs and habits," "mobilizing people," "controlling turmoil," and promoting "state building." The governor wanted to ensure that officials took these issues very seriously as he carried out this radical new policy.[58]

In the meantime, the police of the Sichuan provincial capital issued regulations called Temporary Rules for Regulating Teahouses (Sichuan shenghui jingcha ju guanli chashe ye zanxing banfa), which were even more detailed.[59] Following these regulations, the Chengdu municipal government issued Restrictions of Teahouses in Chengdu (Chengdu shi chaguan ye qudi banfa), which added new limitations: No new teahouses were allowed to open; teahouses in locations that affected public sanitation or blocked traffic were to be removed or shut down; teahouses could not move to a different location unless this became necessary to accommodate a public project such as the widening of roads; any transfer of ownership would not be officially recognized; teahouses that had been closed for longer than three months would not be permitted to reopen and their licenses would be revoked; and violators of the regulations would be punished according to the extent of the violation.[60] These regulations enacted by the provincial authorities, the police, and the municipal government all sought to limit the number of teahouses and the services they offered, but the regulations put forth by the police were the most detailed and concrete and expressed the strongest political orientation. The regulations imposed from the late Qing to the late Republican period not only reflected the state's increasing control over teahouses but also its need to constantly reassert its authority given that these regulations were often ignored.[61]

Conclusion

The teahouse was always a political arena where patrons were consciously or unconsciously drawn into the orbit of politics. Elites and local government officials always had a purpose when they criticized the teahouse and teahouse life. Sometimes it was to improve the city's image, and other times it was to promote cultural enlightenment, attack a "backward" lifestyle, preserve social order and stability, or protect the interests of their own groups and political agendas. Some people regarded the teahouse as a negative influence on society, as a place full of vice, where people wasted time, gossiped, spread rumors, smuggled, and so on, but some considered the social and economic functions of the teahouse an indispensable part of everyday life. These different opinions also reflected attitudes toward popular culture. The elites who held the negative view usually supported government regulation and believed that restricting the teahouse business and teahouse life was necessary, while others—although they thought reform was necessary—believed that the teahouse, despite its various problems, was an important tradition in urban society and contributed to cultural and economic development.

Teahouses played an important role in politics, especially in an era when people received most of their information on current events there and used them as places for political activities. Politics infiltrated the teahouse through other means as well. In fact, it is clear that many people liked to discuss politics in the teahouse. Regardless of their ability to articulate their views, knowledge of current events, or political orientation, people involved in political discussions had an impact on others. "Teahouse politicians" could at least make a voice heard that was different from the official one. Throughout the Republican period the government demanded that teahouse managers report conversations critical of the government and its policies. The public notice "Do not talk about national affairs" that was posted in teahouses might also have been a kind of protest by serving as a proclamation that free speech was not allowed. To a great extent, the teahouse was a barometer of politics, where the topics of conversation and patrons' freedom to express themselves changed along with the political situation. Although most patrons tried to avoid punishment by not talking about sensitive issues, some people, especially leftists like Wen Yiduo, who called for speaking out in the teahouse, struggled to gain rights that the government tried to suppress at all costs. Wen Yiduo paid the ultimate price when he was assassinated after giving a public speech in which he challenged the power of the Nationalist government.[62]

Teahouse culture, while tenacious, inevitably changed under the influence of local and national politics. On the one hand, throughout the four periods discussed, teahouse politics remained more or less the same, with people discussing various topics despite the risks, the government trying to enforce its regulations, authorities suppressing criticism and dissent, many kinds of disputes and conflicts taking place, and social groups and organizations using the space for their activities. But on the other hand, politics in the teahouse was different. From the late Qing to the early Republic, the government paid more attention to the reform of local operas and popular culture while people used the teahouse for political protests. During the New Cultural Movement of the late 1910s and early 1920s, conversations in teahouses focused on more cultural issues, such as one's identity and heritage, and the conflicts between new and old cultures or between Chinese and Western cultures. Teahouse politics reached its zenith during the war, when the teahouse became part of the state's propaganda machine. The government wanted to accomplish several goals through the teahouse: to mobilize people, inspire patriotic zeal, suppress activities that threatened authority, and enforce its absolute power. By using slogans and the Citizens' Pledge, the government wanted people in the teahouse to mobilize and participate in official movements, such as military service and raising money, and wanted to promote patriotism and the New Life Movement. Some of the government's most important targets were so-called traitors, a term for those serving Japanese interests but one that eventually was used to anathematize anyone who challenged the government's power and authority. During the Civil War, any political gathering became taboo and any political talk became dangerous as the democratic movement gained momentum and the economy deteriorated.

Three kinds of politics were evident in the teahouse: Mass politics by ordinary people, elite politics by intellectuals and reformers, and state politics by the government. Thus, politics in the teahouse became very complex, multifaceted, and multileveled. The freedom of commoners to express their political views ultimately was suppressed by the cultural hegemony of the elite and by state power. Elite reformers tried to change the teahouse in order to expand their influence on public politics as the liaison between the people and the state. Sometimes they depended on state power to achieve their goal of teahouse reform, but other times they resented state control of this public forum. The government's role was also comprehensive; the state attacked and suppressed the expression of grass-roots political opinion, while it developed a flexible attitude toward elite politics, in which support or attack was determined by the government's interests. These three kinds of politics coexisted and interacted in the teahouse, making teahouse politics complicated and colorful.

Conclusion:
The Triumph of Small Business and Everyday Culture

THIS BOOK HAS FOCUSED on three issues. First is the booming teahouse business. Teahouses had a unique dynamic and culture, and survived by adopting various business strategies. Nonetheless, they also endured hardships through periods of economic deterioration, social disorder, and political uncertainty. The Teahouse Guild took an active role in dealing with the government and handling issues of pricing and other matters between the profession and the government and between individual teahouses. This book has also analyzed issues pertaining to the workforce, working conditions, employment, and workplace culture. The second issue is the question of teahouse life and teahouse culture. People used the teahouse for leisure, entertainment, and socializing. In the teahouse, people met their friends or watched performances while various social groups such as students, laborers, gangs, and associations conducted their activities there. Women struggled for the right to use this public space. The third issue is the teahouse's role in local and national politics. The teahouse was a scene of conflict and government control and was closely connected with public politics. The teahouse became a political arena that played an important role in the revolution, reformist movement, and wars as it was used by the general public, elites, and representatives of the state.

The process of reforming and controlling teahouses in Chengdu was part of the city's modernization and search for identity, experienced by many other cities in modern China. As Joseph Esherick notes, "Despite the great diversity of modern urban types, there was remarkable uniformity in the modernist agenda of China's urban reformers."[1] The reform measures carried out in Chengdu's teahouses—which addressed entertainment, public order and security, hygiene, business operations, public behavior, morality, new and improved facilities with the introduction of electric lights and running water, indoctrination of patriotism, and so on—were also enacted in many other cities, even though they might not have targeted the teahouse. From this perspective, the teahouse was a microcosm that showcased almost all of the theories and practices of modern urban reform.[2] As Chengdu's ties to the national economy, culture, and politics grew, so did the struggle over the customs and traditions historically found there and those brought in from other places, causing Chengdu's residents to evaluate their identity, as seen in the debate over teahouse life. Modernization weakened the uniqueness of Chengdu's culture, or as Esherick points out, "eclipse[d] the differences of local cultures." The War of Resistance accelerated this process dramatically as the Nationalist government moved to Chongqing and a huge number of refugees flooded the inland cities. This study, however, also shows that the local culture retained its vitality, at least in the teahouse. Although the wave of modernization transformed urban daily life nationwide, the core of everyday culture in Chengdu survived more or less intact.

A study of teahouses gives us not only a better understanding of small businesses, everyday culture, and public politics, but also a broader perspective on the relationship between local history and national culture, on similarities and differences in public drinking customs and public life in China and the West, on small business survival strategies, and finally, on changes and continuity in China's social and cultural life during the first half of the twentieth century. While many traditional businesses disappeared or declined under the burgeoning influence of the West and subsequent economic, political, and cultural transformations, teahouses not only continued to survive but to thrive. As a small business, the teahouse never lost its vitality; as a public space, it never became disconnected from its patrons. By 1950, the teahouse remained the strongest representative of small businesses and local culture in Chengdu.

The Teahouse as Microcosm

Anything and everything could happen in the teahouse, and all sorts of people—scholars, officials, merchants, peddlers, coolies, beggars, shopkeepers, waiters and waitresses, barbers, storytellers, fortune-tellers, and performers—interacted there. Unlike other small shops, which served patrons for a relatively short time and where the interaction was basically between shopkeepers (or employees) and customers, teahouses served those who lingered for many hours or even a whole day and the interaction was largely conducted between patrons. Furthermore, those who made a living in the teahouse, such as peddlers, also played a role. All kinds of people engaged in all kinds of activities there: talking and gossiping, negotiating business deals, settling disputes, smuggling, gambling on games and bird fights, playing games such as chess and cards, looking for a job or hiring, collecting information, complaining about life or politics, holding meetings, arguing, and even fighting. The complexity of teahouses was also reflected in their structure and business operations. A teahouse keeper could be a government official, a prominent merchant, a well-known scholar, a master of the Gowned Brothers, or an absentee landlord, but he could also be a hand-to-mouth laborer, a farmer from the countryside, a formerly wealthy man who was now bankrupt, a peddler, or a low-ranking soldier. A teahouse keeper could be a native Chengdunese or an immigrant, a city sophisticate or a rural rube, or a man or a woman. Teahouse keepers' different backgrounds—education, native place, occupation, families, and so forth—led to different ways of running the business, and different approaches to management, decor, taste in tea, and the treatment of customers.

The teahouse reflected economic, political, cultural and social changes. The prices teahouses charged always fluctuated with the rate of inflation; when the cost of raw materials increased, the price of tea rose; when the economy slumped or when a natural disaster occurred, the number of beggars in the teahouses increased. Likewise, political changes were first evident in the teahouse. Early every morning, the hot topic of conversation was always the latest local and national news. When analyzed over a long period, the specifics of teahouse conversations about politics paralleled the nation's political transformation. In the late Qing era, people discussed the nationalization of the railroad; in the 1910s, topics focused more on the wars between warlords; in the 1920s, people were interested in Westernization and new aspects of culture; in the 1930s and early 1940s, discussions concentrated on Japanese aggression; and in the late 1940s, government corruption, inflation, and the Civil War became the most popular subjects. Teahouse conversations were a barometer of political change. Although government regulations focused on hygiene, public order, and the decency and morality of performances, emphases on one or another of these changed constantly. For example, in the late Qing era the government focused on "obscene" and "violent" programs, but during the War of Resistance it required shows to extol patriotism and condemn traitors.

Because of China's geographic and social complexity, both similarities and differences between regions should be considered. Studying the most basic units of society and going deep inside the city should not prevent historians from examining overarching and significant events and answering larger questions. On the one hand, studies of social fixtures such as teahouses lead us to the deepest levels of the city from which we can see phenomena that have hitherto been largely ignored. On the other hand, an exploration of significant events can enhance our understanding of the relationship between political and social transformations at the national level and daily life at the local level. Therefore, when I focus on teahouses in Chengdu, I inevitably bring local issues into the national arena. For instance, if we deal with the emergence of waitressing, we must also consider the issue of war refugees, who brought characteristics of their more open coastal culture to Chengdu. Such a combination of studies ensures a consideration of macrohistorical questions when we look at history from a microhistorical perspective.

Analyzing the teahouse as a "microcosm" also raises several problems: Can the microcosm represent the larger society and can the experience of the microcosm explain that of the larger society? Also, is a conclusion based on a small sample applicable to the entire population? Chinese social anthropologists, who often study small communities but try to establish a pattern that can provide a greater understanding of the larger society, have been troubled by the same questions. The smaller community is an inseparable subset of the larger society, yet it hardly represents the larger society, because it stems only from "local knowledge" or "local experience." Despite this limitation, local knowledge at least provides a piece of the puzzle. This study is not intended to offer a universal model or pattern of Chinese urban public life, but provides some local experience that can enrich our understanding of history as a whole. Regardless, microhistory is significant because it raises the case study to a level that makes possible generalizations about urban history and helps us understand not only Chengdu but also other Chinese cities.

The process by which modernity brought cultural uniformity to China varied by region. Chengdu, as an inland city, had its particular transformation. Compared with cities in East China, where the Western influence first took hold in the nineteenth century, in Chengdu the weakening of cultural distinctiveness occurred much later and much slower. Through the study of the teahouse and everyday culture, we see that resistance to change was substantial. Under the mighty Westernized discourse of culture, "civilization," and "patriotism," those who favored cultural uniqueness lost their voice, but the underlying local culture and lifestyle retained their vitality. Even though Chengdu could not stop the wave of modernist uniformity, to a large extent it survived. The trend toward the uniformity of modernity met enduring resistance, and this became a theme in the relationship between modernity and traditional culture, along with the growing role of the state in public space and public life during the first half of the twentieth century.

The State's Growing Role in Public Life

The government always paid more attention to public places than to private spaces, and tried to regulate them. With the adoption of the New Policies in the late Qing, Chengdu's local authorities and reformist elites, like those in other Chinese cities, launched a campaign to improve the city's image by restructuring the city's appearance and landscape. Teahouses, as important public places, became their major targets. Throughout the Republican period the government enacted many regulations concerning teahouses on issues of hygiene, public order, entertainment, and registration and licensure. The evidence indicates that the government based all of its policies on the notion that teahouses, teahouse life, and leisure activities harmed society. The government could not eliminate this traditional business entirely because so many depended on it to make a living, but it could, and did, limit the establishment of new teahouses throughout the Republican period.[3] Any teahouse that wanted to move to a new location or transfer ownership had to endure a long and complex bureaucratic process, and even risked losing its right to do business altogether. The government generally had enough power to enforce its regulations, but it often had to compromise once policies were put into practice.

The government focused much of its efforts on teahouse theaters because it believed that watching operas exerted a strong influence on ordinary people. It made a great effort to infuse popular entertainment with orthodox ideology and lead mass culture into the political arena.[4] Government control also reflected the relationship between the state and society, elites and commoners, and elite culture and popular culture. The process by which regulations were made often revealed the dominance of the state over society, elites over commoners, and elite culture over popular culture. We must be aware that the government often exaggerated the vices found in teahouses in order to bolster its rationale for control. For example, the government constantly used terms such as "lecherous" or "violent" to characterize plays it did not like, revealing a cultural prejudice and motivation for seeking cultural hegemony by adopting standards that forbade notions of love, divinity, and legendary virtues. The attack against popular culture during the early twentieth century led reformist elites to oppose the "unhealthy" influence of any plot that dealt with romantic love or divine powers.[5]

These regulations had different effects. Some were not enforced; some were carried out only for a short time; some were only partially implemented. Some regulations were enforced in the beginning but later relaxed for a variety of reasons. First, the government lacked consistency; any change in the national or local political scene, including the leadership of the local government or police, could influence the implementation of rules, especially given the unstable political situation found between the 1911 Revolution and the War of Resistance. Second, teahouse keepers avoided compliance through any means possible, and the government lacked the resources for thorough oversight, providing one more example of the difficulties of penetrating the bottom levels of society. To a large extent, the government had to rely on the Teahouse Guild and teahouses themselves for enforcement. The Teahouse Guild cooperated with the government in limiting the number of teahouses. Also, in many cases teahouses reported "illegal conduct" by competitors. On the surface, it seems that informants supported the restrictions, but their actions more likely reflected their desire to keep potential competitors at bay.

From studying the various regulations, we have seen that from the late Qing era to the fall of the Nationalist government the basic policies concerning teahouses were very similar, focusing on public order, sanitation, "wholesome" entertainment, and so on. Of course, the government often met resistance, especially when its influence affected commoners' ability to earn a living. Teahouse owners had their own means of resistance and managed to survive. They fought for their individual interests and the Teahouse Guild protected the profession's overall interests. Three groups—elites, social reformers, and the government—each with different agendas, sought to influence the teahouse.[6]

The Teahouse and Its Western Counterparts

To a certain extent, Chinese teahouses are comparable to Western taverns, cafés, coffeehouses, and especially, saloons. Of course, significant differences existed between teahouses and their Western counterparts. Scholars of Western history in recent years have focused on studying public life, which has introduced a new vantage point for examining urban history and political transformation. In the study of American history, for example, there has been a focus on the role of drinking places, alcohol, and the temperance movement, while in European history the social context of the tavern, café, and coffeehouse has been explored. The existing scholarship offers us a frame of reference from which we can see how people in different social arenas conducted their public life and used the public spaces they created.[7]

A discussion of the "public" should consider Jürgen Habermas's model of the "public sphere." Our concern is not whether Habermas's concept can be used to analyze the structure of modern Chinese society—a subject that has long been debated among historians of China—but how his concept considers physical public space as a social arena from which to draw political significance.[8] Habermas recognized that the emergence of new beverages changed people's lifestyles. In the middle of the seventeenth century, tea, chocolate, and coffee became popular, especially in upper-class society. Early eighteenth-century London had more than three thousand coffeehouses, "each with a core group of regulars." They provided places for people to move from the private sphere into the public. Much of the bourgeois public sphere was based on coffeehouses, cafés, salons, and so on, where, Habermas believed, there was "a public sphere still existing largely behind closed doors." In fact, Habermas's "public sphere" is not always a social and political sphere; sometimes it refers to a physical space. As Habermas stated, "The line between private and public sphere extended right through the home. The privatized individuals stepped out of the intimacy of their living rooms into the public sphere of the *salon*." The salon as public sphere was actually located in a private place "where bourgeois family heads and their wives were sociable." People gathered there "out of a private life that had assumed institutional form in the enclosed space of the patriarchal conjugal family." Unlike the salon, the coffeehouse was open to the public and was where people sought liberty in places regarded as "seedbeds of political unrest."[9] Like the European coffeehouse, the Chinese teahouse was an arena where opinions were shared and other forms of social communication took place.

From the perspective of the physical "public sphere," the Chinese teahouse played a similar role in public life and politics to coffeehouses and salons in Europe and saloons in America. Scholars who have studied the tavern, saloon, café, and coffeehouse have found that these were not solely places for drinking, but were multifunctional establishments. In their forms of ownership, services provided, and social functions, teahouses were not fundamentally different from public drinking places in the West. Like teahouses, saloons in the United States were complicated establishments that "touched almost every aspect of city life."[10] A saloon not only provided alcohol and food, but also lodging, an employment office, and a place for political gatherings, as did teahouses.[11] The coffeehouse likewise was comparable. As sociologist Richard Sennett has pointed out, it was a place where "speech flourished" and "distinctions of rank were temporarily suspended." Everyone there "had a right to talk to anyone else" and "to enter into any conversation," regardless of whether he was with strangers or friends.[12]

The teahouse in Chengdu became a political arena during the first half of the twentieth century, but in this respect it was not unique. The use of the public arena as a political stage was found in other Chinese cities as well as in other countries. In eighteenth-century European cities, coffeehouses were major urban institutions where people freely expressed their opinions. By the middle of the century, the café emerged as a place that served liquor and where strangers gathered. Just as the people of Chengdu played a role in the social drama on the teahouse "stage," the "public man," to borrow Richard Sennett's term, behaved "as an actor" in the public spaces of Europe.[13] Indeed, whenever a man entered a public place, whether a teahouse or bar, he both watched others and was watched by others in a "show" performed by "actors." In addition, the Chinese government's attempt to control people's public activities during the late Qing and Republican periods reflected an effort that was not unique to China. Reformers in American cities engaged in a similar effort by attempting to bring the saloon under their control, even trying to shut down all drinking places or to transform saloons into orderly places by enforcing tough regulations that often reflected class discrimination. Often saloon keepers believed these regulations undercut their business.[14]

Chapter 1 reveals that opening a teahouse—like establishing a tavern in France or a saloon in the United States—did not require much capital. A tavern in eighteenth-century Paris could be opened with "little more than a table and chairs with a roof overhead."[15] In nineteenth-century American cities, operating a saloon was "the easiest business in the world" for a person to "break into with small capital."[16] Many saloons, like teahouses, were also family businesses, and thus were "the cheapest places to run," because they were "little more than an extension of the household," with no wages to pay. A family could adapt its living room for business, with the wife and children as helpers. Many small shops were driven out of business during economic downturns, but saloons remained "one of the most stable institutions in the neighborhood," similar to the teahouse trade in Chengdu. Just as many immigrants in Chengdu regarded the teahouse as their "semi-home," their counterparts in American cities, who moved often, adopted the saloons as their permanent mailing address, and just as the teahouse was the most popular and affordable place for ordinary Chengdu residents to relax, saloons enjoyed a stable business largely because of "the lack of alternative space," even though Americans had more options than the people of Chengdu. The saloon business was also flexible: the saloon could serve the mobile population who looked for employment during the day and neighborhood residents in the evening.[17]

Teahouses welcomed patrons from all social classes, but most served ordinary people, like saloons, which were "a center of working-class social life" and "commercial leisure-time" establishments. The rise of saloons resulted from improved working conditions, such as shorter workdays and higher wages. Saloons in the United States, as well as teahouses in China, had gender and ethnic distinctions, as seen, for example, in the Chicago City Council's banning of female workers in 1897.[18] In American cities, each group had its special beverage, spoke its native language, and told its favorite jokes, which could be divided into three categories: ethnic, neighborhood, and occupational. Saloons seemed "as essential as churches to the life of many neighborhoods," but social and ethnic groups used the saloon differently based on their own cultural and economic backgrounds. In this respect, saloons were very similar to the teahouses operated by native-place associations, guilds, and the Gowned Brothers. The teahouses of native-place associations served people who came from the same native place, those of guilds served specific professions, and those on neighborhood street corners mainly served people who lived nearby, but usually did not exclude other customers. Just as the teahouse became the center of operations for the Gowned Brothers, American saloons played a similar role in the activities of gangsters, who chose local saloons as their headquarters.[19]

Saloons also provided some necessary facilities in a neighborhood. In nineteenth-century American cities, clean drinking water and toilets were scarce, so the saloon provided beer and a restroom to attract customers. Furthermore, the saloon offered food, warmth in the winter, a meeting space, check-cashing services, and newspapers, making life more convenient and comfortable, even to the point that workers who did not have a permanent address "picked up their mail, heard the local political gossip, or learned of openings in their trade" in the saloon. The saloon, like the teahouse, also provided entertainment in the form of singing, joke telling, and storytelling, which became a crucial part of saloon life, as well as a site for gambling, illegal liquor sales, and cockfighting. Many men in American cities went to the saloon to find employment, giving the saloon a "role as a labor exchange." People who were unemployed gathered in a particular saloon, usually located near the jobs they sought; employers knew where to find them.[20] The saloon also served as a "natural listening post" for gossip and political news, with the saloon keeper acting as the popular "center of communication."[21] Many of these pictures painted by scholars of American urban history also describe Chengdu teahouses.

Taverns, coffeehouses, cafés, and saloons, as well as teahouses, provide an excellent vantage point from which to observe the relationship between the notions of public and private. In eighteenth-century Paris, public drinking places such as taverns "stood at the juncture between public and private, between work and recreation."[22] A private family home could be turned into a teahouse in Chengdu or a saloon in Chicago or Boston, where customers constantly scrutinized the shopkeeper's family life, including his cooking skills, habits, and marriage. In a teahouse, there was often no boundary between public and private space; for example, patrons could easily glimpse inside the proprietor's bedroom. Following a Chinese custom, young female members of the family were taught to avoid contact with strangers, but the teahouse keeper and his family had little privacy. Their family life was largely carried out in front of teahouse-goers, and private matters might become a topic of conversation or gossip. In such a teahouse, private men became public men as private space was transformed into a semi-public or public space. Also, in the teahouse, the private matters of other patrons were always interesting fodder for "public talk." Just as the saloon played a crucial role "as a center of gossip," the teahouse also was a hub where patrons talked with their neighbors about what was happening with their families, relatives, or friends.[23] In most cases, people in the teahouse did not care much about privacy, but sometimes, conversations or gossip led to conflict.

Of course, the physical "public spheres" in the West and China differed in many ways. First, there are obvious differences in local politics between the teahouse and its Western counterparts. In American cities, the saloon was a site of "sidewalk-level politics."[24] Saloon keepers participated in local politics; some became members of the Common Council, although artisans and small merchants also filled some seats. This suggests that American society supported involvement in city affairs. Saloons also hosted early labor unions, which had experienced many difficulties finding gathering places, and some saloons even became "a regular home for the union." As a social institution, the saloon helped communicate across the "ethnic divisions that fragmented the labor movement." When a strike took place, the saloon could be used as headquarters.[25] Some saloon proprietors became very active in community politics by giving social groups free use of their space. Workers could even use their neighborhood saloons for forming political clubs and organizing political activities. In nineteenth-century Paris, café life helped carry on the working-class movement and café owners played "a vital role" in the development of workers' associations.[26] Whereas saloon and café owners were actively involved in local politics, as discussed in Chapter 8 in most cases teahouse proprietors tried to stay out of politics insofar as possible.

Second, the West had its own cultural and social foundation. The culture of tea drinking developed differently in China and Britain. Before tea was introduced into Britain, middle-class families usually served their guests and friends alcohol in the private space of their own home. Tea gradually replaced alcoholic drinks on such occasions.[27] Britain and other Western countries, however, have never created a public space for drinking tea comparable to saloons for drinking alcohol and coffeehouses for drinking coffee.[28] People in Western cities had more choices for leisure pursuits than the Chinese, such as gardening, bowling, dancing, walking, skating, ball and billiard playing, attending concerts, listening to lectures, visiting reading rooms, and so forth.[29] Chengdu residents, lacking other avenues for public life, depended on teahouses more than people in the West depended on cafés, saloons, and coffeehouses.

Third, women in China faced many more restrictions in public than Western women. While working men went to the saloon, "theater-going was a popular form of entertainment" for working-class women, and the late nineteenth century saw "the emergence of a female audience" along with the development of motion pictures.[30] In the United States, saloons attracted many children, and therefore, alcohol became "one of the greatest threats" to city children.[31] The presence of children in teahouses in Chengdu to watch storytelling, folk performances, and local operas never became an issue, although some people complained that this took time away from studying.

Chinese public places of leisure exerted less control over children but more over women, the opposite of what occurred in the West.

Fourth, the central figures in such public spheres—bartenders and teahouse waiters—behaved in different ways. A bartender generally served customers from one spot, so he could converse while working, unlike the waiter in the teahouse, who moved about the entire room to serve patrons and could not stay in one place long enough to interact with others. As described in Chapter 3, the teahouse waiter usually greeted his guests and exchanged a few polite words while working. The fast-paced nature of the job made him an excellent servant but not a good listener. In addition, barkeepers and teahouse waiters occupied different social stations. It was socially appropriate for a bartender to join patrons' conversations, but this was not a case for a teahouse waiter. Patrons did not mind if the waiter briefly commented on the topic under discussion, they did not expect him to join their conversation.

Of course, taverns, coffeehouses, cafés, and saloons varied significantly depending on their location and era of operation. Although they were counterparts of teahouses, and they did not fall into a universal pattern. This book is not a comparative study and thus does not offer a detailed and systematic comparison of the teahouse with each of its Western counterparts. Nonetheless, this summary of their similarities and differences in terms of both Chinese history and world history can enhance our understanding of teahouses and teahouse life.[32]

The Triumph of Small Business and Everyday Culture

The teahouse survived the urban reform movement, government attacks, economic downturns, and waves of modernization, deftly handling complex relationships with other trades, ordinary people, elites, society, and the state. This dexterity helped the teahouse trade survive economic, political, and other national crises and adapt to issues of supply and demand. The teahouse built a united front with some small businesses, especially with peddlers and ordinary residents, who were used to and appreciated the convenient service of small shops. This was a united front in the sense that everyone faced the common threat of modernity, which worked to displace the small shops that appeared weak, without sufficient capital and government support. When the mighty new industries that gained strong support from the government were placed virtually alongside small shops and their allies, the industries lost some of the power they had accrued in the coastal region. Small shops successfully built a "Great Wall" that prevented this intrusion.

The teahouse business was very flexible, adjusting to economic and other conditions and serving all kinds of people, rich and poor, weak and mighty.

Small businesses had to have a strategy to compete with each other, attract customers, and remain profitable. The teahouse trade endured in part because it did not require a large amount of capital and was relatively easy to operate. It had a steady stream of customers from all walks of life. The business provided a space for all sorts of activities, from leisure pursuits to business transactions, from social gatherings to political meetings, and a broad range of other pursuits, both legal and illegal. Although a dramatic transformation took place from 1900 to 1950, the size of small businesses and their business practices changed little. Some teahouses followed the trend of material culture by adding electric lights and offering distilled water and newspapers in the late Qing; offering telephones and table tennis during the 1910s and 1920s; and hiring waitresses and offering lodging, record players, coffee, and snacks in the 1930s and 1940s. As society became more open, teahouses welcomed women; when the government wanted to disseminate propaganda, teahouses adapted to the new requirements and found a way to profit from performances that promoted the government's political agenda.

The most important characteristic of the teahouse's flexibility was its universal service. Even though teahouses observed class distinctions, there were different levels and styles for different social groups and classes. In some cases, a single teahouse offered different settings for different classes, such as "elegant" seats for wealthy patrons and "regular" seats for everybody else. The teahouse was important for the poor, many of whom depended on it to make a living selling everyday items or offering services such as haircuts and pedicures. The teahouse also was a good place for panhandling; patrons who were in a good mood might give more money. For many poor people, the teahouse might be the only indoor place for leisure that they could afford, and storytelling and other folk performances provided the high point of a day filled with hours of hard manual labor. Even those who could not afford a bowl of tea were allowed to enter and drink the tea left behind, and when a show was under way, they could stand outside and watch for free. This was the case in ordinary street-corner teahouses, but the fancier tea gardens, tea balconies, and opera theaters were surrounded by walls and guarded by gatekeepers.

Teahouses developed close, mutually dependent relationships with nearby residents, social groups, and organizations, and offered irreplaceable services. The teahouse was a public space where everyone felt welcome, an atmosphere deliberately cultivated by the teahouse proprietor and waiters as well as by the patrons themselves. Thus, the teahouse fostered a unique commercial culture, perpetuating local traditions while keeping up with developments in the trade. While other service businesses, such as small shops, restaurants, barbershops, and public bathhouses also cultivated these features, the teahouse was unique because it served as an office space and market as well as a place of leisure. Every social group in Chengdu went to the teahouse and usually had its own favorite. Social groups were based on members' social status, common interests, political views, friends, native places, and other common grounds. People in teahouses discussed all kinds of topics. They got to know each other very well, sharing information about their work, families, happy and sad events, and even about private matters. Someone who needed help might first ask his teahouse buddies for information or advice. This social group, of course, was loosely formed, but still functioned as a social force. Teahouse-goers could also chat with strangers, some of whom eventually became acquaintances. Members of the upper class, such as government officials, rich merchants, prominent scholars, or military officers, all enjoyed going to the teahouse; teahouse life was part of their everyday life. Although the elites constantly criticized teahouses for perpetuating "vice," most still believed that the teahouse was necessary. Elites went to the teahouses frequented by others of their social station, and while they might converse about different topics than the lower classes, the local operas and Peking operas they watched were the same, which indicates the value both placed on Chinese tradition. New elites condemned programs that they considered contrary to orthodox ideology, especially those with plots involving love, the supernatural, and deities. While new elites could not control every aspect of a public place such as the teahouse, they imposed their ideas for reform, inevitably leading to changes in teahouse culture.

The government attacked the teahouse because it claimed that it was a refuge for "evil people." The government, unlike local elites, scarcely considered the role the teahouse played in the lives of ordinary people; its main concern was gaining control over public places and turning the teahouse into what it wanted, which inevitably jeopardized the livelihood of teahouse proprietors and their employees. Therefore, teahouse proprietors often found ways to resist government control. The first was "passive resistance": teahouses might not overtly oppose new policies, but simply fail to follow them. The second was through collective action, especially when dealing with issues of pricing and taxation. In this study, we have seen many examples of this form of resistance, which was always organized and overseen by the Teahouse Guild. The third means was for a teahouse to fight individually, which sometimes was successful. Nonetheless, teahouses, as a small business, were no match for the government's power, and some had to face the fate of being closed down. There is no question that the teahouse as an institution, however, displayed extraordinary vitality and strength. It always found a way to survive, no matter how tough the restrictions were, how bad the economy was, or how fiercely the government attacked. It may not be an exaggeration to say that "the teahouse was the soul of social and public life." As Sha Ting declared, "There was no life without the teahouse." The teahouse was a beloved institution that drew people together. As we have seen, the government never stopped adding restrictions and taxes, while local toughs and out-of-control soldiers tyrannized teahouses, jeopardizing business, but the teahouse overcame these challenges. It adapted to the harsh environment and fostered the flexibility necessary to survive.

Teahouse life, however, changed over time. For example, in the late Qing and early Republican eras, the Gowned Brothers operated covertly in teahouses, and by the late Republican era openly established its turf there; the police and government turned a blind eye to its activities. Also, the teahouse was transformed from a male-only domain to one where females also were accepted, especially after the late 1930s, when women became regular customers and waitresses, leading to a new atmosphere. The most dramatic change in teahouse culture was political. Conversations in teahouses shifted with developments in local and national politics. Government control increased as it issued and brutally enforced a plethora of new regulations concerning sanitation, registration, pricing, hours of operation, locations, and public order. More significantly, the government used the teahouse as a venue for disseminating political propaganda, requiring the display of national and party flags, political slogans, "citizens' pledges," portraits of leaders, censored news, and patriotic books and performances, which created some new phenomena of teahouse culture. In addition, patrons were punished for speaking their mind about certain issues; the mandatory public notice posted on the wall reminded them that any political talk at any time could get them in trouble. Given these developments, the teahouse, teahouse culture, and teahouse life changed greatly.

While some aspects of the teahouse changed dramatically during the first half of the twentieth century, others did not. An examination of this continuity gives an opportunity to better understand the nature of small businesses, public life, and teahouse culture in China. The general business and management practices, competition, and employment issues experienced no significant change. Throughout the first half of the twentieth century, the size of the teahouse trade remained almost the same even though the population of Chengdu increased dramatically. Teahouses provided a venue for public life and people provided nonstop business for teahouses. Political, economic, and social changes could not alter the teahouse's basic function. As long as there was urban life, the teahouse found loyal customers. At the point of the Communist Party's victory in 1949, the teahouse was still a place where local residents followed leisure pursuits and sought entertainment, a market where merchants conducted business negotiations and petty peddlers sold their goods, a place where seasonal workers found jobs, and a social arena where many social groups and associations still gathered. Teahouse proprietors still used the traditional ways of raising capital, renting space, buying the same kinds of utensils and furniture, and decorating their shops. Even when the country was at war, they still tried to open their teahouses earlier and close them later, because longer hours of operation helped business by increasing profits. Except for the short time during the war when waitresses worked in teahouses, "masters of tea" served customers and male stove keepers boiled water; many teahouses were solely family businesses without any paid workers. Although the price of tea increased over the years, it basically kept pace with inflation; there was no radical change in the ratio of the price of tea to the price of rice; tea remained affordable for most people. The Teahouse Guild, from the late Qing era to the demise of the GMD regime, still dominated the profession, playing a crucial liaison role between the state and individual teahouses, and working with the government on registration, pricing, and taxation. Many people desperately wanted to enter the business, but the guild and the state authorities wanted to limit competition and so endeavored to control the number of teahouses in Chengdu.

When the Communists took over Chengdu at the end of 1949, the teahouse business still prospered despite the five-year Civil War that came on the heels of the eight-year War of Resistance. Over a decade of turmoil, economic deterioration, rampant inflation, and political disorder brought down many businesses, but the teahouse trade remained relatively stable. In 1949, Chengdu had 659 teahouses, the most since 1935.[33] But the teahouse trade, like all other businesses in China, faced a turning point that year as teahouses, public life, and everyday culture experienced an unprecedented revolution along with the rest of the country. Their fate under socialism will be the subject of my next study.

Appendix*
Comparison of Tea and Rice Prices, 1909–1948

Time	Tea (1 bowl)	Rice (1 dan)	100 bowls of tea can buy rice (dan/pound)
1909–10	4 wen	7,400 wen	0.054/16.75
1924	20 wen	11.2 yuan	0.071/22.14
1925	70 wen	20.8 yuan	0.08/26.1
1937	2 cents	26.8 yuan	0.075/23.13
Aug. 1940	10 cents	141 yuan	0.071/22.01
Jan. 1941	15 cents	311 yuan	0.048/14.88
Feb. 1941	20 cents	329 yuan	0.061/18.91
Mar. 1941	25 cents	309 yuan	0.081/25.11
Nov. 1941	30 cents	567 yuan	0.053/16.43
Jan. 1942	15 cents	664 yuan	0.023/7.13
Apr. 1942	40 cents	933 yuan	0.043/13.33
May 1942	50 cents	990 yuan	0.051/15.81
July 1942	70 cents	890 yuan	0.079/24.49
Sept. 1942	60 cents	1,077 yuan	0.056/17.36
May 1943	1.2 yuan	3,260 yuan	0.037/11.45
Mar. 1945	12 yuan	27,162 yuan	0.044/13.64
Apr. 1946	45 yuan	44,100 yuan	0.1/31
Aug. 1946	60 yuan	48,727 yuan	0.12/37.2
Sept. 1947	600 yuan	500,000 yuan	0.121/37.51
Nov. 1947	800 yuan	1,670,909 yuan	0.048/14.88
Dec. 1947	1,000 yuan	1,982,222 yuan	0.05/15.5
Jan. 1948	1,800 yuan	3,154,283 yuan	0.057/17.67
Aug. 1948	2 cents	40 yuan	0.05/15.5
Sept. 1948	6 cents	131 yuan	0.046/14.2
Dec. 1948	20 yuan	677 yuan	0.03/9.3

NOTE:

* I have been unable to find a complete inventory of rice prices in Chengdu. Therefore, the table uses a proxy: rice prices in Pi County, one mile from Chengdu's West Gate. The price of rice in Pi County should not have differed significantly from that in Chengdu.

The prices of a bowl of tea are for the most common and least expensive tea sold.

The monetary system changed several times during the period of 1909 to 1948. In this table, in 1909–10, the currency was copper yuan; in 1924, copper yuan (for tea) and silver yuan (for rice); 1 silver yuan was about 2,500–3,000 wen); in 1925, copper yuan (for tea) and silver yuan (for rice); 1 silver yuan was about 4,000 wen); from 1935 to August 1948, fabi; and from August 1948: golden yuan (*jinyuanjuan*). In August 1948, fabi was replaced by golden yuan at the rate of one golden yuan to three million fabi yuan.

To convert dan into pounds is very difficult because there was no standard rate; not only did different regions in China have different weight systems, but even in Chengdu there was no standard. Generally, one dan of rice was about 160–180 pounds in East China, which was much less than that of Sichuan. In late Qing-era Chengdu, 1 dan was between 280 and 300 jin and in the 1940s, it was also 280 jin (CDTL, I: 103; JSWS: 377), or about 307–330 pounds. I use 310 pounds in my conversions of dan into pounds.

SOURCES: Tea prices: CDTL, 2: 252; CSJJD, 93-6-739-1; 93-6-735-1; CSSD, 104-1401; 104-1390; 104-1400; 104-1309; 104-1391; CSZGD, 38-11-807; 38-11-32; 38-11-1535; Shu Xincheng, 1934: 144–45. Rice prices: JSWS: 365–72.

Character List

THIS LIST omits the most common terms that are clear in their English translation, the names of provinces and major cities, and the names of people for whom Chinese characters are not especially needed.

aiqiu shi　哀求式
Anlan chaguan　安瀾茶館
Anlesi chashe　安樂寺茶社
Ba Bo　巴波
Babao jie　八寶街
bai matou　拜碼頭
bai shitiaozi　擺詩條子
baiguan　擺館
Baimeigui (teahouse)　白玫瑰（茶館）
baixiang de ren　白相的人
Banbian jie　半邊街
bandeng xi　板凳戲
bang　幫
Baofeng yuqian　暴風雨前
Baogong an　包公案
baohu fei　保護費
baxian zhuo　八仙桌
Beidong jie　北東街
Beidou zhen　北門鎮
Bianjing　汴京
bufa zhitu　不法之徒

buxiao zhitu　不肖之徒
Caihua ban　彩華班
cha boshi　茶博士
chachuan　茶船
chaci　茶詞
chafang　茶房
chafang　茶坊
chafang jiusi　茶坊酒肆
chagai　茶蓋
Chaguan guan'gai　茶館觀丐
Chaguan shige xiao Chengdu, Chengdu shige da chaguan
　　茶館是個小成都，成都是個大茶館
Chaguan xiaodiao　茶館小調
Chaguan xuanchuan shishi jihua　茶館宣傳實施計劃
chaguan zhengzhijia　茶館政治家
Chaiquan jie　茝泉街
Chaishijie　柴市節
chajian jiugui　茶賤酒貴
Chajiu lun　茶酒論
chajuan fengchao　茶捐風潮
chalou　茶樓
chalun　茶輪
chang shuipeng　唱水棚
chang tanghui　唱堂會
Changhe xuan (teahouse)　暢和軒（茶館）
Changle ban　長樂班
Changshun jie　長順街
chapeng　茶棚
chapu　茶鋪
chashe tingye kangjuan　茶社停業抗捐
chashe　茶社
chashe ye　茶社業
chashi　茶室
chasi　茶肆

chating (tea hall) 茶廳

chating (tea pavilion) 茶亭

chawan 茶碗

chaye 茶業

chayuan 茶園

chazhuo juan 茶桌捐

Chengdu jingbei silingbu 成都警備司令部

Chengdu kuaibao 成都快報

Chengdu shenghui jingcha ju dang'an 成都省會警察局檔案

Chengdu shi canyihui 成都市參議會

Chengdu shi chaguan ye qudi banfa 成都市茶館業取締辦法

Chengdu shi chashe minsheng gonghui 成都市茶社民生工會

Chengdu shi chashe ye zhiye gonghui 成都市茶社業職業工會

Chengdu shi chashe yonggongye zhiye gonghui huiyuan gongzuo gongyue 成都市茶社傭工業職業工會會員工作公約

Chengdu shi gongshang ju dang'an 成都市工商局檔案

Chengdu shi gongshang xingzheng dengji dang'an 成都市工商行政登記檔案

Chengdu shi jinqianban tongsu jiangyan xuanchuan ye zhiye gonghui 成都市金錢板通俗講演宣傳業職業工會

Chengdu shi minggongye zhiye gonghui 成都市茗工業職業工會

Chengdu shi qingyin zhiye gonghui 成都市清音職業工會

Chengdu shi shanghui dang'an 成都市商會檔案

Chengdu shi shizheng gongsuo 成都市政公所

Chengdu shi tongsu pinghua ye zhiye gonghui 成都市通俗評話業職業工會

Chengdu shi yinshidian ji chashe qingjie jiancha banfa 成都市飲食店及茶社清潔檢查辦法

Chengdu shi zhengfu gongshang dang'an 成都市政府工商檔案

Chengdu shizhengfu weisheng shiwusuo 成都市政府衛生事務所

Chengdu weisheng jiancha weiyuanhui 成都衛生檢查委員會

Chengdu xianxiang 成都現象

Chenghua chaan guancha dian 成華茶岸官茶店

Chenghua cheng yishihui 成華城議事會

chi jiangcha 吃講茶

chi xiancha 吃閑茶
chi zaocha 吃早茶
chicha 吃茶
chicha yu guoyun 吃茶與國運
chousha 仇殺
choutai baichu 醜態百出
chuan gezi 穿格子
Chuanren zhi Chuan 川人治川
chunli laojunjuan 春禮勞軍捐
Chunxi dawutai (Chunxi wutai) 春熙大舞臺(春熙舞臺)
Chunxi lu 春熙路
chutangshui 出堂水
Cihui tang 慈惠堂
Cuihua ban 翠華班
Da cuipingshan 大翠屏山
da daoqin 打道琴
da lianxiang 打連響
Daan jie 大安街
Dabo 大波
Dagangzi 打杠子
dagu (or dagushu) 大鼓(或大鼓書)
Daguan chayuan 大觀茶園
Daguanghan gechang 大廣寒歌場
Dahan Sichuan junzhengfu 大漢四川軍政府
Dahoufang 大後方
dan 石
daweigu 打圍鼓
Dawutai 大舞臺
dayang (money) 大洋（錢）
dayongtang 打湧堂
Dayu shouzi 打魚收子
Deng Xihou 鄧錫侯
Derong chashe 德榮茶社
dianguang xi 電光戲

dianxi 電戲
diaojiaolou 吊腳樓
diaotang 吊堂
dingda 頂打
Diyi chashe 第一茶社
Diyi gongyuan chashe 第一公園茶社
Diyilou (teahouse) 第一樓（茶館）
Diyiquan (teahouse) 第一泉（茶館）
Dong dajie 東大街
Dongchenggen jie 東城根街
Dongfang chalou ming'an 東方茶樓命案
Dongpo ting (teahouse) 東坡亭（茶館）
Dongya wutai 東亞舞臺
Dongyiqu 東一區
Dongyu jie 東禦街
Dongyuan chashe 東園茶社
Dongzi kou 洞子口
Dou E yuan 竇娥冤
Duan shuangqiang 斷雙槍
erhu 二胡
Erquan chalou 二泉茶樓
Erquan chating 二泉茶廳
eshao 惡少
fabi 法幣
Fangji chashe 方記茶社
Fangqu zhi 防區制
Fangzheng jie 方正街
Feibing yuan 廢兵院
feijijuan 飛機捐
Feng Yan 封演
Feng Yuxiang 馮玉祥
Feng Zikai 豐子愷
Fengshi wenjianji 封氏聞見記
fengya zhishi 風雅之士

Fengyunting chashe　風雲亭茶社
fenlian chicha　粉臉吃茶
Fu chenghuang miao　府城隍廟
fulang zidi　浮浪子弟
Furong chalou　芙蓉茶樓
Furongting chashe　芙蓉亭茶社
Fushun xian lüsheng tongxiang hui　富順縣旅省同鄉會
Fuxing ban　復興班
Fuxing men　復興門
Gaochalou　高茶樓
gejiu gewei　各就各位
Gexin juyuan　革心劇院
Gexin yuan　革心院
Geyuan (teahouse)　葛園（茶館）
gonghui (guild)　公會
gonghui (union)　工會
Gonghui fa　工會法
Gonghui shishi fa　工會實施法
gongsuo　公所
gongye　公爺
Gongyuan　貢院（街）
Gongyun fa　工運法
Guaizaoshu jie　拐棗樹街
Guande (teahouse)　觀德（茶館）
guangguai luli de shehui　光怪陸離的社會
Guanghan pingju yuan　廣寒平劇院
Guangxinglong (restaurant)　廣興隆（飯館）
Guangyuan　廣元
gui chapu　鬼茶鋪
Guiqulai chalou　歸去來茶樓
Guomin gongyue　國民公約
Guomin jingshen zongdongyuan gangling ji shishi banfa
　國民精神總動員綱領及實施辦法
guomin juan　國民捐

guoyu shili　過於勢利
han chaqian　喊茶錢
hanghui　行會
hanjian　漢奸
he gaiwan cha　喝蓋碗茶
he jiabancha　喝加班茶
he shui xiang cha　河水香茶
hecha　喝茶
Heiyi dang　黑衣黨
Heming chashe　鶴鳴茶社
hongfei heipian　紅飛黑片
hongqian bang　紅錢幫
Hongsheng chashe　鴻陞茶社
Hongxing (teahouse)　鴻興（茶館）
Hu Jingyi　胡景伊
hua chafang　花茶房
Huahua chating　華華茶廳
huaji chehuang shi　滑稽扯謊式
Huan wo heshan　還我河山
Huang Ji'an　黃吉安
Huang Jilu　黃季陸
Huangcheng　皇城
Huangtiandang　黃天蕩
huanguo　換過
Huaxi　華西（大學）
Huaxi ba　華西壩
Huaxi ribao　華西日報
Huaxi wanbao　華西晚報
Huaxing chashe　華興茶社
Huaxing jie　華興街
Huguang guan (street)　湖廣館（街）
Huifeng chashe　惠風茶社
huo chungong　活春宮
huodao nao　夥倒鬧

huodong yehu 活動夜壺
huoqian 火錢
huqin 胡琴
Jiangshangcun (teahouse) 江上村（茶館）
Jianguo chuxu 建國儲蓄
Jianguo fanglüe 建國方略
Jiangxi jie 漿洗街
Jiangyou guan 江油關
Jianping she 建平社
jiaojin ziman, mukong yiqie 驕矜自滿，目空一切
jie gaizi 揭蓋子
Jiesan Xinsijun yu zhengchi junji 解散新四軍與整飭軍紀
Jieyue yundong 節約運動
Jinchun chalou 錦春茶樓
Jinchunlou sanjue 錦春樓三絕
Jing'an chashe 靜安茶社
Jinglanxuan (teahouse) 靜蘭軒（茶館）
Jinjiang chashe 錦江茶社
Jinjiang chayuan 錦江茶園
Jinjiang ge (teahouse) 錦江閣（茶館）
Jinling 金陵（大學）
Jinling nüzi 金陵女子（大學）
jinqian ban 金錢板
Jinquan (teahouse) 金泉（茶館）
Jinquan jie 金泉街
Jinsheng chayuan 近聖茶園
jiudian fafu, chafang buqiong 酒店發富，茶坊不窮
judong qingfu 舉動輕浮
Junle juyuan 均樂劇院
Junping jie 君平街
kaili matou 開立碼頭
kelian de xiaoniao 可憐的小鳥
kewu de shidai 可惡的時代
Keyuan (teahouse) 可園(茶館)

kouzishang chicha　口子上吃茶
Kunshou ji　困獸記
lanbing　爛兵
laojun　勞軍
Leguan chayuan　樂觀茶園
Leng Hongfa chashe　冷洪發茶社
Li Jieren　李劼人
lian'ai changsuo　戀愛場所
Liang Hongyu　梁紅玉
liangdi　亮底
liangjia funü　良家婦女
liangnü　良女
liangtang　亮堂
Liangyuan (teahouse)　梁園（茶館）
Lianhua (teahouse)　聯華(茶館)
Liao Wenchang　廖文長
Lichun chashe　麗春茶社
Lin Zexu　林則徐
Ling Guozheng　淩國正
Lingyunbu　淩雲步
Linjiang yingxi chayuan　臨江影戲茶園
Liu Wenhui　劉文輝
Liu Xiang　劉湘
Liujiang chashe　柳江茶社
liula zhizhan　六臘之戰
liulianliu　柳連柳
liuluo de yishujia　流落的藝術家
liupi　流痞
liuwang genü　流亡歌女
lixiang chaguan　理想茶館
Longchun chayuan　龍春茶園
Longqiao　龍橋
longtou daye　龍頭大爺
longxing hubu　龍行虎步

Longyou chashe 龍友茶社
Lu Xiufu 陸秀夫
Luo Lun 羅綸
Luomei 落梅
lushui fuqi 露水夫妻
Lütian chashe 綠天茶社
Lüyin ge 綠蔭閣
Maiyanzhi 賣胭脂
Mantan Chengdu nü chafang 漫談成都女茶房
matou 碼頭
mazhayi 馬紮椅
Mengding (teahouse) 蒙頂（茶館）
Mengshan 蒙山
miandi 免底
Mianhua jie 棉花街
Mingde tang 明德堂
Mingyuan (teahouse) 茗園（茶館）
Modeng jushe 摩登劇社
moku 魔窟
motan guoshi 莫談國事
Nanjing guoju shuchang 南京國劇書場
niaoshui hudou 尿水胡豆
Nongyin chalou 濃蔭茶樓
Nongyuan (teahouse) 農園（茶館）
nü chafang 女茶房
pangren ruowen qizhong yi, guoshi xiutan qie chicha
　旁人若問其中意，國事休談且吃茶
pao jingbao 跑警報
Paoge 袍哥
paotan 跑灘
peng genü 捧歌女
pengke 捧客
Pingjia hui 評價會
pingmin hua 平民化

Pingmin juyuan 平民劇院
Pingshan xian lüsheng tongxiang hui 屏山縣旅省同鄉會
Pinxian chalou 品仙茶樓
Pinxiang chayuan 品香茶園
pitiao ke 皮條客
Pu Dianjun 蒲殿俊
putong zuo 普通座
Qianfang kangzhan shangbing zhiyou she 前方抗戰傷兵之友社
Qianghua xinjushe 強華新劇社
qiangpo shi 強迫式
qianqian 千錢
Qilu daxue 齊魯大學
Qingcha wodu, wodao, shaoxiang jiemeng, chuanxi xiejiao guize
　清查窩賭、窩盜、燒香結盟、傳習邪教規則
qingchaguan 清茶館
Qingfengting 清風亭
Qinglong chashe 青龍茶社
qingtan wuguo 清談誤國
Qingyang chang 青羊場
Qingyang chang zhengjie 青羊場正街
Qingyang gong 青羊宮
Qingyin dengying xiyuan 清音燈影戲園
qinqiang 秦腔
qipao 旗袍
qiuba 丘八
Qiyi chashe 棋藝茶社
Quanxing (teahouse) 全興（茶館）
Quanye chang 勸業場
Qudi xiqu guize 取締戲曲規則
Qudi xiyuan fa 取締戲園法
Qunxian chayuan 群仙茶園
Qunyi xinjushe 群益新劇社
Qunyi zongshe 群益總社
Ronglu xuan (teahouse) 榮祿軒（茶館）

Ruci de Wang Jingwei 如此的汪精衛
Rujiaohui 儒教會
Rulin waishi 儒林外史
Sandao huiguan 三道會館
Sanhuai chayuan 三槐茶園
Sanhuaishu chashe kezhan 三槐樹茶社客棧
Sanjijiang 三祭江
Sanjinzhong 三盡忠
Sanmin zhuyi dazhong duben 三民主義大眾讀本
Sanqiao nanjie 三橋南街
Sanqinghui 三慶會
sanxian 三弦
Sanyigong (teahouse) 三益公（茶館）
Sanzhan Huayuan 三戰華園
Shaanxi jie 陝西街
Shanbei kangda 陝北抗大
shanggui 商規
Shanhe lei 山河淚
Shaocheng 少城
Shazi bao 殺子報
Shede hui (teahouse) 射德會（茶館）
Sheng dongyuan weiyuanhui 省動員委員會
Shengqing chayuan 聖清茶園
Shentongzi 神童子
Shi canyihui 市參議會
Shidai chashe 時代茶社
Shihui jie 石灰街
Shiliang chayuan 師亮茶園
Shiyu zhuo 拾玉鐲
shuangshou qinwang 雙手擒王
shucha 書茶
shuchang 書場
Shuihong taozi 水紅桃子
shuiqian 水錢

Shunxing (teahouse)　順興（茶館）
Shuwutai　蜀舞臺
Shuxin wutai　蜀新舞臺
Shuyuan nanjie　書院南街
Sichuan dili　四川地理
Sichuan jingcha zongting　四川警察總廳
Sichuan quansheng xuesheng lianhehui　四川全省學生聯合會
Sichuan sheng guanli chaguan banfa　四川省管理茶館辦法
Sichuan shenghui jingcha ju guanli chashe ye zanxing banfa
　四川省會警察局管理茶社業暫行辦法
Sichuan shengli kexueguan　四川省立科學館
Sichun chashe　泗春茶社
Simaqiao xiaoqi　駟馬橋小憩
Siming (teahouse)　四明（茶館）
Siquan chashe　泗泉茶社
Siwei chashe　四維茶社
Suihan chashe　歲寒茶社
Suihua jilipu　歲華記麗譜
Taiheheng (teahouse)　泰和亨（茶館）
taiji　太極
Taiping guangji　太平廣記
Taiping xia jie　太平下街
Tan Chengduren chicha　談成都人吃茶
Tang Minghuang　唐明皇
tangcai　堂彩
tangchang　堂唱
tangguan　堂倌
tangpai　堂派
Tangyuan chashe　棠園茶社
tangzuo　堂座
tanya zuo　彈壓座
Taojin ji　淘金紀
Taoyuan chashe　桃源茶社
tebie zuo　特別座

Tian Hongxing Teahouse　田洪興（茶館）
Tian Songyao　田頌堯
Tianhui zhen　天回鎮
Tianluo diwang　天羅地網
Tianqi miao　天齊廟
Tianxia weiluan Shu xianluan, tianxia yizhi Shu weizhi
　天下未亂蜀先亂，天下已治蜀未治
tihu gongren　提壺工人
tizhengtang　提正堂
Tongchun chalou　同春茶樓
Tongchun chashe　同春茶社
tongxiang　同鄉
Tongxing (teahouse)　同興（茶館）
Tongxing chashe kezhan　同心茶社客棧
tongye gonghui　同業公會
Tongyin chalüdian　桐蔭茶旅店
Toushi shediao　偷詩射雕
tuanti xieyue　團體協約
waiguo chaguan　外國茶館
wancha　晚茶
Wanchun chayuan　萬春茶園
Wang Fu　王敷
Wang Qingyuan　王慶源
Wang Xiushan　王秀山
Wangjiaguai (street)　汪家拐（街）
wannian tai　萬年臺
weichicha er chicha　為吃茶而吃茶
Weijiaci chashe　魏家祠茶社
weijunzi　偽君子
Wen Tianxiang　文天祥
Wen Yiduo　聞一多
wengzi　甕子
wengzi fang　甕子房
wengzi jiang　甕子匠

wenping chu, chadao wang　溫瓶出，茶道亡
Wu Yu　吳虞
Wu Zhihui　吳稚輝
wucha　午茶
wucha wuzuo　無茶無座
Wufu (teahouse)　五福（茶館）
wuguo　誤國
wulao qixian　五老七賢
Wusheng jiangyan hui　武聖講演會
xi chawan　洗茶碗
Xiaheba　下河壩
xiajiangren　下江人
xiancha　閑茶
Xiangguang (teahouse)　祥光（茶館）
xiangmian xiansheng　相面先生
xiangyu　鄉愚
Xianhua nü chafang　閑話女茶房
Xianweijing xia zhi Chengdu shi　顯微鏡下之成都市
Xiao Jun　蕭軍
Xiao Tianzhu jie　小天竺街
xiaoben shangye　小本商業
xiaodan　小旦
xiaofangjuan　消防捐
Xiaofangniu　小放牛
Xiaohuayuan chashe　小花園茶社
Xiaoshangfen　小上墳
Xieji chalou　協記茶樓
Xin shenghuo gushi ji　新生活故事集
Xin yusha jie　新玉沙街
Xinghe chayuan　興和茶園
Xinglong xiang　興隆巷
Xingsheng (teahouse)　興盛（茶館）
Xinminbao wankan　新民報晚刊
Xinshenghuo cujinhui　新生活促進會

Xinshijie chayuan　新世界茶園
Xinyouxin dawutai　新又新大舞臺
Xiong Zhuoyun　熊卓雲
Xitaihou　西太後
Xiutan guoshi　休談國事
Xiyu jie　西禦街
Xiyuan (teahouse)　西園（茶館）
xizai xiang　西崽相
yaming　雅名
yandai pazi　煙袋帕子
Yandai xiang　煙袋巷
Yang Sen　楊森
yangqin　揚琴（洋琴）
Yanshi kou　鹽市口
yanwuju　演武劇
yanxiao yinlang　言笑淫浪
yao jieshou, chaguan zou　要解手，茶館走
yaoshi　麼師
yazuo　雅座
yedian　野店
Yeshui touwu　鄴水投巫
yexi　夜戲
Yichun (teahouse)　益春（茶館）
Yichunlou (teahouse)　宜春樓（茶館）
Yicuihua　遺翠花
Yihe chayuan　頤和茶園
Yihua chashe　益華茶社
Yijia chun (teahouse)　一家春（茶館）
Yileban　頤樂班
Yin Changheng　尹昌衡
Yincha bu　飲茶部
yincha zheng　飲茶證
yindang　淫蕩
yingye ziyou　營業自由

Yingyong shiji 英勇事跡
Yintao 飲濤（茶館）
Yinxiang chalou 吟香茶樓
Yinxiaolou (teahouse) 吟嘯樓
yinyuejuan 音樂捐
Yiyi chayuan 一一茶園
Yiyuan (teahouse) 宜園（茶館）
Yongni (teahouse) 永霓(茶館)
Yongquan ju chashe 湧泉居茶社
yongtang 湧堂
youmang jieji 有忙階級
youshang fenghua, mieshi renquan 有傷風化，蔑視人權
youxian 悠閒
youxian 有閑
youxian jieji 有閑階級
youzuo wucha 有座無茶
Yuanheng chahao 元亨茶號
Yuanyuan chashe 元圓茶社
Yudai qiao 玉帶橋
Yue Fei 岳飛
Yuelai chayuan 悅來茶園
Yuelai Zhongxi canguan 悅來中西餐館
yugong 寓公
yugu 魚鼓
yuqiancha 雨前茶
Yuyuan (teahouse) 俞園（茶館）
Zai Qixiangju chaguan li 在其香居茶館裏
zaocha 早茶
Zengji chashe 曾記茶社
Zhang Dai 張岱
Zhang Henshui 張恨水
Zhang Shijie 張士傑
Zhang Shizhao 章士釗
zhangguan buru fuguan, zhanggui buru tangguan
  長官不如副官，掌櫃不如堂倌

Zhanshatan 戰沙灘
Zhanshi Chengdu shehui dongtai 戰時成都社會動態
Zhao Erfeng 趙爾豐
Zheng Banqiao 鄭板橋
Zhengyu huayuan 正娛花園
Zhenliu chashe 枕流茶社
zhishe 支社
zhiye genü 職業歌女
Zhiye jieshao suo 職業介紹所
Zhiyin shuchang 知音書場
Zhiyu dianyingyuan 智育電影院
Zhongguo Guomindang Chengdu shi renmin tuanti linshi zhidao weiyuanhui 中國國民黨成都市人民團體臨時指導委員會
Zhongguo hongshizihui Huayang fenhui 中國紅十字會華陽分會
Zhonghe (teahouse) 中和（茶館）
Zhonghe yuan (teahouse) 中和園（茶館）
Zhongxin (teahouse) 中心（茶館）
zhuang shuiyan 裝水煙
zhuangyan war 裝煙娃兒
Zhuo Wenjun 卓文君
zhuqin 竹琴
Zhuxianzhen 朱仙鎮
Zhuyuan (teahouse) 竹園（茶館）
Ziluolan (teahouse) 紫羅蘭（茶館）
Zitongqiao xijie 梓潼橋西街
Zongcai gao Chuansheng tongbao shu 總裁告川省同胞書
Zongfu jie 總府街
zongshe 總社
Zouma jie 走馬街
zui minzhu de minzhong fating 最民主的民眾法庭
zuo chaguan 坐茶館
zuochang xi 坐場戲

Notes

Introduction

1. Microhistory is a well developed in the field of European social and cultural history but is virtually absent from the study of China. See, for example, Ginzburg, 1982, 1983, 1989; Muir and Ruggiero, 1990, 1991, 1994. Nonetheless, the work of Jonathan Spence can be seen as a kind of "microhistory" that sometimes uses the stories of an individual or individuals as a lens for viewing history. See, for example, the *Death of Woman Wang* and *Treason by the Book* (Spence, 1978, 2001). Because of a lack of systematic archival sources, I will not adopt the microhistory approach by focusing on a single case to examine the teahouse in depth; rather, I will combine general investigations and case analyses. Regarding "public life," see Di Wang, 2003: 13–14. Here "everyday culture" is the "range of discourses and practices that were widely shared in everyday life" (Ruggiero, 2001: 1142). Regarding studies of everyday culture, see Certeau, 1984; Lüdtke, 1995; Ruggiero, 2001. In this book, I often use the terms "lower class" or "ordinary people," by which I mean those often anonymous and forgotten people who lived below the level of the middle class. I define "elites," and "social (or elite) reformers," in my book *Street Culture in Chengdu* (Di Wang, 2003: 16–18). Here, I use them with the same meaning.

2. Joseph Esherick's edited anthology *Remaking the Chinese City* (2000) focuses on modernity and national identity. The volume has contributions by Michael Tsin on Canton, Ruth Rogaski on Tianjin, Kristin Stapleton on Chengdu, Liping Wang on Hangzhou, Madeleine Yue Dong on Beijing, Charles Musgrove on Nanjing, Stephen MacKinnon on Wuhan, and Lee McIsaac on Chongqing. These essays explore issues such as urban planning, reconstruction, hygiene, identity, and so on. Also, see Tsin, 1999; Rogaski, 2004; Stapleton, 2000a; Dong, 2003; and Di Wang, 2003.

3. This is a book about teahouses, not tea. Tea culture is a different—and fascinating—subject, but it is not my focus. Also, many books have been published on this subject, although most are for a general readership. Therefore, I basically ignore the subject of tea leaves themselves, including the production and transportation of tea, except as this subject is related to the teahouse, teahouse culture, or the custom of public drinking.

4. Bird, 1987 [1899]: 345, 350; Wilson, 1929: 112; Chizuka, 1926: 230.

5. For more detailed information on population in Chengdu, see Table 1.2.

6. Jia Daquan and Chen Yishi, 1988: 1–6; Wang Guoan and Yao Ying, 2000; Wen Wenzi, 1990: 452; Evans, 1992: chap. 2.

7. Wang Guoan and Yao Ying, 2000: 32.

8. The earliest record is *What Feng Saw and Heard* (Fengshi wenjianji), written by Feng Yan during the Tang dynasty, which said that, on the route from Shandong and Hebei to the capital, Chang'an, there were many shops where people paid money to drink tea. Also, in *Old Tang History* (Jiu Tangshu) and *A Record of the Peaceful Era* (Taiping guangji) the term "tea stands" (*chasi*) was used (Wang Guoan and Yao Ying, 2000: 49–50).

9. Gernet, 1970: 49–50; Evans, 1992: 60–61; Wang Guoan and Yao Ying, 2000: 49–50; He Manzi, 2002: 271; Wang Hongtai, 2000.

10. Although Jia Daquan and Chen Yishi's *History of Tea Production in Sichuan* (Sichuan chaye shi) states that "the earliest teahouses in Sichuan were be found before the Tang dynasty," they did not provide concrete evidence to support this claim (1988: 368).

11. Fei Zhu, n.d.: 2a–4a.

12. Here is the poem: "The autumn sun is as hot as a steamer,/ and we stop the cart to rest./Then we call for a bowl of tea / at the end of Four-Horse Bridge" (Gu Ying, 1987: 301). In this book, I use the phrase "bowl (*wan*) of tea" instead of the more common "cup (*bei*) of tea" because Sichuan teahouses used bowls to serve tea and calculated sales per bowl. People throughout Sichuan referred to bowls instead of cups of tea.

13. Dingjinyan, 1805: 63.

14. Zhou Xun, 1987 [1936]: 24; Di Wang, 2003: 152. Bamboo armchairs and low wooden tables are not depicted in the drawings of teahouses from this period; instead, benches or armless wooden chairs are shown.

15. Ye Wen, 1949; Wen Wenzi, 1990: 452.

16. Chen Jin, 1992: 32. Teahouses had a logical connection with lavatories because customers who drank a lot of water had to have a convenient place to relieve themselves. Therefore, most teahouses in Chengdu had their own toilets. Some people even used the number of public toilets to estimate the number of teahouses. For example, He Manzi stated that it is only a slight exaggeration to say that every street in Chengdu had at least one teahouse. Public toilets were built within walking distance for the convenience of teahouse-goers; this was satirically called "streamlined coordination production." In Chengdu, the toilet was either inside or outside a teahouse, or nearby in the neighborhood. He Manzi noted that all public toilets were numbered; from this, a rough estimate of the total of the number of teahouses can be reckoned. He found that one toilet near the North Gate was number 970, so he guessed that Chengdu probably had more than a thousand toilets and an equivalent number of teahouses. During that time Chengdu had a population of four hundred thousand or so; there was an average of one teahouse per every four hundred people (He Manzi, 1994: 139). He Manzi's claim that each teahouse had a toilet might not be accurate, even though many teahouses did have them. Many residents depended on public toilets, and some teahouses might not have had a toilet if there was one already nearby. In fact, some toilets attached to teahouses were not considered "public toilets." According to a 1927 yearbook, Chengdu had 1,259

public toilets (*Chengdu shi shizheng nianjian*, 1927: 506). On the reform of toilets in Chengdu, see Stapleton, 2000a: 137.

17. Davidson and Mason, 1905: 86; Shu Xincheng, 1934: 142; Qiu Chi, 1942; Li Ying, 2002.

18. He Manzi, 2002: 270–71.

19. Most of his writings on teahouses in Chengdu are collected in He Manzi, 1994; and He Manzi, 2002.

20. But the problems were "too much crowding" and "uncomfortable seats." Teahouses, he believed, would be improved if they had comfortable seats, more space between tables, and less noise (XMBWK, Oct. 27, 1943). Wang Qingyuan (1944) offered a comprehensive description of teahouses in the small market towns on the Chengdu Plain, but teahouse culture there was similar to that found in the city proper.

21. For such articles, also see TSRB, Apr. 29, 1910. For the late Qing and early Republican criticisms of popular culture and teahouses, see Di Wang, 2003: chap. 4.

22. GMGB, Aug. 4, 1912. *Mingshan xian zhi* (Gazetteer of Mingshan), 1936, vol. 15, cited in Qin Heping, 2000: 93.

23. Shu Xincheng, 1934: 144–45. Shu mentioned Zhang Shizhao (1881–1973), a well-known scholar and educator who was minister of education during the warlord period. In the 1920s, he published articles and gave lectures praising the traditional agrarian lifestyle and opposing industrialization. These articles and lectures have been collected in Zhang Shizhao, 2000.

24. XXXW, Apr. 29, 1938. For more such articles, also see Jian Fu, 1942; Qiu Chi, 1942.

25. SZSC, 186 v. 1431; Ci Jun, 1942; Qiu Chi, 1942.

26. Lao Xiang, 1942.

27. In 2000, Chengdu had at least three thousand teahouses (*Shangwu zaobao*, May 19, 2000).

28. Suzuki, 1982. The next year he published another article on teahouses in late Qing Shanghai. Although a dearth of sources again prevented him from deepening his discussion, Suzuki's studies opened a door to further exploration by historians. In fact, in 1974, Takeuchi Minoru, a scholar of Chinese literature, published *Teahouses: A General Description of Chinese Customs* (Chakan: Chūgoku no fudo to sekaizo). Despite its title, the book actually is a general introduction to the gamut of Chinese customs, with only one section about teahouses. Takeuchi likely was acknowledging the centrality of the teahouse as a symbol of Chinese culture and customs by giving the book this name and putting the chapter on teahouses first (Takeuchi, 1974). Although John Evans's book *Tea in China* is a general history of the Chinese tea trade, he devotes two chapters to a discussion of teahouses in the Song and Qing periods, which provide a useful account of the development of teahouses in China. However, Evans does not address how geographical factors and regional culture affected teahouses and teahouse life in different areas (Evans, 1992: 60–66, 140–43).

29. Nichizawa Haruhiko published two articles on Chinese teahouses. The first, a general overview published in 1985, provides a helpful overview of Chinese teahouses and their history. His second, from 1988, is probably the first to examine teahouses in Chengdu. It is especially valuable considering that most scholars of

urban history have focused only on China's coastal regions. This article, like Suzuki's, also was limited to a few sources, but the scope of the article is from the late Qing era to contemporary times, giving a general picture of teahouses in Chengdu over a long period. For example, his information on teahouses before 1949 was derived almost solely from Chen Maozhao's memoir, "Teahouses of Chengdu" (Chengdu de chaguan). The most interesting part of Nichizawa's article is its description of the revitalization of teahouses in Chengdu after the Cultural Revolution (Nichizawa, 1985, 1988; Chen Maozhao, 1983). Japanese scholars, however, have published some extensive studies of the teahouse in Japan (see Nakamura Toshinori, 1992; Satō, 1993).

30. Wang Hongtai, 2000. One of the earliest studies in this category, *Daily Life in China on the Eve of the Mongol Invasion*, by Jacques Gernet, published in the late 1950s, gives a short description of teahouses in Southern Song Hangzhou (Gernet, 1970: 49). There are a few other relevant studies in Chinese. In his book on rural market towns and social transformation in modern Jiangnan, Xiao Tian relates how teahouses were used for social and commercial activities. Liu Fengyun, in her book on urban space in the Ming and Qing, compares teahouses in major cities such as Beijing and Shanghai. She finds that Beijing, in addition to having large teahouses, also was home to many smaller ones, called "pure teahouses" (*qingchaguan*), the crudest of which were "tea sheds" (*chapeng*). All of these became a "space of sociability," where people enjoyed entertainment and conducted various social activities (Xiao Tian, 1997: 215–22, 237–41, 262–67; Liu Fengyun, 2000: 197–215). In recent years, the culture of tea (not teahouses) has become a hot topic in popular literature in China. A few dozen books on the subject have been published, but almost all are cultural introductions rather than historical studies. See, for example, Gang Fu, 1995; Yang Li, 1997; Chen Xiangbai, 1998; Qin Hao, 1999; Lin Zhi, 2000; Wang Guoan and Yao Ying, 2000; Hao Geng and Mei Zhong, 2001; Peng Guoliang, 2003. Most are for a general readership and feature similar content. The only books that focus on the teahouse itself are *Sichuan's Teahouses* (Sichuan chapu), a photo collection of contemporary teahouses in Sichuan that presents vivid pictures of teahouse life (Chen Jin, 1992), and *Teahouses* (Chaguan), aimed at a general readership (Tao Wenyu, 2005). In 1988, Jia Daquan and Chen Yishi published *A History of Tea in Sichuan* (Sichuan chaye shi), which covers tea production and trade in Sichuan.

31. Skinner, 1964–65: 38–39; Rowe, 1989: 60.

32. Skinner 1964–65: 20, 37–39, 41.

33. Rowe, 1989: 60, 64, 196. In their studies of the working class in Tianjin, Beijing, and Shanghai, Gail Hershatter, David Strand, and Elizabeth Perry, respectively, describe a connection between the teahouse and workers' daily life, with particular attention to the role of the teahouse as a place for leisure and entertainment. Hershatter, for example, finds that people played chess, listened to storytelling, and watched folk performances at teahouses. Similarly, Strand emphasizes that rickshaw pullers in Beijing liked to spend time in teahouses, even during working hours, where their own kind gathered. Perry, who studied the community of Ningbo immigrants in early twentieth-century Shanghai, notes that teahouses were the primary place where people could gather and relax by watching a Shaoxing opera or listening to storytellers or ballad singers in the Suzhou dialect. Performers and

fortunetellers were able to make a living. Bird lovers also often gathered there (Hershatter, 1986: 185–86; Strand, 1989: 58; Perry, 1993: 22).

34. Shao, 1998: 1010; Di Wang, 1998; 2000: 412, 432; Goldstein, 2003: 753–54.

35. Shao, 1998: 1010.

36. Goldstein, 2003: 753–54. Some other articles discuss the relationship between entertainment and the teahouse but their focus is not on the teahouse. For example, Walter Meserve and Ruth Meserve, in their article "From Teahouse to Loudspeaker," published in 1979, analyze folk performances in the teahouses from a theatrical perspective. Carlton Benson's "From Teahouse to Radio" examines how elites used popular culture to control and mobilize urban dwellers in Shanghai in the 1930s, but his work concentrates on performances and radio broadcasts, not really the teahouse itself. In her article "Teahouse, Shadowplay, Bricolage," Zhen Zhang focuses on the short feature *Laborer's Love* in the early 1920s to discuss the connection in Shanghai between traditional shows in the teahouse and early Chinese films. The teahouse itself is not her major concern, but she delves deeply into the cultural background and environment in which Chinese cinema developed in a major city during the 1920s and 1940s. Also, her article takes a literary, not historical, approach (Meserve and Meserve, 1979; Benson, 1996; Zhen Zhang, 1999).

37. Di Wang, 1998; 2000: 412, 432.

38. See Suzuki, 1982; Xiao Tian, 1997: 215–22, 237–41, 262–67; Shao, 1998; Di Wang, 2000; He Manzi, 1994: 192–94; 2002: 270–73; Goldstein, 2003.

39. Li Changli, 2002: 427–55.

40. Wang Qingyuan, 1944: 29–30. In fact, the teahouse did not play an important role in daily life in Shanghai. Leo Ou-fan Lee notes that coffeehouses, "as a public place fraught with political and cultural significance in Europe, especially in France," were also popular in 1930s Shanghai as gathering places for scholars and intellectuals. The teahouses of Shanghai became a "decoration of modern urban life" (1999: 17, 22). Whereas people in Shanghai sought a "modernized life" by frequenting coffeehouses, residents of Chengdu preferred their "traditional" lifestyle by staying with teahouses.

41. Shu Xincheng, 1934: 142; Wang Qingyuan, 1944: 30; He Manzi, 2002: 271; Shao, 1998: 1012–13, 1032; Goldstein, 2003: 754–60.

42. Zhou Zhiying, 1943: 247; He Manzi, 1994: 192.

43. Huang Shang, 2003: 299. Of course, these were superficial observations. In Chapter 6, I point out that there were class distinctions in the teahouses.

44. Hsu and Hsu, 1977: 308. People created various tea customs in different regions. For example, northerners called the act of drinking tea *hecha*, and southerners called it *yincha*, while people along the Yangzi River called it *chicha* (CDWB, Sept. 7, 1948). Cui Xianchang, a writer who lived in Chengdu, also noted that the teahouse in North China usually used high square tables, long benches, and teapots. The seats were uncomfortable and the teapots were not the best for tea, but the worst thing was that customers were charged each time hot water was added to their tea. Therefore, people called these teahouses "no tea and no seat" (*wucha wuzuo*). In Canton, old people called teahouses "tea chambers" (*chashi*). These teahouses mainly sold snacks, but their chairs were much more comfortable. Therefore, these were called "having seats but no tea" (*youzuo wucha*) (Cui Xianchang, 1982: 92–93).

45. Regarding this region, see Skinner, 1964–65; Di Wang, 2003: 4–6.
46. Wang Qingyuan, 1944: 33–35; He Chengpu, 1986: 350; Xue Shaoming, 1986: 166.
47. Wang Qingyuan, 1944: 32.
48. Ibid.: 32–35; Yang Wuneng and Qiu Peihuang, 1995: 731.
49. The Chengdu Plain had abundant underground water, and wells generally could be established by digging eight to ten feet. A shallow well could supply enough water for more than one hundred people, regardless of how much water was used or wasted. However, well water could only be used for washing. In 1927, the city had 2,795 wells. Some families bought river water for drinking but used well water for cooking and washing. On the other hand, the river within the city was shallow and narrow, and people discarded rubbish and washed clothes in it, so its water was undrinkable (Chen Maozhao, 1983: 187; Li Jieren, 1980 [1937]: 414; Zhou Xun, 1987 [1936]: 24; *Chengdu shi shizheng nianjian*, 1927: 526).
50. Xue Shaoming, 1986: 166; Zhou Xun, 1987 [1936]: 24; Chen Maozhao, 1983: 189; Yang Wuneng and Qiu Peihuang, 1995: 731; Li Jieren, 1980 [1937]: 853. In the late nineteenth century river water cost thirty to forty wen per two wooden buckets. In 1910, hot water was sold at one wen per kettle and in 1942, twenty to thirty cents per bucket (about 50 bowls) (CDTL, 2: 253; Ci Jun, 1942). Many residents routinely bought hot water from teahouses for washing. In his novel, Li Jieren described a merchant thus: As soon as he got up, he asked the servant boy "to buy hot water for one wen" from the neighborhood teahouse to wash his face (Li Jieren, 1980 [1937]: 853).
51. On the Chengdu Plain, landowning peasants constituted only 20 percent of the rural population and tenants, 62 percent. Larger landowners lived in the city while the smaller ones lived in the market towns. These landowners did not have access to many outlets for entertainment, although they had money, so they spent a great deal of time in teahouses (Wang Qingyuan, 1944: 32). According to one investigation, in the 1930s on the Chengdu Plain, the percentage of tenants was as high as 80 percent (Guo Hanming and Meng Guangyu, 1944: 15–19; Di Wang, 1993: 138).
52. Fortune, 1853; Nakamura Sakujirō, 1899; Davidson and Mason, 1905; Inoue, 1921; Nakano, 1913 (thanks to Suzuki Tōmō for sending this document to me); Sewell, 1971; Brace, 1974; Service, 1989; Naitō, 1991.
53. Including the Archives of the Chengdu Police Department (Chengdu shenghui jingcha ju dang'an, hereafter CSJJD), Archives of the Chengdu Chamber of Commerce (Chengdu shi shanghui dang'an, hereafter CSSD), Archives of Industry and Commerce in Chengdu (Chengdu shi zhengfu gongshang dang'an, hereafter CSZGD), Archives of Industrial and Commercial Registrations in Chengdu (Chengdu shi gongshang xingzheng dengji dang'an, hereafter CSGXD), and Archives of the Chengdu Bureau of Industry and Commerce (Chengdu shi gongshang ju dang'an, hereafter CSGJD).
54. For instance, from the *West China Evening News* (Huaxi wanbao) of 1942 alone I found at least five such articles. See Ci Jun, 1942; Lu Yin, 1942; Zhou Zhiying, 1942; Ju Ge, 1942; Lao Xiang, 1942.
55. Li Jieren, 1980 [1937]; Sha Ting, 1982 [1940], 1984 [1941], 1984 [1944]. Li Jieren's *Great Wave* was so realistic and factual that some critics said that it was more

"like a chronicle of 1911 Sichuan than a novel." Li himself acknowledged that his "description is too dependent on facts without enough imagination," and that it "reflected social life at that time, but with too many unnecessary details." After criticism that his work contained too much "naturalism," which was discouraged by Marxist writers, Li felt that his first volume of the novel was "like an unsuccessful record of events" (Li Jieren, 1980 [1937]: 951–52).

Chapter 1

1. On studies of modern enterprises, see Cochran, 1980; Cochran, 2000; Köll, 2003; Kubo, 2005. On large successful firms, see Chan, 1982; Zelin, 1988, 1990, 2005; Gardella, 1992; Pomeranz, 1997. There are relatively many more studies of shops in the West, especially in England and France, that examine business practices from various angles. See Davis, 1966; Adburgham, 1967; Forster, 1980; Mui and Mui, 1989.
2. Di Wang, 1993: 324–48.
3. He Yimin, 2002: 182–201; Zhang Xuejun and Zhang Lihong, 1993: 240–48.
4. Wang Guoan and Yao Ying, 2000: 49–50.
5. The control of the number of teahouses is discussed in Chapter 2.
6. Lai Yeyi, 1932.
7. This figure came out in 1951. According to another investigation by the local government that same year, there were 563 teahouses (CSGJD, 119-2-167). Both were reliable sources; perhaps their figures differ because the surveys were conducted at different times of the year.
8. CSJJD, 93-6-2635. The number of streets in Chengdu grew as follows: 1850, over four hundred; 1909, 516; 1939, 576; 1944, 684; 1950, 734 (see Wu Haoshan, 1855: 69; CDTL, 1: 25; He Yimin, 2002: 278, 473, 478; Sichuan sheng wenshi guan, 1987: 305).
9. CSJJD, 93-5-1046.
10. Ibid.
11. Ibid., 93-6-739-3.
12. Saloons in American cities and comparable drinking places elsewhere in the West were similar in many ways to teahouses, but probably had a higher density. In Chicago, for example, "there were always several saloons at the ends of the streetcar lines" (Duis, 1983: 176). Two maps from 1894, one of New York and the other of San Francisco, show that some streets had as many as twelve or thirteen saloons (Powers, 1998: 156–57). Wrexham, Wales, had a population of eight thousand to nine thousand during the 1860s and 1870s, and had eighty-five drinking places, an average of one per 100 to 110 people (Lambert, 1983: 48).
13. CSJJD, 93-6-2635.
14. For a comparative purpose, I give the lowest estimate: By multiplying each table by four people (that is, each seat for one person/day on average), we would have forty thousand customers, or more than one-tenth of the population of Chengdu. However, by looking at other sources, this figure is obviously too low. In 1924, for example, a bowl of tea cost 30 wen, but a square table was taxed at 30 wen per day (ibid., 93-6-739-1). If a square table served an average of only four people daily, this meant that the tax rate was 25 percent—impossibly high. The tax rate in the 1940s was 2 to 3 percent (CSZGD, 38-11-650; CSSD, 104-1390). If we assume that the tax

rate in 1924 was 10 percent (it should actually be less than 10 percent), the turnover of each table could be 300 wen, which means that each table served at least ten customers daily. Other sources also indicate a single seat in an average teahouse served more than ten customers each day (Zhang Fang, 1995: 96; CSJJD, 93-6-739-2).

During the 1930s and 1940s, there were some other estimates, listed below for reference. Most estimates are higher. Statistics from 1931, although incomplete and covering only 261 teahouses, provide useful and detailed information: There were 203,716 customers; 870 waiters, shopkeepers, and water-carriers; 3,088 tables; and 29,551 tea bowls. Average daily costs were 134 yuan for tobacco; 792 jin for tea leaves; and 25,699 jin for wood and coal. Daily average total income was 3,948 yuan and the monthly average total was 118,600 yuan. These 261 teahouses had slightly more than three thousand tables (an average of 11.8 each) and nearly thirty thousand bowls (an average of 113 each). About 870 people worked in these teahouses as proprietors, waiters, and water-carriers. These figures, compared to those from other sources, are problematic. We know there were 621 teahouses in 1931 (see Table 1.1), but if 261 teahouses could have over two hundred thousand customers, the number of the customers for 621 teahouses would be far beyond the population at that time (see Table 1.2) (*Sichuan yuebao* 3, 1933: 126–27).

A 1932 report covered two hundred teahouses in Chengdu, with average daily sales of eight hundred bowls of tea, which meant that, on average, each teahouse had eight hundred patrons per day; the number for the whole city would be 160,000. Total expense was 4,800 yuan per day, or 144,000 per month, or 1,728,000 yuan per year. This amount could support 864,000 hungry people for one month or construct 3,200 li (1 li is about one-third mile) of roads (Bing Fei, 1933). Bing Fei's count was much lower than the actual number of teahouses, but I believe that the estimate of eight hundred customers per teahouse was high. In 1914, for example, there were 9,958 tables in 681 teahouses, for an average of 14.6 tables each. If each teahouse served eight hundred people, each table had to serve an average of fifty-five people per day, an apparent impossibility, although the average teahouse of the 1930s might have been larger than that of the 1910s.

15. Ci Jun, 1942. But, later that year, another source estimated that each teahouse averaged fifty customers per day, for a total of 30,550 customers daily (Qiu Chi, 1942).

16. Yang Zhongyi, 1992: 116. Yang's total is 120,140, which is a miscalculation. I recount and add up all numbers as 133,100.

17. If we add some women and children who went to teahouses too, the number would be larger. Thanks to Joseph Esherick for suggesting this.

18. *Sichuan guanbao* 2, 1910.

19. CDKB, Apr. 23, 1932. A different source from that same year provides a different count: more than eight thousand people, including proprietors and managers and other employees, relied on the teahouse trade, but this survey did not count their family members (XXXW, Apr. 27, 1932). According to a 1936 police investigation, 3,403 men and 415 women were in the teahouse business (XXXW, Apr. 29, 1936).

20. Chen Maozhao, 1983: 178. According to a 1951 investigation, the total number of people making a living in the teahouse business was 3,885, for an average of nearly seven people per teahouse (CSGJD, 119-2-167).

21. XXXW, Jan. 11, 1935. However, these numbers seem also incomplete because just one year earlier, in 1934, the Department of Household Registration of the Capital City Police Headquarters (Shenghui jingbeibu huji chu) conducted an individual census of all the households in Chengdu. The result, according to the report, was "very detailed and accurate." The investigation did not put teahouses in a separate category, but counted them with food providers, for a total of 6,552, which accounted for 8 percent of all households (ibid., Apr. 5, 1934).

22. Shu Xincheng, 1934: 142. As a small business and public space, the teahouse was related to the restaurant in a way similar to how the café and the restaurant in the West were related. Rebecca Spang distinguishes the restaurant from the café in Paris by saying that a café could serve more than five hundred patrons at any one time, and provided light lunches, beverages, newspapers, and other reading materials. A restaurant, however, hardly held more than two hundred people, but it might offer small rooms for smaller parties. Therefore, restaurant service "characterized not commonwealth but compartmentalization." While café customers read newspapers and "thought about the world around them," restaurant patrons read the menu and "thought about their own bodies" (Spang, 2000: 79).

23. The requirements were so simple that somebody said that two or three tables with five or six chairs could meet the most basic needs (Ye Wen, 1949). In fact, more items were needed. A document about a dispute between a teahouse and its landlord provides a good overview of what was needed to run a typical teahouse: one hundred bamboo chairs; twenty wooden square tables; seven folding square tables; three stone vats; four pottery vats; one stove; one electricity meter; seven lamps; one brass jar; one small iron pan; one counter; 116 tea bowls; 102 tea lids; 116 brass tea saucers; 77 small brass tea saucers; six brass water smoking pipes; three brass basins for face washing; five brass kettles; one brass hanging kettle; two water buckets; one brick stand; one flower stand; fifty-five panes of window glass; two bamboo water pipes; two clothing sheds; eight glass tiles; five old wooden square tables; and one wooden cabinet (CSZGD, 38-11-2322).

24. Chen Maozhao, 1983: 183; Jiang Mengbi, seventy-eight years old, interviewed by author, Joy Teahouse, June 22, 1997. A report in a local newspaper indicated this was a common method of raising capital. After Zou, a teahouse keeper, died, his widow wanted to keep the business to support herself. She collected deposits for a total of more than 400 yuan from a hot-towel man and many other small traders. However, after the landlord terminated her lease and asked her to leave, she ran away with the money (GMGB, Aug. 14, 1929).

25. Actually, Chengdu had 640 teahouses in 1936 (see Table 1.1).

26. CSZGD, 38-11-1539. There is a different number: 614 teahouses had a combined capital of 230,800 yuan in 1940 (Chen Maozhao, 1983: 182), equal to 820 dan of rice. Each teahouse thus had only 380 yuan, which could buy only a little over eight hundred pounds of rice (but just half a year later, it could only buy four hundred pounds due to a dramatic rise in rice prices; see the Appendix).

27. JSWS: 369.

28. See the Appendix for prices of rice and a bowl of tea, which changed over time. Another detailed record of capital appeared in 1951. It provided summary data on 328 of the 563 teahouses in Chengdu. The largest amount of capital among

the first thirty teahouses in that account was 14,178,180 yuan, while the smallest was 2,014,640. The capital of the thirty teahouses totaled 174,762,180 yuan, with an average of 5,825,406 per teahouse. Of the thirty teahouses, seventeen were in debt to various extents, including some teahouses with a large capital investment, such as the Prosperous and Peaceful Tea Garden (Xinghe chayuan), which had a fixed capital of 15,096,360 yuan and circulating capital of 1,413,190, but also had 2,864,400 of debt. The total debt of the thirty teahouses was 13,952,090 (CSGJD, 119-2-167).

29. According to the license, the Peach Land Teahouse (Taoyuan chashe) had capital of 2,000 yuan when it opened in October 1940 (CSZGD, 38-11-298).

30. Ibid., 38-11-2192. There is an exception. In 1947, the government also tried to get involved in the teahouse business. The Social Bureau of the Provincial Government set up a Pastime Entertainment Ground in Sun Yat-sen Park, where it established an official teahouse, the Tea Drinking Division (Yincha bu). The bureau provided 500,000 yuan (*fabi*) in funding for this project. Bamboo sheds were built in the empty space between two gardens and enclosed with a bamboo fence. The teahouse, which could serve two hundred customers, had electricity and numerous plants, making it a "quiet and elegant environment." It was controlled by the bureau, which appointed a manager and an accountant to run the business. However, all other employees were wage employees whose incomes varied with the amount of business (SZSC, 186-3367).

31. TSRB, Aug. 3, 1911. John Evans notes the advantage of the teahouse: "It was well known that teahouses always had plenty of cash on hand; many acted as unofficial banks to guarantee gamblers' wagers or accord loans at usurious interest rates for marriage dowries, buying a house, setting up a shop, or funding business deals such as trading in tea, precious metals, or real estate. Several teahouse owners made enough money to prepare sons for the Civil Service Exams and many a great mandarin counted among his ancestors a hard-working teahouse owner" (Evans, 1992: 61). Chen Maozhao estimated that if all costs, including tea, fuel, labor, and rent, were counted as one unit per day, then the sale of more than 100 bowls of tea, boiled water, and hot water would equal 2.5 to three units. Therefore, a teahouse could earn two to three times its investment in profit (Chen Maozhao, 1983: 185). Based on information available to us, Evans and Chen probably overestimated the profits of the average teahouse.

32. More extensive discussion of this issue is given in Chapter 2.

33. GMGB, Jan. 15, 1931.

34. Ibid.

35. But some well-known teahouses were in the B and C levels; for instance, the Joy Tea Garden was classified in Level C (CSZGD, 38-11-97).

36. Ibid., 38-11-1539.

37. Ibid., 38-11-650.

38. CSSD, 104-1390.

39. CSZGD, 38-11-1539.

40. Johnson, Nathan, and Rawski, 1985: ix.

41. CGTGD, 52-128-2.

42. Lin Kongyi, 1986: 165; TSRB, Oct. 19, 1909.

43. Xiong Zhuoyun, eighty-five years old, interviewed by author, Joy Teahouse, June 22, 1997; Chen Maozhao, 1983: 184.
44. CSJJD, 93-6-739-3.
45. Chen Maozhao, 1983: 183–85.
46. Zhang Chengchun, 1986: 23; Chen Maozhao, 1983: 183. Hoh-Cheung Mui and Lorna Mui have studied petty shopkeepers, their business practices, and customers in eighteenth-century England (1989: 200–220).
47. Lai Yeyi, 1932; CDKB, Apr. 23, 1932; Jia Daquan and Chen Yishi, 1988: chap. 7; Chen Maozhao, 1983: 183; Wen Wenzi, 1990: 456; Wang Zehua and Wang He, 1999: 112.
48. Wang Qingyuan, 1944: 34; Ci Jun, 1942.
49. TSRB, Oct. 20, 1909.
50. GMGB, Sept. 7, 1912; May 8, 1918; Qiu Chi, 1942. Xiong Zhuoyun, eighty-eight years old, interviewed by author, Xiong's home, Aug. 9, 2000.
51. Good performances virtually guaranteed repeat customers, as discussed extensively in Chapter 5.
52. GMGB, Oct. 17, 1929; Wang Qingyuan, 1944: 34; Hai Su, 1999: 141; Xiong Zhuoyun, eighty-eight years old, interviewed by author, Xiong's home, Aug. 9, 2000.
53. Xiong Zhuoyun, eighty-eight years old, interviewed by author, Xiong's home, Aug. 9, 2000.
54. Ci Jun, 1942; Chen Jin, 1992: 33. Teahouse names could be placed in the following categories: names based on literary pursuits and interests, such as the Pleasant Spring Balcony (Yichunlou), Reflection of the Moon (Yinyue), Drinking Waves (Yintao), and Bamboo Garden (Zhuyuan); names based on tea, such as Tea Garden (Mingyuan), Fragrant Taste (Pinxiang), Top of Mount Meng (Mengding), and Lu Yu (Lu Yu); names based on the owner's name, such as Fang's Teahouse (Fangji chashe), Zeng's Teahouse (Zengji chashe), and Shiliang Tea Garden (Shiliang chayuan); names based on the names of streets, such as China's Revival Teahouse (Huaxing chashe) and Green Dragon Teahouse (Qinglong chashe); names based on a location, such as Eastern Garden (Dongyuan), Western Garden (Xiyuan), and Central (Zhongxin); names based on numbers, such as First Balcony (Diyilou), Two Fountains (Erquan), Three Sages (Sanyigong), Four Brightnesses (Siming), and Five Happinesses (Wufu); names based on lucky words, such as Rising Prosperity (Hongxing), Rising Fluency (Shunxing), Co-Prosperity (Tongxing), and Flourish (Xingsheng); and names based on foreign words, such as Broadway (Bailaohui), White Roses (Baimeigui), and Violet (Ziluolan) (Chen Maozhao, 1983: 180–81). In this book, I will not only transliterate the names of teahouses, but will also try to translate them into English because the names were also indicators of teahouse culture.
55. Chen Maozhao, 1983: 179; Li Ying, 2002; GMGB, Jan. 29, 1918.
56. Qing Youzheng, 1999: 20.
57. Li Ying, 2002; Shu Xincheng, 1934: 170; GMGB, May 8, 1918; June 25, 1929; Li Jieren, 1980 [1937]: 122. On the relationship between parks and teahouses, see Li Deying, 2003.
58. Wu Yu, 1984, II: 775; GMGB, Mar. 5, 1919. Temporary teahouses within the city typically were bamboo sheds, built by hired laborers, that contained a stove, tables, and chairs.

59. Yao Zhengmin, 1971: 18; GMGB, Feb. 25, 1928; Li Sizhen and Ma Yansen, 1996: 379.

60. For a recent study of hygiene in modern China, see Rogaski, 2004. On Chengdu, see Di Wang, 2000; Di Wang, 2003: chaps. 4 and 5.

61. *Sichuan tongsheng jingcha zhangcheng*, 1903.

62. *Chengdu shi shizheng nianjian*, 1927: 510–11; CDKB, Apr. 2, 1932; CSSD, 104-1388; CSJJD, 93-4-1631.

63. The New Life Movement promoted by Chiang Kai-shek began in 1934. For more about this, see Dirlik, 1975; Chu, 1980; Averill, 1981.

64. CSZGD, 38-11-298, 38-11-335, 38-11-1441.

65. CSSD, 104-1406.

66. XXXW, Mar. 16, 1945; CSZGD, 38-11-298. This document can also be seen in CSSD, 104-1388.

67. Li Jieren, 1980 [1936]: 601–2; Li Jieren, 1980 [1937]: 1060.

68. Wang Shian and Zhu Zhiyan, 1989: 155–56.

69. Li Ying, 2002; Hai Su, 1999: 140.

70. Chen Maozhao, 1983: 183; Wen Wenzi, 1990: 456; Wang Zehua and Wang He, 1999: 112; Hai Su, 1999: 141; Long Zaitian, 1996: 527–28; Zhang Chengchun, 1986: 23.

71. After the war, teahouses by the river experienced a sharp decline. The Village on the River closed, and performers in the teahouse on the south bank went downtown to make a living. Another lower-class teahouse on the south bank was operated by the Gowned Brothers. It hired folk entertainers to perform and did good business (Hai Su, 1999: 143–46).

Chapter 2

1. Golas, 1977; Rowe, 1984. Chinese scholars still debate the nature of native-place and professional associations, despite extensive study. Wang Rigen (1996) points out three factors in the formation of *huiguan*: the exclusion of local people, the value placed on native place, and the need for professional management. Several scholars, including Jiang Zhaocheng (1994), Peng Zeyi (1995), Zhu Ying (1997), and Wu Hui (1999), have found that the *huiguan* contained the functions of the *hanghui*, and not only organized people who came from the same location, but also regulated trade. But other scholars have taken a different approach. Xie Junmei (2000) states, for example, that most Chinese professional organizations existed within the workplace and had connections to the *huiguan*, and that they used *huiguan* to control workers. Unlike scholars who do not distinguish *huiguan* from *gongsuo*, Ma Min (1995) has tried to separate the two, and points out that in Ming- and Qing-era Suzhou, *huiguan* were geographical associations based on native places only, and did not fit the contemporary meaning of *hanghui*, but the functions of *gongsuo* were more like those of the guilds found in the West. Some studies by Chinese historians suggest that the importance of geographical connections gradually weakened in the late Qing, while affiliations related to one's profession or trade became more important (Wang Weiping, 1997). Some Chinese scholars have recognized the gap that exists because, although many works have been published about *huiguan* and *hanghui*, most focus

on the Ming and Qing periods and few deal with the period following the 1920s. In fact, no important work has been published on Republican *huiguan, gongsuo,* and *hanghui* (Feng Xiaocai, 2000; Zhu Ying, 2003).

2. Goodman, 1995: 40.
3. Golas, 1977: 556, 559.
4. Pickett, 2000.
5. Rowe, 1984: 252.
6. Ho Ping-ti (1966), for example, chose the German term *Landsmannschaften* to translate *huiguan*.
7. Golas, 1977: 559.
8. Rowe, 1984: 254. Imahori Seiji was probably the first to challenge Max Weber's notion that China did not have organizations equivalent to Western guilds (Imahori, 1953: 303; Rowe, 1984: 339). Qiu Pengsheng (1990: 2–3) does not use the term *hanghui* in his book on commercial organizations in order to avoid confusion with Western guilds.
9. On reviews of studies of *huiguan* and *hanghui*, see Zhu Ying, 2003.
10. Rowe, 1984: 75–76, 252–53, chaps. 8 and 9.
11. Goodman, 1995: 31, 44–45. Bryna Goodman believes almost all professional organizations considered their members' native places important. She categorizes these organizations into native-place trade associations, native-place multiple-trade associations, trade associations subdivided by native place, nonexclusive trade associations with a strong native-place bias, and native-place associations subdivided by trade (1995: 32–37).
12. Di Wang, 1993: 558–67.
13. Ibid.: 558–67; Di Wang, 2003: chap. 2; Sun Xiaofen, 1997: 248–50.
14. CDTL, 1: 108–9; 2: 462–551; Di Wang, 1993: 568–76; CSJJD, 93-5-1046, 93-6-2635; Zhong Maoxuan, 1984: 40.
15. Li Deying, 2004: 227–28; Zhu Ying, 2004: 361–63; *Chengdu shi zhengfu zhoubao* 1.2 (Jan. 14, 1939): 11–15.
16. CSZGD, 38-11-1539. Such a structure can be seen as a legacy of traditional guilds. H. B. Morse found that the internal management of guilds was, "as might be expected, more democratic." For example, the Tea Guild in 1880s Shanghai had "at its head an annually elected committee of twelve, each committee-man acting in rotation for one month as chairman, or manager; no gild member may refuse to serve on this committee" (Morse, 1967 [1932]: 16). A notebook of the board of directors of the Chengdu Teahouse Guild includes some very useful information, such as the meeting date and place, person chairing the meeting, and the agenda of each meeting of the guild from June 1940 to November 1942. During this period, the guild held thirty-six meetings, at least one per month. Each meeting addressed at least one issue, and sometimes as many as eleven. During this period, the full membership met only once (CSSD, 104-1401).
17. CSSD, 104-1400, 104-1401.
18. CSZGD, 38-11-1539. From this list, I found that President Wang Xiushan had two teahouses: the Brocade Spring Tea Balcony on East City Corner Street (Dongchenggen jie), with capital of 800 yuan, and the Good Morality (Guande) in the Smaller City Park, with capital of 500 yuan (ibid.). Liao, the owner of the largest

teahouse in Chengdu, the Prosperity Tea Hall (Huahua chating), became president of the Teahouse Guild later based on his business skills and good reputation. Access to capital appears to have played a role in the selection of others for positions in the guild.

19. CSSD, 104-1401.

20. Ibid., 104-1400. The fee later was reduced somewhat. In January 1947 the guild set up its standard membership fee based on four classes of teahouses: Class A, 5,000 yuan; Class B, 4,000; Class C, 3,000; and Class D, 2,000 (ibid.). The guild generated income from property it owned as well as from membership fees. In 1941, it sold a piece of land for 3,200 yuan and applied the proceeds toward the purchase of five houses for 5,000 yuan (ibid., 104-1400, 104-1601).

21. CSJJD, 93-6-2635; CSSD, 104-1400. While the members of the Union of Teahouse Workers in Chengdu had many problems—especially their resistance to the membership fee, as discussed in the next chapter—I did not find any similar stories about the guild, which might indicate that teahouse proprietors needed the guild much more than teahouse workers needed the union.

22. CSSD, 104-1401.

23. For more information about late Qing prices, see CDTL, 1: 501–6, 2: 252–56; Zhou Xun, 1987 [1936]: 24.

24. CSJJD, 93-6-739-1.

25. The price of tea was unusually low in January 1942, when one hundred bowls cost the same as about 0.023 dan (about eight pounds) of rice and was unusually high in August 1946, when one hundred bowls were worth 0.12 dan (about forty pounds), and in September 1947, when one hundred bowls were worth 0.121 dan (thirty-eight pounds).

26. CSSD, 104-1401.

27. Ibid.

28. Ibid.; CSSD, 104-1390; CSZGD, 38-11-1530.

29. CSSD, 104-1401.

30. The committee consisted of one member selected to represent each of the five districts, and one each for the special area (that is, Warm Spring Road) and parks, for a total of seven people.

31. CSZGD, 38-11-1540.

32. For unknown reasons, this transition of power did not take place until July 1946, when Liao Wenchang, the owner of the Prosperity Tea Hall, one of the largest teahouses in Chengdu in the 1940s, became president of the guild (CSSD, 104-1400). His presidency lasted until January 1947.

33. CSZGD, 38-11-807.

34. Ibid. Natural disasters could make the situation much worse. For instance, Chengdu suffered enormous damage from flooding in the summer of 1947. Many teahouses along the river were damaged and at least forty-four requested government relief. Some were left as "an empty shell" while others were completely swept away. The guild confirmed their claims and asked the government to grant relief and reissue their licenses (CSSD, 104-1408).

35. CSZGD, 38-11-32; Feuerwerker, 1983: 114.

36. CSZGD, 38-11-1535; CSSD, 104-1391.

37. GMGB, Mar. 13, 1916; CDKB, Apr. 23, 1932.
38. CSJJD, 93-6-2635.
39. Ibid., 93-6-739-1.
40. Ibid.
41. Of the twenty-one teahouses, seven had six tables or fewer, eight had seven to ten tables, four had eleven to fourteen tables, and two had fifteen to eighteen tables (Ibid., 93-6-739-1).
42. I question this claim, because it seems likely that it would still have had patrons on cloudy days, except during winter.
43. CSJJD, 93-6-739-1. But, the Hidden Garden still paid more taxes than any other teahouse in the subdistrict even though it had fewer tables than some. This is because the Hidden Garden charged the highest prices for tea (ibid.).
44. Ibid.
45. Ibid., 93-6-739-3.
46. This is another example of how simple it was to open a teahouse, a question also addressed earlier in this chapter.
47. CSJJD, 93-6-739-3.
48. In fact, numerous teahouses were operated by social organizations under the guise of "internal service." With this in mind, the total number of teahouses might be much larger than that in Table 1.1.
49. CSJJD, 93-5-1046.
50. GMGB, Dec. 11, 1928; Dec. 12, 1928.
51. Ibid., Dec. 13, 1928.
52. Ibid., Jan. 7, 1931; Jan. 13, 1931; CDKB, Feb. 27, 1932.
53. CSSD, 104-1401. Sometimes the government had to compromise. For instance, in 1938, after Chengdu's merchants went on strike to protest a tax increase, the government reduced the tax hike to 2 percent. Small businesses that had less than 100 yuan in goods were exempt (CDKB, Mar. 25, 1938). Although the guild and individual teahouses often sought to have their taxes reduced, their tax burden—based on the number of tables—was not as heavy as claimed. For example, the tax rate was just 2 percent of total operating costs in 1945 (CSSD, 104-1390).
54. CSZGD, 38-11-951.
55. CSSD, 104-1401; CSZGD, 38-11-298.
56. CSZGD, 38-11-1440, 38-11-1441.
57. Ibid., 38-11-1440.
58. Ibid., 38-11-425. A trading group opened a teahouse on East Great Street without a legal license. The teahouse was nominally a gathering place for the group's members, but in fact it served anyone (ibid.). In 1946, when North City Park became the site of the Sichuan Provincial Scientific Hall (Sichuan shengli kexueguan), the Bright Spring Teahouse (Lichun chashe) was ordered to close. The owner could not find an appropriate new location and asked the government for more time until he found a place the next year (ibid., 38-11-1441).
59. Ibid., 38-11-298, 38-11-1441.
60. Ibid., 38-11-1441.
61. Ibid., 38-11-2192.
62. Ibid.

63. Ibid., 38-11-1530.
64. Ibid.
65. Ibid.
66. Ibid., 38-11-1466.
67. Ibid.
68. The following is their explanation: They were afraid that illegal transactions in the teahouse would disrupt business, so in December 1948 they asked the government to send policemen to maintain order, but none were sent. During that period, in order to protect their own interests and keep the business legal, they repeatedly reported relevant information in secret to the local branch of the police. However, on June 21, the government suddenly searched the teahouse and caught some illegal traders (ibid., 38-11-1440).
69. Ibid.
70. Ibid.
71. CSSD, 104-1401.
72. Ibid.
73. Ibid.
74. Ibid.
75. Ibid.
76. CSZGD, 38-11-752. This problem had actually existed since the late Qing. When running water first appeared in Chengdu, water still had to be hand carried from the station (Di Wang, 2003: 124).
77. CSZGD, 38-11-752.
78. Goodman, 1995: 291–314; Morse, 1967 [1932]: 9, 13.

Chapter 3

1. I am indebted to Stephen Averill for the translation of *cha boshi*. Originally, I translated the term literally as "doctor of tea," but he suggested that the word "master" might be more appropriate than "doctor," since the primary meaning is that of an expert who has learned through experience, rather than an expert who has learned through scholarly research. Personal communication with Stephen Averill on May 8, 2001.
2. A few studies of waiters and waitresses in the West have been published. See Spradley and Mann, 1975; Paules, 1991; Cobble, 1991; Walton and Smith, 1994.
3. Chesneaux, 1968; Honig, 1986; Perry, 1993. David Strand's *Rickshaw Beijing* (1989) and Gail Hershatter's *The Workers of Tianjin* (1986) are exceptions. Strand focuses on coolies who made a living on the street. Hershatter, though she also examines factory workers, has excellent descriptions of the workers in the small ironworking shops and in the transportation trade in Santiaoshi (chaps. 4 and 5).
4. Chesneaux, 1968: 42; Di Wang, 1993: 346.
5. Chesneaux, 1968; Perry, 1993.
6. CSZGD, 38-11-1530.
7. For example, the Reviving Teahouse (Quanxing) had five workers (including the proprietor), but only one, the water-carrier, was paid (CSGXD, 40-65-1). Family-run teahouses were like some saloons in late-nineteenth-century American

cities, which were small, family operated affairs. Saloons paid no wages and were little more than an extension of the household, with the family living in back rooms or in an apartment upstairs (Duis, 1983: 49). In this case, they were also like the stores in living rooms described by Hanchao Lu (1995).

8. CSGJD, 119-2-167.
9. William Rowe found that in Hankou, many—but not all—occupations established a system of apprenticeships, especially those that required a high level of skill (Rowe, 1989: 41).
10. During the late Republican and early Communist regimes, Chengdu was divided into five major districts: East (with five subdistricts), South (with six), West (with five), North (with five), and Outer East (with four). The number of streets in each subdistrict varied, while the whole city had 734 (CSGJD, 119-2-169; Sichuan sheng, 1987: 304-05).
11. CSGJD, 119-2-167.
12. He Yimin, 2002: 915; Chen Maozhao, 1983: 185; CSZGD, 38-11-650.
13. Even the month is crucial because the price kept soaring. For example, one dan of rice was 248 yuan in January, but 633 yuan by December (JSWS: 327).
14. Chen Maozhao, 1983: 185; Cui Xianchang, 1982: 101–2.
15. Cui Xianchang, 1982: 99.
16. Chen Haodong and Zhang Siyong, 1991: 1569.
17. Yang Zhongyi, 1992: 116. One *sheng* is about 3.1 pounds.
18. Chen Maozhao, 1983: 183–84.
19. Luo Shang, 1965: 21.
20. Cui Xianchang, 1982: 100. The situation could also be the opposite: the newcomer would tell the waiter that he would take care of all payment even though his friends' tea had already been paid for. The waiter then had to decide whether or not to return the money to his friends and get the money from him. See more about this custom in Chapter 4.
21. On the operating hours of teahouses, see the section under the heading "Management" in Chapter 1.
22. Cui Xianchang, 1982: 101. The stove room was important in a teahouse. The stove usually consisted of two parts. One was a "tea-water oven," made from clay, with a thick iron plate that had a dozen holes called "fire eyes" on the top. One kettle was placed on each to boil. The other part was a big hot-water vat, locally known as a *wengzi*, which could contain one to two tons of water, heated by the surplus heat from the tea-water oven. Thus, the stove keeper could put warm water in the kettles to boil faster, and also sell hot water to nearby residents. That is why local people called the stove room "the house of the big hot-water vat" (*wengzi fang*), and called the stove keeper the "big hot-water-vat man" (*wengzi jiang*) (see Figure 3.2).
23. In Shanghai, women entered the service professions much earlier. In the late 1860s, in the face of serious competition, some opium dens hired young women called *nü tangguan* (waitresses) to serve smoking equipment and tea (Li Changli, 2002: 392–414).
24. Lu Yin, 1942.
25. Di Wang, 2003: chap. 6.

26. Some pointed out that the history of teahouse waitresses can be traced back to as early as the Tang dynasty, when some tea balconies in Suzhou called "flower teahouses" (*hua chafang*) hosted prostitutes (Zhou Zhiying, 1942). I would argue, however, that these women were not waitresses but entertainers comparable to the singers of "tea poems" in Yuan dynasty (1279–1368) Chengdu (see Fei Zhu, n.d.: 2–4).

27. Lu Yin, 1942. The phenomenon was so new that many people were curious about it or even ridiculed it. The prominent scholar Wu Yu wrote in his diary that he "could not help laughing" when he "saw so-called waitresses in a teahouse" (Wu Yu, 1984, II: 774).

28. Lu Yin, 1942.

29. HXWB, June 16, 1941.

30. Lu Yin, 1942.

31. CSZGD, 38-11-983. Another petition tells a slightly different story regarding how Ling took over the union. Huang Yisheng formally held the position of president, but was corrupt. He was afraid of criticism and secretly turned over the membership list and seal to newcomer Ling Guozheng. She "brazenly accepted the position of president" and changed the Union of Tea Workers into the Union of Chengdu Teahouse Workers (ibid., 38-11-758).

32. I have found that some other unions adopted virtually identical regulations. See below.

33. CSZGD, 38-11-982; Hershatter, 1986; Honig, 1986; Strand, 1989; Perry, 1993; Zhu Ying, 2004: 332–34.

34. CSZGD, 38-11-982.

35. Ibid. We can find a similar situation in Shanghai, where unions were legalized but largely controlled by the government (Kohama, 2000: chap. 4).

36. CSZGD, 38-11-982, 38-11-983, 38-11-984.

37. Ibid., 38-11-982.

38. Ibid., 38-11-983, 38-11-984.

39. Ibid., 38-11-984.

40. The phenomenon of workers refusing to pay for membership was not unique to Chengdu; we can find similar stories in other cities, including those with a well-developed labor movement. In Shanghai, for example, when some workers refused to pay the annual fee for the carpentry guild, the guild took them to court (Perry, 1993: 33–34).

41. CSZGD, 38-11-758.

42. Fan Rongwu's petition against Ling Guozheng stated that Ling falsely accused them of being members of the Sworn Brotherhood Society (*Gelaohui*) (ibid.). Although Fan denied Ling's accusation, Ling was probably right. On the relations between teahouses and the Gowned Brothers (the Sworn Brotherhood Society was known as the Gowned Brothers in Sichuan), see Chapter 6; see also Di Wang, 2000.

43. Lu Yin, 1942.

44. CSZGD, 38-11-1115. For a comparison with the regulations of the Union of Chengdu Teahouse Workers, see ibid., 38-11-982.

45. Ibid., 38-11-1115.

46. Membership was open to men and women who were at least sixteen and

were current or former workers in this profession or former clerks in the union. Anyone who violated the regulations and damaged the reputation of the union would receive a warning, or have his or her union privileges withdrawn, or be expelled from the union, depending on the severity of the violation. Expulsion required approval of at least two-thirds of the members (ibid., 38-11-1103).

47. Ibid.
48. Ibid., 38-11-1103, 38-11-1115.
49. Little research regarding conflict between men and women in the workplace in China has been conducted, but a few works in other areas have been published. For example, Diane Koenker examines the language, behavior, and attitudes of men toward women in the early Soviet printing industry, and poses new ways of thinking about the history of the Russian working class (1995: 1438–64).
50. CSZGD, 38-11-983; Lu Yin, 1942.
51. CSZGD, 38-11-983.
52. Ibid., 38-11-758.
53. Cobble, 1993: 6.
54. Lu Yin, 1942.
55. CSZGD, 38-11-758, 38-11-983, 38-11-984.
56. Ibid., 38-11-908.
57. Ibid.
58. Ibid.
59. Ibid. As noted previously, waitresses came from a variety of backgrounds, but here the union's emphasis on "the wives of officers and soldiers" was probably a tactic to win sympathy.
60. Ibid.
61. Di Wang, 1998, 2000, and 2003.
62. Cui Xianchang, 1982: 101; CDKB, Mar. 28, 1932; HXWB, May 21, 1941.
63. Lu Yin, 1942; Zhou Zhiying, 1942.
64. Zhou Zhiying, 1942.
65. Lu Yin, 1942; HXWB, June 12, 1941.
66. Lu Yin, 1942; HXWB, June 16, 1941; Di Wang, 2000.
67. CSSD, 104-1388.
68. Lu Yin, 1942. In the West, prostitution could also be a problem in public drinking establishments. See Haine, 1996: 190–91.
69. Lu Yin, 1942; XXXW, Mar. 16, 1945.
70. Elizabeth Perry has pointed out that in Shanghai "workshop segregation" and "widespread illiteracy" could "inhibit class consciousness," but this, she believes, did not prevent collective action among unskilled workers (Perry, 1993: 60). An analysis of teahouse workers in Chengdu, however, reveals that workplace segregation not only constrained the development of a class consciousness but also prevented the development of collective action. Recent studies of the Chinese working class and labor movement have stressed the influence of workers' native places and cultural orientations in the formation of the labor movement. Also, recent scholarship has noted that in Shanghai, a worker's occupation was often determined by his or her place of origin; people who came from the same area dominated certain

trades. Perry argues that such a pattern of hiring laborers "fostered strong solidarity" among immigrants (Honig, 1986, 1992; Perry, 1993: 27).

71. On native-place associations and guilds in Sichuan, see Di Wang, 1993: 558–67. For studies of this topic in other Chinese cities, see Rowe, 1984 and Goodman, 1995.

Chapter 4

1. Evans, 1992: 61; Cui Xianchang, 1982: 92–93. Drinking tea in the teahouse never became a ritual or ceremony, which was practical for teahouse-goers. But in Japan, drinking tea in the teahouse was more of a symbolic matter; the ritual and process were more important than the actual drinking of tea. As Murai Yasuhiko says, "chanoyu (tea ceremony) is not the same thing as merely drinking tea" (1989: 3). Paul Varley and Kumakura Isao edited a volume that thoroughly examines chanoyu, from its development, culture, and historical significance, to masters of chanoyu, and tea and Zen (1989).
2. Han, 1965: 96.
3. This is discussed in Chapter 6.
4. Ye Wen, 1949. Regarding elite criticism of the teahouse, see Chapter 8.
5. Hu Tian, 1938: 62; Yi Junzuo, 1943: 194.
6. Ci Jun, 1942; Chen Maozhao, 1983: 188.
7. Li Jieren, 1980 [1937]: 53.
8. Ibid.: 210–11, 214–15.
9. Ibid.: 355.
10. GMGB, Jan. 19, 1918.
11. Shu Xincheng, 1934: 144–45.
12. Hai Su, 1999: 141–42.
13. GMGB, Mar. 22, 1930; HXWB, Dec. 27, 1941; Jing Chaoyang, 1999: 26.
14. Zhou Wen, 1999: 228.
15. Hu Tian, 1938: 69. In 1943, the *New Citizens' Nightly* (Xinminbao wankan) mocked teahouse-goers under the headline "Mr. Ma Er Sets a New Record of Visiting Teahouses," stating that some people of Chengdu stayed in teahouses too long, especially during the summer. Some of those "teahouse patrons" visited teahouses three times a day, just like "Mr. Ma Er," a character in the famous classic novel *The Unofficial History of Academic Circles* (Rulin waishi). Therefore, people called them "Mr. Ma Er of Chengdu," and considered them even crazier than the original Ma Er in the novel (XMBWK, Aug. 6, 1943).
16. Qiu Chi, 1942; Hai Su, 1999: 141.
17. HXRB, June 1, 1947; Cui Xianchang, 1982: 102. In American cities, people had a similar motivation for going to the saloon: "drink provided an escape from misery" and the saloon was "an extension of the home." It is interesting that Duis believes that the saloon "could function as a family safety valve, a convenient way for men to escape from the crowded tenements" (1983: 88, 105, 109).
18. HXRB, June 1, 1947; Ye Wen, 1949.
19. Li Jieren, 1980 [1936]: 339.
20. Ci Jun, 1942; Lin Kongyi, 1986: 70; Hai Su, 1999: 139. From Li Jieren's novel,

we can see that a host would tell his guests, "Let's go a teahouse to have a bowl of tea!" Or, if two acquaintances met on the street, one might say, "Later we should go to the teahouse on the corner, my treat." Often this was just a polite gesture that no one took seriously. But because people often met at the teahouse, this gesture was appropriate (Li Jieren, 1980 [1937]: 122).

21. Hu Tian, 1938: 69; Yi Junzuo, 1943: 194; Wu Yu, 1984, I: 177.
22. SZSC, 186-1431; Ci Jun, 1942; Sewell, 1971: 131–32.
23. Li Jieren, 1980 [1937]: 117, 542, 1327; Lin Wenxun, 1995: 142.
24. Heller, 1984: 226, 236.
25. Qiu Chi, 1942; Wen Wenzi, 1990: 454; He Manzi, 1994: 194; Ran Yunfei, 1999: 182.
26. I will discuss political speech in Chapter 8.
27. GMGB, Mar. 16, 1917.
28. Ci Jun, 1942; Wu Yu 1984, I: 195–96, 199; Li Ying, 2002.
29. XXXW, May 24, 1936; Li Ying, 2002.
30. Sha Ting, 1984 [1941]: 4, 125–26.
31. Zhou Zhiying, 1943: 225; Ye Wen, 1949.
32. Li Jieren, 1980 [1936]: 340; Cui Xianchang, 1982: 94; Chen Maozhao, 1983: 187; Chen Jin, 1992: 32; Wen Wenzi, 1990: 453; Sewell, 1986: 64.
33. Cui Xianchang, 1982: 94; Chen Maozhao, 1983: 187; Chen Jin, 1992: 32–33.
34. CDWB, Nov. 18, 1948.
35. The items listed were: 185 tea bowls, 165 saucers, 171 lids, 2 kettles, 75 chairs, 7 tables, 35 smoking pipes, 45 boxes of cigarettes, 4 benches, 31 stools, 240 rolls of tobacco, 25 boxes of balm, 18 boxes of Eight-Diagram Pills, 5 bunches of vegetables, 7 bags of Golden Spirit Pills, 12 bags of headache powder, 134 bowls of tea leaves, and payment for 265 bowls of tea served (CSSD, 104-1397).
36. Xiong Zhuoyun, eighty-nine years old, interviewed by author, Xiong's home, Aug. 9, 2000; Huang Shangjun, 2002: 140–41.
37. Liu Zhenyao, 1999: 147–48; Hao Zhicheng, 1997: 39–40.
38. Zhang Zhenjian, 1999: 320–21.
39. Wang Qingyuan, 1944: 34; Wen Wenzi, 1990: 455. Tian Lai, a well-known Sichuan opera actor, was one of them. In the years just after the 1911 Revolution, he had nothing to occupy his time, so he went to the Eternal Spring (Wanchun) Teahouse for "beating on drums" and became a famous amateur performer within a couple of years. After his family went bankrupt, he became a professional performer of Sichuan-style opera (Luo Xiangpu, 1986: 278–82).
40. XXXW, May 24, 1936; Zhou Zhiying, 1943: 236; Cui Xianchang, 1982: 96.
41. Chai Yuyan, 1999: 105–6.
42. Chen Maozhao, 1983: 181–82. In his investigation of social customs, Fu Chongju collected some tea jargon (CDTL, 2: 43).
43. Li Jieren, 1980 [1937]: 602; Chen Shisong, 1999: 205–6; Di Wang, 2003: chap. 4.
44. Anthropologists have studied relationships among the Chinese and explored the significance of gifts and favors in social networks (see Mayfair Yang, 1994; and Yunxiang Yan, 1996). For more general studies on gift-giving, see Gregory, 1982; and Cheal, 1988.

45. Cui Xianchang, 1982: 100–101.
46. Cited in Rosenzweig, 1983: 58–59.
47. Ibid.: 59. Similarly, treating was common in American saloons, but it was governed by rules and customs: "The first rule of barroom treating was that the recipient was expected to reciprocate, in drinks or favors or some other mutually acceptable manner." There were a variety of treats, including honorable treats, unrequited treats, celebratory treats, keeper's treats, politician's treats, and so on (Powers, 1998: 94–111).
48. De Grazia, 1962: 3; Dumazedier, 1974: 208, 212.
49. However, class distinctions were still observed in the teahouse, a subject discussed in Chapter 6.
50. Duis, 1983; Rosenzweig, 1983; Brennan, 1988; Haine, 1996; Powers, 1998; Cowan, 2005. For more comparative analyses, see the Conclusion.

Chapter 5
1. Liu Zhenyao, 1999: 148–49.
2. For the changes, see Di Wang, 2003.
3. Goldstein, 2003.
4. CDTL, 1: 279; TSRB, Feb. 11, 1910.
5. Ci Jun, 1942; Qu Xiaoqiang, 1999; Li Ying, 2002; Xiong Zhuoyun, eighty-nine years old, interviewed by author, Xiong's home, Aug. 9, 2000.
6. Ci Jun, 1942; Zhou Zhiying, 1943: 225; Luo Shang, 1965: 22–23; Zhang Dafu, 1981: 109; Di Wang, 2003: 80.
7. CSJJD, 93-2-3282; Luo Shang, 1965: 22; Chen Maozhao, 1983: 184–85; Zhang Henshui, 1999: 281.
8. Luo Ziqi and Jiang Shouwen, 1994: 61.
9. Zhou Zhiying, 1943: 225; Hai Su, 1999: 143.
10. Yan Dinggao and Zhou Shaoji, 1996: 387–88; Che Fu, 2003.
11. HXWB, May 21, 1941; Li Zicong, 1998: 574. Dulcimer singers had their own organization, the Three Deities Society (Sanhuang hui), which met on the third day of the third lunar month and on the ninth day of the ninth lunar month (Zhou Zhiying, 1943: 220–21).
12. Zhou Zhiying, 1943: 220–21; Di Fan, 1966: 23.
13. Li Zicong, 1998: 576.
14. Qu Xiaoqiang, 1999: 153–55; Liu Zhenyao, 1999: 148–49.
15. Che Fu, 1985; Liu Zhenyao, 1999: 148.
16. Wen Wenzi, 1990: 457; Gao Huanru, 1999: 23; Zhou Zhiying, 1943: 221; Li Ying, 2002.
17. CSZGD, 38-11-950.
18. The programs could be ascertained from advertisements in local newspapers, which provide the names of the programs, show times, and sometimes the programs' major themes and prices, and even descriptions of the sets. Also, local newspapers sometimes published reviews of plays and the performances of influential actors; from these, we can see how audiences responded to performances.
19. *Sichuan tongsheng jingcha zhangcheng*, 1903. Thanks to Kristin Stapleton for

providing me a handwriting copy of this document. See also TSRB, Apr. 29, 1910. The sources show that violators were punished. For example, during a show at the Joy Tea Garden one night in March 1910, two actors who were charged with "all kinds of ugly behavior" and "harming social customs" were arrested (TSRB, Mar. 22, 1910).

20. Ibid., July 27, 1909.
21. Ibid., Apr. 12, 1910.
22. CDTL, 1: 279–82.
23. Sichuan sheng chuanju, 1999: 379.
24. GMGB, Mar. 29, 1916; Lin Kongyi, 1986: 106.
25. GMGB, Apr. 20, 1914; June 1, 1914.
26. Ibid., June 2, 1917.
27. CSJJD, 93-6-2718.
28. According to an advertisement, the Eternal Spring presented eight plays during the day and seven at night. The Fragrant Taste offered ten titles both during the day and at night (GMGB, Oct. 31, 1912; Mar. 27, 1913).
29. TSRB, Mar. 31, May 5, June 15, July 11, July 16, Sept. 18, Sept. 26, 1909.
30. GMGB, Apr. 26, 1912. For more details about the play, see Di Wang, 2003: 234.
31. GMGB, May 22, 1912; Jan. 20, 1929.
32. Ibid., Apr. 16, 1917.
33. Tan Qingquan, 1985b: 255.
34. *Jiangyou Pass* was a story of the war between the states of Wei and Shu. When the troops of the Wei approached Jiangyou Pass in northern Sichuan, Ma Miao, the Shu general responsible for guarding the pass, recognized that he had no chance of repelling the Wei troops and discussed with his wife the option of surrendering. His wife insisted that he fight and she later committed suicide out of disappointment with her husband's betrayal. Ma was executed after the Wei troops seized the pass (Sichuan sheng chuanju, 1999: 405).
35. Some of his plays were related to current events. To explore the evil of opium, he wrote *Breaking Two Guns* (Duan shuangqiang); to criticize superstition, he wrote *Throwing the Witch into the Ye River* (Yeshui touwu); and to promote natural feet instead of bound feet, he wrote *Striding with Large Steps* (Lingyunbu) (Tan Qingquan, 1985a: 251).
36. Zhou Zhiying and Gao Sibo, 1987: 55; CSJJD, 93-6-964; CDKB, Oct. 22, 1931.
37. Di Wang, 2003: chap. 7.
38. CSWHJ, 124-2-1; GMGB, Mar. 31, 1917; TSRB, Feb. 20, 1910.
39. Wu Yu, 1984, I: 195–96; GMGB, July 19, 1912; Apr. 10, 1913; Apr. 12, 1917.
40. TSRB, June 17, 1909; Dec. 15, 1909; Mar. 28, 1910; CSZGD, 38-11-950. Ping opera was a genre found throughout North China.
41. CSWHJ, 124-2-1.
42. The Joy, however, as the finest theater in town, probably hired employees who were relatively better educated.
43. CSWHJ, 124-2-1.
44. TSRB, Oct. 19, 1909; GMGB, Mar. 1, 1931.

45. TSRB, Sept. 1, 1909.
46. Yingjin Zhang, 1999: 32. On Chinese cinemas, movies, and urban culture, see Yingjin Zhang, 1996 and 1999; Donald, 2000.
47. TSRB, July 27, 1909.
48. CSJJD, 93-6-2723.
49. In the 1920s and 1930s, most cinemas were still attached to teahouses. For example, the Cultivating Wisdom Cinema (Zhiyu dianyingyuan) was located in the Deities Gathering Tea Garden (Qunxian chayuan) and controlled by shareholders.
50. GMGB, Oct. 4, 1927; Jan. 16, 1930.
51. Jing Chaoyang, 1999: 168–69.
52. GMGB, Dec 26, 1916. The shows attracted not only adults but also children, some of whom went alone to see operas every day. A gardener attempted to rape a thirteen-year-old girl who went to the Eternal Spring Tea Garden by herself one evening, but a patrolling security team came to her rescue (GMGB, May 15, 1930).
53. CSJJD, 93-6-964; XXXW, Oct. 29, 1933.
54. GMGB, May 21, 1929. Business at the Eternal Spring Tea Garden boomed after a complimentary essay was published. A few days later, the essay's author went back to the teahouse and found many patrons already seated in the first four rows at 9 AM, the time he arrived (GMGB, May 26, 1929).
55. CSJJD, 93-6-739-1, 93-6-964.
56. Wang Zehua and Wang He, 1999: 129; Hai Su, 1999: 143.
57. CDKB, May 24, 1938.
58. CSJJD, 93-6-2718.
59. Ibid.
60. These included *Picking Up a Jade Bracelet* (Shiyu zhuo), *Beating with a Stick* (Dagangzi), *Great Green Mountain* (Da cuipingshan), *The Little Widow Goes to the Graveyard* (Xiaoshangfen), *Selling Rouge* (Maiyanzhi), *The Fight on the Sandy Beach* (Zhanshatan), *Leaving Cui Hua* (Yicuihua), *Stealing Poems and Shooting Vultures* (Toushi shediao), *A Fisherman Who Adopted a Son* (Dayu shouzi), and *The Little Cowherd in the Pasture* (Xiaofangniu) (CSJJD, 93-6-2718).
61. Ibid. For example, *Selling Rouge* is about a woman who sells rouge for a living. A young scholar falls in love with her and uses buying rouge as an excuse to talk with her and express his love. *Picking Up a Jade Bracelet* is set in the Ming dynasty. A young scholar passes by a farm girl doing embroidery in front of her house, and the two fall in love at first sight. The man deliberately loses one of his jade bracelets as a token of his love (Sichuan sheng chuanju, 1999: 572, 693).
62. CSJJD, 93-6-2718.
63. Regarding the incident, see Di Wang, 2003: 228–29.
64. CSJJD, 93-6-2718.
65. These rules addressed behavior as well as management practices. Patrons could be admitted only after standing in line and buying a ticket, and no one could enter after all the tickets were sold. The regulations also defined the treatment of customers. Government investigators had to show identification to enter the theater for inspections, but military police who were charged with keeping order did not. Military personnel paid a reduced price of 50 wen per ticket, but had to sit in an assigned area in the balcony and could not force their way inside if tickets were sold

out. The reduced-priced tickets were only sold to men in uniform; military personnel in civilian clothes had to buy regular tickets. The regulations also detailed the policy for readmission: patrons who left had to get a pass to return. Patrons were not to change their seats or block the view of others. If someone needed to find a patron, a teahouse worker would hold up a board with the patron's name without interrupting the show. As soon as a show started, audience members had to be quiet, and could not yell "bravo." Those who violated any of these rules were punished accordingly (GMGB, Dec. 26, 1916).

66. Reform and control of popular entertainment was a national trend. See Wakeman, 1995; Goldstein, 2003: 770–75.

67. CSJJD, 93-4-1789.

68. Ibid.

Chapter 6

1. Lao Xiang, 1942; Chen Maozhao, 1983: 189–90.
2. Han, 1965: 228–29; Hubbard, 1923: 125.
3. Hu Tian, 1938: 70; Chen Maozhao, 1983: 190.
4. GMGB, Sept. 11, 1914; Ci Jun, 1942; Qiu Chi, 1942; Lao Xiang, 1942; Chen Maozhao, 1983: 191; Wen Wenzi, 1990: 456–57; Hai Su, 1999: 141.
5. Wang Qingyuan, 1944: 35.
6. There is an old picture of a Chengdu teahouse in *Canadian School in West China*, edited by Brockman Brace (1974: 245). In this picture, several people—old and young, and men and women—are seated around a table and talking; next to the table is a shabbily dressed man sitting on a small, low stool and concentrating intently on something. It is obvious that is not sipping tea or joining the conversation. Most likely, he is repairing shoes.
7. Wang Qingyuan, 1944: 34; Lin Kongyi, 1986: 113; He Manzi, 1994: 193.
8. CSSD, 1927: 512; CDWB, Feb. 28, 1949.
9. Zheng Yunxia and Jia Shu, 1989: 72.
10. Cui Xianchang, 1982: 102. The teahouse provided space for a "floating" population. For many, especially those who did not have a place to live in the city, the teahouse became a place for rest, similar to the saloon in American cities. As Perry Duis noted, "The rise of the mobile worker was one of the most important developments in the last half of the nineteenth century." Saloons served "an endless flow of people who were sometimes far from home [and] competed to develop services and attractions that often differed from those in residential neighborhoods" (Duis, 1983: 172).
11. Chen Kongzhao, 1999: 127; Zhou Shaojie, seventy-five years old, interviewed by author, Joy Teahouse, June 22, 1997. Li Jieren described a tobacconist this way: "The short man [who served tobacco] came and used his yellow brass pipe, which was more than two feet long, to touch Wu's shoulder as he was smoking a cigarette. Wu said, 'Are you blind? Do I have two mouths, one smoking a cigarette and the other your water-pipe?' The short man gave him an angry look and said, 'Why are you in such a bad temper?' Fortunately, a customer called for water-pipe tobacco just then, so the man left while muttering with irritation" (Li Jieren, 1980 [1937]: 154–55).

12. Wang Qingyuan, 1944: 34; Skinner, 1964–65.
13. CDWB, Feb. 28, 1949; Yang Huai, 1982: 67.
14. CDWB, Mar. 20, 1949.
15. For example, the teahouse in Sun Yat-sen Park had a few dozen wooden boards listing various native-place associations, including the Association of Fushun Sojourners in Chengdu (Fushun xian lüsheng tongxiang hui) and the Association of Pingshan Sojourners in Chengdu (Pingshan xian lüsheng tongxiang hui). See Chen Maozhao, 1983: 191–92; Ci Jun, 1942.
16. GMGB, Oct. 17, 1929; CSJJD, 93-6-1062.
17. CSZGD, 38-11-2322.
18. According to the owner of the Sleeping Stream, teachers generally did not go to this teahouse, and students never went to the Cry of the Crane, because seeing each other would be awkward. Teachers did not think students should go to teahouses, while students did not feel comfortable having to pay respect to their teachers there. In the Smaller City Park, the Eternally Together Teahouse (Yongju chashe) had matchmakers who arranged meetings between male and female customers (Wang Shian and Zhu Zhiyan, 1989: 152–54).
19. Ci Jun, 1942; Qiu Chi, 1942; CDWB, Mar. 15, Mar. 20, 1949; Chen Maozhao, 1983: 191–92; Wang Shian and Zhu Zhiyan, 1989: 152–54; He Manzi, 1994: 193; Liang Deman and Huang Shangjun, 1998: 55; Li Ying, 2002.
20. Liu Zhenyao, 1999: 147–48; Qiu Chi, 1942.
21. Ci Jun, 1942.
22. GMGB, June 18, 1929; HXWB, June 5, 1941.
23. CSJJD, 93-2-1011.
24. CSZGD, 38-11-544.
25. Hai Su, 1999: 143.
26. GMGB, July 8, 1914; CSSD, 104-1397; Di Wang, 2000.
27. For studies of the Gowned Brothers in Sichuan, see Liu Ch'eng-yun, 1985; Di Wang, 1993: chap. 8; Stapleton, 1996; and McIsaac, 2000a. For studies of the Sworn Brotherhood Society elsewhere, see Cai Shaoqing, 1984; Murray, 1994; Ownby, 1996; and Martin, 1996.
28. Qiu Chi, 1942. Gold bars were traded at the True Entertainment Garden (Zhengyu huayuan), White Roses (Baimeigui), and Violet (Ziluolan) Teahouse. Guns, bullets, and opium were smuggled at the Fragrant Taste Tea Garden, Chinese-Scholar Tree Shadow (Huaiyin), Pleasant Tea Garden (Yiyuan), Wei Family Temple Teahouse (Weijiaci chaguan), and Ge Garden (Geyuan) (Chen Maozhao, 1983: 192).
29. CSJJD, 93-6-1525.
30. *Sichuan tongsheng jingcha zhangcheng*, 1903; Cui Xianchang, 1982: 96; Xiong Zhuoyun, eighty-eight years old, interviewed by author, Xiong's home, Aug. 9, 2000.
31. Li Ying, 2002; Hai Su, 1999: 142. For further discussion of this practice, see Chapter 4.
32. Chen Maozhao, 1983: 186.
33. "Chengdu shi paoge de yige jingtou," 1949–50; "Chengdu shi paoge zuzhi diaocha biao," 1949–50.
34. Chen Maozhao, 1983: 186.

35. CSJJD, 93-3-1322.
36. CSZGD, 38-11-1466.
37. Hu Tian, 1938: 70; Zhou Zhiying, 1943: 247.
38. Ci Jun, 1942.
39. The amount of capital is noted for fourteen of the thirty-three Class A teahouses mentioned above. Of these fourteen, six had 1,000 yuan or more (the highest, 2,500 yuan) in capital, and the rest had 400 to 800 yuan. These fourteen teahouses had a total capital of 14,800 yuan, with an average of a little more than 1,000 yuan each (CSZGD, 38-11-1821). On the subjects of capital; the number of hired workers, tables, and chairs; total sales; and the amount of taxes, see also Chapters 1, 2, and 3.
40. Li Jieren, 1980 [1936]: 457; Hai Su, 1999: 139; Yi Junzuo, 1943: 194.
41. HXWB, Sept. 20, 1941.
42. HXRB, Mar. 11, 1947; Shu Xincheng, 1934: 142–43.
43. Shu Xincheng, 1934: 143.
44. GMGB, July 17, 1928.
45. Chen Maozhao, 1983: 192; Zhou Zhiying, 1943: 247.
46. Ba Bo, 2003: 295.
47. Lao She, 1944.
48. Cui Xianchang, 1982: 98.
49. Some recent studies of women in traditional Chinese society also pay attention to women's domestic roles, and focus on elite women (Ko, 1994; Mann, 1997). Some examine working women in the People's Republic (Sheridan and Salaff, 1984). In the nineteenth and early twentieth centuries women typically were banned from public drinking places in many countries around the world. On the issue of gender in American saloons, see Powers, 1998: chap. 2; Murdock, 1998: chap. 1; Parsons, 2003: chap. 2. On women's public drinking in American cities, see MacAndrew and Edgerton, 1969; Douglas, 1987; Blocker, 1985; Peiss, 1986: chap. 1; Rosenzweig, 1983: chap. 2. Emmanuel Akyeampong examines gender in public drinking in Africa (Ghana) (1996: chap. 3; 149–53). In England, women had a long history of working in the brewery business (Bennett, 1996). On women in the temperance movement in American cities, see Dannenbaum, 1984. In late-nineteenth-century American cities, women were encouraged to frequent ballrooms, restaurants, and other public arenas, where they could buy alcohol, and drink and dance with men. Although this caused concern among social reformers, it was a widespread practice (Murdock, 1998: 77). The saloons in nineteenth-century North America were basically a man's world, and regulations were enacted to restrict women because "men defined pub space as both public and out of bounds to women" (Murdock, 1998: 8; see also Erenberg, 1981: 5; Campbell, 2001: 5, 7, 129). However, some working-class women also visited saloons, although most working men chose the saloon as a "gendered space free of heterosexual tensions." Some men came to saloons "to get away from wives," but some "might also have been getting even with them" (Powers, 1998: 46–47). In Paris, however, the situation was different, and working-class women could frequent cafés, even "when they were alone," which became "one of the main spaces of male-female interaction." The French Revolution of 1789 "brought women into [the] café in an unprecedented

fashion." Women increasingly took part in political mobilization and played a role in café life, which in the Paris Commune marked "the peak of women's participation in café politics" (Haine, 1996: 179, 200).

50. Goldstein, 2003: 765; Zhen Zhang, 1999: 33; Li Changli, 2002: 427–55.
51. Di Wang, 2003: chap. 6; Wang Zehua and Wang He, 1999: 108.
52. Men entered the Joy Tea Garden from the front gate on China's Revival Street (Huaxing jie) and women entered from the side door on West Chinese Catalpa Bridge Street (Zitongqiao xijie). The best seats were in the boxes at the front on the first floor (*tangzuo*), while the seats underneath the balcony, called "regular seats" (*putong zuo*), were the cheapest, separated from the boxes by a wire screen. In addition to the boxes, there were more than a dozen "enforcement seats" (*tanya zuo*) for the soldiers who kept order in the theater. Later, the boxes were dismantled and on the back of each chair a small wooden board was installed for holding tea bowls. The balcony curtains were also removed so that men and women could see each other (CDTL, 1: 277–79; Wang Zehua and Wang He, 1999: 129).
53. Li Jieren, 1980 [1937]: 232.
54. Qiu Chi, 1942.
55. Li Jieren, 1980 [1937]: 1464.
56. TSRB, Aug. 1, Aug. 3, Aug. 15, 1911.
57. Ibid., Apr. 29, 1910.
58. GMGB, Apr. 25, Oct. 31, 1912; Mar. 8, 1914.
59. Lin Kongyi, 1986: 100, 196.
60. CDKB, Mar. 16, 1932; Ci Jun, 1942.
61. According to Li Jieren, prostitution in the teahouse was not a new phenomenon. Before the emergence of the police in Chengdu, as Li described it, "women of good families" did not frequent the teahouse (Li Jieren, 1980 [1936]: 339). Although decent people despised the custom, prostitutes and their customers were a constant presence in the teahouse. Prostitution caused problems such as fighting for men's favor, gossiping, overcrowding by curious onlookers, and even violence. Therefore, the government enacted measures to control prostitution in the teahouses.
62. GMGB, Oct. 7, 1914; CDKB, Aug. 7, 1938.
63. HXWB, Nov. 27, 1941.
64. Hai Su, 1999: 143–46.
65. Ibid. In 1944, Sha Ting wrote *Caged Beast* (Kunshou ji), a novel set in a market town on the Chengdu Plain in 1940. One of major scenes was in a teahouse: "This teahouse was opened by a well-known member of the local gentry. It is a special place, where the majority of patrons are young intellectuals, but women also come here. Therefore, it attracts a lot of attention. Now, the open-minded and interesting old gentry have moved to Chengdu, but the atmosphere remains. . . . The major entertainment here is pure conversation (*qingtan*) about everything from important national affairs to the dead rat that was found somewhere on the street" (Sha Ting, 1984 [1944]: 423).

Chapter 7

1. GMGB, July 27, July 29, 1929. For more detailed reports on this case, see ibid., Aug. 1, Aug. 18, Sept. 15, Sept. 16, 1929; May 29, 1930.
2. Regarding "drinking settlement tea," see Chapter 6, and Di Wang, 2003: 99–101.
3. Yerkovich, 1977: 192–93. Agnes Heller considered gossip an important part of everyday life: News "has always played a more or less important part in our everyday life—starting with gossip, the oldest form of newscasting in everyday contexts" (Heller, 1984: 223).
4. TSRB, May 15, 1910. This case may support Heller's finding that "friction in everyday life contacts usually takes the form of the quarrel. This can be defined as the collision of two or more sets of particularistic interests" (Heller, 1984: 247).
5. TSRB, Oct. 21, Dec. 21, 1909; July 31, 1911; GMGB, Mar. 26, 1914.
6. CSJJD, 93-6-2723.
7. CSSD, 104-1397.
8. CSJJD, 93-2-3282. The list of damage provides further information about the supplies used in a teahouse: 149 tea bowls, 182 lids, five tea pots, one hot water vat, and one dirty-water vat. Two-thirds of the teahouse was damaged. There was also an attached kitchen, which lost the following items: one iron frying pan, one stove, one kitchen cabinet, five small pottery bowls, one pottery jar, thirty-one bowls, five porcelain rice bowls, eleven rough pottery rice bowls, eight spoons, one rice basin, one ceramic water vat, nine dishes for cooked vegetables, and one jar with cooked meat and turnips, for a total loss of 86,000 yuan.
9. CDWB, Sept. 19, 1948.
10. CSJJD, 93-2-3282.
11. Xiong Zhuoyun, eighty-eight years old, interviewed by author, his home, Aug. 9, 2000; CSSD, 104-1397; CSZGD, 38-11-544.
12. Li Ying, 2002; CSSD, 104-1397; CSZGD, 38-11-544.
13. CDKB, Mar. 28, 1932.
14. See examples in TSRB, May 3, Aug. 29, 1909.
15. An example in 1915 can be seen in CSJJD, 93-6-2723.
16. GMGB, Mar. 28, Mar. 29, 1928.
17. Di Wang, 2003: chap. 7.
18. Ibid.: chap. 2.
19. In May 1913, for instance, a policeman wrote a report on the Fragrant Taste Tea Garden's delay in paying 13.2 yuan per day as a "protection fee" (*baohu fei*). The teahouse owed 528 yuan for forty days' worth of shows, but it refused to pay, saying that business had been slow (CSJJD, 93-6-2723).
20. Wang Zehua and Wang He, 1999: 134–35.
21. CSZGD, 38-11-534, 38-11-544.
22. Ibid., 38-11-1465. During this period the currency, fabi, became enormously devalued.
23. Ibid., 38-11-444.
24. GMGB, July 17, 1928; Sept. 24, 1930.
25. CSZGD, 38-11-984.
26. For more cases about local toughs, see CSJJD, 93-3-1333.

27. GMGB, Apr. 7, 1914; CSJJD, 93-2-1012.

28. The teahouse claimed more than 30 million fabi yuan in damages, including the destruction of 326 tea bowls, 335 lids, seventeen wooden tables, and thirty-four bamboo chairs. The man responsible was arrested after the municipal government transferred this case to the police (CSZGD, 38-11-1535).

29. On political chaos and turmoil in early Republican Sichuan in general and Chengdu in particular, see Kapp, 1973; and Di Wang, 2003: chap. 7.

30. In the early Republican era, the police decreed that soldiers in uniform could be charged only 50 wen to watch performances in teahouse theaters. Teahouses tried to curry favor with officers to gain protection as the social order crumbled. The Joy Tea Garden, for instance, gave all of its tickets for a day of performances to military officers (Di Wang, 2003: chap. 7; GMGB, Dec. 30, 1913; Dec. 26, 1916).

31. CDKB, Sept. 23, 1930. The *Citizens' Daily* reported four cases of violence in August and September 1930 alone. One was when a few hoodlums drank tea with prostitutes in the Common Spring Teahouse (Tongchun chashe) in the Smaller City Park, and a group of "hoodlum soldiers" became "jealous" and tried to sit next to the prostitutes, resulting in an argument. The soldiers threw tea bowls at the hoodlums, accidentally hitting a child on the head and causing him to bleed. The violence caused "public resentment," and the patrons who saw what happened demanded that those responsible take the child to the hospital (GMGB, Aug. 5, 1930). Another case occurred the next day at the Archery and Morality Society (Shede hui) Teahouse, which was also in the Smaller City Park. Several soldiers forced a restaurant keeper to kneel before a young woman. The woman, the wife of a military officer, had felt humiliated and asked her husband to seek revenge after she was served a dish in his restaurant in a crude pottery bowl (GMGB, Aug. 6, 1930). That same month, the military police sent two squads to the Gushing Fountain Chamber Teahouse (Yongquan ju chashe) and arrested four hooligans and two "hoodlum soldiers" who had instigated mass violence (GMGB, Aug. 17, 1930). In September, the *Citizens' Daily*, under the notable headline "A Teahouse-Goer Is Shot to Death during the Day in Successful and Peaceful Street," reported that more than a dozen soldiers rushed into the crowded High Tea Balcony (Gaochalou) and shot a man in the chest and head numerous times to ensure his death. Nobody knew why they wanted to kill him (GMGB, Sept. 24, 1930).

32. CDKB, Mar. 14, 1932.

33. Ibid., May 24, May 25, 1938.

34. CSJJD, 93-2-2780.

35. CSZGD, 38-11-1465.

36. CDKB, Apr. 28, 1932; CSZGD, 38-11-328.

37. CSJJD, 93-2-5117.

38. Chiang Kai-shek, who was also governor of Sichuan at that time, signed an order for the Chengdu Police Force to handle this matter (CSZGD, 38-11-520).

39. Ibid., 38-11-328. There is no evidence regarding the outcome of their requests.

40. GMGB, June 25, 1929; Aug. 8, 1930; CDKB, Apr. 28, 1932.

41. GMGB, June 25, 1929.

42. CSZGD, 38-11-1530.

Chapter 8

1. There is a famous saying in China: "When the empire is peaceful, Sichuan is the first to have a rebellion; when order is established in the empire, Sichuan is still in chaos" (*Tianxia weiluan Shu xianluan, tianxia yizhi Shu weizhi*). This saying emphasizes Sichuan's uniqueness and strategic position in national politics and also the difficulties in governing the province, which has been first among the provinces in population since the nineteenth century.

2. See Di Wang, 2003: chap. 2.

3. On the development of urban administration in Chengdu, see Stapleton, 2000a; Di Wang, 1993: 401–2; Di Wang, 2003: chaps. 2, 4, 5; Qiao Zengxi, Li Canhua, and Bai Zhaoyu, 1983; He Yimin, 2002: chap. 3.

4. *Sichuan tongsheng jingcha zhangcheng*, 1903; CSJJD, 93-2-2559 and 93-6-2718; GMGB, Dec. 16, Dec. 26, 1916; CSSD, 1927: 510–12; CDKB, Apr. 2, 1932; XXXW, Mar. 16, 1945; Jia Daquan and Chen Yishi, 1988: 369; CSSD, 104-1388 and 104-1406; CSZGD, 38-11-298; *Sichuan sheng zhengfu shehuichu dang'an*, vol. 186: 1431. The general regulations pertaining to all service occupations or informal policies that were implemented are not included. Therefore, one surmises teahouses suffered even more restrictions than those discussed here.

5. Di Wang, 2003: chap. 7.

6. For more detailed information of this period, see Stapleton, 2000a; and Di Wang, 2003: chaps. 4, 5.

7. Qin Shao has discussed how reformist elites regarded the teahouses in Nantong as "backward" establishments and tried very hard to reform them (Shao, 1998). I have also discussed how teahouses in Chengdu were a convenient target of urban reform (Di Wang, 2000; Di Wang, 2003: chap. 5).

8. *Sichuan tongsheng jingcha zhangcheng*, 1903; *Shengyuan jingqu zhangcheng*, n.d.: 27, 30.

9. Regarding the movement, see Di Wang, 2003: chap. 7. The leaders of the constitutional movement and the Railroad Protection Movement, including Pu Dianjun and Luo Lun, negotiated with Zhao Erfeng, acting governor-general, with the result that Pu was made governor. But, when Qing soldiers rioted and looted banks and other businesses in most of Chengdu's commercial districts in early December 1911, Pu and other major officials in the new government fled for their lives. The riots were soon quelled and Zhao Erfeng was killed by the allied forces of the New Army headed by Yin Changheng and the revolutionaries. Yin then became governor of the Sichuan Military Government (Sichuan jun zhengfu), which was established on December 10, 1911 (Wei Yingtao, 1981: chaps. 4, 5; Stapleton, 2000a: chaps. 3, 5; Di Wang, 2003: chaps. 5, 7).

10. Di Wang, 2003: 228–30; Stapleton, 2000a: chap. 7; Kapp, 1973: chaps. 1, 2.

11. Li Jieren, 1980 [1937]: 788; Han, 1965: 228–29.

12. TSRB, Aug. 6 1909; May 25, 1910; GMGB, June 14, 1912; Oct. 7, 1929.

13. GMGB, May 5, July 29, 1917.

14. Ibid., July 1, 1916; Aug. 20, 1917; Wu Yu, 1984, I: 265–66.

15. Di Wang, 2003: 228–30; Stapleton, 2000a: chap. 7; Kapp, 1973: chaps. 1, 2.

16. These five warlords were Liu Xiang, Liu Wenhui, Deng Xihou, Tian Songyao, and Yang Sen. Chengdu had five mayors during this period, all of whom were gen-

erals under these warlords. During this period, Sichuan was commonly regarded as one of the most unstable provinces but in fact, under this power structure, Chengdu was relatively peaceful, avoiding war as it did in 1917 (Kapp, 1973: chap. 3). At the end of 1932 war broke out between Liu Xiang and Liu Wenhui and another war broke out the next year between Deng Xihou and Liu Wenhui. Both wars were fought in the streets of Chengdu, resulting in many deaths and an enormous loss of property in the worst catastrophe since 1917. These warlords struggled to grab more financial resources by dramatically increasing taxes, smuggling opium, and controlling the economy. High taxes and economic instability, exacerbated by the presence of bandits, forced many landlords to sell their land and move to the city. Many ended up in Chengdu and became new customers of the teahouses there.

17. Kapp, 1973: chaps. 3, 4, 5; Qiao Zengxi, Li Canhua, and Bai Zhaoyu, 1983: 15; Zhang Xuejun and Zhang Lihong, 1993: 296; He Yimin, 2002: 345–46.

18. GMGB, Apr. 9, 1917.

19. Ibid., Feb. 10, 1922.

20. Lu Xun, 1973 [1921]: 359–416.

21. On the regulation of teahouse theaters and performances, see Chapter 5.

22. CDKB, Apr. 2, 1932; Jia Daquan and Chen Yishi, 1988: 369.

23. In order to have more control, Chiang Kai-shek himself concurrently held the post of governor of Sichuan.

24. In 1940 Chengdu suffered serious food shortages that resulted in rice riots. To address this problem, as well as the increasing number of Japanese air raids, the government ordered residents to evacuate. People lived in the shadow of war, and "running for their lives whenever sirens sounded the alert" (*pao jingbao*) became a part of daily life from 1938 to 1941. People began moving back to the city in 1941 and 1942 after the Japanese shifted their focus to the Pacific War and stopped bombing. From October 1938 to August 1941, there were thirteen air raids. The worst attacks, on June 11, 1939, October 27, 1940, and July 27, 1941, killed and wounded several thousand people and made homeless countless more, and reduced many streets and districts to rubble (Liu Xiyuan, 1998: 148–51).

25. XMBWK, Oct. 27, 1943. There is no study of wartime Chengdu but a few of wartime Chongqing. See McIsaac, 2000b; Zhang Jin, 2005.

26. Zhou Wen, 1999: 229; XXXW, Apr. 9, 1938; Zhou Zhiying, 1943: 224. Teahouses and teahouse theaters took part in patriotic activities, especially fundraising, from the early stages of the War of Resistance (CDKB, Aug. 25, Aug. 27, Sep. 1, 1938).

27. HXWB, June 16, Nov. 23, 1941.

28. Jian Fu, 1942; Qiu Chi, 1942; Zhou Zhiying, 1943: 246.

29. Wang Qingyuan, 1944: 37–38; Zhou Zhiying, 1943: 224.

30. CSZGD, 38-11-1103.

31. This story described crimes of the Japanese invaders and called on fellow countrymen to organize for self-protection as all Chinese fought for their lives. The script claimed, "We will fight for victory in recovering our motherland. We would rather die as a hero than live as a slave without a country" (CSZGD, 38-11-1103). Regarding Yue Fei in historical memory, see Huang Donglan, 2004.

32. CSZGD, 38-11-1103.
33. Ibid., 38-11-950, 38-11-951.
34. The guild especially organized a committee called the Committee on Lecture Platforms (Jiangtai weiyuanhui), which had three to five members per district, for a total of nineteen people (CSSD, 104-1401).
35. CSZGD, 38-11-952.
36. Class A teahouses were required to display the GMD and national flags, and portraits of the founding father Sun Yat-sen as well as the president and chairman of the national government (the chairman's portrait on the left and president's on the right). A blackboard, a lectern, magazines and newspapers, pictures, and slogans were also required. Class B and C teahouses had to have all of above items except the lectern. Those that did not meet the requirements by a certain deadline were to be fined, and those that refused to follow this order were to be shut down. The mayor also required the Teahouse Guild to report the names, locations, and owners of all teahouses in Chengdu (CSSD, 104-1384). The government enacted "The Setting of Teahouses," which gave concrete instructions about décor based on a teahouse's economic capacity, size, and class. Class A teahouses had to post cartoons, slogans, charts, and pictures, had to provide books and newspapers for patrons to read, and had to have a blackboard for displaying propaganda and news. Class B teahouses had most of the same requirements, but pictures and books were optional and the blackboard was smaller. Class C teahouses had to display the cartoons, slogans, and charts, but not the pictures, and did not have to have newspapers or a blackboard (ibid., 104-1388).
37. Ibid., 104-1390.
38. Ibid., 104-1388.
39. Here are some examples of the slogans. On transportation: "Develop transportation for taking military supplies to the frontlines," "Transportation in the rear areas is just like fighting on the frontlines," "Transportation plays a key role in the War of Resistance," and "Transportation depends on the power of humans and animals." On air defense: "No air defense, no national defense," "Develop air defense," "Building air defense is strengthening national defense," and "Everyone contributes to buying aircraft for killing the enemy." On economizing and saving: "Practicing strict economy promotes saving," "Economizing and saving establishes a foundation for our children," "Savings bonds benefit us and the nation," and "Economizing promotes the fight against the Japanese." The government also sought financial support and stressed the importance of raising money: "It is natural that the rich should donate more money," "To donate money for the military is to improve the morale of soldiers," and "Respond enthusiastically to the call to donate rice and money" (ibid.).
40. Ibid.
41. Some praised the heroes of the War of Resistance and some, such as *Stories of Bravery* (Yingyong shiji) and *Yue Fei*, the heroes of ancient wars. Anti-Communist themes characterized some books, such as *Disbanding the New Fourth Army and Strengthening Military Discipline* (Jiesan Xinsijun yu zhengchi junji). Some were about traitors, such as *Nets Above and Snares Below* (Tianluo diwang) and *This Is Wang Jingwei* (Ruci de Wang Jingwei). Some promoted GMD ideology, such as *A*

Popular Reading of the Three Principles of the People (Sanmin zhuyi dazhong duben) and *A Brief Plan of National Construction* (Jianguo fanglüe). Some addressed mobilization of the masses in the resistance movement, such as *The President's Call for Sichuan Folk-followers* (Zongcai gao Chuansheng tongbao shu) and *Outline for Mobilizing the National Spirit and Its Implementation* (Guomin jingshen zongdongyuan gangling ji shishi banfa). There were also some general-interest publications on social reform, such as *Sichuan Geography* (Sichuan dili) and *A Collection of Stories about the New Life* (Xin shenghuo gushi ji) (ibid.).

42. Ibid., 104-1401.
43. Ibid., 104-1388, 104-1401.
44. Ju Ge, 1942.
45. Propaganda in the teahouse became so important and common that someone wrote an article entitled "The Theory and Practice of Teahouse Propaganda," which discusses the importance and functions of teahouses, the value of teahouse propaganda and its relation to the war, and the preparation of teahouse propaganda, as well as how to do teahouse propaganda (Bo Xing, 1941). The GMD government continued this strategy even after the war ended. In 1948, the Sichuan Provincial Government enacted Regulations on Teahouses in Sichuan, which still required teahouses to hang slogans and pictures of the New Life Movement and enact sanitation, air defense, and poison-prevention measures. The government also called on teahouses to provide books and newspapers for customers (CSZGD, 38-11-298).
46. Ibid. These regulations detailed requirements for hygiene, which has been discussed in Chapter 1.
47. Yu Xi, 1943.
48. Ci Jun, 1942.
49. Bai Yuhua, 1945.
50. Lao She, 1978: 78, 92, 113.
51. Yu Xi, 1943.
52. Zhang Zhenjian, 1999: 321–22.
53. Qiao Zengxi, Li Canhua, and Bai Zhaoyu, 1983: 9–11; He Yimin, 2002: 347, 585–86; Kapp, 1973: chap. 8; Li Wenfu, 1998. In early December 1949 thirty-five Communists were executed at Twelfth Bridge (Shier qiao) (Liao Junyi, 1998; Tang Tiyao, 1998).
54. CSSD, 104-1397. The original document is not dated, but Mayor Chen Bingguang held the position in 1946-47 (He Yimin, 2002: 354), indicating that this public notice was issued during that time.
55. CSJJD, 93-2-759. There is a similar case in CSJJD, 93-2-3101.
56. CSSD, 104-1388.
57. On gambling in the teahouse, see Suzuki, 1982: 534; Di Wang, 2003: chap. 6.
58. CSJJD, 93-2-2559.
59. Ibid.
60. CSSD, 104-1388.
61. Teahouse managers did not support most of the restrictions, but they definitely favored the policy of limiting the number of new teahouses. Their motivation was clear: They did not want the competition that new teahouses would bring. See Chapter 2.

62. Communists often used teahouses for meetings and networking. It was said that they often met in the teahouses on Horse Walking Street, Green Stone Bridge, East City Corner Street (Dongchenggen jie), Warm Spring Road, the Smaller City Park, and Long Fluent Street. Ma Shitu wrote the drama *Three Challenges in the Prosperous Tea Garden* (Sanzhan Huayuan) about the struggles between the CCP and special agents of the GMD (Chen Maozhao, 1983: 192–93). According to the keeper of the Sleeping Stream Teahouse, CCP members often held secret meetings there because secret agents did not pay much attention to a place that mainly attracted high school students. The teahouse keeper knew their identity but pretended to know nothing about their activities (Wang Shian and Zhu Zhiyan, 1989: 156).

Conclusion

1. Esherick, 2000: 7.
2. For recent studies of these reforms, see ibid.
3. The Teahouse Guild supported this policy. See Chapter 2.
4. This phenomenon was not unique to Chengdu; during the same period, this became a national trend, defined by Fredric Wakeman as the "licensing of leisure" (Wakeman, 1995).
5. Di Wang, 2003: chap. 7.
6. Governments around the world sought to increase control over public drinking places such as the saloons of the United States, cafés of France, and teahouses of China. In American cities in the late nineteenth century, "All of these antisaloon efforts essentially failed despite some minor successes," because the poor depended on saloons. In France, proprietors of cafés resisted restrictions: "Whenever confronted with police repression, café owners turned these benefits into excuses, citing 'freedom of commerce' or 'private property' and claiming that the police had no right to enter their establishments" (Duis, 1983: 113; Haine, 1996: 190).
7. See Pittman and Snyder, 1962; Austin, 1985; Duis, 1983; Rosenzweig, 1983; Peiss, 1986; Murdock, 1998; Parsons, 2003. On public drinking in Europe, especially in France, see Prestwich, 1988; Brennan, 1988; and Haine, 1996. Also see Lambert, 1983, for Wales; Warsh, 1993, and Campbell, 2001, for Canada; and Akyeampong, 1996, for Africa. The density of teahouses in China was lower than that of saloons in America or cafés in France. Paris had 30,000 drinking establishments or cafés from the late 1880s until the early twentieth century. In 1909, London had 5,860 drinking establishments or cafés and New York had 10,821. This means that London had one shop per thousand residents; New York had 3.15, and Paris had 11.25 (Haine, 1996: 3–4, 153). Chengdu, which had the highest density of teahouses in China during this period, had 1.5 teahouses per thousand residents (518 for 350,000 residents).
8. On the scholarship and debates over the notion of the "public sphere" in China, see Rowe, 1989, 1990; Rankin, 1986, 1990; Strand, 1989; Philip Huang, 1993; Wakeman, 1993.
9. Habermas, 1989: 32, 35, 45–46, 59. On recent studies of coffeehouses, see Cowan, 2005.
10. Duis, 1983: 1.
11. Campbell, 2001: 4.

12. Sennett, 1977: 81.
13. Ibid.: 80, 107.
14. Rosenzweig, 1983: 117; Duis, 1983: 116.
15. Brennan, 1988: 8.
16. A saloon keeper in Chicago recalled that all a saloon needed was "the key to the place." After he paid the first month's rent, he went to a brewery agent "with the lease for the place and the rent receipt and they'll have the fixtures out at the dump" (Duis, 1983: 47).
17. Ibid.: 49, 120–21.
18. Rosenzweig, 1983: 36; Duis, 1983: 49.
19. Rosenzweig, 1983: 58; Duis, 1983: 87, 102, 145. More examples of the similarities can be found in other studies: Saloons became a kind of social club in the "the everyday lives of the millions of workers" who considered them a "poor man's club" (Powers, 1998). Professional, ethnic, and neighborhood ties could be found in the saloon. Local theaters became a center of "plebeian culture" in Pittsburgh, where working-class audiences enjoyed comedies and melodramas based on local stories (Couvares, 1983: 142). In Germany, although alcohol "pervaded all spheres of urban working-class life" in the workplace and at home, in both public life or private life, "none of the new mass commercial leisure forms was the sole province of the working class in general or of any group within it." Workingmen visited the cinemas, sports arenas, and fairs "where the classes, religions, ethnic groups and sexes could mix." Therefore, "some degree of social harmony in leisure was achieved" (Abrams, 1992: 66, 183). Cafés in nineteenth-century Paris experienced a similar trend, where working-class café-goers "produced a distinctive subculture." Workingmen, more than any other group, "made the café their home." Scott Haine regards the café as "an annex to the workshop and factory." The café could also be a political arena, often used for strikes and demonstrations (Haine, 1996: 2, 59, 79–87).
20. Duis, 1983: 112, 180; Rosenzweig, 1983: 53–55.
21. Duis, 1983: 126.
22. Brennan, 1988: 12.
23. Duis, 1983: 141.
24. Jones, 1986: 164; Duis, 1983: 127.
25. Duis, 1983: 136, 178–79.
26. Powers, 1998: 65; Haine, 1996: 215.
27. Walvin, 1997: 11–12; Macfarlane and Macfarlane, 2004: 82.
28. Although I have found some documentation of business strategies, very detailed and systematic materials are lacking, and no accounting records have been found to date. Scholars of British economic history have access to daily accounting records because shops in England, especially those that sold tea, were "required to keep an account of their sales and purchases of tea in the books," although this rule was often disregarded. These records also provide a comprehensive study of competition between shops, specifically regarding the retailing of tea. Tea was one of the principal goods handled by grocers, "one on which a considerable part of their profit depended. Although large quantities of sugar were sold, it was not an item that yielded a high margin of profit. Indeed, it was often used as a leading article to attract custom for tea or coffee" (Mui and Mui, 1989: 201, 208, 250).

29. Rosenzweig, 1983: 56. But, despite many options, "probably only the church and the home rivaled the saloon as working-class social centers." Workers spent their leisure time in a wide range of pursuits: "gossiping with neighbors, lounging in pool halls, studying in night classes, visiting dance halls, mending worn clothing, organizing temperance societies, tending gardens, raising money for their churches, arguing over trade union strategy, and watching melodramas." But, Rosenzweig points out, "for many, drinking occupied an important portion of their growing, but still limited, leisure hours. Indeed, it is hardly surprising that a diversion like drinking, which had once played such a central role during work time, would also have a central place in leisure time" (ibid.: 40, 56). This, to a certain extent, is similar to the situation in early twentieth-century Chengdu.

30. Peiss, 1986: 140, 142.

31. Duis, 1983: 101.

32. When we compare the teahouse with the saloon, it may be useful to compare tea with alcohol as beverages. Although both tea and alcohol have made successful inroads worldwide, tea remains the world's most popular drink largely because of its nature. The world consumption of tea "easily equals all the other manufactured drinks in the world put together—that is, coffee, chocolate, cocoa, sweet fizzy artificial drinks and all alcoholic drinks" (Macfarlane and Macfarlane, 2004: 32). Overconsumption of alcohol can lead to social and health problems, but tea drinkers face no similar threats. Furthermore, alcohol consumption has been regulated and controlled over time, but tea has always had a green light everywhere; the Chinese government regulated the teahouse as a public space, but not the beverage itself. The government was never able to galvanize a social movement comparable to the temperance movement in nineteenth-century America. Going to the teahouse differed from going to the saloon in many ways. Alcohol was a powerful lure to the point of being addictive. A man might forego a meal to stop "at a nearby saloon" (Duis, 1983: 89). On studies of drunkenness and drunkards, also see Brennan, 1988: chap. 4; Crowley, 1999; Parsons, 2003. Although drinking "provided an escape from misery" for many working-class Americans (Duis, 1983: 88), it also wrought widespread financial and social devastation, which has been fully explored in Western literature. Tea drinking hardly had the same result. Tea is not addictive although some people drink it habitually every day, and its effects are mild compared to alcohol's. Any tea drinking "addiction" has more to do with the atmosphere in the teahouse than with the beverage itself, which is not the case with alcohol addiction. History is full of accounts of people who act violently after drinking too much alcohol, while drinking tea in public was solely a means of socializing. As we know, alcohol addiction is often uncontrolled, and alcoholism causes serious problems. In contrast, tea drinking is gentle, peaceful, and rational; tea drinking does not affect the emotions or lead to violent behavior. Drinking in a saloon, though cheaper than most other forms of entertainment, was still costly, because saloon-goers had to pay for every glass of beer. Drinking in a teahouse, however, was cheap, because a customer who paid for a cup (or bowl) of tea was entitled to as many free refills of water as he desired. Furthermore, the effects of alcohol are cumulative, but the effects of cup after cup of increasingly diluted tea are not. A teahouse-goer's mind and body were not affected, regardless of how long he stayed. This made it easy for a man to linger

in a teahouse for an entire day, but it was very difficult for a saloon-goer to do the same even if he could afford it.

Both tea and alcohol (wine) have a long tradition in China and have contributed much to Chinese civilization. When we discuss the social impact of tea and alcohol in China, we have to ask the following: Was there a serious problem in China's alcohol consumption? What was the relationship between tea drinking and wine drinking in China? How did drinking alcohol differ in China and the West? What different social problems resulted from drinking alcohol and tea in China and the West? Wine and tea have a complex relationship in China; at times, people chose one over the other, but most of the time, people used them in a way that was complementary. For example, people in Chengdu often went to a teahouse after drinking alcohol in a wine shop or restaurant. When one product can substitute completely for another, then their functions must be identical. Although wine and tea are beverages, their physiological effects are different, so one is not a direct replacement for the other. Anthropologists have pointed out that from earliest times wine (*jiu*) drinking was "a basic part of Chinese living," especially in religious ceremonies (Schafer, 1977: 119). Tea eventually replaced wine as the national drink. The relationship between wine and tea in ancient China is vividly described in Wang Fu's Tang dynasty essay "A Debate on Tea and Wine" (Chajiu lun), discovered in the Dunhuang caves. The author anthropomorphized wine and tea and let them "debate" their virtues. According to the essay, wine could make people "high" and lead them to act more bravely and with more imagination, but could also make them drunk and crazy. Also, drinking wine was costly; it has always been the case that "tea is cheap and wine is expensive" (*chajian jiugui*). However, tea could not be used in important ceremonies or to boost people's spirits, and drinking too much could cause stomach pain. The essay concludes by pointing out that both tea and wine depend on each other, making "wine shops rich while teahouses are not poor" (*jiudian fafu, chafang buqiong*) (Wang Fu, 2000: 174–75). Wine shops and teahouses never became serious rivals, at least from what we have seen in Chengdu.

33. See Table 1.1 in Chapter 1.

Works Cited

Abrams, Lynn. 1992. *Workers' Culture in Imperial Germany: Leisure and Recreation in the Rhineland and Westphalia.* London: Routledge.
Adburgham, Alison. 1967. *Shops and Shopping, 1800–1914.* London: George Allen & Unwin.
Akyeampong, Emmanuel Kwaku. 1996. *Drink, Power, and Cultural Change: A Social History of Alcohol in Ghana, c. 1800 to Recent Times.* Portsmouth, Eng.: Heinemann.
Austin, Gregory. 1985. *Alcohol in Western Society from Antiquity to 1800: A Chronological History.* Santa Barbara, CA: ABC-Clio Information Services.
Averill, Stephen C. 1981. "The New Life in Action: The Nationalist Government in South Jiangxi, 1934–37." *China Quarterly* 88 (Dec.): 594–628.
Ba Bo. 2003. "Zuo chaguan" [Sitting in the teahouse], 294–98 in Peng Guoliang, 2003.
Bai Yuhua. 1945. "Tantan 'Xiutan guoshi'" [A chat on "Do not talk about national affairs"]. XXXW, Mar. 18.
Bennett, Judith M. 1996. *Ale, Beer, and Brewsters in England: Women's Work in a Changing World, 1300–1600.* New York: Oxford University Press.
Benson, Carlton. 1996. "From Teahouse to Radio: Storytelling and the Commercialization of Culture in 1930s Shanghai." Ph.D. diss., University of California, Berkeley.
Bing Fei. 1933. "Xiaofei xiao tongji" [Brief statistics on consumption]. XXXW, Oct. 29.
Bird, Isabella. 1987 [1899]. *The Yangtze Valley and Beyond: An Account of Journeys in China, Chiefly in the Province of Sze Chuan and Among the Man-sze of the Somo Territory.* First published by John Murray in 1899. Rept., Boston: Beacon Press, 1987.
Blocker, Jack S., Jr. 1985. *"Give to the Wind Thy Fears": The Women's Temperance Crusade, 1873–1874.* Westport, CT: Greenwood.
Bo Xing. 1941. "Chaguan xuanchuan de lilun yu shiji" [The theory and practice of teahouse propaganda]. *Fuwu yuekan* [Service monthly] 6 (May): 5–10.
Brace, Brockman, ed. 1974. *Canadian School in West China.* Published for the Canadian School Alumni Association.

Brennan, Thomas. 1988. *Public Drinking and Popular Culture in Eighteenth-Century Paris*. Princeton, NJ: Princeton University Press.
Cai Shaoqing. 1984. "On the Origin of the Gelaohui." *Modern China* 10.4 (Oct.): 481–508.
Campbell, Robert A. 2001. *Sit Down and Drink Your Beer: Regulating Vancouver's Beer Parlours, 1925–1954*. Toronto: University of Toronto Press.
Certeau, Michel de. 1984. *The Practice of Everyday Life*. Trans. Steven F. Rendall. Berkeley: University of California Press.
Chai Yuyan. 1999. "Huashuo niaoshui hudou" [Stories of urinated broad beans], 105–7 in Feng Zhicheng, 1999.
Chan, Wellington K. K. 1982. "The Organizational Structure of the Traditional Chinese Firm and Its Modern Reform." *Business History Review* 56.2 (Summer): 218–35.
Chang, K. C., ed. 1977. *Food in Chinese Culture: Anthropological and Historical Perspectives*. New Haven, CT: Yale University Press.
Che Fu. 1985. "Jia Shusan" [A biography of Jia Shusan], 268–70 in Ren Yimin, ed., *Sichuan jinxiandai renwu zhuan* [Biographies of figures of modern Sichuan], vol. 1. Chengdu: Sichuan sheng shehui kexueyuan chubanshe.
———. 1995. "Zhou lianzhang chaguan yu Li Yueqiu" [Company Commander Zhou's teahouse and Li Yueqiu]. *Longmenzhen* [Folk tales] 2 (86): 1–6.
———. 2003. *Jincheng jiushi* [Old stories of the brocade city]. Chengdu: Sichuan wenyi chubanshe.
Cheal, David. 1988. *The Gift Economy*. New York: Routledge.
Chen Haodong, and Zhang Siyong, eds. 1991. *Chengdu minjian wenxue jicheng* [A treasury of Chengdu folklore]. Chengdu: Sichuan renmin chubanshe.
Chen Jin. 1992. *Sichuan chapu* [Sichuan's teahouses]. Chengdu: Sichuan renmin chubanshe.
Chen Kongzhao. 1999. "Yeziyan ganr, shuiyan dai yu xisu" [Smoking pipes, tobacco pouches, and social customs], 125–27 in Feng Zhicheng, 1999.
Chen Maozhao. 1983. "Chengdu de chaguan" [Teahouses of Chengdu]. *Chengdu wenshi ziliao xuanji* [Selections of literature and historical materials on Chengdu] 4: 178–93.
Chen Shisong. 1999. *Tianxia Sichuan ren* [Sichuanese]. Chengdu: Sichuan renmin chubanshe.
Chen Xiangbai. 1998. *Zhongguo chawenhua* [Tea culture in China]. Taiyuan: Shanxi renmin chubanshe.
Chengdu kuaibao [Chengdu daily bulletin]. 1929–49.
Chengdu shenghui jingcha ju dang'an [Archives of the Chengdu Police Department]. Republican period. Chengdu Municipal Archives, *quanzhong* 93.
Chengdu shi difang zhi bianzuan weiyuanhui, ed. 2000. *Chengdu shizhi—Gongshang xingzheng guanli zhi* [Gazetteer of Chengdu: Administration of industry and commerce]. Chengdu: Sichuan cishu chubanshe.
Chengdu shi gehang geye tongye gonghui dang'an [Archives of all occupations in Chengdu]. Chengdu Municipal Archives, *quanzhong* 52.
Chengdu shi gongshang ju dang'an [Archives of the Chengdu Bureau of Industry and Commerce]. Chengdu Municipal Archives, *quanzhong* 119.

Chengdu shi gongshang xingzheng dengji dang'an [Archives of industrial and commercial registrations in Chengdu]. Chengdu Municipal Archives, *quanzhong* 40.
"Chengdu shi paoge de yige jingtou" [A view of the Gowned Brothers in Chengdu]. 1949–50. In *Chengdu shi gongan ju dang'an* [Archives of the Chengdu Police Department]. No date. From the contents, I estimate the document dates to about 1949–50.
"Chengdu shi paoge zuzhi diaocha biao" [A table of the investigation of the Gowned Brothers organization in Chengdu]. No date. Based on the contents, it was likely prepared in late 1949 or 1950. Archives of the Chengdu Police Department.
Chengdu shi qunzhong yishuguan, ed. 1996. *Chengdu zhanggu* [Anecdotes of Chengdu], no. 1. Chengdu: Chengdu chubanshe.
———. 1998. *Chengdu zhanggu* [Anecdotes of Chengdu], no. 2. Chengdu: Sichuan daxue chubanshe.
Chengdu shi shanghui dang'an [Archives of the Chengdu Chamber of Commerce]. Republican period. Chengdu Municipal Archives, *quanzhong* 104.
Chengdu shi shizheng nianjian [Annals of municipal administration in Chengdu]. 1927.
Chengdu shi wenhua ju dang'an [Archives of the Chengdu Bureau of Culture]. Chengdu Municipal Archives, *quanzhong* 124.
Chengdu shi zhengfu gongshang dang'an [Archives of industry and commerce in Chengdu]. Republican period. Chengdu Municipal Archives, *quanzhong* 38.
Chengdu shi zhengfu zhoubao [Weekly journal of the Chengdu Municipal Government]. 1939.
Chengdu wanbao [Chengdu evening news]. 1948–49.
Chesneaux, Jean. 1968. *The Chinese Labor Movement, 1919–1927*. Trans. H. M. Wright. Stanford, CA: Stanford University Press.
Chizuka Reisui. 1926. *Shin nyū-Shoku ki* [An account of a recent trip to Sichuan]. Tokyo: Osaka yagō shoten.
Chu, Samuel C. 1980. "The New Life Movement before the Sino-Japanese Conflict: A reflection of Kuomintang Limitations in Thought and Action," 37–68 in F. Gilbert Chan, ed., *China at the Crossroads: Nationalists and Communists, 1927–1949*. Boulder, CO: Westview Press.
Ci Jun. 1942. "Chengdu de chaguan" [Teahouses of Chengdu]. Pts. 1–2, HXWB, Jan. 28–29.
Cobble, Dorothy Sue. 1991. *Dishing It Out: Waitresses and Their Unions in the Twentieth Century*. Urbana: University of Illinois Press.
———, ed. 1993. *Women and Unions: Forging a Partnership*. Ithaca, NY: ILR Press.
Cochran, Sherman. 1980. *Big Business in China: Sino-Foreign Rivalry in the Cigarette Industry, 1890–1930*. Cambridge, MA: Harvard University Press.
———. 2000. *Encountering Chinese Networks: Western, Japanese, and Chinese Corporations in China, 1880–1937*. Berkeley: University of California Press.
Couvares, Francis G. 1983. "The Triumph of Commerce: Class Culture and Mass Culture in Pittsburgh," 123–52 in Michael H. Frisch and Daniel J. Walkowitz, eds., *Working-Class America: Essays on Labor, Community, and American Society*. Urbana: University of Illinois Press.

Cowan, Brian. 2005. *The Social Life of Coffee: The Emergence of the British Coffeehouse.* New Haven, CT: Yale University Press.
Crowley, John W., ed. 1999. *Drunkard's Progress: Narratives of Addiction, Despair, and Recovery.* Baltimore: Johns Hopkins University Press.
Cui Xianchang. 1982. "Jiu Chengdu chaguan sumiao" [A literary sketch of the teahouses of old Chengdu]. *Longmenzhen* [Folk tales] 6 (12): 92–102.
Dannenbaum, Jed. 1984. *Drink and Disorder: Temperance Reform in Cincinnati from the Washingtonian Revival to the WCTU.* Urbana: University of Illinois Press.
Davidson, Robert J., and Isaac Mason. 1905. *Life in West China: Described By Two Residents in the Province of Sz-chwan.* London: Headley Brothers.
Davis, Dorothy. 1966. *Fairs, Shops, and Supermarkets: A History of English Shopping.* Toronto: University of Toronto Press.
De Grazia, Sebastian. 1962. *Of Time, Work, and Leisure.* New York: Twentieth Century Fund.
Di Fan. 1966. "Chengdu zhi yangqin" [The dulcimer in Chengdu]. *Sichuan wenxian* [Documents on Sichuan] 5 (45): 22–23.
Dingjinyan Qiaosou. 1805. *Chengdu zhuzhici* [Bamboo-branch poetry of Chengdu], 59–69 in Lin Kongyi, 1986.
Dirlik, Arif. 1975. "The Ideological Foundations of the New Life Movement: A Study in Counter-revolution." *Journal of Asian Studies* 34.4 (Aug.): 945–80.
Donald, Stephanie Hemelryk. 2000. *Public Secrets, Public Spaces: Cinema and Civility in China.* Lanham, MD: Rowman & Littlefield.
Dong, Madeleine Yue. 2000. "Defining Beiping: Urban Reconstruction and National Identity, 1928–1936," 121–38 in Esherick, 2000.
———. 2003. *Republican Beijing: The City and Its Histories.* Berkeley: University of California Press.
Douglas, Mary, ed. 1987. *Constructive Drinking: Perspectives on Drink from Anthropology.* Cambridge, Eng.: Cambridge University Press.
Downer, Lesley. 2001. *Women of the Pleasure Quarters: The Secret History of the Geisha.* New York: Broadway Books.
Duis, Perry R. 1983. *The Saloon: Public Drinking in Chicago and Boston, 1880–1920.* Urbana: University of Illinois Press.
Dumazedier, Joffre. 1974. *Sociology of Leisure.* Trans. Marea A. McKenzie. New York: Elsevier.
Erenberg, Lewis A. 1981. *Steppin' Out: New York Nightlife and the Transformation of American Culture, 1890–1930.* Westport, CT: Greenwood Press.
Esherick, Joseph W., ed. 2000. *Remaking the Chinese City: Modernity and National Identity, 1900–1950.* Honolulu: University of Hawai'i Press.
Evans, John C. 1992. *Tea in China: The History of China's National Drink.* New York: Greenwood.
Fei Zhu. n.d. (Yuan dynasty). *Suihua jilipu* [Record of festivals]. In *Mohai jinhu* [Golden kettle in a sea of ink], vol. 3.
Feng Xiaocai. 2000. "Zhongguo dalu zuijin zhi huiguan shi yanjiu" [Recent studies of the history of *huiguan* in mainland China]. *Jindai Zhongguo shi yanjiu tongxun* [Newsletter of modern Chinese history] 30: 90–108.

Feng Zhicheng, ed. 1999. *Shimin jiyizhong de lao Chengdu* [Old Chengdu in the memories of its residents]. Chengdu: Sichuan wenyi chubanshe.
Feuerwerker, Robert. 1983. "Economic Trends, 1912–49," 28–127 in John K. Fairbank ed., *Cambridge History of China*, vol. 12, pt. 1. Cambridge, Eng.: Cambridge University Press.
Forster, Robert. 1980. *Merchants, Landlords, Magistrates: The Depont Family in Eighteenth-Century France*. Baltimore: Johns Hopkins University Press.
Fortune, Robert. 1853. *Two Visits to the Tea Countries of China*. 2 vols. London: John Murray.
Fu Chongju. 1909–10. *Chengdu tonglan* [An investigation of Chengdu]. Originally eight volumes, printed by Chengdu tongsu baoshe. Reprinted in two volumes by Bashu shushe, Chengdu, 1987. (The texts cited in this book are from the 1987 version, but the illustrations are from the 1909–10 version.)
Gang Fu. 1995. *Chawenhua* [Tea culture]. Beijing: Zhongguo jingji chubanshe.
Gao Huanru. 1999. "Cong Wanli qiao dao Wangjiang lou" [From the Thousand-*li* Bridge to the River View Tower], 22–24 in Feng Zhicheng, 1999.
Gao Shunian, and Wang Yongzhong. 1985. *Chengdu shichang daguan* [General information about Chengdu's markets]. Beijing: Zhongguo zhanwang chubanshe.
Gardella, Robert. 1992. "Squaring Accounts: Commercial Bookkeeping Methods and Capitalist Rationalism in Late Qing and Republican China." *Journal of Asian Studies* 51.2 (May): 317–39.
Gernet, Jacques. 1970. *Daily Life in China on the Eve of the Mongol Invasion, 1250–1276*. Stanford, CA: Stanford University Press.
Ginzburg, Carlo. 1982. *The Cheese and the Worms: The Cosmos of a Sixteenth-Century Miller*. Trans. John and Anne Tedeschi. New York: Penguin.
———. 1983. *The Night Battles: Witchcraft & Agrarian Cults in the Sixteenth & Seventeenth Centuries*. Trans. John and Anne Tedeschi. Baltimore: Johns Hopkins University Press.
———. 1989. *Clues, Myths, and the Historical Method*. Trans. John and Anne C. Tedeschi. Baltimore: Johns Hopkins University Press.
Golas, Peter J. 1977. "Early Ch'ing Guilds," 555–80 in Skinner, 1977.
Goldstein, Joshua. 2003. "From Teahouses to Playhouse: Theaters as Social Texts in Early-Twentieth-Century China." *Journal of Asian Studies* 62.3 (Aug.): 753–79.
Goodman, Bryna. 1995. *Native Place, City, and Nation: Regional Networks and Identities in Shanghai, 1853–1937*. Berkeley: University of California Press.
Gregory, C. A. 1982. *Gifts and Commodities*. London: Academic Press.
Gu Ying. 1987. *Jincheng shicui* [A collection of poems of the brocade city]. Chengdu: Sichuan renmin chubanshe.
Guo Hanming, and Meng Guangyu. 1944. *Sichuan zudian wenti* [The tenant issue in Sichuan]. Chongqing: Shangwu yinshuguan.
Guomin gongbao [Citizens' daily]. 1912–49.
Habermas, Jürgen. 1989. *The Structural Transformation of the Public Sphere: An Inquiry into a Category of Bourgeois Society*. Trans. Thomas Burger. Cambridge, MA: MIT Press.
Hai Su. 1999. "Chapu zhongsheng xiang" [Various faces in the teahouse], 139–46 in Feng Zhicheng, 1999.

Haine, Scott W. 1996. *The World of the Paris Café: Sociability among the French Working Class, 1789–1914*. Baltimore: Johns Hopkins University Press.

Han Suyin. 1965. *The Crippled Tree: China: History, Autobiography*. New York: G. P. Putnam's Sons.

Hao Geng, and Mei Zhong, eds. 2001. *Aichazhe shuo* [Tales from people who love tea]. Hangzhou: Zhejiang sheying chubanshe.

Hao Zhicheng. 1997. "Fuqin de gushi" [Stories about my father]. *Longmenzhen* [Folk tales] 1 (97): 37–44.

He Chengpu. 1986. *Chengdu yehua* [Night talks in Chengdu]. Chengdu: Sichuan renmin chubanshe.

He Manzi. 1994. *Wuzakan* [Five series of random talks]. Chengdu: Chengdu chubanshe.

———. 2002. *He Manzi xueshu lunwenji* [An essay collection of He Manzi's academic writings]. Pts. 1–3. Fuzhou: Fujian renmin chubanshe.

He Yimin, ed. 2002. *Biange yu fazhan: Zhongguo neilu chengshi Chengdu xiandaihua yanjiu* [Reform and development: A study of modernization in the interior Chinese city of Chengdu]. Chengdu: Sichuan daxue chubanshe.

Heller, Agnes. 1984. *Everyday Life*. Trans. G. L. Campbell. London: Routledge & Kegan Paul.

Hershatter, Gail. 1986. *The Workers of Tianjin*. Stanford, CA: Stanford University Press.

Hirayama Shu. 1911. *Shina kakumei oyobi himitsu kessha* [Revolutionaries' organizations and secret societies in China]. *Nihon oyobi Nihonjin* [Japan and Japanese], no. 56. Tokyo: Seikyōsha.

Ho Ping-ti. 1966. "The Geographic Distribution of Huikuan (Landsmannschaften) in Central and Upper Yangtze Provinces." *Tsinghua Journal of Chinese Studies* n.s. 5.2 (Dec.): 120–52.

Honig, Emily. 1986. *Sisters and Strangers: Women in the Shanghai Cotton Mills, 1919–1949*. Stanford, CA: Stanford University Press.

———. 1992. *Creating Chinese Ethnicity: Subei People in Shanghai, 1850–1980*. New Haven, CT: Yale University Press.

Hsu, Vera Y. N., and Francis L. K. Hsu. 1977. "Modern China: North," 295–316 in K. C. Chang, 1977.

Hu Tian. 1938. *Chengdu daoyou* [Guidebook to Chengdu]. Chengdu: Shuwen yinshuashe.

Huang Donglan. 2004. "Yue Fei miao: Chuangzao gonggong jiyi de 'chang'" [Yue Fei temple: Creating the 'field' of public memory], 158–77 in Sun Jiang, *Shijian, jiyi, xushu* [Events, memory, and narrative]. Hangzhou: Zhejiang renmin chubanshe.

Huang, Philip C. C. 1993. "'Public Sphere'/'Civil Society' in China? The Third Realm between State and Society." *Modern China* 19.2 (Apr.): 216–40.

Huang Shang. 2003. "Chaguan" [Teahouses], 299–301 in Peng Guoliang, 2003.

Huang Shangjun. 2002. *Sichuan fangyan yu minsu* [Sichuan dialect and folklore]. Chengdu: Sichuan renmin chubanshe.

Huaxi ribao [West China daily news]. 1947.

Huaxi wanbao [West China evening news]. 1934–49.

Hubbard, George D. 1923. *The Geographic Setting of Chengdu*. Oberlin, OH: Oberlin College.
Imahori Seiji. 1953. *Chūgoku no shakai kōzō: Anshan rejiimu ni okeru "kyōdōtai"* [Chinese social structure: "Community" in the ancient regime]. Tokyo: Yūhikaku.
Inoue Kōbai. 1921. *Shina fūzoku* [Chinese customs]. Tokyo: Nihondō shoten.
Jia Daquan, and Chen Yishi. 1988. *Sichuan chaye shi* [A history of Sichuan tea]. Chengdu: Bashu shushe.
Jian Fu. 1942. *Xianhua Rongcheng* [Random talks on Chengdu]. HXWB, June 17.
Jiang Zhaocheng. 1994. *Ming-Qing Hang Jia Hu shehui jingji shi yanjiu* [The social and economic history of Hangzhou, Jiaxing, and Taihu during the Ming and Qing dynasties]. Hangzhou: Hangzhou daxue chubanshe.
Jing Chaoyang. 1999. "Jiu dianying yuan yiwen" [Anecdotes about old cinemas], 167–69 in Feng Zhicheng, 1999.
Jingwu xunkan [Journal of police affairs]. 1936.
Johnson, David, A. J. Nathan, and E. S. Rawski, eds. 1985. *Popular Culture in Late Imperial China*. Berkeley: University of California Press.
Jones, Stephen G. 1986. *Workers at Play: A Social and Economic History of Leisure, 1918–1939*. London: Routledge & Kegan Paul.
Ju Ge. 1942. "Lixiang de chaguan" [Ideal teahouses]. HXWB, Oct. 17.
Kapp, Robert A. 1973. *Szechwan and the Chinese Republic: Provincial Militarism and Central Power, 1911–1938*. New Haven, CT: Yale University Press.
Ko, Dorothy. 1994. *Teachers of the Inner Chambers: Women and Culture in Seventeenth-Century China*. Stanford, CA: Stanford University Press.
Koenker, Diane P. 1995. "Men against Women on the Shop Floor in Early Soviet Russia: Gender and Class in the Socialist Workplace." *American Historical Review* 100.5: 1438–64.
Kohama Masako. 2000. *Kindai Shanhai ni okeru kōkyōsei to kokka* [The public and the state in modern Shanghai]. Tokyo: Kenbun shuppan.
Köll, Elisabeth. 2003. *From Cotton Mill to Business Empire: The Emergence of Regional Enterprises in Modern China*. Cambridge, MA: Harvard University Asia Center.
Kubo Tōru. 2005. *Senkanki Chūgoku no mengyō to kigyō keiei* [The cotton industry and the management of enterprises in wartime China]. Tokyo: Kyūko shoyin.
Lai Yeyi. 1932. "Chengdu shi chashe zhi jinxi" [The past and present of Chengdu's teahouses]. XXXW, Apr. 27.
Lambert, W. R. 1983. *Drink and Sobriety in Victorian Wales, c. 1820–c. 1895*. Cardiff: University of Wales Press.
Lao She. 1944. "Chaguan guan'gai" [Observing beggars in the teahouse]. XMBWK, Jan. 9.
Lao She. 1978. *Chaguan* [The teahouse], 73–144 in *Lao She juzuo xuan* [Selected plays of Lao She]. Beijing: Renmin wenxue chubanshe.
Lao Xiang. 1942. "Tan Chengduren chicha" [A chat on the tea drinking of Chengdu people]. Pts. 1–3. HXWB, Dec. 26–28.
Lee, Leo Ou-fan. 1999. *Shanghai Modern: The Flowering of a New Urban Culture in China, 1930–1945*. Cambridge, MA: Harvard University Press.
Li Changli. 2002. *WanQing Shanghai de shehui bianqian—Shenghuo lunli de jindaihua* [Social change in late Qing Shanghai: Modernization of life and ethics]. Tianjin: Tianjin renmin chubanshe.

Li Deying. 2003. "Gongyuan li de shehui chongtu—yi jindai Chengdu chengshi gongyuan weili" [Social conflict in parks: A case study of modern Chengdu]. *Shilin* [Journal of history] 1: 1–11.

———. 2004. "Tongye gonghui yu chengshi zhengfu guanxi chutan: Yi minguo shiqi Chengdu weili" [A study of the relationship between guilds and urban administration: A case study of Republican Chengdu], 223–42 in *Chengshi shi yanjiu* [Studies of urban history], vol. 22. Tianjin: Tianjin shehui kexueyuan chubanshe.

Li Jieren. 1980 [1936]. *Baofeng yuqian* [Before the storm], 275–662 in *Li Jieren xuanji* [A selection of Li Jieren's works], vol. 1. Originally published in Shanghai by Zhonghua shuju in 1936. Chengdu: Sichuan renmin chubanshe.

———. 1980 [1937]. *Dabo* [Great wave], 3–1631 in *Li Jieren xuanji*, vol. 2, pts. 1–3. Originally published in Shanghai by Zhonghua shuju in 1937. Chengdu: Sichuan renmin chubanshe.

Li Sizhen, and Ma Yansen. 1996. "Jinchun lou 'sanjue'—Jia Xiazi, Zhou Mazi, Si Pangzi" [Three bests in the Bright Spring Tea Balcony: Blind Jia, Pockmarks Zhou, and Fatso Si], 378–83 in Chengdu shi qunzhong yishuguan, 1996.

Li Wenfu. 1998. "Kangri zhongqi Chengdu 'qiangmi' shijian" [The Chengdu rice riots in the middle of the war], 66–72 in Chengdu shi qunzhong yishuguan, 1998.

Li Ying. 2002. "Jiu Chengdu de chaguan" [Teahouses in old Chengdu]. *Chengdu wanbao* [Chengdu evening news], Apr. 7.

Li Zhuxi, Zeng Dejiu, and Huang Weihu, eds. 1987. *Jindai Sichuan wujia shiliao* [Materials on prices in modern Sichuan]. Chengdu: Sichuan kexue jishu chubanshe.

Li Zicong. 1998. "Sichuan yangqin 'tangpai' de youlai he fazhan" [Origin and development of the "Tang school" of the Sichuan dulcimer], 574–78 in Chengdu shi qunzhong yishuguan, 1998.

Liang Deman, and Huang Shangjun. 1998. *Chengdu fangyan cidian* [A dictionary of the Chengdu dialect]. Nanjing: Jiangsu jiaoyu chubanshe.

Liao Junyi. 1998. "Wo canjia Shier qiao datusha de huiyi" [My recollections of participating in the massacre at Twelfth Bridge], 84–90 in Chengdu shi qunzhong yishuguan, 1998.

Lin Kongyi, ed. 1986. *Chengdu zhuzhi ci* [A collection of Chengdu bamboo-branch poems]. Chengdu: Sichuan renmin chubanshe.

Lin Wenxun. 1995. *Chengdu ren* [Chengdunese]. Hangzhou: Zhejiang renmin chubanshe.

Lin Zhi. 2000. *Zhongguo chadao* [The way of Chinese tea]. Beijing: Zhonghua gongshang lianhe chubanshe.

Liu Ch'eng-yun. 1985. "Kuo-lu: A Sworn Brotherhood Organization in Szechwan." *Late Imperial China* 6.1: 56–82.

Liu Fengyun. 2000. *Ming-Qing chengshi kongjian de wenhua tanxi* [A cultural examination of urban space in the Ming and Qing]. Beijing: Zhongyang minzu daxue chubanshe.

Liu Xiyuan. 1998. "Pao jingbao" [Running whenever sirens sounded the alert], 148–51 in Chengdu shi qunzhong yishuguan, 1998.

Liu Zhenyao. 1999. "'Anlan' chaguan yiwang" [Memories of the Anlan Teahouse], 147–49 in Feng Zhicheng, 1999.

Long Zaitian. 1996. "Huahua chating" [Prosperous Tea Hall], 526–28 in Chengdu shi qunzhong yishuguan, 1996.

Lu, Hanchao. 1995. "Away from Nanking Road: Small Stores and Neighborhood Life in Modern Shanghai." *Journal of Asian Studies* 54.1: 93–123.

Lu Xun. 1973 [1919]. "Yao" [Medicine], 289–310 in *Lu Xun quanji* [The complete works of Lu Xun], vol. 1. Beijing: Renmin wenxue chubanshe.

———. 1973 [1921]. "A Q zhengzhuan" [The true story of Ah Q], 359–416 in *Lu Xun quanji* [The complete works of Lu Xun], vol. 1. Beijing: Renmin wenxue chubanshe.

Lu Yin. 1942. "Xianhua nü chafang" [A chat about teahouse waitresses]. HXWB, Feb. 25–28.

Lüdtke, Alf. 1995. *The History of Everyday Life: Reconstructing Historical Experiences and Ways of Life*. Trans. William Templer. Princeton, NJ: Princeton University Press.

Luo Shang. 1965. "Chaguan fengqing" [Customs and practices of teahouses]. *Sichuan wenxian* [Documents on Sichuan] 10 (38): 21–23.

Luo Xiangpu. 1986. "Tian Lai" [A biography of Tian Lai], 278–82 in Ren Yimin, ed., *Sichuan jinxiandai renwu zhuan* [Biographies of figures in modern Sichuan], vol. 2. Chengdu: Sichuan sheng shehui kexueyuan chubanshe.

Luo Ziqi, and Jiang Shouwen. 1994. "Pingshu yiren Zhong Xiaofan quwen" [Interesting stories about storyteller Zhong Xiaofan]. *Longmenzhen* [Folk tales] 4 (82): 58–61.

Ma Min. 1995. *Guanshang zhijian: Shehui jubian zhong de jindai shenshang* [Between officials and merchants: Modern gentry in dramatic social change]. Tianjin: Tianjin renmin chubanshe.

MacAndrew, Craig, and Robert B. Edgerton. 1969. *Drunken Comportment: A Social Explanation*. Chicago: Aldine.

Macfarlane, Alan, and Iris Macfarlane. 2004. *The Empire of Tea: The Remarkable History of the Plant That Took Over the World*. Woodstock, NY: Overlook Press.

MacKinnon, Stephen R. 2000. "Wuhan's Search for Identity in the Republican Period," 161–73 in Esherick, 2000.

MacLeod, Christine. 1999. "Negotiating the Rewards of Invention: The Shop-Floor Inventor in Victorian Britain." *Business History* 41.2: 17–36.

Mann, Susan. 1997. *Precious Records: Women in China's Long Eighteenth Century*. Stanford, CA: Stanford University Press.

Martin, Brian. 1996. *The Shanghai Green Gang: Politics and Organized Crime, 1919–1937*. Berkeley: University of California Press.

McIsaac, Lee. 2000a. "'Righteous Fraternities' and Honorable Men: Sworn Brotherhoods in Wartime Chongqing." *American Historical Review* 105.5: 1641–55.

———. 2000b. "The City as Nation: Creating a Wartime Capital in Chongqing," 174–91 in Esherick, 2000.

McNeill, William H. 1989. "The Historical Significance of Tea," 255–63 in Varley and Kumakura, 1989.

Meserve, Walter J., and Ruth I. Meserve. 1979. "From Teahouse to Loudspeaker: The Popular Entertainer in the People's Republic of China." *Journal of Popular Culture* 8.1: 131–40.

Morse, Hosea Ballou. 1967 [1932]. *The Gilds of China, with an Account of the Gild Merchant or Co-hong of Canton*. 2nd edition, 1932,. Rept., 1967. New York: Russell & Russell, 1967.

Mui, Hoh-cheung, and Lorna H. Mui. 1989. *Shops and Shopkeeping in Eighteenth-Century England.* Kingston, Ont.: McGill-Queen's University Press.

Muir, Edward, and Guido Ruggiero, eds. 1990. *Sex and Gender in Historical Perspective.* Baltimore: Johns Hopkins University Press.

———. 1991. *Microhistory and the Lost Peoples of Europe: Selections from Quaderni Storici.* Trans. Eren Branch. Baltimore: Johns Hopkins University Press.

———. 1994. *History from Crime.* Trans. Corrada Curry, Margaret Gallucci, and Mary Gallucci. Baltimore: Johns Hopkins University Press.

Murai Yasuhiko. 1989. "The Development of Chanoyu: Before Rikyu," 3–32 in Varley and Kumakura, 1989.

Murdock, Catherine Gilbert. 1998. *Domesticating Drink: Women, Men, and Alcohol in America, 1870–1940.* Baltimore: Johns Hopkins University Press.

Murray, Dian H. 1994. *The Origins of the Tiandihui: The Chinese Triads in Legend and History.* Stanford, CA: Stanford University Press.

Musgrove, Charles D. 2000. "Building a Dream: Constructing a National Capital in Nanjing, 1927–1937," 139–57 in Esherick, 2000.

Naitō Rishin. 1991. *Sunde mita Seito: Shoku no kuni ni miru Chūgoku no nichijo seikatsu* [Chengdu as I lived it: The Chinese today in the land of Shu]. Tokyo: Saimaru shuppankai.

Nakamura Sakujirō. 1899. *Shina man yūdan* [Travelogue of China]. Tokyo: Sesshikai.

Nakamura Toshinori. 1992. "Early History of the Teahouse." Pts. 1–3. *Chanoyu Quarterly* 69: 7–32; 70: 22–40; 71: 31–44.

Nakano Kozan. 1913. *Shina tairiku ōdan yūshoku zaso* [Travel notes on Sichuan on a trip across China]. Printed in 1913 without a publisher. Collected in the Toyo Bunko, Tokyo.

Nichizawa Haruhiko. 1985. "Yamucha no hanashi" [Tales on drinking tea]. *GS—Tanoshii chisiki* [GS—Pleasant knowledge] 3: 242–53.

———. 1988. "Gendai Chūgoku no chakan—Shisen shō Seiito no jirei kara" [Teahouses in China: The case of Chengdu, Sichuan]. *Fūzoku* [Folklore] 26.4: 50–63.

Ownby, David. 1996. *Sworn Brotherhoods and Secret Societies in Early and Mid-Qing China: The Formation of a Tradition.* Stanford, CA: Stanford University Press.

Parsons, Elaine F. 2003. *Manhood Lost: Fallen Drunkards and Redeeming Women in the Nineteenth-Century United States.* Baltimore: Johns Hopkins University Press.

Paules, Greta Foff. 1991. *Dishing It Out: Power and Resistance among Waitresses in a New Jersey Restaurant.* Philadelphia: Temple University Press.

Peiss, Kathy. 1986. *Cheap Amusements: Working Women and Leisure in Turn-of-the-Century New York.* Philadelphia: Temple University Press.

Peng Guoliang, ed. 2003. *Bairen xianshuo: Cha zhi qu* [Chats of a hundred people: The charm of tea]. Zhuhai: Zhuhai chubanshe.

Peng Qinian. 1963. "Xinhai geming hou chuanju zai Chengdu de xin fazhan" [A new development of Sichuan opera in Chengdu after the 1911 Revolution]. *Sichuan wenshi ziliao xuanji* [Collections of literary and historical materials in Sichuan] 8: 159–72.

Peng Zeyi. 1995. *Zhongguo gongshang hanghui shiliao ji* [A collection of sources on Chinese guilds]. Beijing: Zhonghua shuju.

Perry, Elizabeth J. 1993. *Shanghai on Strike: The Politics of Chinese Labor*. Stanford, CA: Stanford University Press.
Pickett, Joseph P., et al., eds. 2000. *The American Heritage Dictionary of the English Language*. 4th ed. Boston: Houghton Mifflin.
Pittman, David J., and Charles R. Snyder, eds. 1962. *Society, Culture and Drinking Patterns*. New York: J. Wiley.
Pomeranz, Kenneth. 1997. "'Traditional' Chinese Business Forms Revisited: Family, Firm, and Financing in the History of the Yutang Company." *Late Imperial China* 18.1 (June): 1–38.
———. 2000. *The Great Divergence: Europe, China, and the Making of the Modern World Economy*. Princeton, NJ: Princeton University Press.
Porter, David L. 2002. "Monstrous Beauty: Eighteenth-Century Fashion and the Aesthetics of the Chinese Taste." *Eighteenth-Century Studies* 35.3: 395–411.
Powers, Madelon. 1998. *Faces along the Bar: Lore and Order in the Workingman's Saloon, 1870–1920*. Chicago: University of Chicago Press.
Prestwich, Patricia E. 1988. *Drink and the Politics of Social Reform: Antialcoholism in France since 1870*. Palo Alto, CA: Society for the Promotion of Science and Scholarship.
Qiao Zengxi, Li Canhua, and Bai Zhaoyu. 1983. "Chengdu shizheng yan'ge gaishu" [General information about the course of change and development of Chengdu's municipal administration]. *Chengdu wenshi ziliao xuanji* [Selections on literature and historical materials of Chengdu] 5: 1–22.
Qin Hao, ed. 1999. *Chayuan* [Fate of tea]. Hohhot: Neimenggu renmin chubanshe.
Qin Heping. 2000. "Ersanshi niandai yapian yu Sichuan chengzhen shuijuan guanxi zhi renshi" [Relations between opium and taxes in the cities and towns of Sichuan in the 1920s and 1930s], 76–96 in *Chengshi shi yanjiu* [Studies of urban history], vols. 19–20. Tianjin: Tianjin shehui kexueyuan chubanshe.
Qing Youzheng. 1999. "Jincheng nan'an yi xiaojie" [A small street on the southern bank of Brocade City], 19–21 in Feng Zhicheng, 1999.
Qiu Chi. 1942. "Chengdu de chaguan" [Teahouses of Chengdu]. XXXW, Aug. 7–8.
Qiu Pengsheng. 1990. *Shiba shijiu shiji Suzhou cheng de xinxing gongshang ye tuanti* [New organizations of industry and commerce in eighteenth- and nineteenth-century Suzhou]. *Taida wenshi congkan* [Taiwan National University series on culture and history], no. 86. Taipei: Guoli Taiwan daxue chuban weiyuanhui.
Qu Xiaoqiang. 1999. "Zhuqin jueji Jia Shusan" [The incredible art of Jia Shusan's bamboo dulcimer], 153–56 in Feng Zhicheng, 1999.
Ran Yunfei. 1999. *Cong lishi de pianpang jinru Chengdu* [Looking at Chengdu from another side of history]. Chengdu: Sichuan wenyi chubanshe.
Rankin, Mary B. 1986. *Elite Activism and Political Transformation in China: Zhejiang Province, 1865–1911*. Stanford, CA: Stanford University Press.
———. 1990. "The Origins of a Chinese Public Sphere: Local Elites and Community Affairs in the Late Imperial Period." *Etudes Chinoises* 9.2: 14–60.
Rogaski, Ruth. 2000. "Hygienic Modernity in Tianjin," 30–46 in Esherick, 2000.
———. 2004. *Hygienic Modernity: Meanings of Health & Disease in Treaty-Port China*. Berkeley: University of California Press.

Rosenzweig, Roy. 1983. *Eight Hours for What We Will: Workers and Leisure in an Industrial City, 1870–1920.* New York: Cambridge University Press.
Rowe, William T. 1984. *Hankow: Commerce and Society in a Chinese City, 1796–1889.* Stanford, CA: Stanford University Press.
———. 1989. *Hankow: Conflict and Community in a Chinese City, 1796–1895.* Stanford, CA: Stanford University Press.
———. 1990. "The Public Sphere in Modern China." *Modern China* 16.3 (July): 309–29.
Ruggiero, Guido. 2001. "The Strange Death of Margarita Marcellini: Male, Signs, and the Everyday World of Pre-Modern Medicine." *American Historical Review* 106.4 (Oct.): 1141–58.
Satō Yōjin. 1993. *Edo mizu chaya fūzoku kō* [A study of teahouses in Edo]. Tokyo: Miki shobo.
Schafer, Edward H. 1977. "T'ang," 85–140 in K. C. Chang, 1977.
Sennett, Richard. 1977. *The Fall of Public Man: On the Social Psychology of Capitalism.* New York: Vintage.
Service, John S., ed. 1989. *Golden Inches: The China Memoir of Grace Service.* Berkeley: University of California Press.
Sewell, William G. 1971. *The People of Wheelbarrow Lane.* South Brunswick, NJ: A. S. Barnes.
———. 1986. *The Dragon's Backbone: Portraits of Chengdu People in the 1920's.* Drawings by Yu Zidan. York: William Sessions Limited.
Sha Ting. 1982 [1940]. "Zai Qixiangju chaguan li" [In the Fragrant Chamber Teahouse], 140–56 in *Sha Ting xuanji* [Selections from the works of Sha Ting], vol. 1. Chengdu: Sichuan renmin chubanshe.
———. 1984 [1941]. *Taojin ji* [Digging gold], 3–293 in *Sha Ting xuanji* [Selections from the works of Sha Ting], vol. 2. Chengdu: Sichuan renmin chubanshe.
———. 1984 [1944]. *Kunshou ji* [Caged beast], 299–625 in *Sha Ting xuanji* [Selections from the works of Sha Ting], vol. 2. Chengdu: Sichuan renmin chubanshe.
Shangwu zaobao [Morning commercial news]. 2000.
Shao, Qin. 1998. "Tempest over Teapots: The Vilification of Teahouse Culture in Early Republican China." *Journal of Asian Studies* 57.4: 1009–41.
Shengyuan jingqu zhangcheng [Regulations of the Chengdu police]. n.d. In *Sichuan jingwu zhangcheng* [Regulations of the Sichuan police], vol. 2. Judging by the contents, this work dates to the late Qing.
Sheridan, Mary, and Janet W. Salaff. 1984. *Lives: Chinese Working Women.* Bloomington: Indiana University Press.
Shi Jufu. 1936. *Sichuan renkou shuzi yanjiu zhi xinziliao* [New materials on the statistics of Sichuan's population]. Chengdu: Minjian yishi she.
Shu Xincheng. 1934. *Shuyou xinying* [My feelings during a tour of Sichuan]. Shanghai: Zhonghua shuju.
Sichuan guanbao [Sichuan gazette]. 1903–11.
Sichuan sheng chuanju yishu yanjiu yuan, et al., eds. 1999. *Chuanju jumu cidian* [A dictionary of Sichuan-opera programs]. Chengdu: Sichuan cishu chubanshe.
Sichuan sheng wenshi guan, ed. 1987. *Chengdu chengfang guji kao* [Materials on

urban construction and historical sites in Chengdu]. Chengdu: Sichuan renmin chubanshe.

Sichuan sheng zhengfu shehuichu dang'an [Archives of the Social Bureau of the Sichuan Provincial Government], *quanzhong* 186.

Sichuan tongsheng jingcha zhangcheng [Regulations of the Sichuan Provincial Police], 1903. From the Archives of the Police Department (1501), vol. 179 in the First Historical Archives (Beijing). Handwritten copy, provided by Kristin Stapleton.

Sichuan yuebao [Sichuan monthly]. 1933.

Skinner, G. William. 1964–65. "Marketing and Social Structure in Rural China." *Journal of Asian Studies* 24.1: 3–43; 24.2: 195–228; 24.3: 363–99.

———, ed. 1977. *The City in Late Imperial China*. Stanford, CA: Stanford University Press.

Spang, Rebecca L. 2000. *The Invention of the Restaurant: Paris and Modern Gastronomic Culture*. Cambridge, MA: Harvard University Press.

Spence, Jonathan. 1978. *Death of Woman Wang*. New York: Viking Press.

———. 2001. *Treason by the Book*. New York: Viking Press.

Spradley, James, and Brenda Mann. 1975. *The Cocktail Waitresses: Women's Work in a Man's World*. New York: Knopf.

Stapleton, Kristin. 1996. "Urban Politics in an Age of 'Secret Societies': The Cases of Shanghai and Chengdu." *Republican China* 22.1: 23–63.

———. 2000a. *Civilizing Chengdu: Chinese Urban Reform, 1875–1937*. Cambridge, MA: Harvard University Asia Center.

———. 2000b. "Yang Sen in Chengdu: Urban Planning in the Interior," 90–104 in Esherick, 2000.

Strand, David. 1989. *Rickshaw Beijing: City People and Politics in the 1920s*. Berkeley: University of California Press.

Sun Xiaofen. 1997. *Qingdai qianqi de yimin tian Sichuan* [Immigrants in early Qing Sichuan]. Chengdu: Sichuan daxue chubanshe.

Suzuki Tōmō. 1982. "Shinmatsu Kō-Seku no chakan ni tsuite" [Teahouses in late Qing Jiangsu and Zhejiang], 529–40 in *Rekishi ni okeru minshū to bunka: Sakai Tadao sensei koki shugaku kinen ronshū* [People and culture in history: An essay collection in honor of Sakai Tadao]. Tokyo: Kokusho kankōkai.

———. 1983. "Shinmatsu no Shanhai chakan ni tsuite" [A study of teahouses in late Qing Shanghai]. *Ryōgen* [Setting the prairie ablaze] 19 (Nov.): 2–5.

Takeuchi Minoru. 1974. *Chakan: Chūgoku no fudo to sekaizo* [Teahouses: A general description of Chinese customs]. Tokyo: Taishukan shoten.

Tan Qingquan. 1985a. "Huang Ji'an" [Biography of Huang Ji'an], 251–54 in Ren Yimin, ed. *Sichuan jinxiandai renwu zhuan* [Biographies of figures in modern Sichuan], vol. 1. Chengdu: Sichuan sheng shehui kexueyuan chubanshe.

———. 1985b. "Kang Zilin" [Biography of Kang Zilin], 255–58 in Ren Yimin, ed. *Sichuan jinxiandai renwu zhuan* [Biographies of figures in modern Sichuan], vol. 1. Chengdu: Sichuan sheng shehui kexueyuan chubanshe.

Tang Tiyao. 1998. "Woshi Shier qiao can'an de zhixing guizishou" [I carried out the massacre at Twelfth Bridge], 91–94 in Chengdu shi qunzhong yishuguan, 1998.

Tao Wenyu. 2005. *Chaguan* [Teahouses]. Shijiazhuang: Huashan wenyi chubanshe.

Tongsu huabao [Popular pictorial]. 1909–11.

Tongsu ribao [Popular daily]. 1909–11.
Tsin, Michael. 1999. *Nation, Governance, and Modernity in China: Canton, 1900–1927*. Stanford, CA: Stanford University Press.
———. 2000. "Canton Remapped," 19–29 in Esherick, 2000.
Varley, Paul, and Kumakura Isao, eds. 1989. *Tea in Japan: Essays on the History of Chanoyu*. Honolulu: University of Hawaii Press.
Wakeman, Frederic, Jr. 1993. "The Civil Society and Public Sphere Debate: Western Reflections on Chinese Political Culture." *Modern China* 19.2 (Apr.): 108–38.
———. 1995. "Licensing Leisure: The Chinese Nationalists' Attempt to Regulate Shanghai, 1927–1949." *Journal of Asian Studies* 54.1: 19–42.
Walton, John K., and Jenny Smith. 1994. "The Rhetoric of Community and the Business of Pleasure: The San Sebastian Waiters' Strike of 1920." *International Review of Social History* 39.1: 1–31.
Walvin, James. 1997. *Fruits of Empire: Exotic Produce and British Taste, 1660–1800*. New York: New York University Press.
Wang, Di. 1993. *Kuachu fengbi de shijie: Changjiang shangyou quyu shehui yanjiu, 1644–1911* [Striding out of a closed world: A study of society in the upper Yangzi region, 1644–1911]. Beijing: Zhonghua shuju.
———. 1998. "Street Culture: Public Space and Urban Commoners in Late-Qing Chengdu." *Modern China* 24.1 (Jan.): 34–72.
———. 2000. "The Idle and the Busy: Teahouses and Public Life in Early Twentieth-Century Chengdu." *Journal of Urban History* 26.4: 411–37.
———. 2003. *Street Culture in Chengdu: Public Space, Urban Commoners, and Local Politics in Chengdu, 1870–1930*. Stanford, CA: Stanford University Press.
Wang Fu. 2000 [Tang dynasty]. "Chajiu lu" [Debate between tea and wine], 174–76 in Wang Guoan and Yao Ying, 2000.
Wang Guoan, and Yao Ying. 2000. *Cha yu Zhongguo wenhua* [Tea and Chinese culture]. Beijing: Hanyu dacidian chubanshe.
Wang Hongtai (Wang Hung-tai). 2000. "Cong xiaofei de kongjian dao kongjian de xiaofei—Ming-Qing chengshi zhong de jiulou yu chaguan" [From consumer space to the consumption of space: Wine shops and teahouses in Ming and Qing cities]. *Xin shixue* [New history] 11.3: 1–46.
Wang, Liping. 2000. "Tourism and Spatial Change in Hangzhou, 1911–1927," 107–20 in Esherick, 2000.
Wang Qingyuan. 1944. "Chengdu pingyuan xiangcun chaguan" [Rural teahouses on the Chengdu Plain]. *Fengtu shi* [Folkways] 1.4: 29–38.
Wang Rigen. 1996. "Diyuxing huiguan yu huiguan de diquxing chayi" [Geographical huiguan and geographical differences among huiguan]. *Zhongguo lishi dili luncong* [Chinese historical geography series] 1: 95–109.
Wang Shian, and Zhu Zhiyan. 1989. "Manhua Shaocheng gongyuan nei jijia geju teshe de chaguan—Huiyi wo jingying Zhenliu chashe de yiduan jingli" [A random talk about the characteristics of the teahouses in the Smaller City Park: Memories of my management of the Sleeping Stream Teahouse]. *Shaocheng wenshi ziliao* [Cultural and historical material of the Smaller City] 2: 150–60.
Wang Weiping. 1997. "Qingdai Suzhou de cishan shiye" [Charities in Qing Suzhou]. *Zhongguo shi yanjiu* [Journal of Chinese history] 3: 145–56.

Wang Zehua, and Wang He. 1999. *Minguo shiqi de lao Chengdu* [Old Chengdu during the Republican era]. Chengdu: Sichuan wenyi chubanshe.
Warsh, Cheryl Krasnick, ed. 1993. *Drink in Canada: Historical Essays*. Montreal: McGill-Queen's University Press.
Wei Yingtao. 1981. *Sichuan baolu yundong shi* [A history of the Sichuan Railroad Protection Movement]. Chengdu: Sichuan renmin chubanshe.
Wen Wenzi, ed. 1990. *Sichuan fengwu zhi* [Customs of Sichuan]. Chengdu: Sichuan renmin chubanshe.
Wen Yiduo. 1985 [1940s]. "Chaguan xiaodiao" [A canzonet of the teahouse]. *Wenshi ziliao xuanji* [Selected literary and historical material], 3, Junlian xian zhengxie wenshi ziliao yanjiu weiyuanhui, ed.: 61–62.
Wilson, Ernest H. 1929. *China: Mother of Gardens*. Boston: Stratford.
Wu Haoshan. 1855. *Benzhuo liyan* [A collection of clumsy slang], 69–77 in Lin Kongyi, 1986.
Wu Hui. 1999. "Huiguan, gongsuo, hanghui: Qingdai shangren zuzhi yanbian shuyao" [Huiguan, gongsuo, and hanghui: A brief introduction to merchant organizations in the Qing]. *Zhongguo jingji shi yanjiu* [Journal of Chinese economic history] 3: 111–30.
Wu Yu. 1984. *Wu Yu riji* [Wu Yu's diary]. Two vols. Chengdu: Sichuan renmin chubanshe.
Xiao Han. 1986. "Chengdu shangye chang de xingshuai" [The rise and fall of the Commercial Center in Chengdu]. *Longmenzhen* [Folk tales] 6 (36): 36–48.
Xiao Tian. 1997. *Jiangnan xiangzhen shehui de jindai zhuanxing* [The social transformation of marketing towns in modern Jiangnan]. Beijing: Zhongguo shangye chubanshe.
Xie Junmei. 2000. "Qingdai Shanghai huiguan gongsuo shulüe" [A brief introduction to the huiguan and gongsuo of Qing Shanghai]. *Huadong shifan daxue xuebao* [Journal of East China Normal University] 2: 36–41.
Xinminbao wankan [Evening edition of New citizens' daily]. 1943–44.
Xinxin xinwen [Latest news]. 1930–50.
Xue Shaoming. 1986 [1936]. *Qian Dian Chuan lüxing ji* [Travel notes on Guizhou, Yunnan, and Sichuan]. Chongqing: Chongqing chubanshe.
Yan Dinggao, and Zhou Shaoji. 1996. "Shendai sanbao, wuren kedi—Ji Chengdu pingshu yiren Zhang Xijiu" [Unchallengeable with three treasures: Stories of storyteller Zhang Xijiu], 387–92 in Chengdu shi qunzhong yishuguan, 1996.
Yan, Yunxiang. 1996. *The Flow of Gifts: Reciprocity and Social Networks in a Chinese Village*. Stanford, CA: Stanford University Press.
Yang Huai. 1982. "Shentongzi yu Mantianfei" [A divine boy and a wandering man]. *Longmenzhen* [Folk tales], 1 (7): 65–70.
Yang Li, ed. 1997. *Cha bolan* [A comprehensive book of tea]. Taiyuan: Shanxi guji chubanshe.
Yang, Mayfair Mei-hui. 1994. *Gifts, Favors, and Banquets: The Art of Social Relationships in China*. Ithaca, NY: Cornell University Press.
Yang Wuneng, and Qiu Peihuang, eds. 1995. *Chengdu da cidian* [Grand dictionary of Chengdu]. Chengdu: Sichuan cishu chubanshe.

Yang Zhongyi. 1992. "Chengdu chaguan" [Teahouses in Chengdu]. *Nongye kaogu* [Agricultural archeology] 4 (special issue on Chinese tea): 114–17.
Yao Zhengmin. 1971. "Chengdu fengqing" [Folk traditions in Chengdu]. *Sichuan wenxian* [Documents on Sichuan] 5 (105): 17–21.
Ye Wen. 1949. "Chengdu chazuo fengqing" [Feelings of Chengdu teahouses]. CDWB, Mar. 20.
Yerkovich, Sally. 1977. "Gossiping as a Way of Speaking." *Journal of Communication* 27.1: 192–96.
Yi Junzuo. 1943. "Jincheng qiri ji" [Seven days in Chengdu], 177–210 in *Chuan-Kang youzong* [Travel notes on Sichuan and Xikang]. N.p.: Zhongguo lüxingshe.
Yu Xi. 1943. "Chaguan zhengzhi jia" [Teahouse politicians]. HXWB, Jan. 15.
Zelin, Madeleine. 1988. "Capital Accumulation and Investment Strategies in Early Modern China: The Case of the Furong Salt Yard." *Late Imperial China* 9.1 (June): 79–122.
———. 1990. "The Rise and Fall of the Fu-Rong Salt-Yard Elite: Merchant Dominance in Late Qing China," 82–109 in Joseph Esherick and Mary Rankin, eds., *Chinese Local Elites and Patterns of Dominance*. Berkeley: University of California Press.
———. 2005. *The Merchants of Zigong: Industrial Entrepreneurship in Early Modern China*. New York: Columbia University Press.
Zeng Zhizhong, and You Deyan, eds. 1999. *Wenhuaren shiyezhong de lao Chengdu* [Old Chengdu in the eyes of intellectuals]. Chengdu: Sichuan wenyi chubanshe.
Zhang Chengchun. 1986. "Jiefang qian Chengdu chaye jingying guanli shihua" [Historical stories of the management of the tea business in pre-liberation Chengdu]. Unpublished manuscript.
Zhang Dafu. 1981. "Gao Baxi" [Magician Gao]. *Chengdu fengwu* [Folk traditions in Chengdu] 1: 109–12.
Zhang Fang. 1995. "Chuantu suibi" [Informal essays on the customs of Sichuan]. *Longmenzhen* [Folk tales] 3 (87): 95–98.
Zhang Henshui. 1999. "Rongxing zagan" [Random thoughts on a trip to Chengdu], 277–87 in Zeng Zhizhong and You Deyan, 1999.
Zhang Jin. 2005. "Faxian shenghuo: Ershi shiji ersanshi niandai Chongqing chengshi shehui bianqian" [Discovering life: Changes in urban society in 1920–30s Chongqing], 329–66 in Li Xiaoti, *Zhongguo de chengshi shenghuo* [Urban life in China]. Taipei: Lianjing.
Zhang Shizhao. 2000. "Wenhua yundong yu nongcun gailiang" [The cultural movement and rural reform], 144–46; "Nongguobian" [A debate on the agricultural state], 266–72; "Zhang Xingyan zai nongda zhi yanshuoci" [Notes of Zhang Shizhao's lecture at the Agricultural College], 403–5. *Zhang Shizhao quanji* [A complete collection of Zhang Shizhao's works], vol. 4. Shanghai: Shanghai wenhui chubanshe.
Zhang Xuejun, and Zhang Lihong. 1993. *Chengdu chengshi shi* [A general history of Chengdu]. Chengdu: Chengdu chubanshe.
Zhang, Yingjin. 1996. *The City in Modern Chinese Literature and Film: Configurations of Space, Time, and Gender*. Stanford, CA: Stanford University Press.

———, ed. 1999. *Cinema and Urban Culture in Shanghai, 1922–1943*. Stanford, CA: Stanford University Press.
Zhang, Zhen. 1999. "Teahouse, Shadowplay, Bricolage: 'Laborer's Love' and the Question of Early Chinese Cinema," 27–50 in Yingjin Zhang, 1999.
Zhang Zhenjian. 1999. "Nanmen you zuo 'Shusan qiao'" [An evacuation bridge at the South Gate], 320–22 in Feng Zhicheng, 1999.
Zheng Yun. 1981. "Yifu duilian de miaoyong" [A smart use for a matched couplet]. *Chengdu fengwu* [Folk traditions in Chengdu] 1: 82–83.
Zheng Yunxia, and Jia Shu. 1989. "Jiushi jianghu" [River and lake runners in the past]. *Longmenzhen* [Folk tales], 3 (51): 1–11; 4 (52): 25–37; 5 (53): 69–79.
Zhong Maoxuan. 1984. *Liu Shiliang waizhuan* [An informal biography of Liu Shiliang]. Chengdu: Sichuan renmin chubanshe.
Zhou Wen. 1999. "Chengdu de yinxiang" [Impressions of Chengdu], 224–31 in Zeng Zhizhong and You Deyan, 1999.
Zhou Xun. 1987 [1936]. *Furong huajiu lu* [Talking about the past of Chengdu]. Chengdu: Sichuan renmin chubanshe.
Zhou Zhiying. 1942. "Mantan Chengdu nü chafang" [A random talk about Chengdu's teahouse waitresses]. HXWB, Oct. 13.
———. 1943. *Xin Chengdu* [New Chengdu]. Chengdu: Fuxing shuju.
Zhou Zhiying, and Gao Sibo. 1987. "Chengdu de zaoqi huaju huodong" [Performances of early modern drama in Chengdu]. *Sichuan wenshi ziliao xuanji* [Collections of literary and historical materials on Sichuan] 36: 53–65.
Zhu Longyuan. 1987. "Zhou Muliang" [A biography of Zhou Muliang], 301–6 in Ren Yimin, ed., *Sichuan jinxiandai renwu zhuan* [Biographies of figures in modern Sichuan] vol. 3. Chengdu: Sichuan renmin chubanshe.
Zhu Ying. 1997. *Zhuanxing shiqi de shehui yu guojia—Yi jindai Zhongguo shanghui wei zhuti de toushi* [Society and state during the transformational period: An examination of Chinese chambers of commerce]. Wuhan: Huazhong shifang daxue chubanshe.
———. 2003. "Zhongguo hanghui shi yanjiu de huigu yu zhanwang" [Retrospective and perspective on studies of the history of Chinese guilds]. *Lishi yanjiu* [Historical research] 2: 155–74.
———, ed. 2004. *Zhongguo jindai tongye gonghui yu dangdai hangye xiehui* [Guilds and professional associations in modern China]. Beijing: Zhongguo renmin daxue chubanshe.

Index

A Fisherman Who Adopted a Son (Dayu shouzi), 308
acrobats, 136
actors, 22, 99, 123, 147, 161, 164, 165, 175, 191, 197, 206, 214, 229, 242, 255, 305n39, 306nn18, 19. *See also* actresses
actresses, 143, 148, 153, 154, 161, 164, 214. *See also* actors
airplane tax (feijijuan), 80
All Joy Theater (Junle juyuan), 158
alley battles, 231
American cities, 132, 255–58 passim, 291n12, 300n7, 304n17, 309n10, 311n49, 319n6
An Investigation of Chengdu (Chengdu tonglan), 30, 123, 129, 145
Archery and Morality Society (Shede hui) Teahouse, 314n31
Archives of Industrial and Commercial Registrations in Chengdu (Chengdu shi gongshang xingzheng dengji dang'an), 290n53
Archives of Industry and Commerce in Chengdu (Chengdu shi zhengfu gongshang dang'an), 290n53
Archives of the Chengdu Bureau of Industry and Commerce (Chengdu shi gongshang ju dang'an), 290n53
Archives of the Chengdu Chamber of Commerce (Chengdu shi shanghui dang'an), 290n53
Archives of the Chengdu Police Department (Chengdu shenghui jingcha ju dang'an), 290n53

Association of Fushun Sojourners in Chengdu (Fushun xian lüsheng tongxiang hui), 310n15
Association of Pingshan Sojourners in Chengdu (Pingshan xian lüsheng tongxiang hui), 310n15
Averill, Stephen, 300n1

Ba Bo, 135
bamboo dulcimer (zhuqin), 142, 143
Bamboo Garden (Zhuyuan) Teahouse, 44, 295n54
bamboo-branch poetry, 6
bang (gangs), 57–60 passim; of tea leaf, 60; of teahouses, 67, 69, 81, 178. *See also* Teahouse Guild
bankruptcy, 93, 100
Bao Legal Cases (Baogong an), 146
baojia, 75, 175, 176, 214, 219. *See also* militia
barbers, 29, 35, 42, 51, 70, 171, 196, 209, 250. *See also* barbershops
barbershops, 53, 55, 171, 260
beating continuous tinkles (da lianxiang), 139
beating on drums (daweigu), 129
beating the Daoist drum (da daoqin), 139
Beating with a Stick (Dagangzi), 308n60
Before the Storm (Baofeng yuqian), 167
beggars, 51, 71, 114, 188, 220, 250, 251
behaving frivolously (judong qingfu), 195
Beneficial and Prosperous (Yihua) Teahouse, 219
Bianjing, 6
Big Dipper Market Town (Beidou zhen), 124

big hot-water-vat man (wengzi jiang), 301n22
black market, 77
bored and idle people (baixiang de ren), 235
Breaking Two Guns (Duan shuangqiang), 307n35
Brief Plan of National Construction (Jianguo fanglüe), 317n41
Bright Spring Teahouse (Lichun chashe), 299n58
Brocade River Pavilion (Jinjiang ge) Teahouse, 37
Brocade River Tea Garden (Jinjiang chayuan), 151
Brocade River Teahouse (Jinjiang chashe), 183
Brocade Spring Tea Balcony (Jinchun chalou), 45, 50, 142–43, 297n18
Buddhist monks, 146
busy class (youmang jieji), 114, 184

café, 23, 134, 155, 254, 255, 258, 293n22, 311n49, 319n6, 320n19
Caged Beast (Kunshou ji), 21, 312n65
calling for tea money (han chaqian), 130–32
Canzonet of the Teahouse (Chaguan xiaodiao), 224
capital (investment), 20, 27, 28, 35–38, 42, 55, 56, 61, 74, 153, 184, 185, 222, 256, 259, 260, 262, 286n8, 293nn24, 26, 28, 294n29, 297n18, 311n39
card for drinking tea (yincha zheng), 239
Center for Promoting Industry and Commerce (Quanye chang), 40, 42, 46, 116, 151, 154, 189, 190. *See also* Commerical Center
center of communication, 3, 257
Central (Zhongxin) Teahouse, 295n54
central government, 2, 29, 60, 71, 223, 225, 231, 232, 234
Central Green Goat Market Street (Qingyang chang zhengjie), 73
Central Peace Garden Teahouse (Zhonghe yuan), 73
Chamber of Commerce, 20, 60, 80, 209, 290n53
Charitable and Benevolent Hall (Cihui tang), 141
Chen Maozhao, 30, 287n29, 294n31
Chengdu Bulletin (Chengdu kuaibao), 195

Chengdu City Council (Chengdu shi canyihui), 73. *See also* City Council
Chengdu Garrison Headquarters (Chengdu jingbei silingbu), 220
Chengdu phenomenon (Chengdu xianxiang), 235
Chengdu Plain, 4, 13, 17, 18, 41, 172, 287n20, 290nn49, 51, 312n65
Chengdu Security Army, 243
cheongsam (qipao), 91, 106
Chess Art Teahouse (Qiyi chashe), 175
Chiang Kai-shek, 231, 235, 237, 243, 296n63, 314n38, 316n23
China's Revival Street (Huaxing jie), 312n52
China's Revival Teahouse (Huaxing chashe), 295
Chinese cities, 2, 18, 93, 108, 211, 223, 252, 253, 255, 304n71
Chinese Flowering Crabapple Teahouse (Tangyuan chashe), 207
Chinese Red Cross (Zhongguo hongshizihui Huayang fenhui), 173
Chongqing, 8, 9, 59, 109, 234, 239, 250, 285n2, 316n25
Citing Fragrant Poems Tea Balcony (Yinxiang chalou), 164
Citizens' Daily (Guomin gongbao), 9, 117, 151, 203, 211, 314n31
Citizens' Pledge (Guomin gongyue), 238, 243, 247
citizens' tax (guomin juan), 230
City Council (Shi canyihui), 73, 225, 226. *See also* Chengdu City Council
City Council of Chengdu and Huayang (Chenghua cheng yishihui), 225. *See also* Chengdu City Council
city gates, 4, 118, 169, 170; East Gate, 32, 118, 140, 174; New South Gate, 55, 143, 182; North Gate, 123, 143, 286n16; Revival Gate, 119–20; South Gate, 128, 221; West Gate, 47, 49, 121, 123, 140
city wall, 4–5, 32, 122, 128
Civil War (1945-49), 2–3, 14, 63, 66, 119, 208, 219, 220, 226, 243–45, 247, 251, 263
coffeehouses (coffee shops), 12, 23, 134, 254–55
Cold Winter Teahouse (Suihan chashe), 212
Collection of Stories about the New Life (Xin shenghuo gushi ji), 318n42
collective contracts (tuanti xieyue), 95

Coming and Going Tea Balcony (Guiqulai chalou), 143
Commercial Center (Shangye chang), 40, 43–46, 119, 175, 185. *See also* Center for Promoting Industry and Commerce
commercial codes (shanggui), 73
Committee to Investigate Hygiene in Chengdu (Chengdu weisheng jiancha weiyuanhui), 51
common geographic origin (tongxiang), 58
Common Prosperity Restaurant (Guangxinglong), 117
Common Spring Teahouse (Tongchun chashe), 45, 314n31
Communists (Communist Party or CCP), 83, 87, 119, 152, 177, 182, 208, 225–26, 231, 238–39, 244, 262, 263, 301n10, 318n53, 319n62
community, 3, 71, 86, 168, 175, 184, 197, 203, 204–5, 211, 225, 252, 288n33; activities, 59; center, 133, 168; information center, 121; leaders, 76, 204; life, 17, 168; politics, 258; self-control and autonomy, 178; sense of, 197; service, 58.
competition of teahouses, 2, 28, 40, 55, 71–74 passim, 76, 82, 86, 103, 108, 152, 175, 209, 211, 262–63, 301n23, 318n61, 320n28
Confucian Society (Rujiaohui), 69
Constructive Peace Society (Jianping she), 173
Cooperation Tea Balcony (Xieji chalou), 141
Co-Prosperity Teahouse and Inn (Tongxing chashe kezhan), 74–75, 295n54
corrupt soldiers or army riffraff (lanbing), 105, 217. *See also* hoodlum soldiers
costs, 35, 37–39, 55–56, 64–66 passim, 82, 220, 246, 291n14, 294n31, 299n53; labor, 28, 38, 62, 80
Cotton Street (Mianhua jie), 40, 141
Cry of the Crane Teahouse (Heming chashe), 43–45, 61, 88, 175, 208, 310n18
Cui Xianchang, 289n44
Cultivating Wisdom Cinema (Zhiyu dianyingyuan), 308n49
cultural diversity, 2, 249
customers (patrons), 3, 7–8, 20, 22, 27, 38, 40–43, 50, 52, 54–56, 62, 66, 68, 73, 77, 84–85, 89, 92, 96–97, 103, 105–7, 109, 113, 115, 117, 119, 120–1, 125, 127–35, 138, 140–43, 158–59, 162, 164, 167, 170, 176, 182, 185–87, 195–96, 198, 204, 206, 209, 213, 215, 217–18, 220, 224–25, 227, 234–35, 239–40, 250, 257, 286n16, 289n44, 299n42, 308n54, 312n61; attract, 28, 42–63, 86, 91, 101, 140, 147–48, 157, 163, 171, 257; behavior of, 118–19, 126, 242, 246; classes of, 16, 175, 184, 188, 256, 260, 312n65; competition for, 20, 152; control of, 228; female, 9, 20, 23, 105, 108, 157, 168, 189, 191–92, 194, 196, 198–99, 207, 310n18; harassing or bullying, 23, 222; number of, 17, 20, 27, 34, 38–39, 44, 47, 53–54, 157, 171, 186, 188, 291n14, 292n15, 294n30; occupations of, 54, 179; regular, 41, 55, 115, 131, 172, 262, 295n51, 304n15; treatment of, 43, 84, 89, 98, 170–71, 185, 204, 221, 251, 259–60, 263, 308n65, 317n36, 318n45, 321n32

Dai Kan, 141
daily resistance, 199
dan (of rice), 36–37, 62–63, 66, 88, 157, 293n26, 298n25, 301n13
Date Tree Street (Guaizaoshu jie), 215
De Grazia, Sebastian, 133
Debate on Tea and Wine (Chajiu lun), 321n32. *See also* Wang Fu
Deities Gathering Tea Garden (Qunxian chayuan), 157, 161, 308n49
Deity of Tasting Tea Balcony (Pinxian chalou), 99
Deng Xihou, 315n16
Department of Household Registration of Capital City Police Headquarters (Shenghui jingbeibu huji chu), 293n21
devil's den (moku), 11
Digging Gold (Taojin ji), 21, 123
dingda, 73
Disbanding the New Fourth Army and Strengthening Military Discipline (Jiesan Xinsijun yu zhengchi junji), 317n41
disputes, 11, 13, 15, 20, 23, 61, 64, 78–79, 95–96, 98, 106, 115, 159, 167–68, 175–78 passim, 182, 204–6 passim, 208, 210–11, 215, 221–23, 226, 228, 247, 251
Divine Boy (Shentongzi), 172
Divine Military Society for Public Lectures (Wusheng jiangyan hui), 174
Do not talk about national affairs (xiutan guoshi or motan guoshi), 241–42, 246

donation, 39, 62, 80, 138, 149, 150, 154, 159, 174, 188, 229, 317n39
Dongpo Pavilion (Dongpo ting), 175
down-river people (xiajiangren), 143
Dragon Bridge (Longqiao), 120
Dragon Friends Teahouse (Longyou chashe), 217
dragon head masters (longtou daye), 181
drank leisure tea (chi xiancha), 119
Dream of Red Chambers (Honglou meng), 145
drink early tea (chi zaocha), 121
drinking lidded-bowl tea (he gaiwan cha), 126
drinking overtime tea (he jiabancha), 128
drinking settlement tea (chi jiangcha), 168, 175–78, 197–98, 204, 223, 313n2
Drinking Waves (Yintao) Teahouse, 45, 295n54
Duis, Perry, 304n17, 309n10
dulcimers (yangqin), 135, 141
Dumazedier, Joffre, 132, 133

earwax pickers, 125, 171, 196, 209
East Asian Theater (Dongya wutai), 151
East City Corner Street (Dongchenggen jie), 45, 297n18, 319n62
East District, 33, 67, 87
East Garden Teahouse (Dongyuan chashe), 207
East Great Street (Dong dajie), 32, 40, 44–45, 54, 140, 299n58
East Imperial Street (Dongyu jie), 175
Eight Heads from Eight Provinces (Basheng shoushi), 59
Eight Treasures Street (Babao jie), 183
eight-deity tables (baxian zhuo), 117
electric operas (dianxi), 155
electric-light operas (dianguang xi), 155
elegant name (yaming), 85
elegant seats (yazuo), 185, 260
Elegant Tea Garden (Keyuan), 45, 136–37, 147–48, 152, 157, 189, 194, 229
elite culture, 138, 166, 253
Emperor Returns Town (Tianhui zheng), 123
employment of teahouses, 2, 22, 87, 90, 95–96, 101, 132, 170, 188, 197, 249, 255–57 passim, 262
employment office (zhiye jieshao suo), 96
enforcement seats (tanya zuo), 312n52

entertainment, 2–3, 15, 52, 92–93, 98, 115, 119, 135–66, 167, 220, 226–27, 235, 249, 253–54, 257–58, 262, 288nn30, 33, 289n36, 290n51, 312n65, 321n32; cheap, 9; folk, 47; noble, 237; patriotic, 236; popular, 22–23, 236, 253, 258, 309n66; public, 236
Era Teahouse (Shidai chashe), 177
Esherick, Joseph, 249–50, 285n2, 292n17
Eternal Spring Tea Garden (Wanchun chayuan), 45, 148, 150–51, 155, 157–58, 161, 173, 191, 194, 230, 305n39, 307n28, 308nn52, 54
evening tea (wancha), 12
everyday culture, 1–2, 8, 22, 44, 134, 150, 223, 250, 252, 259, 263, 285n1
everyday life (daily life), 1–4 passim, 8, 11, 15, 21, 23, 27, 84, 113–14, 120–22 passim, 127, 131, 134, 151, 155, 157, 164, 170, 198, 204, 219, 232, 234–35, 238, 246, 250, 252, 261, 285n1, 288nn29, 33, 289n40, 313nn3, 4, 316n24
Examination Yuan Street (Gongyuan), 175

fabi (legal tender), 37, 63, 294n30, 313n22, 314n28
Fallen Calyx Canthus (Luomei), 149
Fang's Teahouse (Fangji chashe), 295
Farm Garden Teahouse (Nongyuan), 118
Feng Yan, 286n8
Feng Yuxiang, 84
Feng Zikai, 16
Fight on the Sandy Beach (Zhanshatan), 308n60
fire control tax (xiaofangjuan), 80
fire money (huoqian), 88
First Balcony (Diyilou), 46, 131, 151, 190, 295
First Fountain Teahouse (Diyiquan), 118, 182
First Park Teahouse (Diyi gongyuan chashe), 159
First Subdistrict of the East District (Dongyiqu), 87
First Teahouse (Diyi chashe), 68
fish drum (yugu), 139
Five Happinesses (Wufu), 295n54
Five Seniors and Seven Sages (wulao qixian), 141
Flourish (Xingsheng) Teahouse, 295n54
Flower Fair, 34, 47, 49, 50

flower teahouses (hua chafang), 302n26
folk performances, 9, 117, 125, 136, 138–44, 147, 160, 164, 165, 258, 260, 288n33, 289n36
folksingers, 50, 136
foreign teahouses (waiguo chaguan), 8. *See also* coffeehouses
forever stages (wannian tai), 136
fortune-tellers, 171–73, 196, 250
Four Brightnesses (Siming) Teahouse, 295n54
Four Dimensions Teahouse (Siwei chashe), 174
Four Fountains Teahouse (Siquan chashe), 72
Four Springs Teahouse (Sichun chashe), 142, 176
Fragrant Herb and Fountain Street (Chaiquan jie), 45, 210
Fragrant Taste Tea Garden (Pinxiang chayuan), 44–45, 123, 148, 151, 155, 157, 170, 206, 295n54, 307n28, 310n28, 313n19
fragrant tea made with river water (he shui xiang cha), 18
freedom to do business (yingye ziyou), 73
Friendship Society of Wounded Soldiers on the Frontlines (Qianfang kangzhan shangbing zhiyou she), 80
frivolous young people (fulang zidi), 119
Fu Chongju, 145, 305n42. *See also An Investigation of Chengdu*
Fu River, 55
fuel, 18, 37–38, 64–65, 74, 294n31

gamblers, 8, 213, 294n31
Gangsters in Black (Heiyi dang), 156
Ge Garden (Geyuan), 310n28
gender, 3, 15, 22–23, 86, 90, 100, 107–8, 168, 211, 256, 311n49
General Mass Benevolent Society (Qunyi zongshe), 182
Gernet, Jacques, 288n30
ghost teahouses (gui chapu), 40
gifts from the Spring Festival for the military (chunli laojunjuan), 80
going through booths (chuan gezi), 138
Golas, Peter, 58
Golden Fountain (Jinquan) Teahouse, 75
Golden Fountain Street (Jinquan jie), 72
golden-clipper chatting (jinqian ban), 139

Goldstein, Joshua, 14
gonghui (union), 3, 43, 98–100, 258. *See also* Union of Teahouse Workers in Chengdu
gongsuo, 57–59, 81, 296n1
Good Morality (Guande) Teahouse, 297n18
good women (liangnü), 105
Goodman, Bryna, 59, 81, 297n11
gossip, 10, 115, 121, 189, 205, 227, 245, 257, 313n3
Gowned Brothers (Paoge), 53, 76–77, 97, 103, 168, 170, 176–84, 198–99, 214–15, 217, 251–56, 257, 262, 296n71, 302n42, 310n27
Grand Stage (Dawutai), 150
Grand Stage of Warm Spring (Chunxi dawutai or Chunxi wutai), 157–58
Grand View Tea Garden (Daguan chayuan), 151, 161, 206, 217
Great Green Mountain (Da cuipingshan), 308n60
Great Han Military Government (Dahan Sichuan junzhengfu), 228
Great Heavenly Singing Theater (Daguanghan gechang), 195
Great Peace Street (Daan jie), 209
Great Rear Area (Dahoufang), 84
Great Wave (Dabo), 21, 116, 189, 290n55
Green Dragon Teahouse (Qinglong chashe), 295n54
Green Goat Market (Qingyang chang), 32, 40, 68, 73, 124
Green Goat Temple (Qingyang gong), 47, 49
Green Shadow Pavilion (Lüyin ge), 45, 221
Green Sky Teahouse (Lütian chashe), 43, 47, 174
Guangyuan, 27
Guizhou army, 141, 228, 231
Gushing Fountain Chamber Teahouse (Yongquan ju chashe), 314n31

Habermas, Jürgen, 254–55
Hai Su, 118, 141, 178, 185
Half Side Street (Banbian jie), 187
Han Suyin, 114, 169, 229
hanghui, 58, 296n1, 297nn8, 9. *See also* guild
hanging around the hall (diaotang), 40, 128
hanging balconies (diaojiaolou), 47
Hangzhou, 6, 13, 15, 17, 285n2, 288n30
Hankou, 13, 58–59, 301n9
Happy Troupe (Yileban), 148

hate killing or revenge killing (chousha), 215
He Manzi, 7, 16–17, 175, 286n16
headquarters, of gangsters, 257; of garrisons, 220, 237; of guilds, 174; of GMD party, 96; of Gowned Brothers, 23, 97, 168, 178–79, 182, 198–99; of labor movement, 258; of lottery, 123; of police, 293n21; of social organizations, 3, 173–74; of union, 99
Heart of Reform Theater (Gexin juyuan or Gexin yuan), 151
Heaven's Ping Opera Theater (Guanghan pingju yuan), 152
Heavenly Temple (Tianqi miao), 146. *See also Nemesis of the Murderous Son*
Heller, Agnes, 121, 313nn3, 4
Hibiscus Pavilion Teahouse (Furongting chashe), 45, 163
Hibiscus Tea Balcony (Furong chalou), 44, 141–42
High Tea Balcony (Gaochalou), 314n31
Home for Disabled Soldiers (Feibing yuan), 68
hoodlum soldiers (qiuba), 217. *See also* corrupt soldiers
hoodlums, 102, 212, 215, 314n31. *See also* hoodlum soldiers
Horse Walking Street (Zouma jie), 175, 319n62
horse-shape chairs (mazhayi), 184
hotels (inns), 51, 74–76 passim, 132, 171, 183, 195, 244
hot-towel men (yandai pazi), 91, 159, 171–72, 196
house of the big hot-water vat (wengzi fang), 301n22
Hu Jingyi, 228
Hu Tian, 114, 184
Huang Ji'an, 149–50
Huang Jilu, 221
Huang Shang, 16–17, 27
Huayang Branch of the Chinese Red Cross (Zhongguo hongshizihui Huayang fenhui), 173
Hubei and Hunan Guild Hall Street (Huguang guan), 40
huqin, 142
hygiene, 2, 20, 50–52, 56, 72, 74, 130, 171, 226, 240, 249, 251, 253, 285n2, 296n60, 318n46

ideal teahouse (lixiang chaguan), 239–40. *See also* municipal teahouse
identity, 2, 81, 134, 160, 177, 180, 211, 232, 247, 249–50, 285n2
idle class (youxian jieji), 16, 114
Imperial Banner Troupe (Cuihua ban), 148
Imperial City (Huangcheng), 4, 230, 237
In the Fragrant Chamber Teahouse (Zai Qixiangju chaguan li), 21
income, 19, 35, 37–38, 43, 61, 143, 150, 162, 197, 213, 229–30, 292, 294, 298n20; average, 38; of guild, 99; of laborers, 139; sale, 65; soft, 88; sources of, 38, 105, 197, 203; supplementary, 159
inflation, 36, 62, 64, 66, 97, 235, 243, 251, 263
Injustice of Dou E (Dou E yuan), 146
Institute of Hygienic Affairs of the Chengdu Municipal Government (Chengdu shizhengfu weisheng shiwusuo), 51

Jade Belt Bridge (Yudai qiao), 27
Japanese air raids, 55, 128, 196, 220, 316n24
Jia Shusan, 142
Jiangsu, 13, 237
Jiangyou Pass (Jiangyou guan), 150
jie gaizi (uncovering the lid), 130
Jinling University, 221
Jinling Woman's (Jinling nüzi) University, 221
jinyuanjuan (golden yuan), 63
Joy Garden Chinese and Western Restaurant (Yuelai Zhongxi canguan), 151
Joy Tea Garden (Yuelai chayuan), 9, 37, 44, 45, 136, 147–55 passim, 157, 161, 174, 186, 189–91 passim, 195, 205, 212–14 passim, 229, 294n35, 307nn19, 42, 312n52, 314n30
Juicy Red Peach (Shuihong taozi), 195
Junping Street (Junping jie), 188

kettles, 27, 41, 74, 85, 90, 114, 127, 142, 220, 293n23, 301n22, 305n35
Kingdom of Tea and Teahouses, 1
Knight, Luther, 41, 49, 229–30

Labor Movement Code (Gongyun fa), 97
Lao She, 241
laojun, 80
Laundry Street (Jiangxi jie), 31
Law on Union Operations (Gonghui shishi fa), 99

Law on Unions (Gonghui fa), 99
lawless brigands (bufa zhitu), 221
Leaving Cui Hua (Yicuihua), 308n60
lecherous plays, 147, 160–61
leisure activities, 2, 15, 17, 120, 133, 227, 253
leisure tea (xiancha), 119, 196
Leng Hongfa Teahouse (Leng Hongfa chashe), 67
Li Jieren, 53, 117, 120, 131, 167–68, 185, 189–90, 228, 241, 290n50, 309n11, 312n61
Liang Garden (Liangyuan), 50
Liang Hongyu, 150
liangdi (showing secrets), 180
Liao Wenchang, 54, 57, 65, 298n32
lighting the hall (liangtang), 127
Lime Street (Shihui jie), 174
Lin Zexu, 150
Ling Guozheng, 92, 100, 302n42
Little Cowherd in the Pasture (Xiaofangniu), 308n60
Little India (Xiao Tianzhu) Street, 31
Little India Teahouse (Xiao Tianzhu chashe), 174
Little Widow Goes to the Graveyard (Xiaoshangfen), 308n60
Liu Wenhui, 315n16
Liu Xiang, 315n16
liula zhizhan (fights every sixth and twelfth lunar month), 175
local authorities, 3, 57, 60, 62, 70–71, 74–75, 79, 82, 93, 98, 102, 104, 106, 108–9, 144, 163, 171, 178–79, 181–82, 199, 204, 210–11, 222–23, 226, 241, 252. *See also* local government; municipal government; police
local culture, 1–2, 14, 22–23, 39, 44, 131, 166, 169, 199, 250, 252
local elites, 8, 13–14, 40, 103, 119, 144, 151, 168, 174, 225, 227, 261
local government, 3, 20, 27, 29–30, 42, 56, 60, 62, 64, 69, 71, 75, 79, 81–83 passim, 106, 109, 147, 157, 165, 174, 178, 184, 218, 223, 226, 233, 239, 244, 246, 253, 291n7
local politics, 3, 23, 100, 223, 258
London, 14, 254, 319n7
Long Fluent Street (Changshun jie), 76, 183, 319n62
Long Happiness Troupe (Changle ban), 148
Lower Peace Street (Taiping xia jie), 47
Lower River Bank Street (Xiaheba), 72

lower-class people, 8, 16, 23, 28, 35, 50, 62, 106, 120, 133, 154, 160, 167, 185–89 passim, 285n1
lower-class teahouses, 17, 50, 54, 56, 91, 123, 126, 139, 142, 186, 296n71
Lu Xiufu, 150
Lu Xun, 233
Lu Yin, 106
Lucky Light Teahouse (Xiangguang) Teahouse, 175
Luo Lun, 315n9

mahjong, 10, 53, 123, 212
Main Mansion Street (Zongfu jie), 43, 196, 235
management of teahouses, 3, 22, 28, 37, 39–44, 54–55, 162, 210, 251, 262, 308n65
managers, 18, 52, 70, 73, 77, 78, 153, 160, 209, 219, 222, 231, 242, 246, 292n19, 318n61
Manchu City (Shaosheng), 4
marriage brokers (pitiao ke), 190
martial law, 141, 150
masters of tea (cha boshi), 84–85, 87–90, 107, 263
material culture, 126–27, 233, 260
matou, 178, 183, 228. *See also* turf
mediation, 61, 93, 177, 198, 203–4
members' pledge of the union, 95
membership, 153; of guild, 39, 58, 60–62, 77, 81, 185, 297n16, 298nn20, 21; of Nationalist Party, 39, 61; of union, 93, 95–101 passim, 302nn31, 40, 46
men's clubs, 13
merchants, 16–17, 42, 54, 60, 70, 73, 76–78 passim, 108, 114, 151, 154, 162, 169–72, 174, 183, 196–97, 207–8, 250, 258, 261–62, 299n53
mere talk hurts the country (qingtan wuguo), 11
miandi, 128
microcosm, 1–2, 23, 168, 204, 211, 250–52
microhistory, 1, 252, 285n1
Military Police, 218–19, 243–44, 308n65, 314n31
Military Security Committee, 244
militia, 176–77, 210–11. *See also* baojia
Ming dynasty (1368-1644), 6, 308n61
Ministry of Agriculture, Industry, and Commerce (Nonggongshang bu), 86
modern drama (huaju), 150

Modern Drama Society (Modeng jushe), 150
modernist transformation, 1, 14
modernist uniformity, 1–2, 14, 22–23, 56, 109, 134, 166, 199, 249, 252
modernization, 1–2, 14, 28, 249–50, 259
Moral and Prosperous Teahouse (Derong chashe), 177
Moral Integrity at the Firewood Market (Chaishijie), 150
Mount Meng (Mengshan), 47
Mouth Hole (Dongzi kou), 123
Movement to Economize (Jieyue yundong), 79–80
movie, 125, 155–57, 165, 166, 175, 212, 308n46
moving night pots (huodong yehu), 156
municipal government, 38, 51–52, 60, 64, 69, 71–72, 75, 77–78, 81, 209, 213, 220, 225. *See also* local government
municipal teahouse, 239–40. *See also* ideal teahouse
Murai Yasuhiko, 304n1
Murder at the Oriental Tea Balcony (Dongfang chalou ming'an), 203–4
music tax (yinyuejuan), 80

Nanjing National Opera Theater (Nanjing guoju shuchang), 237
Nanjing, 6, 8, 13, 16–17, 109, 148, 186, 237, 285n2
Nantong, 14–16, 315n7
National Protection Movement, 162
Nationalist government, 2, 14, 29, 60, 70–71, 93, 98, 119, 166, 176, 223, 243, 246, 250, 254
Nationalist Party (Guomindang or GMD), 2, 7, 14, 39, 60–61, 79, 92, 96, 100, 218, 225–26, 231, 236–38 passim, 240, 243, 263, 317nn36, 41, 318n45, 319n62
Near Sage Tea Garden (Jinsheng chayuan), 212
neighborhood, 3, 18, 43, 59, 75, 115, 121, 127–28, 130, 133, 140, 168, 175, 178, 189, 203, 211, 228, 231, 256–58, 286n, 290n50, 320n19. *See also* neighbors
neighbors, 132, 175–77, 207, 211–14, 219, 222, 257, 321n29. *See also* neighborhood
Nemesis of the Murderous Son (Shazi bao), 146
Nets Above and Snares Below (Tianluo diwang), 317n41

New Chengdu (Xin Chengdu), 60, 188, 235
New Citizens' Nightly (Xinminbao wankan), 304n15
New Cultural Movement, 47, 118, 155, 174, 233, 247
New Life Movement, 51–52, 238, 247, 296n63, 318n45
New Life Promotion Association (Xinshenghuo cujinhui), 220
New Play Society for Strengthening China (Qianghua xinjushe), 147
New Play Society for the Public Interest (Qunyi xinjushe), 147
New Policies, 29, 152, 223, 227, 252
New Sichuan Stage (Shuxin wutai), 157
New World Tea Garden (Xinshijie chayuan), 141
Newest Grand Stage (Xinyouxin dawutai), 157
Nichizawa Haruhiko, 13, 287n29
night operas (yexi), 151
noon tea (wucha), 12
North East Street (Beidong jie), 212
numbers of teahouses, 29–35

Observing Beggars in the Teahouse (Chaguan guangai), 188
Official Tea Leaf Store of Chengdu (Chenghua chaan guancha dian), 42
old masters (gongye), 195
One and One Tea Garden (Yiyi chayuan), 230
One Family's Spring (Yijia chun) Teahouse, 151
one-night stands (lushui fuqi), 190
open turf time (kaili matou), 183
operas, 9–10, 145, 237, 253; audience of, 157–60; licentious, 161; local (Sichuan), 7, 9, 11, 22, 43, 104, 114, 129, 136, 138, 144, 147, 149, 151, 155, 157–60 passim, 160–61, 163–66 passim, 186, 189, 247, 258, 261, 308n52; new (reformed), 145, 147–50 passim, 152, 155, 165, 174, 191; Peking, 175; Ping, 152, 261
opium, 8, 15, 167, 170, 183, 213–14, 301n23, 307n35, 310n28
Optimistic Tea Garden (Leguan chayuan), 129
Oriental Tea Balcony (Dongfang chalou), 45
Outline for Mobilizing the National Spirit and

Its Implementation (Guomin jingshen zongdongyuan gangling ji shishi banfa), 318n41
out-of-hall water (chutangshui), 128
ownership, 22, 28, 35, 55, 72–73, 77, 245, 253, 255

pao jingbao (running for their lives whenever sirens sounded the alert), 316n24
Paris, 7, 14, 23, 155, 256–58 passim, 293n22, 311n49, 319n7, 320n19
parks, 15, 47, 51, 117, 126, 185, 220, 221, 295n57, 298n30; Central City Park, 47; First Park, 68; North City Park, 123, 299n58; Smaller City Park, 6, 34, 42, 45, 47–48, 53, 116, 121, 172, 174, 184–85, 190, 197, 208, 221, 297n18, 310n18, 314n31, 319n62; Sun Yat-sen Park, 45, 129, 143, 185, 194, 218, 220, 294n30, 310n15; Zhiji Temple Park, 47, 221
partnership (partners), 37–38, 74–75, 171. *See also* shareholders
patron deity associations (tudi hui or qingming hui), 59
Peace and Happiness Temple Teahouse (Anlesi chashe), 45, 179
Peace and Quiet Teahouse (Jing'an chashe), 123
Peaceful and Prosperous (Taiheheng) Teahouse, 40
Peach Land Teahouse (Taoyuan chashe), 294n29
peddlers, 35–36, 40, 42, 51, 104–5, 114–17 passim, 121, 133–34, 143, 154, 159, 169–72, 182, 188, 196, 209–10, 220, 250–51, 259, 262
pedicurists, 51, 171, 196
peng genü (a member of a singing girls' group), 195. *See also* pengke
pengke (members of the group), 195. *See also* peng genü
People's Theater (Pingmin juyuan), 218
performance tea (shucha), 196
performed in teahouses (baiguan), 141
performing violent opera (yanwuju), 176
physiognomists (xiangmian xiansheng), 172. *See also* fortune-tellers
Picking up a Jade Bracelet (Shiyu zhuo), 308n60

place of lovers (lian'ai changsuo), 104
Plan for Inspecting the Sanitation of Restaurants and Teahouses in Chengdu (Chengdu shi yinshidian ji chashe qingjie jiancha banfa), 51
Plan of Propaganda in Teahouses (Chaguan xuanchuan shishi jihua), 237
playing the poem game (bai shitiaozi), 122
Pleasant and Peaceful Chamber (Changhe xuan) Teahouse, 125
Pleasant Spring Balcony (Yichunlou), 45, 151, 190, 206, 295n54
Pleasant Tea Garden (Yiyuan), 45, 50, 78, 310n28
Pleasant Wind Teahouse (Huifeng chashe), 45, 143
Pleasure Spring (Yichun) Teahouse, 136
poems, 4, 6, 123, 164, 180, 186, 302n26
police, 9, 50, 51–53 passim, 56, 60, 66–70 passim, 75, 96, 106, 146, 150, 155, 157, 160–64 passim, 174, 176–83 passim, 189, 191, 195, 203, 204–13 passim, 215–21 passim, 223, 225, 226, 228, 231, 238–40 passim, 243–45 passim, 253, 262, 293n21, 312n61, 314nn28, 30, 38, 319n6; archives of, 20, 290n53; arrest, 208, 213; branches, 33, 206, 300n68; chief, 149, 159; collecting taxes, 66–67, 70; control, 194, 199, 221; department, 68, 70, 103, 106, 159, 161, 206–8, 220; establishment of, 50; investigation, 30, 68, 161, 205, 292n19; military, 218, 243, 244, 308n65, 314n31; officers, 53, 118, 159, 163, 228; regulations of, 20, 50, 162, 178; secret agents, 183; station, 78, 195; subdistrict of, 69, 75
political arena, 3, 14, 23, 225, 246, 249, 253, 255, 320n19
politics of resistance, 234–40
popular culture, 8–9, 14, 22, 39, 126, 138, 144–45, 160, 166, 227–28, 246–47, 253, 287n21, 289n36
Popular Daily (Tongsu ribao), 144–45, 191, 205–6
populations, 4, 30–34 passim, 47, 55, 73, 135, 235, 252, 256, 262, 285n5, 286n16, 290n51, 291n14, 309n10, 315n1
pre-rain tea (yuqiancha), 4
President's Call for Sichuan Folk-followers (Zongcai gao Chuansheng tongbao shu), 318

Price Evaluation Committee (Pingjia hui), 63, 79
prices, 10, 16, 18, 38, 42, 57–58, 62–66, 78–79, 82, 88, 106, 156, 162, 251, 293nn26, 28, 298n23, 299n43, 306n18
professional singing girls (zhiye genü), 195
Prosperity Tea Hall (Huahua chating), 43, 45, 54, 170, 182, 208, 297n18, 298n32
Prosperous and Happy Chamber (Ronglu xuan) Teahouse, 175
Prosperous and Peaceful Tea Garden (Xinghe chayuan), 294n28
prostitutes, 6, 11, 15, 90, 98, 102, 105, 106, 121, 145, 163, 189, 192, 194, 195, 199, 215, 243, 302n26, 303n68, 312n61, 314n31
protection fee (baohu fei), 313n19
provincial capital, 1, 4, 22, 76, 103, 121–22, 162, 225, 233, 245
Provincial Mobilization Committee (Sheng dongyuan weiyuanhui), 237
Provincial Police Department, 206–8, 220. *See also* police
Pu Dianjun, 315n9
public life, 1, 5, 15, 22–23, 151, 168, 204, 226, 252, 254, 262–63
public man, 255
public notice, 67, 75, 77, 103, 174, 178, 194–95, 204, 220, 221–22, 241, 243–44, 246, 262, 318n54
Public Office of Chengdu Municipal Affairs (Chengdu shi shizheng gongsuo), 225
public places, 15, 23, 51–52, 85, 90, 102, 107, 115, 159, 166, 168, 179, 195, 197–98, 204, 206, 220, 222–23, 231, 252–53, 255, 259, 261, 289n40
public politics, 3, 224–47, 249–50
public sphere, 254–55, 258–59, 319n8
public talks, 2
pure teahouses (qingchaguan), 288
Pure Wind Pavilion (Qingfengting), 142

Qilu University, 221
Quiet Orchid Chamber Teahouse (Jinglanxuan), 180
Quieting Waves Teahouse (Anlan chaguan), 128, 142, 175

Railroad Protection Movement, 21, 226, 228, 315n9

Reading of the Three Principles of the People (Sanmin zhuyi dazhong duben), 318n41
real pictures of pornography (huo chungong), 191
Reciting (Yongni) Teahouse, 136
Reciting and Whistling Balcony (Yinxiaolou), 175
Record of Festivals (Suihua jilipu), 6
Record of the Peaceful Era (Taiping guangji), 286n8
Recovering the Motherland (Huan wo heshan), 236
red and black boards (hongfei heipian), 180
Red Army, 231
Red Deity Town (Zhuxianzhen), 150
red money gang (hongqian bang), 53
reformist elites, 8, 10, 138, 145, 165, 192, 223, 227, 252–53, 315n7. *See also* Westernized elites
refugee singing girls (liuwang genü), 195
refugees, 29–30, 86, 90, 252
registration of businesses, 10, 60–61, 73–75 passim, 93, 96, 153, 226, 253, 262–63, 290n53
regular seats (putong zuo), 185, 190, 260, 312n52
Regulations for Restricting Theaters (Qudi xiyuan fa), 162
Regulations for the Inspection of Gambling, Thieves' Dens, the Sworn Brotherhood, and Heterodox Sects (Qingcha wodu, wodao, shaoxiang jiemeng, chuanxi xiejiao guize), 180–81
Regulations on Local Operas and Folk Performances (Qudi xiqu guize), 160
Regulations on Professional Organizations in Industry and Commerce, 60
Regulations on Teahouses in Sichuan (Sichuan sheng guanli chaguan banfa), 52, 240, 318n45
regulations, 2–3, 20, 28, 40, 50–52 passim, 56, 59–60, 72, 76–79 passim, 82, 96–97, 144, 148, 157, 179–80, 199, 205, 207, 210, 226, 228, 233–34, 238–40 passim, 244–45, 247, 251, 253–54, 256, 262, 302nn32, 44, 308n65, 311n49, 315n4, 318nn45, 46; guild, 72, 73; licensing, 72, 75, 183; performances, 138, 160–63 passim, 166; sanitation (hygiene), 50–51, 56; waitresses, 96, 106–8; union, 92–95, 98–100 passim

rent, 35, 39, 43, 44, 74, 76, 120–21, 136, 138, 168, 173, 203, 210, 294n31, 320n16
residents, 1, 10, 12, 18–19, 32–34, 38–39, 43, 52, 55, 62, 73, 92, 97, 115, 118–19, 122, 126–27, 128, 130–31, 140, 161, 168, 177–78, 183, 198–99, 205, 207–8, 210–14 passim, 217–18, 223, 226, 228–29, 231–32, 235, 241, 250, 256, 258–60, 262, 286n16, 289n40, 290n50, 301n22, 316n24, 319n7
Resistance University of Northern Shaanxi (Shanbei kangda), 239
restaurants, 7, 13, 18, 29, 35, 42, 51–52, 54–55, 60, 85–86, 104, 117, 121, 151, 171, 195, 260, 311n49
Restrictions of Teahouses in Chengdu (Chengdu shi chaguan ye qudi banfa), 245
Revival Gate (Fuxing men), 220
Revival Troupe (Fuxing ban), 148
Reviving Teahouse (Quanxing), 300n7
rickshaw pullers, 115, 169, 288n33
Rising Dragon Alley (Xinglong xiang), 139
Rising Fluency (Shunxing) Teahouse, 295n54
Rising Prosperity (Hongxing) Teahouse, 295n54
Riverside Shadow Play Tea Garden (Linjiang yingxi chayuan), 191
Rosenzweig, Roy, 132, 321n29
Rowe, William, 13–14, 58–59, 301n9
rube (xiangyu), 75
ruffians (liupi), 215
Rules for Watching and Patrolling, 228
rumors, 10, 226, 231, 246
running on the beach (paotan), 138
running water, 54, 65, 80–81, 250, 300n76
rushing into the hall (dayongtang), 127

Sacred and Pure Tea Garden (Shengqing chayuan), 141, 143
salaries (wages), 37–39, 62, 88, 91–93, 97, 154, 159, 256, 300n7
salons, 254–55
saloons, 7, 132, 254–59 passim, 291n12, 301n7, 306n47, 309n10, 311n49, 319nn6, 7, 320n19
Salt Market Corner (Yanshi kou), 37
sanxian (three-stringed instrument), 142
Saving for Rebuilding the Country (Jianguo chuxu), 80

School of the Hall (tangpai), 141
second-hand goods business, 160
secret society rituals (bai matou), 228
sedan-chair carriers, 104, 115, 187–88
self-government movement, 225, 227, 231
Selling Rouge (Maiyanzhi), 308n60
Sennett, Richard, 255
Sewell, William, 120, 126
Sha Ting, 21, 123, 125, 261, 312n65
Shaanxi opera (qinqiang), 152
Shaanxi Street (Shaanxi jie), 31, 164, 188
Shanghai, 8, 10, 14–16, 18, 27, 29, 43, 59, 108, 118, 155, 188–89, 287n28, 288nn30, 33, 289nn36, 40, 297n16, 301n23, 302nn35, 40, 303n70
Shao, Qin, 14, 315n7
shareholders, 37, 42–43, 155, 206–7, 210, 308n49. *See also* partnership
Shiliang Tea Garden (Shiliang chayuan), 295n54
shoe polishers, 171, 209
shopkeepers (proprietors), 27–28, 35, 39–41, 56–57, 61–62, 67, 70, 73–74, 78–79, 82–83, 88, 91, 105, 107–9, 127, 134, 168, 170, 182–83, 198, 209–10, 214, 244, 250, 261–62, 258, 291n14, 292n19, 295n46, 298n21, 319n6
shops, 3, 13, 28–29, 35, 39–41 passim, 55, 60, 72, 86, 107–8, 117, 119, 127, 154, 169–71, 174, 184, 211, 213, 222, 231, 235, 250, 256, 259–60, 263, 286n8, 291n1, 300n3, 320n28; barber, 51, 171, 260; butcher, 171; lottery, 123; tea, 5–6; weaving, 188; wine, 6, 13, 85, 221, 322n32. *See also* small businesses
Shu Xincheng, 7, 9, 12, 17, 35, 47, 117, 186
Sichuan Military Government (Sichuan jun zhengfu), 315n9
Sichuan people govern Sichuan (Chuanren zhi Chuan), 231
Sichuan Police Department (Sichuan jingcha zongting), 161
Sichuan Provincial Capital Police, 244
Sichuan Provincial Scientific Hall (Sichuan shengli kexueguan), 299n58
Sichuan Stage (Shuwutai), 157
Sichuan Student Association (Sichuan quansheng xuesheng lianhehui), 150
Sichuan University, 174, 207, 221
silver yuan (dayang), 118, 156, 203, 209, 231, 266

singing for the event in the hall (chang tanghui), 136
singing stories with drums (dagu or dagushu), 143
singing under the water shed (chang shuipeng), 138
sitting arena operas (zuochang xi), 151
sitting in the teahouse (zuo chaguan), 120, 135
sitting operas (daweigu), 129. *See also* stool opera
Skinner, William, 13, 172
Sleeping Stream Teahouse (Zhenliu chashe), 38, 45, 53, 174, 310n18, 319n62
small businesses with little capital (xiaoben shangye), 27
small businesses, 2–3, 27–60, 62, 66, 69, 85, 107, 109, 127, 167, 250, 259–60, 262, 299n53. *See also* shops
Small Garden Teahouse (Xiaohuayuan chashe), 175
smuggle, 179, 183, 246, 310n28
Social Bureau of the Provincial Government, 294n30
social reform, 3, 9, 145, 226, 318n41. *See also* social reformers
social reformers, 14, 144, 146, 148, 155, 191, 194, 198, 227, 254, 285n1, 311n49. *See also* social reform
Social Situation in Wartime Chengdu (Zhanshi Chengdu shehui dongtai), 10
Society of the Hall of Righteousness and Morality (Mingde tang), 163–64
Society of the King of Water-Carriers (Shuigong wangye hui), 62
sojourner masters (yugong), 115
soldiers, 10, 23, 68–69, 80, 91, 102, 141, 150, 154, 159, 162, 177, 182, 205, 209, 212, 214, 217–20, 222–23, 244, 262, 303n59, 312n52, 314nn30, 31, 315n9, 317n39. *See also* corrupt soldiers; hoodlum soldiers
Song dynasty (960-1279), 6, 13, 122, 150, 199, 236, 287n28, 288n30
South Fu River, 128
South Private Academy Street (Shuyuan nanjie), 218
South Three Bridges Street (Sanqiao nanjie), 175
Southwest Union University, 225

special area, 38, 63, 298n30. *See also* Warm Spring Road
special seats (tebie zuo), 185, 190
Spence, Jonathan, 285n1
Splendid Troupe (Caihua ban), 148
Spring Dragon Tea Garden (Longchun chayuan), 102
Spring Tea Balcony (Tongchun chalou), 45, 185
Square Street (Fangzheng jie), 205
Stapleton, Kristin, 285n2, 306n19
state's growing role, 1–2, 15, 22, 134, 225, 252
Stealing Poems and Shooting Vultures (Toushi shediao), 308n60
stool opera (bandeng xi), 129. *See also* sitting operas
Stories of Bravery (Yingyong shiji), 317n41
storytellers, 98, 114–15, 125, 135, 138, 140–41, 144, 165–66, 177, 228, 235, 250, 288n33. *See also* storytelling
Storytelling Arena for Bosom Buddies (Zhiyin shuchang), 143
storytelling arenas (shuchang), 140, 143, 237
storytelling, 40, 43, 98, 135–36, 139–41, 143, 164–65, 236, 257–58, 260, 288n33. *See also* storytellers
stove keepers, 87–89, 92, 171, 189, 263, 301n22
Striding with Large Steps (Lingyunbu), 307n35
strike, 69–71, 93, 174, 258, 299n53, 320n19
students, 11, 17, 43, 121, 128, 133, 162, 174, 190, 197, 207–8, 221, 234, 239, 249, 310n18, 319n62
Summer Palace Tea Garden (Yihe chayuan), 144
Suzuki Tōmō, 13, 290n52
Sworn Brotherhood Society (Gelaohui), 13, 23, 168, 177–78, 302n42, 310n27. *See also* Gowned Brothers
System of Defense Districts (Fangqu zhi), 231

Takeuchi Minoru, 287n28
Tang dynasty (618-907), 6, 144, 286nn8, 10, 302n26, 321n32
Tang Minghuang, 144
Tangchang, 141
tangguan, 85, 88. *See also* masters of tea
tavern, 23, 134, 254–56 passim
taxes, 28, 39, 60, 66–71, 230, 290n14; evasion,

34, 214; exemption, 71, 174; protests, 228, 299n53, 70–71
tea and wine shops (chafang jiusi), 6
tea boats (chachuan), 126
tea booths or tea sheds (chapeng), 5, 220, 288
tea bowl formations (chawan zhen), 180
tea bowls (chawan), 43, 50–51, 53–54, 74, 85, 120, 126–27, 162, 176–77, 185, 208–9, 210–11, 217, 219–22, 292n14, 293n23, 305n35, 312n52, 313n8, 314nn28, 31
tea chambers (chashi), 5–6, 289
tea drinking (chicha), 4–7 passim, 17, 126–27, 165, 234–35, 239, 258, 294n30, 316n25, 321n32
Tea Drinking Division (Yincha bu), 294n30
Tea Garden (Mingyuan) Teahouse, 295n54
Tea Guild, 297n16
tea halls (chating), 5
tea pavilion (chating), 5
tea poems (chaci), 6
tea rooms (chafang), 5–6
tea rotations (chalun), 128
tea shops (chapu), 5–6
tea stands (chasi), 286n8
Tea Tax Unrest (chajuan fengchao), 71
teachers, 115, 121, 175, 197, 310n18
Teahouse Guild, 3, 30, 35, 37, 39, 42, 51–52, 57–83, 88, 106, 108, 123, 178, 185, 207–9, 219–20, 239, 261, 263, 298n32, 317nn34, 36, 319n3; account of, 20, 297n16; business registration, 71–78; classification of teahouses, 185; control of pricing, 63–66; control of teahouse business, 40; functions, 22; membership, 38, 62, 298nn20, 21; organization, 60–62; relationship with state, 60, 78–81, 213, 217, 237, 239, 249, 254; relief, 298n34; rights of teahouses, 220, 254; tax protests, 66–71, 299n53; transformation of, 60. *See also* guild
teahouse men (chafang), 85. *See also* masters of tea
teahouse politician (chaguan zhengzhijia), 227, 241–43 passim, 246
teahouse-goers, 8, 10–11, 16, 22, 42, 47, 115, 119, 131, 168, 171, 186, 198, 232, 257, 261, 286n16, 304nn1, 15. *See also* customers
teahouses strike against taxes (chashe tingye kangjuan), 69
Tears of Mountains and Rivers (Shanhe lei), 150

tea-table tax (chazhuo juan), 69, 70
temple fairs, 47, 50, 136
temples, 11, 47, 49, 117, 136, 146, 160–61, 170, 215, 221; Prefectural City God Temple, 215; Temple of the City God, 187. *See also* temple fairs
Temporary Instruction Committee of the Chinese Nationalist Party for People's Organizations in Chengdu (Zhongguo Guomindang Chengdu shi renmin tuanti linshi zhidao weiyuanhui), 236
Temporary Rules for Regulating Teahouses (Sichuan shenghui jingcha ju guanli chashe ye zanxing banfa), 245
The 1911 Revolution, 4, 6, 30, 50, 117, 148, 151, 161, 178, 194, 207, 217, 223, 226, 230, 233, 253, 305n39
Theater of Pure Ballad Singing and Shadow Plays (Qingyin dengying xiyuan), 116
theaters, 3, 9, 14–15, 22, 116, 125, 136, 138, 144, 147–48, 150, 151–66, 186, 189–95 passim, 206–7, 212, 214–15, 217–19 passim, 226, 233–37 passim, 253, 258, 260, 307n42, 308n65, 312n52, 314n30, 316nn21, 26, 320n19
thefts, 20, 182, 208, 221
Thick Shadow Tea Balcony (Nongyin chalou), 42, 45, 174
This Is Wang Jingwei (Ruci de Wang Jingwei), 317n41
Three Bests in the Bright Spring Tea Balcony (Jinchunlou sanjue), 84, 143
Three Celebrations Society (Sanqinghui), 148–49, 152, 154
Three Challenges in the Prosperous Tea Garden (Sanzhan Huayuan), 319
Three Chinese-Scholar Trees Tea Garden (Sanhuai chayuan), 76
Three Chinese-Scholar Trees Teahouse and Inn (Sanhuaishu chashe kezhan), 76
Three Deities Society (Sanhuang hui), 306n11
Three Kingdoms (220–65), 142
Three Loyalties (Sanjinzhong), 150
Three Sacrifices at the River (Sanjijiang), 142
Three Sages (Sanyigong) Teahouse, 38, 45, 53–54, 91, 175, 195, 295n54
Three Way Guild (Sandao huiguan), 174
Throwing the Witch into the Ye River (Yeshui touwu), 307n35

Tian Hongxing Teahouse, 79
Tian Lai, 305n39
Tian Songyao, 315n16
tizhengtang, 85. See also tangguan; masters of tea
Tobacco Bag Lane (Yandai xiang), 187
tobacconists, 35, 70, 171–72, 196. See also water-pipe tobacco servants
toilets, 35, 50, 52, 124, 130, 156, 257, 286n16
tongye gonghui, 58–59. See also guild
Top of Mount Meng (Mengding) Teahouse, 295n54
traffic, 2, 47, 72, 183, 212, 214, 245
traitors (hanjian), 11, 106, 150, 236, 317n41
True Entertainment Garden (Zhengyu huayuan), 38, 45, 54, 184, 188, 310n28
True Story of Ah Q, 233
Tung-Tree Shadow Teahouse and Inn (Tongyin chalüdian), 183
turf, 13, 178, 181–83, 262; branches, 180, 182, 211, 215; generals, 182
Two Fountains Tea Balcony (Erquan chalou), 45, 175, 185
Two Fountains Tea Hall (Erquan chating), 38

Uncle Tom's Cabin, 148
Union of Chengdu Teahouse Workers (Chengdu shi chashe ye zhiye gonghui), 86–87, 92–100, 108–9, 302nn31, 44
Union of Chengdu Teahouse Workers' Livelihood (Chengdu shi chashe minsheng gonghui), 92
Union of Tea Workers of Chengdu (Chengdu shi minggongye zhiye gonghui), 92
Union of the Ballad Singing Profession of Chengdu (Chengdu shi qingyin zhiye gonghui), 98
Union of the Golden Coin Bamboo Clippers' Popular Lecture and Propaganda Profession of Chengdu (Chengdu shi jinqianban tongsu jiangyan xuanchuan ye zhiye gonghui), 98–99
Union of the Popular Storytelling Profession of Chengdu (Chengdu shi tongsu pinghua ye zhiye gonghui), 98
United China Teahouse (Lianhua), 118
Unofficial History of Academic Circles (Rulin waishi), 17, 304n15
unworthy people (buxiao zhitu), 243

urban reform, 1–2, 8, 50, 205, 227–28, 250, 259, 315n7
urheen (erhu), 142

vagrant artists (liuluo de yishujia), 138
Village on the River (Jiangshangcun) Teahouse, 55, 296n71
violence, 53, 56, 102, 109, 176–78, 183, 197, 204–5, 207, 209, 212, 214–17 passim, 222–23, 312n61, 314n31
Violet (Ziluolan) Teahouse, 43, 207, 295n54, 310n28

wage workers, 37, 87–88
waiters, 27, 51–53 passim, 84–92 passim, 96–98 passim, 100–04 passim, 107–8, 114, 116, 125, 127, 130, 132, 134–35, 141–43, 156, 159, 170–71, 180, 182, 185–86, 193, 195, 198, 204, 209, 214–15, 221, 224–25, 250, 259–60, 291n14, 300n2, 301n20. *See also* masters of tea
waitresses (nü chafang), 85–86, 90–92, 119, 196, 209, 235, 240, 250, 260, 262–63, 300n2, 301n23, 302nn26, 27, 303n59
Wang Family Corner (Wangjiaguai), 188
Wang Fu, 322n32. *Also see* Debate on Tea and Wine
Wang Hung-tai, 13
Wang Qingyuan, 18, 172, 287n20
Wang Xiushan, 61, 64–65, 79, 88, 213, 219, 297n18
War of Resistance (1937-45), 2–3, 7–8, 10, 14, 30, 51–52, 86, 95, 107, 151, 163–64, 166, 176, 219, 226, 234–40 passim, 241, 243, 250–51, 253, 263, 316n26, 317nn39, 41
Warm Spring Road (Chunxi lu), 27, 38, 40, 44–46, 53–54, 63, 91, 119, 140, 144, 158, 175, 182, 184–85, 203, 235, 298n30, 319n62
Water Gang (Shuibang), 60
water money (shuiqian), 88
water-carriers, 18, 37, 62, 65, 70, 73, 92, 117, 209, 291n14
water-pipe tobacco servants (zhuang shuiyan or zhuangyan war), 172. *See also* tobacconists
Weber, Max, 297n8
Wei Family Ancestral Temple Teahouse (Weijiaci chashe), 96

Wen Tianxiang, 150
Wen Yiduo, 224–27, 240, 246
wengzi, 301n22
West China (Huaxi) University, 221
West China Daily (Huaxi ribao), 119
West China Evening News (Huaxi wanbao), 11, 239
West China Square (Huaxi ba), 174
West Chinese Catalpa Bridge Street (Zitongqiao xijie), 312n52
West Imperial Street (Xiyu jie), 45, 175
Western Empress Dowager (Xitaihou), 149
Western Garden (Xiyuan) Teahouse, 295n54
Western influence, 4, 252
Westernization, 1, 28, 39, 155, 161, 166, 251
Westernized elites, 9–10, 118, 199, 233. *See also* reformist elites
What Feng Saw and Heard (Fengshi wenjianji), 286n8
White Roses Teahouse (Baimeigui), 43, 295n54, 310n28
wild shops (yedian), 174
willow and willow (liulianliu), 139
Willow River Teahouse (Liujiang chashe), 73
Wind and Cloud Pavilion Teahouse (Fengyunting chashe), 45, 210–11
wine shops, 6, 13, 85, 213, 221, 321n32
wine, 77, 117, 177, 213, 321n32
women of good families (liangjia funü), 189
women, 9, 23, 93, 119, 142, 153, 155–57 passim, 160, 168, 198–99, 206–7, 211, 215, 240, 249, 258–60 passim, 262, 292nn17, 19, 302nn26, 46, 303n49, 309n6, 312nn52, 61, 65; customers, 9, 15, 20, 116–17, 150, 163, 186, 188–96; elderly, 189–90; harassed, 218; of good families (liangjia funü), 189; in the theater, 206; lower-class, 15, 258, 311n49; prostitutes, 194; middle and upper-class, 15, 119, 189–90, 196; restrictions, 191–94, 199, 207, 258; singers, 8; waitressing, 86, 90–92, 98, 102–9, 240, 301n23; young women, 189, 196. *See also* waitresses
workers carrying kettles (tihu gongren), 85. *See also* masters of tea
workers, 29, 80, 86, 117–18, 133, 207, 213, 257, 258, 288n33, 296n1, 300nn3, 7, 302nn40, 46, 303n70, 320n19, 321n29; female, 100, 108–9, 256; restaurant, 40, 170; seasonal, 170, 262; shop, 119, 154;

teahouse, 3, 22, 35, 37–38, 40, 51, 56, 66, 71, 85–86, 87–100, 102–3, 105, 107–9, 117, 153–54, 169–70, 177, 190, 203–4, 209, 215, 234, 298n21, 311n39. *See also* wage workers
working class, 86, 108, 256, 258, 288n33, 303nn49, 70, 311n49, 320n19, 321n29
workplace culture, 15, 22, 86, 107, 109, 249
workplaces, 85–86, 98, 101–2, 107–9, 114, 117, 170, 296n1, 303nn49, 70, 320n19
Wu Yu, 47, 120, 123, 151, 231, 295n58, 302n27
Wu Zhihui, 7
Wuhan, 8, 285n2

xi chawan (washing tea bowls), 127
Xiao Jun, 7
xiaodan, 147, 206
Xiong Zhuoyun, 43, 180, 208
Xue Tao Well, 47–48

Yang Sen, 183, 231, 315n16
Yangzhou, 6, 7, 15, 16, 195
Yellow Heaven Lake (Huangtiandang), 150
Yi Junzuo, 114, 185
Yin Changheng, 228, 315n9
young masters (yaoshi), 85. *See also* masters of tea
young ruffian (eshao), 8
youxian (idle or relaxed), 133
youxian (leisure or pastime), 133
Yu Garden (Yuyuan) Teahouse, 157
Yuan dynasty (1271–1368), 6, 302n26
Yuan Garden Teahouse (Yuanyuan chashe), 102
Yuanheng Tea Firm (Yuanheng chahao), 42
Yue Fei, 150, 236, 316n31, 317n41
Yunnan army, 228, 231

Zeng's Teahouse (Zengji chashe), 295n54
Zhang Henshui, 17, 113
Zhang Shijie, 150
Zhang Shizhao, 9, 287n23
Zhang Xijiu, 141
Zhao Erfeng, 315m9
Zhejiang, 13, 59
Zheng Banqiao, 4
Zhonghe Teahouse, 73
Zhou Wen, 118, 234
Zhuo Wenjun, 174

Printed by Printforce, United Kingdom